Strategy for Public and Nonprofit Organizations

"I have long admired Sandro Cabral for his brilliance and for using frontier ideas from the field of Strategy in the public interest. The book you hold in your hands has me admiring him more than ever. Full of powerful examples and practical insights, this book will make you optimistic that private and public organizations can conquer the world's most pressing problems by working together."

—Anita McGahan, *Professor of Strategic Management, Rotman School of Management, University of Toronto, Canada*

"Effective strategies in the public and nonprofit realm (and in the business world, too) involve good ideas, worth implementing, that can be implemented—along with the coalition of support necessary to adopt and implement them. Sandro Cabral has written an excellent, academically grounded book aimed especially, but not exclusively, at developing really good ideas. I do not know of another work like it."

—John M. Bryson, *McKnight Presidential Professor Emeritus, University of Minnesota, USA*

"Cabral's book addresses the gap in the literature by taking central principles in strategic management research and practice and modifying them so that they can be applied in the public and non-profit sectors. The result not only gives clear guidance to managers in these kinds of organizations in developing and implementing strategies, it also has implications for managers in privately owned for profit firms."

—Jay Barney, *Presidential Professor of Strategic Management and Lassonde Chair of Social Entrepreneurship Eccles School of Business, The University of Utah, USA*

"This book is much-needed: it provides an outstanding resource for graduate students, managers, and researchers aiming to promote the strategic management and performance of public and nonprofit organizations. Readers will find evidence-based coverage of a full range of key topics in strategy; engaging writing; and useful examples throughout."

—Thomas D'Aunno, *Professor of Management at the Robert F. Wagner Graduate School of Public Service, New York University*

Sandro Cabral

Strategy for Public and Nonprofit Organizations

An Applied Perspective

palgrave
macmillan

Sandro Cabral
Insper Institute of Education
and Research
São Paulo, Brazil

ISBN 978-3-031-64968-4 ISBN 978-3-031-64969-1 (eBook)
https://doi.org/10.1007/978-3-031-64969-1

This Palgrave Macmillan imprint is published by the registered company Springer Nature Switzerland AG
The registered company address is: Gewerbestrasse 11, 6330 Cham, Switzerland

To Renata, Luiza, and Leticia

Preface

Like many others, I grapple with the belief that my achievements are unearned, illegitimate, and merely a stroke of luck. Regardless of the publications and several teaching and research awards accumulated, the persistent feeling of being a fraud lurks, akin to the unmasking at the end of a Scooby-Doo episode. Needless to say, impostor syndrome has haunted me relentlessly from the moment Palgrave McMillan offered me a contract to write this book, through the writing process, and even now that I have completed all the chapters.

I have built my academic career advocating for the importance of building bridges between strategy and public management. I can testify to the growing number of works in the 2010s and 2020s examining not only how strategic management lenses can help public and nonprofit organizations create public value but also how private firms can benefit from a careful consideration of government and the third sector. Despite these facts, a myriad of questions arose in my mind when conceiving this book. Do you have something new to say, really? How will you avoid producing a shallow piece that, in attempting to promote cross-fertilization and interdisciplinary dialogues, may overlook important concepts on both sides of the fence? Will your book adopt a "fill in the blanks" approach and be limited to demonstrating how strategic management theories apply to the context of public and nonprofits? How will your book add to previous works focused on the interface between strategy and public administration, such as Mark Moore's seminal book on the relationships between strategic management and public value creation[1], the excellent works of John Bryson on strategic planning in public and nonprofits[2], the carefully conceived book of Ewan Ferlie and Edoardo Ongaro[3], and the work of Rhys Andrews, George Boyne, Jeniffer Law, and Richard Walker[4]?, all published by public administration and public management scholars? How can your book benefit strategic management scholars and managers from private organizations seeking to understand the functioning of governments and nonprofit organizations? Will your book be useful to public managers to design and implement policies that can improve the lives of the communities they serve?

The list of questions above is not exhaustive, and of course, I am not confident that I have found convincing and satisfactory responses to all of them. Nevertheless, I have accepted the challenge and made some self-centered resolutions to make this personal endeavor possible.

I made a promise to myself: if I was not having fun while writing the book, I would quit. As you can see, I did not quit. Despite the pressure of deadlines and other professional and personal duties that never cease, I can confidently say that writing this book brought me joy. I relished in finding suitable empirical examples, in crafting and revising sentences, and in acquiring new knowledge along the way.

Inspired by the principal-agent theory, I also convinced myself that the only thing I can control is my efforts. This realization was pivotal in dealing with impostor syndrome, and I have dedicated all my efforts to encapsulating in this book what I have been doing for over two decades: connecting abstract concepts to reality or to configurations students can grasp. Since my undergraduate studies in engineering and throughout my master's and doctoral studies in management, understanding the links between theory and practice has been the most effective way for me to learn. The professors I have most admired were those who helped me connect the dots, understand the peculiarities of the context under examination, and utilize accumulated knowledge to understand different contexts in the future. Hence, the inclusion of empirical examples to facilitate these connections is essential.

[1] Moore (1995).

[2] Bryson (2018).

[3] Ferlie and Ongaro (2015).

[4] Andrews, Boyne, Law, and Walker (2011).

Consistently, I have strived to integrate both the recent advancements in the literature on strategic management in the context of public and nonprofit organizations and the findings of my own research. This area has gained significant traction in recent years, as evidenced by numerous contributions and special issues in leading business and management journals[5]. Indeed, it is interesting to note that most existing books advocating for connections between strategy and public and nonprofit management have been authored by scholars from the public and nonprofit sectors. This fact presents a unique opportunity to produce a book that emphasizes the strategic management perspective. Along these lines, in addition to the contributions of public and nonprofit authors, the present book sheds light on the efforts made by business and management scholars. It also explores the contributions of organizational and managerial economics to the realm of strategy in the context of public and nonprofit organizations and examines the strategic actions undertaken by private and for-profit firms in a world characterized by multiple stakeholders with conflicting demands.

I also drew upon my personal experiences to write this book. Growing up in a suburb of São Paulo, Brazil, I was surrounded by poverty, structural inequities, police brutality, and deficient infrastructure. These firsthand experiences allowed me to witness the hardships caused by incapable governments in the lives of those most in need. Later, living in Salvador, Bahia, I encountered the issues of racial and gender inequities from a different perspective, which only served to amplify my indignation and sense of mission. Nearly two decades since completing my doctoral studies, I am certain that the decision I made to harness my capabilities and energy to seek solutions for addressing major societal problems through the lens of management was the right thing to do.

All these elements above helped me to mitigate the effects of impostor syndrome, persevere, and complete this book. While I understand that some readers may dislike my approach, this book is a personal effort that reflects my truth, intentions, aspirations, and passions. The examples from Motown, carnival, movies, and various public, private, and nonprofit organizations—some drawn from works of people whom I

[5] Refer to Barney (2005); Cabral, Mahoney, McGahan, and Potoski (2019); Mahoney, McGahan, and Pitelis (2009); McGahan, Zelner, and Barney (2013); Quélin, Kivleniece, and Lazzarini (2017).

deeply admire—alongside my personal trajectory were essential for amplifying my voice and thoughts.

The book expresses the way I perceive the world: as a place where solutions to the problems faced by disenfranchised populations can be discovered, attenuated, or at least understood by integrating elements from public, private, and nonprofit organizations. Complex challenges faced by businesses and society at large are seldom overcome without integrating complementary elements, which, when combined, produce stronger effects than when isolated. The recent example of the COVID-19 pandemic illustrates that the development of vaccines would not have been possible without the orchestrated efforts of public, private, and nonprofit organizations. Similarly, major technological innovations often emerge from the combined efforts of passionate entrepreneurs, nonprofit research institutes, and massive public investments. This reinforces my belief in the importance of understanding how strategic management perspectives are crucial for enhancing the performance of public and nonprofit organizations and fostering successful cross-sector collaborations.

Overall, I cannot guarantee that reading this book will be a valuable and worthwhile experience for every reader. The only assurance I can offer is that my friends, coauthors, scholars, managers, and the students with whom I have had the privilege to interact will recognize my voice throughout the pages.

Despite its flaws, this book would not have come to fruition without the support of numerous individuals and organizations. I am especially indebted to some mentors who eventually became coauthors and friends. Marcus Alban, my master's and doctoral advisor at the Federal University of Bahia in Brazil, was the first person to encourage me to write this book and reminded me of this need every time we met. Sergio Lazzarini played a pivotal role in my academic journey and saw value in me that I had not recognized myself; without his encouragement, I doubt I would have become a strategy scholar. Furthermore, Sergio provided detailed comments on the initial version of this manuscript, which significantly contributed to improving the book, or at the very least, making it less deficient. Paulo Furquim de Azevedo was also instrumental in my life, first by introducing me to the world of organizational economics as my mentor during my bachelor's in engineering at the Federal University of São Carlos, and later by being an incredible coauthor. Anita McGahan has been a constant source of inspiration, whether through her beliefs in the importance of strategic management lenses for addressing major societal needs or by opening doors to the mainstream strategy for scholars like me who were outside the main cliques. Bertrand Quélin, with his astuteness, discipline, and unique sense of humor, taught me a great deal about navigating the field of strategy. I have also benefited from interactions with several coauthors over the years. A huge thanks to all of you.

I acknowledge the students of undergraduate, graduate, and executive education programs I had the privilege to interact with in my regular courses at the Federal University of Bahia and at Insper, as well as students from institutions such as HEC-Paris, New York University, EMLV-Paris, and Agostinho Neto University in Angola, whom I had the opportunity to meet during visiting positions or exchange programs. Believe me, I learn more from you than one can imagine. I am also deeply indebted to Guilherme Fowler Monteiro and Sergio Lazzarini for their course materials, which shaped some of my teaching notes that served as the basis for several chapters of this book. Your generosity is immense. I am also grateful to Marcelo Marchesini and Bruno Varela for their suggestions and dialogues about strategy in the context of the public sector.

This book would not be possible without the academic council of Insper that offered all the institutional support I needed to make my intentions possible. I also thank Milton Seligman and Leticia Piccolloto from Brava Foundation who believed in this project from the outset and provided me with the necessary funding for a sabbatical leave at the New York University between August 2023 and January 2024 to write this book. Andre Marques and Aline Marcon from Insper offered invaluable support with the administrative burdens and I am indebted with both.

Special thanks to Salo Coslovsky, Thomas D'Aunno, and Sherry Glied from the New York University's Robert F. Wagner Graduate School of Public Service and to Sinziana Dorobantu from the NYU Stern School of Business for hosting me during my sabbatical and granting me access to all I needed from NYU to complete this book. I also thank Leandro Pongeluppe for his support, friendship, and informal conversations while I was in the United States.

Crucial in this journey is my family, who provided all the necessary emotional and logistical support to make this project a reality. My parents, "Dona" Claudia e "Seu" Cabral, and my mother-in-law, Helia Ruas Gaspar, not only offered invaluable encouragement but also lent a helping hand during my absence from Salvador. I am deeply indebted to my daughter, Luiza, for understanding my absence, and to my younger daughter, Leticia, who bravely accepted the challenge of joining me and living with her father in New York City, away from her family and friends. Finally, I am immensely grateful to my partner, the love of my life, Renata, for being an exemplar of kindness and resilience, for embracing the distance, and for letting me be myself.

São Paulo, Brazil Sandro Cabral
New York City, USA

Contents

Part I Foundations

1	**Introduction**	3
	Why Do Public and Nonprofit Organizations Need Strategic Management?	10
	Why Do Private Organizations Need to Pay Attention to Public and Nonprofit Relationships?	14
	Book Structure	19
	References	21
2	**Strategy Beyond Private and For-profit Organizations**	25
	Strategy: Genesis and Evolution in the Management Realm	26
	What Is Strategy?	33
	Strategy in the Context of Public and Nonprofit Organizations	35
	Differences Between Public and Private Organizations	35
	Public Policy Cycle and Strategy	37
	Strategy in Public Organizations: Cooptation by Private Interests? Really?	39
	Strategy and Public Administration/Management: More Dialogues Are Needed	41
	Conclusions	44
	References	45

3 Public Value Creation 51
What Is Value? A Strategic Approach 53
About Public Value 56
The Public Value Creation Dynamics 58
The Importance of Mission for Public Value Creation 59
Public Value Creation: The Strategic Triangle 62
Public Values and Public Value Creation 64
Conclusions 67
References 67

Part II Inside the Organizational Boundaries

4 Incentives in Public and Nonprofit Organizations 73
Principal-Agent Relationships 74
Agency Costs 76
Incentive Contracts with Complete Information 77
Incentive Contracts with Asymmetric Information 80
Group-Based Incentives and Relational Contracts in Public and Nonprofit Organizations 88
The Free-Rriding Problem 92
Relational Contracts 94
Conclusion 104
References 105

5 Performance Management in Public and Nonprofit Organizations 107
Objective Versus Subjective Performance Indicators 110
Distortions and Problems in Objective and Subjective Measures 113
Multitask 113
Ratchet Effect 115
Gaming 117
Social Comparison 120
Distortions in Subjective Measures 121
Defining Relevant Performance Indicators: The Importance of Theory of Change 122
Selecting Key Performance Indicators (KPIs) 126
Conclusion 127
References 128

6 Centralization Versus Decentralization in Public and Nonprofit Organizations 131
Centralization Versus Decentralization of Decision Rights: Pros and Cons 135
Benefits of Decentralization 136
Problems of Decentralization 141
Balancing Centralization and Decentralization 145
Organizational Structures 148
The Unitary Form (U-Form) 150
Multidivisional Forms (M-Form) 151
Matrix Forms 154
Conclusions 156
References 157

7 Strategy Implementation 161
Defining the Concept of Strategy Implementation 163
Drivers of Successful Implementation 165
The Importance of External and Internal Fit in Strategy Implementation 170
External Fit and Strategy Implementation 173
Internal Fit and Complementarities During Strategy Implementation 177
Strategy Implementation and Organizational Inertia 179
Conclusion 183
References 184

Part III Outside the Organizational Boundaries

8 Stakeholder Management in the Public Interest 191
Stakeholder Management: What Is? 194
Stakeholder Management Beyond Profit-Oriented Organizations 198
Stakeholder Approaches and Public Management 200
Firms and Collective Action Problems: A New Stakeholder Orientation 203
Stakeholder Analysis: The Identification Issue 207
The Power-Grid Model 208
The Stakeholder Identification and Salience Model 210
Conclusion 213
References 214

9	**On the Government Boundaries**	219
	Setting the Boundaries: Drivers of Scope Choices	224
	Organizational Boundaries: The Contributions of Property Rights Theory and Transaction Cost Economics	224
	Organizational Boundaries: The Contributions of Public Eonomics and Policy Analysis	227
	The Different Modes of Provision	232
	Full Government Provision	233
	Outsourcing	235
	Public–Private Partnerships and Concessions	237
	Privatization	238
	Choosing the Mode of Provision	240
	Probity Concerns	240
	Capable Suppliers	241
	Private Investments and Ownership	243
	An Integrative Model for Selecting the Mode of Delivery	244
	Conclusion	247
	References	248
10	**Cross-Sector and Public-Public Collaborations**	251
	Cross-Sector Collaborations: Definition and Forms	255
	Strategic Alliances and Cross-Sector Collaborations: Differences and Similarities	259
	Divergent Points Between Alliances and Cross-Sector Collaborations	261
	Convergent Points Between Alliances and Cross-Sector Collaborations	263
	Collaborative Governance in Cross-Sector Collaborations	268
	The Ansell and Gash Model of Collaborative Governance	271
	Collaborative Governance and Performance: The Role of Cross-Sector Capabilities and Public-Public Capabilities for Cross-Sector Collaborations Involving Governments	272
	Collaborative Governance and Accountability Issues	276
	Conclusion	278
	References	279

11 Conclusions 285
Reference 290

References 291

Index 317

List of Figures

Fig. 2.1	Policy cycle and strategic elements	39
Fig. 3.1	Value creation and value appropriation in private organizations	55
Fig. 3.2	The public value governance triangle (PGVT): Illustration from conditional cash-transfer programs	65
Fig. 4.1	Principal-agent model	75
Fig. 4.2	Sequence of decisions in the incentive contract between Herod and Matthew	82
Fig. 4.3	Example of a principal-agent decision tree	98
Fig. 5.1	Theory of change: an illustrative example in education	125
Fig. 6.1	U-form in public organizations—example of a maternity hospital	151
Fig. 6.2	M-form in public organizations—police department example	153
Fig. 6.3	Matrix organization—multicampus university example	155
Fig. 7.1	External fit and strategy implementation at US gymnastics	174
Fig. 8.1	Power-interest grid—example of the decision of reopening schools during the COVID-19 pandemic	210
Fig. 9.1	Types of goods	230
Fig. 9.2	Modes of provision of public services	234
Fig. 9.3	Choosing the mode of delivery	245

List of Tables

Table 8.1	Stakeholder typology based on power, legitimacy, and urgency attributes	212
Table 10.1	Major divergent and convergent points between strategic alliances and cross-sector collaborations	267

PART I

Foundations

CHAPTER 1

Introduction

In 1959, Berry Gordy Jr., a songwriter and producer, who was also a former blue-collar auto plant worker, founded Motown Records in Detroit, Michigan, United States. Motown became one of the most successful businesses in the history of the music industry. Superstars like Marvin Gaye, Michael Jackson, Smokey Robinson, Martha Reeves, Diana Ross, Stevie Wonder, and groups like The Four Tops, The Jackson Five, The Marvelettes, The Supremes, and The Temptations, to name a few, sparked an esthetic revolution in the show business with their unique songs and style.

The value created by Motown is immense. Now belonging to the giant Universal Music, Motown's catalog, filled with soul and pop hits, has an economic value that is hard to calculate. While Motown's artists generated economic rents for firm's shareholders and executives and contributed to social and economic inclusion by activating supply chains in the entertainment industry, they have also influenced significant changes in modern society. These artists played a crucial role in disseminating African American heritage across the world and breaking racial barriers present in larger portions of US society in the decades of the 1960s and 1970s by entertaining both Black and white audiences. Their high-quality artistic expressions fostered feelings of pride and belonging within Black communities. These expressions played a supportive role in the efforts of the

S. Cabral, *Strategy for Public and Nonprofit Organizations*,
https://doi.org/10.1007/978-3-031-64969-1_1

Black Baptist church and other organizations in the civil rights movement, aiming to promote integration and challenge racial stereotypes.

Although the value created by Motown was appropriated unevenly among certain stakeholders compared to others, this organization serves as a prime example of how for-profit firms can facilitate the creation of both economic and social value.

Several factors explain Motown's success. One obvious explanation is the entrepreneurial and far-sighted orientation of Berry Gordy, who was able to create a successful business model. Drawing from his experience in Detroit's assembly lines, he translated operational strategies proven successful in the automotive industry to the music business. Specialization, standardization, division of labor, and processes to ensure quality control were implemented at Hitsville, USA, Motown's headquarters at 2648 West Grand Boulevard, Detroit, where most of the soul and pop music hits of the 1960s were conceived, produced, and recorded. In addition to his business mindset, as a songwriter and producer, Mr. Gordy also had an acute perception of music, enabling him to identify promising artists, producers, and choreographers and to acquire the best equipment for song production. In other words, he could identify, attract, and orchestrate the necessary resources and capabilities to achieve the envisioned goals.

A significant factor contributing to Motown's success hinged on the ability to engage with audiences beyond Detroit (indeed, the label's name alludes to Detroit as the Motor City in the United States—Motor Town). The so-called Motown Revue comprised tours featuring the label's roster in various Eastern and Southern locations in the US, fostering connections among both Black and non-Black audiences, including segregated cities where Black artists faced violent assaults from white supremacists. The capability to manage relationships with a myriad of stakeholders and recognize shared and differing interests was crucial in disseminating Black culture, even in racialized and hostile areas. And, of course, these tours also helped to increase sales records, revenues from concerts, and advertising.

Goal setting, a clear sense of mission, resources, and practices to achieve expected goals and abilities to identify stakeholders' needs and manage relationships with relevant actors to assure the creation of value represent, indeed, some strategic management concepts deployed by several private organizations to attain their economic objectives. It is true that a massive portion of Motown's success can be attributed to the utilization of strategic management concepts, but it is essential to acknowledge that value creation for Motown would not have occurred without the contribution of public and nonprofit organizations.

The most invaluable asset of a music record company is its artists. In the 1950s, Detroit had plenty of groups formed by young talented artists singing in the streets without any instrumentation. Among them was the influential artist Smokey Robinson, future leader of The Miracles, author of hits like "The track of my tears" and "My Girl" who eventually became Vice President of Motown. Duke Fakir and Levi Stubbs members of the Four Tops as well as Otis Williams and Melvin Franklin, founders of the Temptations, were also among the high-quality teenagers harmonically signing loving songs with the doo-wop styles in Black neighborhoods of the motor town, who eventually became Motown's major stars in the next decades.

But how was it possible to have such an amount of talented and musically liberated teenagers in the same city, at the same time? Was it just a coincidence? Was it about something in the water people drank in Detroit that gave musical gifts to anyone who drank those waters? None of these possibilities seems to be plausible. Yet, the reason Motown in the 1950s and 1960s was able to access highly qualified musicians has its roots exactly to what inspired Berry Gordy to define the name of his company: the auto industry in Detroit.

Driven by the booming automotive industry, in the first half of the twentieth century, Detroit experienced a huge population increasing from around 300,000 in the 1900s to almost 2 million inhabitants in the mid-1950s. Immigrants and migrants from other parts of the United States have moved to Detroit in pursuit of better living conditions. The establishment of major firms like Chrysler, Ford, and General Motors has increased the demands for public services, especially in education. A new middle class in the city pressured the city council to invest more in education over the first decades of the century, and more schools were built, more teachers were hired, and innovative programs to assure that children were well-educated were made, benefiting not only white populations, which until the decade of 1970 comprised most of the population in Detroit, but also Black populations living in underserved regions.[1]

[1] For more information about the economic rise and fall of Detroit during the twentieth century, please refer to Farley et al. (2000). A comprehensive history about how the Detroit's education system evolved can be seen in Mirel (1999).

Among these initiatives, a massive program of music education in public schools played a leading role in the nurturing of future Motown's artists. Guided by high-caliber and professional music teachers, students were exposed to music theory and classical European music, in addition to the traditional marching-based music. Actions to incentivize students to attend classic music and opera concerts and other artistic manifestations complemented the music training enabled by public investments and fostered the emersion of a unique esthetic among young Black students combining appropriate musical training, African heritage, and the cultural background from the US Southern States. Most Motown performers and songwriters of classical hits like the brothers Eddie and Brian Holland were exposed to music in public schools. Groups like the Supremes, led by Diana Ross, met, and rehearsed at their schools. Other Detroit' artists not attached to Motown, like Aretha Franklin, and artists outside of Detroit, like Michael Jackson, born and raised in Gary, Indiana, benefited from public investments in music education. Without public investments in education for individuals with visual impairments, probably one of the most talented artists ever, Steve Wonder, could not develop their abilities in plenitude.[2]

Despite the importance of government investments in public education in enabling private interests, in the case of Motown, a special type of nonprofit organization also contributed to nurture gifted musicians: the Black Baptist church. This nonprofit organization is one of the most prominent Black institutions in the United States. It represents a substantial portion of the Black community in the country, not only by influencing the values and the morality of communities but also by addressing structural problems faced by African Americans, being a pivotal institution in the Civil Rights movement. Churches also accompanied the mass migration from southern to northern states in the twentieth century and promoted support to Black communities in the regions where they were settled, which included Detroit.[3]

Along with the preaching, the signing is central to worship in Black Baptist churches. Both are "*magnets of attraction and the primary vehicles*

[2] Early (2004) and McCarthy (2013) provide evidence on the role played by public investments in music programs in Detroit's schools for the development of Motown and of the pop and Black music.

[3] Refer to Soule and Dyke (1999) for depiction of the importance of churches in political organization of Black communities in the United States.

of spiritual transport"[4] and play a leading role in attracting audience to churches. The vocal ornamentation that characterizes the soul music is largely inspired by the gospels of Black Baptist churches. As several icons of soul music, almost all of Motown's artists had their first contact with music in the wooden benches of churches and eventually became singers during worship. In Black Baptist churches, since their childhood, future musicians like Aretha Frankin, Marvin Gaye, and Diana Ross[5] exercised the moaning, the pitch glides, the syncopation, and the elongation that were later transferred to the popular music.[6]

Although such a value-creating combination of business policies conceived in the private sphere with public and nonprofit policies explains a significant portion of the success of Motown, this story is not an isolated case. The successful examples of Silicon Valley in California, Route 128 in Massachusetts, and the Research Triangle in North Carolina exhibit the same pattern of complementarities between the entrepreneurial spirit present in private enterprises, public investments, and nonprofit organizations. Examples of nonprofits include Stanford, Duke, and Harvard, all committed to education and research. Without cross-sectoral synergistic efforts among organizations that are oftentimes seen as silos that do not interact, though they do, several technological innovations present in our lives from smartphones to solar energy would not be possible without efforts from public, private, and nonprofit organizations.[7]

Complementary actions between organizations of several types also contribute to addressing grand challenges such as climate change, health, and well-being. Effective responses to the unprecedent pandemic of

[4] Abbington (2009, p. 40).

[5] In an interview, Duke Fakir, the legendary singer of the Four Tops exemplifies the role of churches to nurture musicians in Detroit: "*first of all, Detroit is full of churches. It's one of those cities in which gospel music has always been prevalent, jazz music had always been prevalent. Back in the day this was a jazz town. Big bands back in the day used to just come and hang around Detroit because there were so many great musicians here. It's been like that, always down through the years. And when I was born we went to church, just like a couple of the other guys, so we sang all our lives, pretty much. I've sang all my life! My mother worked at church and my cousins and I, we all went to choir, we grew up there*" https://thequietus.com/articles/03956-the-four-tops-interview.

[6] See Legg (2010) for more about the characteristics of music played in Baptist Black churches.

[7] See Adams (2005) and Mazzucato (2013).

COVID-19 hinged on intense coordination of efforts among governments, for-profit pharmaceutical companies, and nonprofit research institutes to perform research and development activities to obtain effective vaccines. Without efforts involving public authorities, firms like Pfizer, BioNTech, Astra Zeneca, and nonprofits like Oxford University, probably, I would not be able to draft this book after the pandemic, and, probably, readers would not be able to read it.

Coordinated actions led by for-profit firms articulating public and nonprofit organizations have also been contributing to the attainment of the United Nations Sustainable Development Goals (SDGs). Natura, a world-class firm in cosmetics is known for engaging communities, and public and nonprofit stakeholders in actions that reduce deforestation in the Amazon Forest and promote economically and environmentally sustainable supply chains through the principles of polycentric governance idealized by the Nobel Prize winner, Elinor Ostrom. In some cases, shareholders can guide actions to help the firm reconcile financial and social goals, creating private and public values appropriated by several stakeholders beyond shareholders and financiers.[8]

Likewise, public organizations can engage firms and nonprofits in the pursuit of several policy goals. Corfo, the Chilean agency of economic development played a leading role in the development of the local salmon industry by putting together nonprofit organizations, local firms, and multilateral organisms and coordinating actions for technological transferring, cultivation, and access to global markets that were key to make Chile one of the world leaders in the trout and salmon exports.[9] Governments can also articulate firms and nonprofits for the provision of services normally supplied by public authorities through public–private partnerships[10] and other contractual arrangements to benefit citizens, like in social impact bonds, whereas governments can support cross-sector alliances to address a major problem triggering payments to cross-sector

[8] Anita McGahan and Leandro Pongeluppe (2023) as well as Aline Gatignon and Laurence Capron (2023) illustrate how Natura can simultaneously pursue financial and social goals through extensive collaboration with local communities, nonprofits, suppliers, and governmental bodies. Evidence also suggests that shareholders play a pivotal role in supporting relational strategies between Natura and the surrounding communities, by blending instrumental and morally oriented principles. See Lazzarini et al. (2020).

[9] Lazzarini (2015).

[10] See Quelin et al. (2019).

partners contingent to the attainment of goals.[11] In a similar vein, nonprofits can lead collaborative efforts with firms, governments, and multilaterals to attain their missions and create public value as in the case of the *Médicins Sans Frontières* providing healthcare in underserved regions or Greenpeace in its actions to protect the environment.[12]

The examples above provoke significant reflections aligned with the objectives of this book. Firstly, they underscore the critical role of strategic management for public and nonprofit organizations. Despite having distinct missions, objectives, and constraints compared to their private counterparts, these organizations must strategize effectively to accomplish their organizational goals. As evidenced by the Motown example mentioned earlier, whether strategizing independently or in collaboration with private entities, the strategic processes of public and nonprofit organizations can carry profound implications for both public policies and business strategies. These implications can enable the creation of value for a broader range of stakeholders.

Likewise, either through collaborations with governments and nonprofits or simply by considering the aspirations of these actors and leveraging the externalities facilitated by public and nonprofit organizations in their strategizing, for-profit firms can enhance their capacity to pursue organizational goals and create value embraced by myriad of stakeholders, including shareholders. Specifically, understanding how government operates becomes crucial for firms reliant on governmental support to achieve their financial objectives and, eventually, their socially oriented goals. Such enhanced understanding is key for effective business policies in regulated sectors and in industries where public and private interests overlap and coevolve.

Along these lines, in a world where boundaries between public, nonprofit, and private organizations are blurred, and some degree of cross-sector collaboration is needed, understanding the aspirations and the potential of non-governmental actors, either private or nonprofit, is necessary for public managers and policymakers responsible for designing, implementing, and evaluating public policies. The accumulated knowledge in strategic management can be instrumental for governments in

[11] Lazzarini et al. (2021), Economy et al. (2023), and Faulk et al. (2020) discuss social impact bonds and some of their economic and social implications.

[12] More about cross-sector collaborations in Chapter 10.

identifying the conditions under which public service performance and public value creation can be achieved concomitantly.

Why Do Public and Nonprofit Organizations Need Strategic Management?

There is a vast number of definitions for the term strategy, and most of them are crafted to deal with settings characterized by competition and rivalry among firms, and built under behavioral assumptions that firms are focused only on reaping financial goals, which may mismatch with the public and nonprofit context. Within the integrative view of this book, a general definition must be broad enough to encompass the peculiarities of public, private, and nonprofit organizations, but narrow enough to be actionable, meaningful, and senseful. In line with this approach, I propose that the strategizing process is inherently scientific and theory-based. Managers across public, private, and nonprofit sectors develop theories and hypotheses to address organizational objectives, akin to equations where organization-specific theories, reflecting decisions and rules, are placed on the right-hand side to achieve value creation objectives on the left side.[13]

In this book, I define strategy as *structured processes that assist organizations of all types in identifying, acquiring, and preserving the distinctive factors that enable them to translate their ambitions into superior performance, while accounting for the interdependence between their internal and external environment.*

While the definition above aligns well with organizations of all types, it is particularly applicable to public and nonprofit entities. Consistent with the theory-based view of strategy, these organizations can formulate theories of change to attain desired performance levels, considering their specific goals and constraints. Notably, disparities exist between private and public/nonprofit organizations regarding goals, incentives,

[13] Teppo Felin and Todd Zenger (2017) provide an insightful portrait about the importance of strategies based on unique theories at the firm-level. In the "theory-based view", managers function as theorists by crafting theories to assist organizations in creating value. There is a growing consensus regarding the role of the strategist within an organization as someone responsible for guiding the organization towards a position of enhanced value, supported by causal paths established by established theories and/or causal-based evidence—see Lazzarini and Zenger (2023).

constraints, and accountability standards.[14] Recognizing these distinctions when applying the accumulated knowledge in strategic management to public and nonprofit sectors is crucial for enabling effective contributions to public policy.

Like private firms, public and nonprofit organizations may also benefit from strategic planning to define their goals, identify the necessary resources, and devise actions and processes conducive to achieve these goals, eventually in collaboration with organizations from different sectors.[15]

Formed by individuals typically acting in their self-interest and subject to extrinsic and intrinsic sources of motivation, organizations of all types can rely on structures of rewards and punishments to influence efforts from employees, managers, and suppliers to achieve strategic intents. Payments (or sanctions) contingent upon the attainment of expected outcomes can occur in private organizations when salespersons meet (or do not meet) expected sales goals, in nonprofits when managers attain (or do not attain) fundraising targets, and in public organizations, such as when bonuses are offered to police officers if homicides and street robbery records in territories under their authority reduce. Similarly, public, private, and nonprofits frequently provide non-pecuniary awards and recognitions that induce efforts as effectively as monetary-based accolades.

Organizational design and decisions related to the allocation of decision rights are strategic and can also exert a positive (or negative) influence on performance, whether in the context of public or nonprofit organizations independently, or in tandem with incentives and performance management systems.[16]

For instance, consider a scenario where a government alters the allocation of decision rights, opting to enhance tax collection by granting greater autonomy to revenue agents, allowing them to determine which taxpayers are more likely to engage in tax fraud and evasion. While the specific knowledge of these agents is pivotal for maximizing expected results in a more decentralized setting, their efforts may be suboptimal if the government does not implement payment systems that reward agents

[14] Ring and Perry (1985).

[15] John M. Bryson (2018).

[16] See Brickley et al. (2001) for insights into the importance of the triad: incentives, decision rights, and performance management for organizational performance.

for their additional efforts. It is important to note that in many countries, revenue agents and tax collectors are tenured civil servants with job security and fixed salaries, regardless of their efforts. In the absence of mechanisms rewarding extra efforts or penalizing a lack thereof, inducing different behavioral responses from these agents is unlikely. Even if incentives are promised, additional efforts might not be observed without performance measurement systems capable of assessing the outcomes of each agent. This situation can be even worse in the absence of incentives (rewards and punishments) and performance management systems, which is a common feature in public and nonprofit organizations. Without these motivating factors, unless the agents are intrinsically motivated to perform their duties, their fixed salaries and the absence of performance assessment or consequences for lack of effort or misbehavior may not lead to public value creation and the attainment of strategic goals.

While necessary to achieve strategic objectives, the existence of organizational structures to oversee the conduct of agents and hold them accountable is not a sufficient condition to ensure the creation of public value, especially when principals are uninterested or uninformed. Consider the strategic problem of oversighting intelligence activities in democratic settings, which involves handling sensitive information that could potentially threaten the security of nations. Despite the secrecy surrounding certain intelligence functions, such as covert actions in foreign countries and anti-terrorism missions, effective oversight from elected representatives—typically carried out by congressional members of the Senate and the House of Representatives—is crucial to ensure that these activities are performed within the bounds of existing laws. However, the effectiveness of oversight can face challenges not only due to inherent information asymmetries between committee members and intelligence officers but also as a result of inadequate monitoring by disengaged or uninterested politicians. Historical trends of abuses by intelligence agencies in the United States[17] and more recently in Brazil, where intelligence officers of the Brazilian Intelligence Agency (Abin) were investigated for structuring an illegal apparatus within the agency for personal and political benefits during 2019 and 2022,[18] serve as

[17] Johnson (2014).

[18] For more details about the Brazilian intelligence issues, refer to https://apnews.com/article/brazil-ramagem-bolsonaro-police-spying-18d039c5e11e18341afe8ee2fb4428d and https://www.france24.com/en/americas/20240131-lula-fires-brazil-s-intel-agency-no-2-over-alleged-illegal-espionage.

illustrative examples highlighting the strategic importance of organizational design in the government context. Definitely, there is nothing more favorable for malicious agents than having uninterested or uninformed principals. If the principals themselves are also malicious, the issues become even more severe.

These examples also highlight why the lack of alignment between incentives, organizational design, and performance management can impede productivity and the delivery of goods and services with an adequate cost versus benefit relationship. This mismatch often results in government services being perceived as inferior to those provided by the private sector. Strategic management lenses are crucial in helping public and nonprofit organizations understand why certain configurations, instead of being value-creating, are value-destroying. Understanding these aspects is essential for taxpayers, donors, and especially for strategists responsible for designing, implementing, and evaluating business and public policies to address pressing social needs. This is particularly important for policies targeting those who are more vulnerable in society and lack the means to afford private services, relying instead on public and nonprofit organizations.

In addition to emphasizing important aspects affecting performance within the internal organization, strategic management lenses can also prove useful for public and nonprofit organizations managing relationships with stakeholders beyond their boundaries and engaging in cross-sector relationships. Similar to private firms, a strategic management orientation is crucial for public and nonprofit organizations when making scope and diversification decisions. Over the past decades, several governments have adopted market-friendly reforms, promoting the involvement of private and nonprofit actors in delivering goods and services that were traditionally provided by public authorities. However, even as some governments have reduced their scope and delegated functions to external actors, they still play a leading role in providing various services. This may involve regulating activities with positive and negative externalities and natural monopolies or orchestrating cross-sector collaborations with private and nonprofit organizations through a myriad of organizational arrangements, such as concessions, public–private partnerships, and management contracts.

In this regard, governments need to understand the aspirations of private and nonprofit organizations and reconcile these interests with those of citizens, while also taking into account the inherent limitations of the public sector in terms of incentives, flexibility, and accountability standards. Furthermore, in a world where stakeholders are more aware of their rights, there is increased pressure for improved visibility of government functioning. This is more pronounced than ever, and in a context where political and ideological polarization is widespread globally, the management of stakeholder relationships has become even more relevant.

Governments that are genuinely committed to ensuring a more equitable appropriation of the public value created across stakeholders, especially those who are particularly disenfranchised, need to develop the ability to map stakeholders and determine how they are affected by policies and how they can influence the effectiveness (or ineffectiveness) of the designed policies. This becomes central when policy changes alter how the created value is distributed across stakeholders, particularly when certain groups stand to benefit more than others or when some stakeholders incur greater losses than others. In such cases, effectively managing tensions involves nurturing coalitions among stakeholders to support desired changes or block undesired ones, which underscores the importance of increased attention by public and nonprofit actors on strategic stakeholder-related features.

Why Do Private Organizations Need to Pay Attention to Public and Nonprofit Relationships?

Bridging strategic management with public and nonprofit perspectives is also important for private for-profit firms. This connection can foster valuable insights into the creation of value by firms operating in regulated industries, businesses significantly affected by government decisions, and activities involving collaborative or adversarial relationships with public and nonprofit organizations, with the potential to create or destroy value. Enhanced attention to public and nonprofit organizations by private firms is strategic. It enables firms to develop strategies based on features of the institutional environment that are typically outside of regular market arenas. This attention may allow firms to contribute to alleviating pressing social problems and addressing major global challenges. Additionally, it can help firms to navigate the complex landscape of myriad stakeholders, often with conflicting interests, and enhance the visibility of management scholarship in police debates.

First, a closer examination of how public and nonprofit organizations shape the institutional environment can help firms anticipate competitors by devising successful strategies considering the influence of communities, public bodies, and other actors outside of regular market forces that are conducive to improved overall performance. These institutional-based strategies are known, for a lack of a better expression, as nonmarket strategies (NMS). David Baron posits that "*the nonmarket environment includes those interactions that are intermediated by the public, stakeholders, government, the media, and public institutions*" and that "*these institutions differ from those of the market environment because of characteristics such as majority rule, due process, broad enfranchisement, collective action, and publicness*".[19]

To adapt to or influence the institutional environment, firms may adopt several corporate political activities. These activities may include lobbying, campaign contributions, and mobilization of stakeholders, among other actions aimed at influencing government decisions on behalf of firms.[20] Firms and business syndicates from regulated industries, for instance, tend to achieve superior financial results by engaging with regulators and other civil servants. This involves informing them about their actions, intentions, and industry-specific knowledge, particularly when firms possess accumulated experience in corporate political activities.[21] In industries prone to generating negative externalities for communities, firms may collaborate and promote self-regulatory institutions. This is particularly true when misconduct by one firm harms others in the industry.[22] For the same reason, in a world where firms' actions are increasingly visible and

[19] Baron (1995, p. 51).

[20] Katic and Hillman (2023).

[21] The works of Bonardi et al. (2006) as well as Hadani and Schuler (2013) demonstrate the importance of nonmarket strategies for improving the performance of firms in regulated industries.

[22] Barnett and King (2008) analyze the effects of the formation of self-regulation institutions aimed at increasing safety standards in the chemical industry. Their study focuses on actions taken by major chemical firms in response to a major accident in a pesticide plant in India owned by Union Carbide, which resulted in the deaths of thousands of citizens.

pressure for environmental, social, and governance (ESG) aspects is escalating, firms can also pursue collaborations with social movements. This can help restore their image and reputation with prominent stakeholders through nonmarket strategies.[23] Unique and differentiated investments in corporate social responsibility (CSR) can even generate positive returns for firms, especially in industries with a lower number of CSR areas that are considered material.[24] Overall, an enhanced understanding of public and nonprofit organizations surrounding the firm and the industries in which they operate is crucial for firms to navigate through the institutional environment and devise adequate strategies.

Secondly, the combined knowledge from the fields of strategic management and public and nonprofit sectors can aid organizations in contributing to efforts addressing global challenges related to structural violence, inclusion, gender and racial diversity, migration crises, natural disasters, and poverty alleviation, among others. Of course, firms may not need to address all the boxes of the United Nations' sustainable development goals (SDGs). This would be implausible, as even purpose-oriented firms may lack the necessary capabilities to address major problems individually. However, since "grand challenges" can often be tackled through orchestrated and coordinated efforts by multiple actors, firms may choose to engage in collective action efforts to address issues affecting at least their surrounding communities, potential customers, or beneficiaries of their goods and services. Paying attention to public and nonprofit organizations can help firms comprehend the limits (and possibilities) of actions oriented toward addressing these goals, while also ensuring their long-term financial sustainability.

Along these lines, focusing on the grand challenge of healthcare, Keyvan Vakili and Anita McGahan analyze the efforts of research and development activities for neglected diseases. These are diseases that primarily affect the poorest populations who cannot afford medical treatment. They examine the role of a multilateral policy designed to protect intellectual property rights, which is supposed to stimulate scientific activity by securing producers' rights. However, they have identified that

[23] Odziemkowska (2022) analyze collaborations between firms and social movement organizations (SMOs). With the support of 25 years of data involving environmental movements and Fortune 500 firms, she finds conditions under which firms and social movements collaborate.

[24] See Nardi et al. (2022).

although the United Nations World Trade Organization's Agreement on Trade-Related Aspects of Intellectual Property Rights (TRIPS) has led to an increase in basic science research on neglected diseases, it did not result in an increase in applied research on neglected diseases in low-income countries. If delays in commercialization challenge the effectiveness of intellectual property protection policies in providing healthcare for those in need, these findings highlight the importance of firms working in tandem with public authorities and multilateral organizations to craft adequate business and public policies to address grand challenges.[25] Likewise, strategic management scholars can play a decisive role in identifying models and configurations that overcome organizational design problems and facilitate collaboration between firms, governments, nonprofits, and multilateral organizations to address grand challenges in a viable manner.[26]

Third, further attention to public and nonprofits can facilitate stakeholder management strategies and assist purpose-oriented firms in identifying suitable strategies to reconcile financial and social goals and ensure the equitable distribution of value across multiple stakeholders. From an instrumental perspective, mapping all stakeholders surrounding the firm, including public and nonprofit organizations, and classifying them according to their current and potential relevance can be a key aspect for firms, regardless of their purpose. Recognizing which stakeholders have legitimate claims, which stakeholders can affect or be affected by actions or omissions of the organization, and understanding their respective stakes are primary steps in the strategizing process. By interacting with their public and nonprofit stakeholders, firms have the opportunity to adapt and eventually revise their strategies, implementing different courses of action that promote better alignment between the demands of the external environment and the internal aspects of the organization deemed necessary for the attainment of strategic objectives.

Firms can also engage with stakeholders based on normative grounds. Instead of guiding their interactions with suppliers, customers, employees, shareholders, governments, communities, and other organizations of civil society solely based on instrumental and economic aspects, firms can

[25] Vakili and McGahan (2016).

[26] George et al. (2024) pay particular attention to SDG-17 "Partnership for the Goals", and focus on the existing barriers to promote further collaboration aimed at addressing grand challenges affecting modern societies.

use corporate values and purpose to shape their decisions. The adoption of relational approaches based on reciprocity and common values and beliefs shared by firms and communities can help strengthen firms' attachments with stakeholders. This, in turn, can increase trust levels in the relationships and induce stakeholders' commitment to projects proposed by the firm. In a study conducted by Thomaz Teodorovicz, Sergio Lazzarini, Anita McGahan, and myself, we analyzed the relationship between a major firm and two sets of stakeholders—managers and employees under flexible arrangements. We found that investments made by the firm in general human capital, which increase the outside options of workers under flexible arrangements and may even benefit competitors, result in improved performance and prolonged relationships with these workers when the training opportunities are framed using relational terms.[27] Therefore, purpose-oriented organizations aiming to foster collective action and address social problems can "*…earn their legitimacy and competitive power from the utility that they represent for their stakeholders*".[28] For that reason, managing relationships with public and nonprofit stakeholders is crucial.

Last, by providing implications for both business policies and public policies, this interdisciplinary view can also facilitate the education of future managers with a mindset distinct from the financially-oriented tradition. This, in turn, has the potential to increase the influence of management lenses in addressing the major problems affecting the interface between business and society. The management community must have a seat at the table for major decisions and occupy a space equivalent to that of lawyers and economists.[29] The organization-oriented mindset inherent in management approaches can contribute to ongoing efforts to improve conditions for certain groups without causing harm to others, leading to win–win-win situations. In such scenarios, businesses, society, and politicians sponsoring successful arrangements all benefit from the outcomes produced.

[27] Teodorovicz et al. (2023).

[28] See Durand (2023, p. 153).

[29] I owe the idea that "managers are out of the table" to my coauthor and friend Anita McGahan, who mentioned it in a presentation in São Paulo, Brazil, in 2009. In large part, my subsequent papers and this book would not be possible without that inspiring talk.

Book Structure

This book is structured in three parts. **Part I** covers the foundations and concepts that underpin the analyses and developments made throughout the book (this chapters, Chapters 2 and 3). **Part II** focuses on aspects related to the internal organization and how they can be articulated to lead to improved performance (Chapters 4, 5, 6, and 7). **Part III** delves into the strategic features of public and nonprofit organizations at the external level (Chapters 8, 9, and 10).

While this chapter introduces this book, Chapter 2 examines why conversations between strategy and public and nonprofit organizations are necessary. It paints a portrait of the evolution of strategic management scholarship and illustrates the convergences and divergences between strategy and public and nonprofit fields.

Chapter 3 introduces the concepts of value creation and public creation, both of which are cornerstones for the relationships between public, private, and nonprofit organizations. The chapter also discusses the forces shaping value creation and explores appropriation dilemmas that arise when a myriad of stakeholders are present.

Chapter 4 inaugurates Part II of the book and addresses a central point for the attainment of strategic objectives in public and nonprofit organizations: the structure of incentives. Departing from the organizational economics literature, the chapter offers readers information about the potential (and limitations) of pay-for-performance schemes to incentivize individuals and groups to exert superior efforts conducive to enhanced performance and public value creation.

Chapter 5 sheds light on performance management systems and their importance for the attainment of strategic objectives in public and nonprofit organizations, as well as in public–private arrangements. Besides discussing the differences between subjective and objective performance, the chapter highlights the potential of the theory of change in choosing performance indicators that effectively assess the value created. The chapter also maintains that appropriate indicators must reflect actions from agents that are associated with performance, are not subject to incentive distortions, and have reduced measurement costs.

Chapter 6 delves into the intricate dilemmas surrounding the allocation of decision rights within public and nonprofit organizations. It examines the advantages and drawbacks of both centralized and decentralized structures, emphasizing the criticality of balancing between central authority and autonomy. Furthermore, the chapter delineates the circumstances under which unitary, multidivisional, and matrix structures must be invoked within the realm of public and nonprofit sectors.

Chapter 7 sheds light on the often overlooked aspect of strategy implementation, contrasting it with the typically emphasized strategic planning process. It outlines the essential components necessary for successful strategy implementation. Moreover, the chapter underscores the critical role of change management in ensuring effective implementation, stressing the significance of aligning the internal organization with external contingencies (external fit), and identifying complementarities among its internal elements (internal fit).

In Chapter 8, the pivotal importance of stakeholder management is explored, particularly within the contexts of public and nonprofit organizations, as well as within private organizations engaging with governments and the potential for generating or destroying public value. The chapter discusses the process of identifying pertinent stakeholders and delineates effective stakeholder strategies under both normative and instrumental approaches.

In Chapter 9, the drivers behind scope choices in governmental settings are dissected through the lenses of organizational economics and policy analysis. The chapter explores various modes of provision and explicates the circumstances under which governments must select the most appropriate modes, considering factors such as probity concerns, the availability of capable partners, and the challenges surrounding property rights and governance.

In Chapter 10, the focus shifts to how cross-sector collaborations (CSCs) offer a viable approach to tackling wicked problems that challenge resolution or mitigation by individual organizations in isolation. The chapter not only presents various forms of collaborations but also delves into the distinctions and similarities between CSCs and strategic alliances. Furthermore, it explores the significance of collaborative governance models, particularly in arrangements where governments assume a substantial orchestrating role. It also emphasizes the crucial role of public–public collaborations for fostering effective public–private partnerships.

Finally, Chapter 11 concludes by summarizing the main topics covered in this book, explaining why strategists, policymakers, and researchers can benefit from it, and shedding light on some important aspects that, although not developed in this work, are crucial for those interested in strategies for public and nonprofit organizations. These aspects include capability-based perspectives and nonmarket strategies.

References

Abbington, J. (2009). Music wars: A perspective from the Black Church. *Liturgy, 24*(4), 40–47.

Adams, S. B. (2005). Stanford and Silicon Valley: Lessons on becoming a high-tech region. *California Management Review, 48*(1), 29–51.

Barnett, M. L., & King, A. A. (2008). Good fences make good neighbors: A longitudinal analysis of an industry self-regulatory institution. *Academy of Management Journal, 51*(6), 1150–1170.

Baron, D. P. (1995). The nonmarket strategy system. *MIT Sloan Management Review, 37*(1), 73.

Bonardi, J.-P., Holburn, G. L., & Vanden Bergh, R. G. (2006). Nonmarket strategy performance: Evidence from US electric utilities. *Academy of Management Journal, 49*(6), 1209–1228.

Brickley, J. A., Smith, C. W., & Zimmerman, J. L. (2001). *Managerial economics and organizational architecture* (2nd ed.). McGraw-Hill.

Bryson, J. M. (2018). *Strategic planning for public and nonprofit organizations: A guide to strengthening and sustaining organizational achievement*. Wiley.

Durand, R. (2023). From the boardroom: Making purpose research relevant for practice. *Strategy Science, 8*(2), 149–158. https://doi.org/10.1287/stsc.2023.0182

Early, G. L. (2004). *One nation under a groove: Motown and American culture*. University of Michigan Press.

Economy, C., Carter, E., & Airoldi, M. (2023). Have we 'stretched' social impact bonds too far? An empirical analysis of SIB design in practice. *International Public Management Journal, 26*(3), 413–436.

Farley, R., Danziger, S., & Holzer, H. J. (2000). *Detroit divided*. Russell Sage Foundation.

Faulk, L., Pandey, S., Pandey, S. K., & Scott Kennedy, K. (2020). Donors' responses to profit incentives in the social sector: The entrepreneurial orientation reward and the profit penalty. *Journal of Policy Analysis and Management, 39*(1), 218–242. https://doi.org/10.1002/pam.22179

Felin, T., & Zenger, T. R. (2017). The theory-based view: Economic actors as theorists. *Strategy Science, 2*(4), 258–271.

Gatignon, A., & Capron, L. (2023). The firm as an architect of polycentric governance: Building open institutional infrastructure in emerging markets. *Strategic Management Journal, 44*(1), 48–85.

George, G., Fewer, T. J., Lazzarini, S., McGahan, A. M., & Puranam, P. (2024). Partnering for grand challenges: A review of organizational design considerations in public–private collaborations. *Journal of Management, 50*(1), 10–40.

Hadani, M., & Schuler, D. A. (2013). In search of El Dorado: The elusive financial returns on corporate political investments. *Strategic Management Journal, 34*(2), 165–181.

Johnson, L. K. (2014). Intelligence shocks, media coverage, and congressional accountability, 1947–2012. *Journal of Intelligence History, 13*(1), 1–21.

Katic, I. V., & Hillman, A. (2023). Corporate political activity, reimagined: Revisiting the political marketplace. *Journal of Management, 49*(6), 1911–1938.

Lazzarini, S. G. (2015). Strategizing by the government: Can industrial policy create firm-level competitive advantage? *Strategic Management Journal, 36*(1), 97–112.

Lazzarini, S. G., Boehe, D., Pongeluppe, L. S., & Cook, M. L. (2020). *From instrumental to normative relational strategies: A study of open buyer-supplier relations.* Paper presented at the Academy of Management Proceedings.

Lazzarini, S. G., Cabral, S., Pongeluppe, L. S., Ferreira, L. C. d. M., & Rotondaro, A. (2021). The best of both worlds? Impact investors and their role in the financial versus social performance debate. In *A research agenda for social finance*. Edward Elgar Publishing.

Lazzarini, S. G., & Zenger, T. (2023). Strategy as (a causal) theory of change. *Academy of Management Proceedings, 2023*(1), 11924. https://doi.org/10.5465/AMPROC.2023.11924abstract

Legg, A. (2010). A taxonomy of musical gesture in African American gospel music. *Popular Music, 29*(1), 103–129.

Mazzucato, M. (2013). *The entrepreneurial state: Debunking public vs private sector myths*. Anthem Press.

McCarthy, M. (2013). The young musicians of Motown: A success story of urban music education. *Music Educators Journal, 99*(3), 35–42.

McGahan, A., & Pongeluppe, L. S. (2023). There is no planet B: Aligning stakeholder interests to preserve the amazon rainforest. *Management Science, 69*(12), 7860–7881. https://doi.org/10.1287/mnsc.2023.4884

Mirel, J. (1999). *The rise and fall of an urban school system: Detroit, 1907–81.* University of Michigan Press.

Nardi, L., Zenger, T., Lazzarini, S. G., & Cabral, S. (2022). Doing well by doing good, uniquely: Materiality and the market value of unique CSR strategies. *Strategy Science, 7*(1), 10–26.

Odziemkowska, K. (2022). Frenemies: Overcoming audiences' ideological opposition to firm–activist collaborations. *Administrative Science Quarterly, 67*(2), 469–514.

Quelin, B. V., Cabral, S., Lazzarini, S., & Kivleniece, I. (2019). The private scope in public–private collaborations: An institutional and capability-based perspective. *Organization Science, 30*(4), 831–846.

Ring, P. S., & Perry, J. L. (1985). Strategic management in public and private organizations: Implications of distinctive contexts and constraints. *Academy of Management Review, 10*(2), 276–286.

Soule, S. A., & Dyke, N. V. (1999). Black church arson in the United States, 1989–1996. *Ethnic and Racial Studies, 22*(4), 724–742.

Teodorovicz, T., Lazzarini, S., Cabral, S., & McGahan, A. M. (2023). Investing in general human capital as a relational strategy: Evidence on flexible arrangements with contract workers. *Strategic Management Journal, 45*, 902–938.

Vakili, K., & McGahan, A. M. (2016). Health care's grand challenge: Stimulating basic science on diseases that primarily afflict the poor. *Academy of Management Journal, 59*(6), 1917–1939.

CHAPTER 2

Strategy Beyond Private and For-profit Organizations

Public and private organizations are more alike than we can imagine. On the one hand, private for-profit organizations are no longer oriented to solely focused on addressing the interests of shareholders. Instead, other stakeholders have been incorporated in the decision-making process, thus adding other performance dimensions that are beyond profits. In an era of important socioenvironmental challenges and sustained development goals, the ever-growing pressure of clients, suppliers, and a myriad of social movements have been shaping how firms run their businesses. Firms have been paying increased attention to how their practices harm the environment, how to manage their supply chains to mitigate the depletion of natural resources, how to enhance gender and race diversity in their operations, and how to incorporate purpose aspects in their routines. By being accountable to other stakeholders than profit-oriented owners, firms are more responsive to societal demands and, hence, become more alike to governments.

On the other hand, governments and public agencies have been implementing several organizational practices that are commonplace in businesses, such as performance-contingent payments, measures of client satisfaction, cross-sector collaborations with non-governmental actors (private and nonprofit), and strategic management tools, to name a few. Along these lines, the United States government through the Government Performance and Results Act (GPRA) of 1993 (P.L. 103–62) and

S. Cabral, *Strategy for Public and Nonprofit Organizations*,
https://doi.org/10.1007/978-3-031-64969-1_2

the GPRA Modernization Act of 2010 (P.L. 111–352) explicitly requires strategic planning at the organizational level to define agency's objectives and how the established objectives will be attained. The pursuit for effectiveness in governments and public agencies makes them more alike to for-profit firms.

In the past few decades, elected officers, bureaucrats, and scholars from both disciplines, public administration, and strategic management, have been arguing about the importance of strategy principles to improve citizens' conditions. Some strategy scholars claim that public and private interests are interdependent and that they need to be seen in tandem to engender global sustainable value creation.[1] In turn, Ewan Ferlie and Edoardo Ongaro, two prominent scholars in the public management scholarship, argue that some strategic management models are largely applicable to public organizations, and efforts to promote the integration of these disciplines are needed.[2]

Yet, considering that strategy and public management disciplines have evolved separately, it is worth delineating how the strategy field changed over time in the management realm and how its lenses can be infused in public and nonprofit organizations.

Strategy: Genesis and Evolution in the Management Realm

The concept of strategy originally referred to military operations and the various tactics that could be used to gain an advantage over the enemy. Sun Tzu in ancient China and Carl Von Clausewitz in the Prussian Kingdom recognized the critical importance of planning, coordination, and an understanding of one's own capabilities when engaged in warfare. Similarly, the Italian philosopher Nicolau Machiavelli associated strategic behavior with conscious adjustments between means and ends to achieve prosperity or, at the very least, survival. He believed that individuals act in their own self-interest, and this drives their strategic decision-making.[3]

[1] See Mahoney et al. (2009).

[2] Ferlie and Ongaro (2022) offer several real-world cases with applications of strategic management models in public organizations.

[3] Niccolò Machiavelli's masterpiece, "The Prince", was published in 1532. It was and still is influential in discussions related to power in organizations and the corresponding strategic implications.

Although the importance of strategic thinking has long been recognized in military circles, the field of strategy gained wider relevance during the twentieth century with the emergence of management programs, particularly in the aftermath of World War II. In the post-war era, businesses and industries were eager to expand and rebuild, and management schools such as Harvard Business School responded by introducing new subjects and courses that would prepare future executives for the challenges of strategic decision-making in the upper echelons of corporate leadership.[4]

In response to the growing demand for effective strategic decision-making in the post-war era, management schools introduced new subjects and courses designed to help students recognize the external and internal factors that affect organizations, as well as develop analytical processes to evaluate and develop alternative solutions under different scenarios. These courses focused on nurturing competencies related to problem-solving, enabling students and practitioners to weigh the pros and cons of different courses of action in a rational manner. To achieve this, the teaching and research of strategy drew on a range of fields, including economics, general management, political science, organizational theory, psychology, sociology, and others. This interdisciplinary approach has allowed strategy to develop a pluralistic and multifaceted identity, characterized by a diverse range of perspectives, theories, and methodologies. As a result, the study of strategy continues to be an important area of research and practice, with relevance across a broad range of industries and sectors.

The strategy field's evolution has always been closely tied to changes in the external environment, the challenges faced by businesses and governments, and the available resources at any given time. In this context, the decades of the 1950s and 1960s were marked by the emergence and expansion of business conglomerates, which created a demand for a deeper understanding of the dynamics of corporate organizations. This period saw the development of new frameworks and models for analyzing and managing corporate structures and operations, including the creation of strategic planning processes, the introduction of management information systems, and the growing emphasis on organizational culture and human resources management. These developments helped to establish

[4] For further information about the history of the Harvard Business School, one of the main responsible by the development of the strategy field, see Copeland (1958).

strategic management as a distinct field of study, with its own set of tools and methodologies for addressing complex organizational challenges.

The initial efforts to understand the details of the corporate world were largely descriptive and inductive, based on observations of real-world organizations. These early studies sought to identify patterns and trends in corporate behavior and performance and to develop frameworks for understanding the factors that contributed to success or failure in the business world. The works of scholars like Alfred Chandler were instrumental in cementing the research on corporate diversification. His research helped to highlight the importance of organizational structures in shaping corporate behavior and performance. Chandler's research suggested that firms needed to adapt their internal structures in response to changes in their external environments or changes in their corporate strategies.[5] Similarly, Igor Ansoff's work provided valuable insights with in-depth case studies to describe best practices within firms and industries. Ansoff's research provided a normative perspective on strategic thinking, outlining what managers should and should not do to achieve success. While the use of prescriptions based on single cases lacks generalizability, Ansoff's approach remains popular among public and private managers more than 50 years after its introduction.[6]

During the decades of 1970 and 1980, the strategy field shifted its focus to financial control in response to external environmental forces and changes within the academic community. This shift was driven in part by the two major oil shocks of the 1970s and the monetary crisis that impacted several developing countries in the 1980s. Incorporating advances from Economics, Mathematics, and Statistics has allowed the strategy field to better understand competitive dynamics under uncertainty. Decision theory, game theory, and advancements in computer processing have narrowed the gap between strategy research and "hard sciences". These advancements have facilitated the development of falsifiable theoretical propositions and empirical tests, including simulations, experiments, and analysis of large datasets with detailed organizational

[5] Alfred Chandler pioneered in studying the relationship between strategy and organizational structures, such as the so-called M-Forms and U-Forms (Chandler, 1962).

[6] With a remarkable career in both public and private sector, Igor Ansoff is one of the founders of the Corporate Strategy stream. He is still one of the most influential strategic management authors of all times (Ansoff, 1965).

data over time. As a result, the strategy field has become more evidence-based and rigorous in its approach.[7]

Advances in behavioral theories made it possible to incorporate sociology, psychology, and political science traits to understand a myriad of strategic phenomena in organizations, including the configuration of organizational networks,[8] the dynamics of organizational survival and strategic changes experienced by organizations,[9] as well as processes involving strategic decisions under bounded rationality and subject to cognitive biases.[10]

However, unlike descriptive and prescriptive works, formal models can be challenging for managers who are not familiar with mathematical notations, as they may find it difficult to absorb the content presented in a dry and technical language. Despite the efforts of leading journal editors and scientific associations in the field to bridge the gap between academics and practitioners, much of the theoretical developments in the strategy realm have limited practical utility for those who ultimately should benefit from scientific advancements. Michael Porter, a renowned scholar from Harvard Business School, is a remarkable exception whose works are widely embraced by both academia and practice.[11]

Michael Porter's contributions to the field of strategy, including his Five Forces Framework and the Diamond Model, have had a significant impact. These frameworks have helped organizations better understand their competitive environment and make informed decisions about their strategic positioning. The Five Forces Framework considers the threats posed by new entrants, substitutes, buyers, suppliers, and competitors, while the Diamond Model looks at the factors that contribute to a country's competitive advantage, including factor conditions, related, and

[7] For a detailed view about the historical evolution of the strategy field see Bownan et al. (2002), Durand et al. (2017), and Hoskisson et al. (1999).

[8] See Granovetter (1982) and Uzzi (1996).

[9] See the works of Hannan and Freeman (1977, 1984).

[10] The Nobel Prize Awards in Economics to Herbert Simon (1982), Daniel Kahneman (2002) and Richard Thaler (2017) highlight the importance of behavioral aspects in individual decision-making and their strategic implications to both public and private organizations. For further information, see Simon (1965, 1973, 1991), Khaneman and Tversky (1982), and Thaler and Ganser (2015).

[11] See Porter (1980, 1990).

supporting industries, firm strategy, structure, and rivalry, and demand conditions.

In addition to Porter's works, various strategic diagnosis tools have become popular in organizations worldwide. For instance, the SWOT matrix, which identifies internal and external environmental factors such as strengths, weaknesses, opportunities, and threats, and the Growth-Share matrix developed by the Boston Consulting Group to aid companies in managing their corporate portfolio. These tools have been incorporated into the routine of many organizations, helping them to evaluate their current positions and to plan future strategies.

The technological and geopolitical changes experienced after the decade of 1990 brought about significant implications for organizations. The observed increase in the flows of goods, services, and information demands not only a set of clear rules to ensure predictability in the game played by organizations. In other words, as Douglass North, the Nobel Prize Winner in 1993, pointed out, institutions or the rules of the game are needed to reduce transaction costs and enable effective governance.[12]

Given the potential impact of the alignment or misalignment between institutions, governance structures, external environment, internal resources, and organization's stakeholders on organizational performance, a significant portion of the strategy field has focused on understanding the configurations that lead to organizational success or failure.

Transaction Cost Economics (TCE) was developed to explain how firms minimize transaction costs when exchanging goods and services. Scholars such as Ronald Coase (1991) and Oliver Williamson (2009), both Nobel Prize winners, contributed to TCE's development. Many strategy scholars have been inspired by TCE to investigate a variety of topics, including buyer–supplier relationships,[13] relationships between firms and governments,[14] internal organization and the interplay between formal and informal structures,[15] strategies out of the market arena

[12] See North (1990).

[13] The works of Dyer (1997) and Kale et al. (2002) on buyer–supplier relationships and of Lumineau and Henderson (2012) on interorganizational relationships in dyads and networks are good examples of the use of TCE in strategy.

[14] See Argyres (1999) and Lazzarini (2015).

[15] See Nickerson and Zenger (2002) and Poppo and Zenger (2002).

(nonmarket strategies),[16] and relationships with a myriad of stakeholders surrounding the focal organization.[17]

In the twenty-first century, there has been a significant shift in the focus of strategy. As boundaries between the public and private sectors have become more fluid, the joint action of public, private, and nonprofit organizations to solve complex problems has become widely accepted. This is particularly true in the face of persistent social dilemmas such as hunger, violence, social exclusion, inequity, and inadequate health and education provision, which has increased the pressure on different actors to find effective solutions. In fact, some of the major problems affecting modern societies cannot be easily addressed by governments in isolation.

For example, neglected diseases such as malaria, dengue, and leishmaniasis affect disenfranchised populations who cannot afford medicines and medical treatment. Due to these circumstances, pharmaceutical companies and privately owned research laboratories may hesitate to invest in innovative technologies because the returns on investment are uncertain. These firms may end up spending substantial amounts on products for markets that lack the means to afford new drugs. In the end, these disenfranchised populations may end up without access to potentially life-saving treatments.

To address these challenges, various organizations from the public, private, nonprofit, and multilateral sectors have been forming partnerships to support the research and development of drugs and medicines for those in need. These collaborations aim to pool resources, knowledge, and expertise to find solutions to neglected diseases and other health issues affecting disenfranchised populations. Through these collaborations, innovative financing mechanisms have been developed to provide incentives for pharmaceutical companies and research laboratories to invest in the development of new treatments and technologies that may not have been viable in the absence of these partnerships. As a result,

[16] To know more about nonmarket strategies, readers may check Baron (1995), Bonardi et al. (2006), Dorobantu et al. (2017), and Paik et al. (2019).

[17] Debates about the importance of stakeholders in a strategy perspective have been gaining prominence in the past years. See the works of Freeman (1984), Barney (2018), and Dorobantu and Odziemkowska (2017) in strategic management and of Gomes et al. (2010) and John M. Bryson et al. (2006) in public management.

more people have access to life-saving medicines, and progress has been made in reducing health disparities in distinct parts of the world.[18]

The successful development of vaccines against COVID-19 is a prime example of the need for coordinated action between private, public, and nonprofit actors. Without the contributions of pharmaceutical companies, government funding, and nonprofit organizations, it would not have been possible to achieve the widespread distribution of vaccines that we are currently witnessing. The COVID-19 pandemic has reinforced the importance of collaboration among different sectors and highlighted the need for a more holistic approach to solving global challenges.

Understanding the key drivers of successful cross-sectoral collaborations aimed at addressing complex social issues is crucial, despite the inherent differences between public and private organizations regarding incentives, accountability standards, and goal ambiguity.[19] The use of strategic management lenses in policy debates has garnered the attention of not only public management scholars interested in strategy but also mainstream management scholars seeking to enrich their theories through examples outside the realm of conventional private firms, given the existing interdependence between public and private interests and the extensive knowledge accumulated in the strategy field.[20] Connection efforts on the public administration side remain consistent. Scholarly works exploring topics such as strategic planning in public organizations,[21] performance drivers in the public sector,[22] and the role

[18] Rezaie et al. (2008) describe in detail how partnership between public and private actors in developing countries has been fostering health innovations. See also George et al. (2012).

[19] See Ring and Perry (1985).

[20] The works of Jay Barney (2005), and Joe Mahoney et al. (2009) are stepping-stones on the new use of strategy in policy debates in the twenty-first century. In common, the authors sustain that novel and interesting organizational phenomena can be investigated through increased research efforts focused on public and nonprofit organizations, and their interactions with business firms. Subsequent efforts to explore the relationships between strategic management constructs and social dilemmas are present in special issues of leading journals such as Strategic Entrepreneurship Journal (McGahan et al., 2013), Journal of Management Studies (Quélin et al., 2017), and Strategic Management Journal (Cabral et al., 2019).

[21] See Bryson (2018) for a comprehensive view about strategic planning in public organizations.

[22] The work of Andrews et al. (2012) is one of the most remarkable attempts to summarize the major concerns of public service performance dilemmas.

of resources and capabilities achieving enhanced performance[23] have become increasingly prevalent.

Incorporating strategic management principles into public and nonprofit organizations necessitates broadening the definition of "strategy" beyond its traditional association with the private sector, as discussed below.

What Is Strategy?

Having explored the origins and evolution of the strategy field, readers may wonder, what exactly does the term "strategy" entail?

Michael Porter asserts that strategy is what distinguishes an organization from its competitors by viewing it as an inherent element in a competitive environment where current and potential rivals can threaten the organization's position, and where the alignment between internal and external factors can provide a sustainable competitive advantage.[24] In turn, Jay Barney argues that strategy is about a theory on how to achieve superior performance standards in the markets and in the industries that organizations operate. Another professor from the University of Utah, Todd Zenger, posits that strategy sustains the identification of unique assets, activities, and resources that once combined enable synergic configurations with value creation potential.[25] Rajiv Nag, Donald Hambrick, and Ming-Jer Chen conducted a comprehensive literature review and employed mixed methods to conclude that the strategy field encompasses both deliberate and emergent initiatives taken by top-level executives to enhance firm performance in external environments, on behalf of the owners.[26]

Although these conceptions are not exhaustive, they commonly share a finalistic component in which organizational outcomes stem from a combination of identified factors. However, as the strategy field expands beyond for-profit private firms and encompasses public and nonprofit organizations, a more comprehensive definition including other organizational types is necessary. In this context, I define strategy as *structured*

[23] See Bryson et al. (2007) and Cabral (2017).

[24] Porter (1996).

[25] See Barney (1997) and Zenger (2016).

[26] Nag et al. (2007).

processes that assist organizations of all types in identifying, acquiring, and preserving the distinctive factors that enable them to translate their ambitions into superior performance, while accounting for the interdependence between their internal and external environments.

Consistent with the efforts to make strategic management constructs applicable to a large set of organizations, the provided definition connects the choices made by public, private, and nonprofit organizations and the subsequent effects. In the case of public and nonprofit organizations, the dependent variables, or the objectives to be accomplished, are not necessarily financial or profitability measures as is common for private firms. According to this definition, the variables of interest cover a broader set of dimensions related to public value creation. This includes features reflecting the impacts on distinct types of stakeholders and extends beyond the actors that are directly impacted by strategic actions. This definition acknowledges the importance of considering various perspectives and the broader societal consequences of strategic decisions in all types of organizations.

Natura a leading multinational cosmetics, beauty, and personal care company, is widely recognized for being a stakeholder-oriented company with constructive partnerships with local suppliers aiming for fair prices and long-term stability in its supply chains. It is important to note that while value-creating arrangements with suppliers from disenfranchised areas may improve the effectiveness of supply chains and improve financial performance, those actions also reduce deforestation and lead to improved environmental outcomes. Leandro Pongeluppe and Anita McGahan conducted a study examining the impact of Natura on environmental outcomes. Their research highlights how Natura effectively addresses positive externalities associated with environmental protection by actively involving stakeholders in the Brazilian Amazon and sharing value with them. The authors' findings demonstrate Natura's commitment to internalizing and promoting sustainable practices, showcasing the company's positive influence on the environment and local communities.[27] This case illustrates the role of strategic actions on improved performance, such as the presence of stakeholder management abilities

[27] See McGahan and Pongeluppe (2023).

to nurture relationships with surrounding communities that complement the firm's resources.[28]

Strategy in the Context of Public and Nonprofit Organizations

Differences Between Public and Private Organizations

In 1985, James Perry, one of the most prolific existing public administration scholars, and Peter Ring, a leading strategic management researcher, have written a piece for the prestigious journal Academy of Management Review. In their pioneering article, they claimed a more intense use of strategic management content in public organizations. They highlighted the importance of considering the unique features and peculiarities of the public sector when applying strategy models in public organizations. *Grosso modo*, when compared to private organizations, public counterparts tend to be more subject to increased regulatory restrictions, stricter hiring, and procurement norms, as well as more rigid accountability standards.[29]

In the past decades, several elected public officers have been trying to improve public capacities by importing private-sector practices to public organizations. It is common to listen to the allegedly and inherent superiority of private practices, especially by right-wing leaders. While public organizations can benefit from the infusion of practices developed in other contexts, and managerial reforms in the public sector such as the well-known New Public Management (NPM) have reduced the public–private gap, the acknowledgment of the existing differences between public and private spheres is key to avoid inadequate strategies with a low likelihood of success are designed in implemented.

One of the most striking differences between public and private organizations is the *structure of incentives*. Public organizations are characterized by weak and low-powered incentives as they have limited capacity to implement rewards and sanctions mechanisms to induce superior efforts

[28] Cabral et al. (2019) highlight the importance of strategic management lenses for value-creating structures involving firms concerned with broader societal issues.

[29] Ring and Perry (1985).

of civil servants.[30] In most countries, civil servants with job security hardly ever have their contracts terminated due to performance insufficiency. On one side, job security in public organizations reduces the margin of maneuver for terminating job contracts based on patronage grounds, ensuring a more stable workforce that retains the accumulated knowledge. Nevertheless, the impossibility of firing underperforming servants may contribute to deficient service provision to citizens.

Indeed, corporativism and pressure for unions to protect employees are commonplace in public organizations and may hinder the enforcement of severe sanctions against civil servants who misbehave.[31] In addition, implementing stronger incentives in the public sector via rewards is not straightforward as well. Budgetary restrictions along with legal and ideological barriers against performance-contingent payments and difficult-to-measure performance tend to impede the adoption of reward structures that are conducive to improved outcomes. Even when public officers can remove the existing hurdles and implement pay-for-performance programs, public organizations are not free of implementing programs with inadequate targets, low incentive intensity, and incentive distortions caused by free-riding, gaming, and multitask.[32]

Public organizations tend also to serve a more diverse set of stakeholders, which can force them to pursue multiple objectives that can eventually be in conflict with one another. Should a state-owned water and sewage company pursue financial goals or assure services with low costs to citizens? Should the head of a corrections department pursue the promotion of reinsertion strategies or prioritize security and order dimensions in prisons? Would education department managers promote actions toward improved student learning or actions to minimize the costs per student? Answers to these types of questions are not straightforward, of course. All these hypothetical situations illustrate key organizational

[30] For a more detailed account of incentives in public and private organizations, see Williamson (1999) and Dixit (2002).

[31] In a joint research with Sergio Lazzarini, I have investigated the challenges of sanctioning civil servants in police forces. We find that officer-specific features along with investigation features and organizational structure of internal affairs divisions influence hazards of punishment (and acquittal) of officers suspected of misbehavior. See Cabral and Lazzarini (2015).

[32] Heinrich and Marschke (2010) provide an interesting portrait of pay-for-performance challenges in the public sector realm.

problems induced by ***goal ambiguity*** in public organizations. As a result, organizations that prioritize accommodating various interests without explicitly addressing trade-offs and choosing clear courses of action are more prone to obtain lower performance standards.

Public Policy Cycle and Strategy

Although the set of existing constraints in public organizations may foster operational rigidity and frustrate citizens expecting flexible and agile governments, there are opportunities to address such limitations. One possibility involves exploiting accumulated knowledge in strategy to address these problems. Developing specific strategic approaches to public and nonprofit organizations can enable enhanced conversations and collaborations between the fields of strategy and public administration. By embracing these opportunities and stimulating convergences, it becomes possible to integrate the strategic management reasoning with the public policy cycle (design, implementation, and evaluation).

The first connection is between the design phase in the policy cycle and the strategic planning process. Policymakers can reap important benefits from using strategic planning tools when designing new policies. These tools may help policymakers to align current resources and structures with expected (or possible) policy goals. By considering key strategic features such as mission, vision, and organizational values into policymaking, policymakers can ensure greater cohesion and direction. Further, strategic planning enables a comprehensive analysis of both internal and external environments, which allows policymakers to detect critical resources, trade-offs, and other factors that may thwart policy effectiveness.[33] In addition to incorporating strategic planning features, policy designers can leverage the knowledge and past experiences of managers, as well as the outcomes of similar policies implemented in different contexts. By doing so, they can craft effective theories of change that establish connections between inputs, activities, outputs, outcomes, and desired impacts in an evidence-based fashion. Although the theory of change can be applied to implement policies and guide evaluation, its significance in the design stage lies particularly in problem formulation. It supports a theory-based approach, wherein managers and policymakers, acting as strategists, devise

[33] Ferlie and Ongaro (2015) and Bryson (2018) provide comprehensive views of strategic planning in public organizations.

unique theories that involve mobilizing adequate resources to address the problems they want to tackle.[34]

Second, performance management systems may be equally relevant during the evaluation phase. Drawing from the accumulated knowledge in policy analysis, public officers could establish causal connections between strategical resources, practices, and outcomes. Besides identifying existing complementarities between strategic factors, causal-based policy evaluations using counterfactual assessments can not only inform policy evaluation but also activate new accountability standards in public organizations. In fact, evidence-based policymaking can contribute to improving the clarity between efforts (both individual and collective) and outcomes. Further, more stringent policy evaluation techniques can alter current incentive structures and highlight effective, or ineffective, organizational arrangements. Despite the limitations of using experimental and non-experimental techniques based on counterfactual assessment,[35] the pursuit of causal-based evidence reinforces the importance of using strategic management tenets, like performance management systems, in the public policy cycle.

Third, public policy implementation can benefit from the inventory of accumulated knowledge on strategy execution (or strategy implementation).[36] An adequate implementation requires the acknowledgment of the existing interdependence between policy design (strategy formulation) and policy evaluation (performance management). Drawing on a contingent perspective, organizational dimensions present in the implementation process must align with both the external environment and the other dimensions in a complementary fashion. For instance, to provide effective implementations that are conducive to superior performance, it is key to align resources, practices, incentive systems, and allocation of decision rights. This alignment should not only consider aligned environmental forces, such as political, technological, economic, and legal

[34] For connections between theories of change and strategy process, see Lazzarini and Zenger (2023) and Felin and Zenger (2017).

[35] In a joint work with Sergio Lazzarini, Sergio Firpo, Thomaz Teodorovicz, and I, we have established the reasons why counterfactual assessment techniques are not highly disseminated in the outcome-based contracts realm. For further information, see Lazzarini et al. (2022).

[36] For good reviews about strategy execution, see Higgins (2005) and Tawse and Tabesh (2021).

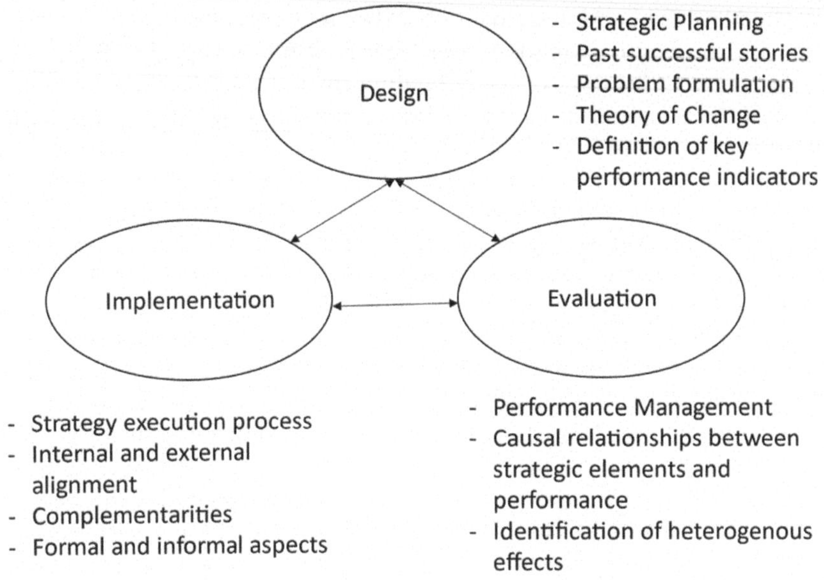

Fig. 2.1 Policy cycle and strategic elements

but also account for the informal aspects surrounding the organization, including culture, codes of conduct, taboos, and so on. In other words, assuring coherence and compatibility among these various dimensions is crucial to effective strategy/policy implementation.

Figure 2.1 illustrates the relationships between strategic elements and the policy cycle.

Strategy in Public Organizations: Cooptation by Private Interests? Really?

Despite an increasing convergence on the feasibility of applying strategy theories to areas addressing urgent societal issues, dissenting opinions against expanding cross-disciplinary dialogues persist. Some of these voices conceive strategy as a body of knowledge exclusive to private firms, while others argue that policy issues are too complex to be informed by strategy theories developed in the context of private sector.

The New Public Management (NPM) paradigm, introduced in countries like the United Kingdom and New Zealand during the 1980s and 1990s, played a leading role in facilitating the infusion of practices developed in the private sector into public organizations. Increased claims for the use of performance management practices in governments created tensions with the traditional modus operandi based on the bureaucratic paradigm. The lack of efficiency and effectiveness of procedural-based approaches reinforced the need for alternative approaches inspired by market mechanisms. These novel approaches were later adapted to the public and nonprofit context.[37]

The implementation of the New Public Management (NPM) approach led many governments to embark on a role redesign journey. Rather than solely functioning as executors, these governments began to assume a more strategic role. They shifted their focus toward defining major guidelines and fostering collaboration with many public and private entities in the delivery of public services. This strategic role resembles the design approach advocated by Igor Ansoff.[38] In this context, top leaders within public organizations play a vital role in setting overarching principles, incentive schemes, and performance evaluation methods to support the implementation of previously designed strategies.

Under the framework of New Public Management (NPM), governments actively encouraged the involvement of external actors in the provision of public services through various modes such as outsourcing, concessions, public–private partnerships, and privatization. Also, governments sought to foster collaborative efforts with the third sector, particularly in education, healthcare, and social services. This shift was accompanied by an increasing emphasis on citizen-centric approaches, where the focus shifted to treating individuals as clients or customers. Buzzwords such as results-oriented, performance-based payments, transparency, and compliance gradually became embedded in the functioning of government institutions.

It is important to acknowledge that the infusion of private-sector practices into the public sector was met with varying degrees of resistance

[37] Hood (1995) provides an excellent account of New Public Management, its aims, and its limitations.

[38] For a further description of the design school, see Ansoff (1965). A portrait of the different schools of the strategic management thought can be seen in Mintzberg et al. (2020).

and inertia in some government entities. This includes several constructs related to the field of strategy. However, overall, there was a noticeable shift toward adopting a more strategic-oriented role. This transformation brought about significant changes, including the increased influence, and expanded scope of audit bodies, which began to exert coercive power and intervene in all phases of the policy cycle. It is now common to witness watchdog agencies scrutinizing decisions made by elected officials, even during the policy design phase. While this enhanced oversight can be viewed as serving the public interest by preventing misconduct by public officials, it also introduces a level of uncertainty due to discretionary interpretations of legal rules. This uncertainty can discourage risk-averse officers from pursuing innovative initiatives in the public sector, as they may hesitate to take action that could be called into question by regulatory bodies. Finding the right balance between accountability and flexibility is key to fostering a conducive environment for innovation. This remains a challenge in this evolving landscape.

Strategy and Public Administration/Management: More Dialogues Are Needed

Some scholars have directed their attention toward integrating some widely accepted strategic management theories into the public administration/management literature. To address the need of adapting internal structures to environmental changes, the utilization of typologies, such as those formulated by Miles and Snow, has become commonplace. These typologies serve as valuable tools for understanding the interplay between strategies, structures, and the external environment.[39] This view inspired public administration scholars such as Kennett Meyer, George Boyne, Peter O'Toole, and Richard Walker, who have sought to develop typologies that capture the unique characteristics of public organizations.

Public administration/management scholars have also been arguing about the importance of strategic planning in public organizations to cope with the trend of increasing citizen's demands in times of decreasing public funds. Over the last decades, John Bryson emerged as one of the most active advocates of the importance of the strategic planning

[39] See Miles et al. (1978) to know more about the foundations of the relationship between strategy, structure, and environment, and Meier et al. (2010) to observe the application of Miles and Snow's theories in public organizations.

process as an inducer of organization's decisions toward established goals. His contributions have been influential in the field of public administration.[40] Recent works suggest a positive association between strategic planning and performance. These works provide support for the proposition that strategic planning serves as a prevailing channel to drive public organizations toward improved outcomes.[41]

While these research efforts have been valuable to raise the awareness of the importance of infusing strategy constructs in public and nonprofit organizations, these research endeavors are not without their share of criticisms. Besides the well-known counterargument surrounding the overreliance on principles derived from competitive environments, which may not fully cover the particulars of the public and nonprofit realm,[42] there are other points that deserve attention. A non-negligible portion of the existing works are descriptive and focus on testing strategic management theories in the context of public organizations. Although the testing of theories in specific contexts is valuable to inform practitioners about what may work and what may not work, it is crucial that current research move beyond to make the existing literature of strategy in public organizations more influential. This involves extending the reach of scholarly works and intervention in practice beyond disciplinary walls and, most importantly, guiding both business and public policymaking. In fact, we see limited involvement of management scholars in decision-making arenas. Instead, these spaces are predominantly occupied by lawyers and economists.

Considering that both relevance and rigor are key features to be considered and heard at the table, there is a growing trend to valorize empirical strategies that are grounded in solid causal foundations in public administration and strategic management research. This requires the employment of experimental (i.e., Randomized Control Trials) and quasi-experimental approaches, such as Difference-in-Differences, Research Discontinuity Designs, or Synthetic Control Methods to assure that the

[40] See Bryson (1988, 2018).

[41] George et al. (2019) performed a meta-analysis in 31 studies and found that strategic planning is effective to lead organizations to achieve their established goals, especially when the strategic planning process is formal. However, despite these efforts, to the date, causal evidence of the relationship between strategic planning and public service performance remains scant.

[42] See Brown (2010).

relationships between strategy constructs and performance hold. These rigorous methods are key to bolstering the credibility of this research agenda with relevant stakeholders.

There is also room for enhanced efforts to connect works that occur in parallel in both fields. One area that would benefit from further integration is the study of pay-for-performance programs.[43] An enhanced conversation between strategy and public management would provide a more comprehensive understanding of how individuals and group members respond to incentives, including in private firms.[44] Another area of potential collaboration is the exploration of resources and capabilities in buyer–supplier relationships, when the buyer is a public agency. This includes a myriad of promising topics, such as public procurement and public–private partnerships, where efforts by public management scholars to be heard and recognized by strategy scholars are becoming increasingly visible.[45] Other areas, such as organizational design,[46] present opportunities for increased conversation. Certainly, exploring the dilemmas of centralization and decentralization, as well as investigating the alignment between principals, agents, and stewards in public and nonprofit organizations, with the support of novel and consistent theoretical and empirical approaches, are avenues for integration between strategy and public and nonprofit scholars.[47]

Overall, there is a promising venue for works that goes beyond mere descriptive accounts, which often resemble consulting reports. Instead,

[43] To know more about incentives in public organizations, see the works of Heinrich (2007), Heinrich and Marschke (2010), and Park and Berry (2014).

[44] The works of Frank and Obloj (2014) and Nyberg et al. (2018) provide interesting insights on the dynamics of individual and collective incentives in private firms.

[45] The work of John Bryson, Barbara Crosby and Melissa Stone on cross-sector collaborations (Bryson et al., 2006) dialogues with contemporary works in strategy either conceptual (Quélin et al., 2017) or empirical (Gatignon & Capron, 2023). In the same vein, some public administration scholars have been attempting to publish their works on the role of capabilities in public procurement in both public administration and strategy outlets. See Alonso and Andrews (2019).

[46] Andrews et al. (2009) bring questions related to centralization and decentralization in public organizations and the corresponding performance implications.

[47] See Van Slyke (2007) for an interesting reflection on how agents can behave like stewards in public organizations and Cabral and Lazzarini (2015) for an analysis of the performance implications from the design of organizations in which the role of agent-monitors and agent-executors are intertwined.

the focus tends to be on identifying the relevant strategic factors that shape performance, determining how value is created, and examining the stakeholders from public, private, and nonprofit organizations who capture that value in both market and nonmarket arenas. More crucially, understanding the conditions under which the value created is appropriated by stakeholders with legitimate claims is essential in a world where previously silent stakeholders are progressively becoming more vocal.[48]

Conclusions

Despite relevant differences in terms of incentives, flexibility, purpose, and accountability standards, public and nonprofit organizations face several challenges that are common to their private counterparts. They need to attract and select adequate employees, motivating them to exert the necessary efforts to produce outcomes. Additionally, they must manage relationships with multiple stakeholders who may have conflicting objectives. Public and nonprofit organizations, as well as private firms, must also pay attention to communicating their actions, managing operations, developing new products and services to serve clients and citizens, controlling their finances, planning their future, and dealing with trade-offs. In line with our definition of strategy as *structured processes that assist organizations of all types in identifying, acquiring, and preserving the distinctive factors that enable them to translate their ambitions into superior performance, while accounting for the interdependence between their internal and external environments*, public and nonprofit organizations, like private firms, need strategies to achieve their goals.

Besides offering a definition of strategy applicable to a wide spectrum of organizations, this chapter illustrates the evolution of strategic management thinking over time. It highlights convergences between public administration and strategy scholars regarding the importance of using strategic management lenses to address pressing societal needs found in most societies worldwide. While recognizing the differences between various types of organizations is crucial for delineating feasible responses to real problems and avoiding superficial one-size-fits-all solutions, efforts to identify under which conditions strategic management approaches can help public and nonprofit organizations create value for a broader range

[48] See Cabral et al. (2019).

of citizens are key. This is essential to ensure that (strategic) management and public administration scholars are heard by decision-makers, inviting them to the table to discuss, inform, and guide important decisions that affect societies at large.

References

Alonso, J. M., & Andrews, R. (2019). Governance by targets and the performance of cross-sector partnerships: Do partner diversity and partnership capabilities matter? *Strategic Management Journal, 40*(4), 556–579.

Andrews, R., Boyne, G. A., Law, J., & Walker, R. M. (2009). Centralization, organizational strategy, and public service performance. *Journal of Public Administration Research and Theory, 19*(1), 57–80.

Andrews, R., Boyne, G. A., Law, J., & Walker, R. M. (2012). *Strategic management and public service performance*. Palgrave Macmillan.

Ansoff, H. I. (1965). *Corporate strategy: An analytic approach to business policy for growth and expansion*. McGraw Hill.

Argyres, N. S. (1999). The impact of information technology on coordination: Evidence from the B-2 "Stealth" bomber. *Organization Science, 10*(2), 162–180.

Barney, J. B. (1997). *Gaining and sustaining competitive advantage*. Addison-Wesley Publishing Company.

Barney, J. B. (2005). Should strategic management research engage public policy debates? *Academy of Management Journal, 48*(6), 945–948.

Barney, J. B. (2018). Why resource-based theory's model of profit appropriation must incorporate a stakeholder perspective. *Strategic Management Journal, 39*(13), 3305–3325. https://doi.org/10.1002/smj.2949

Baron, D. P. (1995). The nonmarket strategy system. *MIT Sloan Management Review, 37*(1), 73.

Bonardi, J.-P., Holburn, G. L., & Bergh, R. G. V. (2006). Nonmarket strategy performance: Evidence from US electric utilities. *Academy of Management Journal, 49*(6), 1209–1228.

Bowman, E. H., Singh, H., & Thomas, H. (2002). The domain of strategic management: History and evolution. In A. Pettigrew, H. Thomas, & R. Whittington (Eds.), *Handbook of strategy and management* (pp. 31–51). Sage.

Brown, T. L. (2010). The evolution of public sector strategy. *Public Administration Review, 70*(s1), s212–s214.

Bryson, J. M. (1988). A strategic planning process for public and non-profit organizations. *Long Range Planning, 21*(1), 73–81.

Bryson, J. M. (2018). *Strategic planning for public and nonprofit organizations: A guide to strengthening and sustaining organizational achievement*. Wiley.

Bryson, J. M., Ackermann, F., & Eden, C. (2007). Putting the resource-based view of strategy and distinctive competencies to work in public organizations. *Public Administration Review, 67*(4), 702–717.

Bryson, J. M., Crosby, B. C., & Stone, M. M. (2006). The design and implementation of cross-sector collaborations: Propositions from the literature. *Public Administration Review, 66*, 44–55.

Cabral, S. (2017). Reconciling conflicting policy objectives in public contracting: The enabling role of capabilities. *Journal of Management Studies, 54*(6). https://doi.org/10.1111/joms.12269

Cabral, S., & Lazzarini, S. G. (2015). The "guarding the guardians" problem: An analysis of the organizational performance of an internal affairs division. *Journal of Public Administration Research and Theory, 25*(3), 797–829.

Cabral, S., Mahoney, J. T., McGahan, A. M., & Potoski, M. (2019). Value creation and value appropriation in public and nonprofit organizations. *Strategic Management Journal, 40*(4), 465–475.

Chandler, A. D. (1962). *Strategy and structure*. MIT Press.

Copeland, M. T. (1958). *An mark an era: The history of Harvard Business School*. Little Brown and Company.

Dixit, A. (2002). Incentives and organizations in the public sector: An interpretative review. *The Journal of Human Resources, 37*(4), 696–727.

Dorobantu, S., Kaul, A., & Zelner, B. (2017). Nonmarket strategy research through the lens of new institutional economics: An integrative review and future directions. *Strategic Management Journal, 38*(1), 114–140.

Dorobantu, S., & Odziemkowska, K. (2017). Valuing stakeholder governance: Property rights, community mobilization, and firm value. *Strategic Management Journal, 38*(13), 2682–2703.

Durand, R., Grant, R. M., & Madsen, T. L. (2017). The expanding domain of strategic management research and the quest for integration. *Strategic Management Journal, 38*(1), 4–16.

Dyer, J. H. (1997). Effective interfirm collaboration: How firms minimize transaction costs and maximize transaction value. *Strategic Management Journal, 18*(7), 535–556.

Felin, T., & Zenger, T. R. (2017). The theory-based view: Economic actors as theorists. *Strategy Science, 2*(4), 258–271.

Ferlie, E., & Ongaro, E. (2015). *Strategic management in public services organizations: Concepts, schools and contemporary issues*. Routledge.

Ferlie, E., & Ongaro, E. (2022). *Strategic management in public services organizations: Concepts, schools and contemporary issues*. Routledge.

Frank, D. H., & Obloj, T. (2014). Firm-specific human capital, organizational incentives, and agency costs: Evidence from retail banking. *Strategic Management Journal, 35*(9), 1279–1301.

Freeman, R. E. (1984). *Strategic management: A stakeholder approach*. Pitman.

Gatignon, A., & Capron, L. (2023). The firm as an architect of polycentric governance: Building open institutional infrastructure in emerging markets. *Strategic Management Journal, 44*(1), 48–85.

George, B., Walker, R. M., & Monster, J. (2019). Does strategic planning improve organizational performance? A Meta-Analysis. *Public Administration Review, 79*(6), 810–819.

George, G., McGahan, A. M., & Prabhu, J. (2012). Innovation for inclusive growth: Towards a theoretical framework and a research agenda. *Journal of Management Studies, 49*(4), 661–683.

Gomes, R. C., Liddle, J., & Gomes, L. O. M. (2010). A five-sided model of stakeholder influence: A cross-national analysis of decision making in local government. *Public Management Review, 12*(5), 701–724.

Granovetter, M. (1982). The strength of weak ties: A network theory revisited. In P. V. Marsden & N. Lin (Eds.), *Social structure and network analysis* (pp. 105–130). Sage.

Hannan, M. T., & Freeman, J. (1977). The population ecology of organizations. *American Journal of Sociology, 83*(929–984).

Hannan, M. T., & Freeman, J. (1984). Structural inertia and organizational change. *American Sociological Review, 49*, 149–164.

Heinrich, C. J. (2007). False or fitting recognition? The use of high performance bonuses in motivating organizational achievements. *Journal of Policy Analysis and Management, 26*(2), 281–304. https://doi.org/10.1002/pam.20244

Heinrich, C. J., & Marschke, G. (2010). Incentives and their dynamics in public sector performance management systems. *Journal of Policy Analysis and Management, 29*(1), 183–208.

Higgins, J. M. (2005). The eight 'S's of successful strategy execution. *Journal of Change Management, 5*(1), 3–13.

Hood, C. (1995). The "new public management" in the 1980s: Variations on a theme. *Accounting, Organizations and Society, 20*(2–3), 93–109. https://doi.org/10.1016/0361-3682(93)E0001-W

Hoskisson, R. E., Wan, W. P., Yiu, D., & Hitt, M. A. (1999). Theory and research in strategic management: Swings of a pendulum. *Journal of Management, 25*(3), 417–456.

Kale, P., Dyer, J. H., & Singh, H. (2002). Alliance capability, stock market response, and long-term alliance success: The role of the alliance function. *Strategic Management Journal, 23*, 747–767.

Khaneman, D., & Tversky, A. (1982). *Judgment under uncertainty: Heuristics and biases*. Cambridge University Press.

Lazzarini, S. G. (2015). Strategizing by the government: Can industrial policy create firm-level competitive advantage? *Strategic Management Journal, 36*(1), 97–112.

Lazzarini, S. G., Cabral, S., Firpo, S., & Teodorovicz, T. (2022). Why are counterfactual assessment methods not widespread in outcome-based contracts? A formal model approach. *Journal of Public Administration Research and Theory, 32*(3), 509–523.

Lazzarini, S. G., & Zenger, T. (2023). Strategy as (a causal) theory of change. *Academy of Management Proceedings, 2023*(1), 11924. https://doi.org/10.5465/AMPROC.2023.11924abstract

Lumineau, F., & Henderson, J. E. (2012). The influence of relational experience and contractual governance on the negotiation strategy in buyer–supplier disputes. *Journal of Operations Management, 30*(5), 382–395.

Mahoney, J. T., McGahan, A. M., & Pitelis, C. N. (2009). Perspective—The interdependence of private and public interests. *Organization Science, 20*(6), 1034–1052.

McGahan, A., & Pongeluppe, L. S. (2023). There is no planet B: Aligning stakeholder interests to preserve the Amazon rainforest. *Management Science, 69*(12), 7860–7881. https://doi.org/10.1287/mnsc.2023.4884

McGahan, A. M., Zelner, B. A., & Barney, J. B. (2013). Entrepreneurship in the public interest: Introduction to the special issue. *Strategic Entrepreneurship, 7*, 1–5.

Meier, K. J., O'Toole, L. J., Boyne, G. A., Walker, R. M., & Andrews, R. (2010). Alignment and results: Testing the interaction effects of strategy, structure, and environment from miles and snow. *Administration & Society, 42*(2), 160–192.

Miles, R. E., Snow, C. C., Meyer, A. D., & Coleman, H. J., Jr. (1978). Organizational strategy, structure, and process. *Academy of Management Review, 3*(3), 546–562.

Mintzberg, H., Ahlstrand, B., & Lampel, J. B. (2020). *Strategy safari*. Pearson.

Nag, R., Hambrick, D. C., & Chen, M. J. (2007). What is strategic management, really? Inductive derivation of a consensus definition of the field. *Strategic Management Journal, 28*(9), 935–955.

Nickerson, J. A., & Zenger, T. R. (2002). Being efficiently fickle: A dynamic theory of organizational choice. *Organization Science, 13*(5), 547–567.

North Douglas, C. (1990). *Institutions, institutional change and economic performance*. Cambridge University Press.

Nyberg, A. J., Maltarich, M. A., Abdulsalam, D. D., Essman, S. M., & Cragun, O. (2018). Collective pay for performance: A cross-disciplinary review and meta-analysis. *Journal of Management, 44*(6), 2433–2472.

Paik, Y., Kang, S., & Seamans, R. (2019). Entrepreneurship, innovation, and political competition: How the public sector helps the sharing economy create value. *Strategic Management Journal, 40*(4), 503–532. https://doi.org/10.1002/smj.2937

Park, S., & Berry, F. (2014). Successful diffusion of a failed policy: The case of pay-for-performance in the US federal government. *Public Management Review, 16*(6), 763–781.

Poppo, L., & Zenger, T. R. (2002). Do formal contracts and relational governance function as substitutes or complements? *Strategic Management Journal, 23*(8), 707–726.

Porter, M. E. (1980). *Competitive strategy*. The Free Press.

Porter, M. E. (1990, March–April). The competitive advantage of nations. *Harvard Business Review*, 73–93.

Porter, M. E. (1996, November–December). What is strategy? *Harvard Business Review*, 61–78.

Quélin, B. V., Kivleniece, I., & Lazzarini, S. (2017). Public-private collaboration, hybridity and social value: Towards new theoretical perspectives. *Journal of Management Studies, 54*(6), 763–792. https://doi.org/10.1111/joms.12274

Rezaie, R., Frew, S. E., Sammut, S. M., Maliakkal, M. R., Daar, A. S., & Singer, P. A. (2008). Brazilian health biotech—Fostering crosstalk between public and private sectors. *Nature Biotechnology, 26*(6), 627–644.

Ring, P. S., & Perry, J. L. (1985). Strategic management in public and private organizations: Implications of distinctive contexts and constraints. *Academy of Management Review, 10*(2), 276–286.

Simon, H. A. (1965). Administrative decision-making. *Public Administration Review, 25*(1), 31–37.

Simon, H. A. (1973). Organization man—Rational or self-actualizing. *Public Administration Review, 33*(4), 346–353.

Simon, H. A. (1991). Bounded rationality and organizational learning. *Organization Science, 2*(1), 125–134.

Tawse, A., & Tabesh, P. (2021). Strategy implementation: A review and an introductory framework. *European Management Journal, 39*(1), 22–33. https://doi.org/10.1016/j.emj.2020.09.005

Thaler, R. H., & Ganser, L. (2015). *Misbehaving: The making of behavioral economics*. Nash Format.

Uzzi, B. (1996). The sources and consequences of embeddedness for the economic performance of organizations: The network effect. *American Sociological Review*, 61, 674–698.

Van Slyke, D. M. (2007). Agents or Stewards: Using theory to understand the government-nonprofit social service contracting relationship. *Journal of Public Administration Research and Theory, 17*(2), 157–187. https://doi.org/10.1093/jopart/mul012

Williamson, O. E. (1999). Public and private bureaucracies: A transaction cost economics perspective. *Journal of Law, Economics and Organization, 15*(1), 306–342.

Zenger, T. (2016). *Beyond competitive advantage: How to solve the puzzle of sustaining growth while creating value*. Harvard Business Review Press.

CHAPTER 3

Public Value Creation

Acclaimed as the greatest basketball player of all time, Michael Jordan was extraordinary both on and off the court. In addition to amassing numerous records in the National Basketball Association (NBA), Michael Jordan remains one of the most valued endorsers for several major brands. Along these lines, the 2023 movie "*Air*", directed by Ben Affleck and based on factual facts, portrays the world-shattering partnership established in 1984 between Nike and Michael Jordan, which sparked a revolution in the global sneaker industry. During that time, rival sports brands like Adidas and Converse signed contracts with basketball players to recommend their shoes for a fixed sum. Nike, to strengthen its position in the basketball shoe market, took an aggressive approach by offering an uncommon deal to Michael Jordan: US$ 250,000 per year for an exclusive line of products known as "*Air Jordan*". This investment amounted to the entire annual budget of Nike's basketball division. Committing such financial resources to a young and talented player who recently had been drafted by Chicago Bulls from the University of North Carolina was an unprecedented and bold move.

Not surprisingly, Adidas, already an established presence in the basketball industry, responded by matching Nike's offer. In a strategic move, Nike reacted by accepting a counteroffer from Deloris Jordan, Michael Jordan's mother. In addition to the fixed amount over five years, she proposed a percentage of each sale of the Air Jordan line. Nike was

S. Cabral, *Strategy for Public and Nonprofit Organizations*,
https://doi.org/10.1007/978-3-031-64969-1_3

initially forecasting sales of US$ 3 million in the first year, but the actual results were above US$ 160 million within that period. Despite the inherent risks, this groundbreaking deal had a transformative effect and altered the trajectory of the industry. This case also offers valuable insights applicable to the context of public and nonprofit sectors, as we will see next.[1]

Bolsa Familia, a conditional cash-transfer program intended to combat extreme poverty, was introduced by the Brazilian federal government in 2003. The program has a very straightforward structure. If children in the family attend school and meet certain medical requirements, such as the completion of the vaccination schedule for children under the age of 7 and attendance at public health units for pregnant and nursing women for monitoring purposes, families with income below a certain threshold are given remuneration.

The program improved health outcomes by increasing infant visits to public health units for preventive services and lowering infant mortality due to malnutrition and diarrhea with a budget of less than 1% of the Brazilian Gross Domestic Product (GDP). Additionally, the program increased girl school enrollment and grade progression, particularly for girls in rural areas and those between the ages of 15 and 17 in urban areas. It also decreased fertility among teenagers. Additionally, there is evidence that Bolsa Familia decreased crime rates, particularly for property crimes.[2]

What connects these two cases?

Both examples represent value creation in a stylized manner. The agreement between Nike and Michael Jordan is a prime example of how value could be created and shared among a broader set of stakeholders beyond Nike's shareholders and executives, by combining financial resources with Michael Jordan's innate traits. The Brazilian conditional cash-transfer program serves as an example of how a low-cost solution can increase public value by alleviating poverty while also enhancing

[1] See https://screenrant.com/michael-jordan-air-jordan-profits-air-movie/.

[2] In the last two decades, the Bolsa Familia program and their policy implications were widely studied. Shei et al. (2014) and Rasella et al. (2013) analyze the impact of Bolsa Familia on health outcomes. An additional analysis on the program's effects on education can be seen in De Brauw et al. (2015). Olson et al. (2019) offer an interesting analysis on how the program influenced pregnancy in Brazilian teenagers, while Chioda et al. (2016) assess the effects of Bolsa Familia on crime outcomes.

outcomes in education, health, and public security by allocating money to disenfranchised families.

The two cases align with the definition of strategy provided in the previous chapter, illustrating the significance of structured processes for organizations to identify and preserve factors that mediate the relationship between intentions and effective outcomes. Both Nike and the Brazilian federal government were able to alter the conversation patterns in their respective environments due to their successful value-creating strategies.

Value creation is at the core of both the strategy and public and nonprofit fields. While initial discussions about value in the strategy field focused on how shareholders can appropriate value created in private organizations, there is now a growing interest among firms in distributing this value among their stakeholders. Some businesses can generate public value without sacrificing the pursuit of financial value by creating goods or services to meet the needs of disenfranchised populations, as illustrated in the Natura example above. Similarly, scholars and practitioners in the public and nonprofit realm are closely observing the increasing trend of cross-sector collaborations involving organizations from different sectors and their implications for public value creation. Businesses and nonprofits can assist governments in creating value for citizens, just as governments can support businesses and nonprofits in pursuing their missions while benefiting targeted populations.

What Is Value? A Strategic Approach

I often teach strategy courses to managers from private, public, and nonprofit organizations. Typically, in my initial classes, I engage students by asking them to reflect on their roles within their respective organizations and the overall outcomes they should strive to achieve. It is common for managers in for-profit organizations to emphasize the importance of value creation as a primary objective. Civil servants and nonprofit managers oftentimes assert that their role is to create public value. However, when I delve deeper and inquire about the specific meaning of "value" and "public value", the responses I receive tend to lack precision.

To promote cross-disciplinary dialogues between strategy and public and nonprofit fields, it is necessary to understand how value creation concepts are framed in both public and private contexts.

With a focus on value creation in the context of private firms, Adam Brandenburger and Harborne Stuart Jr offer[3] a view on the foundations of value creation. In a simplified way, value creation in an organization involves a relationship between the benefits generated from a particular action or set of actions that benefit buyers and the supplier's opportunity costs. In a given transaction where buyers enjoy certain goods or services provided by entities responsible for their provision, the value created (VC) stems from the difference between the buyer's willingness to pay (WTP) and the firm's suppliers opportunity costs (OC), such that: VC = WTP − OC.

Firms, firm's buyers, and firm's suppliers, however, appropriate to a greater or lesser extent the value created from the activity, depending on the nature of the goods or services offered and the power and information asymmetry between the parties. By making efforts to provide goods and services, firms are rewarded with a price (P) paid by buyers. The value appropriated by the firm (VAF) is given by: VAF = P − C, whereas C corresponds to the firm's costs, while the value appropriated by the supplier (VAS) is given by: VAS = OC − C.

Note that the willingness to pay on the part of the buyer is different from the actual price paid. Rational actors, those who consciously adjust their means and ends to seek what is best for themselves to increase their personal satisfaction, will never pay a price higher than their willingness to pay, provided they are fully exercising their mental faculties. Therefore, WTP $\geq$ P. Consequently, the value appropriated by the buyer (VAB) is VAC = WTP − P. The value appropriated by the firm's suppliers corresponds to the difference between the firm's costs and the supplier's opportunity costs, as shown in Fig. 3.1 adapted from the work of Brandenburger and Stuart Jr.

The relationships above help explain why buyers are willing to pay different prices for the same item and why firms are constantly innovating to offer greater value to their buyers. Both quality improvements and cost innovations can result in higher value appropriated by buyers and firms, depending on power asymmetries between the parties and the resources employed in the bargaining process. For example, coffee buyers (final consumers) may prefer to spend higher amounts to enjoy a cup of coffee in a more sophisticated environment, believing that the benefits

[3] Brandenburger and Stuart Jr (1996).

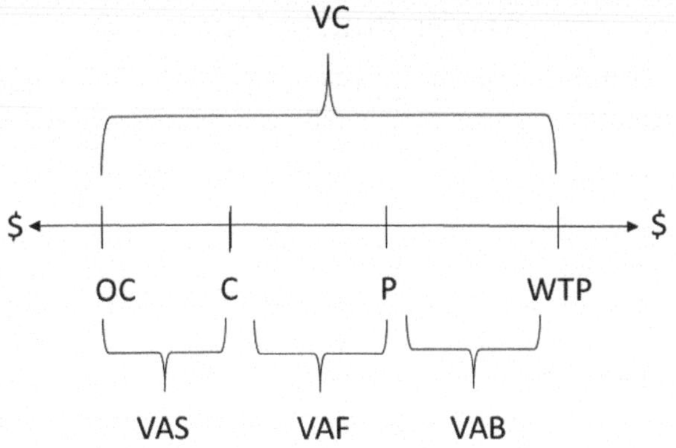

Fig. 3.1 Value creation and value appropriation in private organizations

associated with it outweigh the price paid, depending on their willingness to pay.

It is important to note that even though prices may be high, there is no guarantee of value appropriation by the firm, as it depends on the magnitude of their costs. If their costs are too high due to process inefficiencies or other managerial factors, the buyer may appropriate larger portions of the value created than the firm. The same reasoning applies to firms' suppliers, who can capture greater or lesser value based on their opportunity costs. With that said, the dynamics of value creation and appropriation in private relationships depend on strategic actions by the focal firm to promote perceptions of added value that increase the buyer's willingness to pay, effective cost management, and ultimately, the buyers' and suppliers' ability to bargain and capture the value created.

In the deal between Nike and Michael Jordan, Doloris Jordan's counteroffer enabled her son to capture a larger portion of the value created. Although the deal did not entail a significant increase in Nike's costs, the resulting deal allowed Nike to capture considerably more value than any other available alternative at that time. This was really a "win–win" situation with mutual benefits over time.

About Public Value

The readers of this text are likely asking themselves the following question: What does the story above tell me about how public value is created?

The answer to this question is simple: even public goods and services provided by governments or nonprofit entities are not exempt from the aforementioned logic based on cost–benefit analysis. Reforms around the world aimed at increasing transparency in public spending, the consolidation of democratic values in many societies, the development of government information systems that record transactions carried out by public agents, and communication systems that allow citizens to know what is happening in the world through a mobile phone, coupled with increasing levels of education, have formed more aware citizens capable of questioning what is provided by governments. More precise information disseminated through the press, social media, or government portals enhances dialogues among citizens, politicians, and bureaucrats based on cost–benefit analysis. This enables discussions on the relevance of expenditures vis-à-vis the results obtained.

Therefore, choices regarding the best way to provide public goods and services, whether through direct provision, concessions, public–private partnerships, or privatization, can be made on a common basis grounded in the value created in each alternative, within what is known as *value for money*.[4]

Of course, governments should not solely guide their decisions based on economic aspects. Barry Bozeman (2007) argues that economic principles should not guide in isolation the government actions. A normative consensus about the rights that citizens should be entitled as well as the principles under which governments must act is needed. Ethical, moral, and equity-related aspects, what Bozeman coins as *public values*, should not be disregarded in the decision-making process.[5]

[4] McKevitt (2015) conceives value for money as a combination of three Es: economy, referring to the acquisition of inputs in the appropriate quantity and quality; efficiency, in terms of providing proper service levels for minimum costs; and effectiveness, related to the attainment of envisioned outcomes.

[5] See Bozeman (2007). Public values can include principles rooted on democracy, equity, fairness, social justice, transparency, to name a few.

In this context, a government, for example, may propose delegating prison services to the private sector based on analyses demonstrating that private actors can deliver greater benefits in terms of security and order indicators, as well as services provided to incarcerated individuals, at lower costs compared to direct government provision. Yet, based on existing public values shared by the communities they serve, the government may choose direct provision due to a moral decision by society not to delegate prison services to private organizations, even if, prima facie, the cost–benefit ratio is less favorable to taxpayers.

Similarly, governments may refrain from implementing universal public healthcare systems with substantial government funding due to deeply rooted societal beliefs that governments should not impose redistributive obligations on their citizens, even though such systems generate greater benefits for society as a whole in terms of reducing diseases, absenteeism rates, and increasing the life expectancy of vulnerable individuals. In both cases, ideological aspects and moral choices can influence decisions.

However, decision-making in the public sector becomes more transparent and democratic when the perspective of value creation, based on the relationship between costs and benefits, is incorporated. In this regard, Mark Moore, one of the pioneering authors who has focused on value creation in the public sector, argues that public value is created when public organizations achieve the desired benefits at an appropriate cost.[6] But what sets public value creation apart from the concepts of shareholder value creation commonly found in private organizations?

One way to distinguish between the two is by focusing on the beneficiaries of the action. Private value is created when stakeholders directly benefit from actions intended to generate benefits at a reasonable cost appropriate to the value. Nonetheless, public value arises when the intended actions benefit not only the directly affected stakeholders but also other actors in society.

A conditional cash-transfer program like the before mentioned Bolsa Família creates value that is primarily appropriated by its beneficiaries. By receiving cash allocations, they can address their basic needs, particularly by purchasing food and other essential goods necessary for their survival. However, considering the program's conditionalities, beneficiaries must enroll their children in schools and comply with the vaccination schedule.

[6] See Moore (1995).

This leads to better education and improved health indicators for the children who are part of the program compared to those who are not part of the program. In these cases, in addition to the benefits outweighing the costs, the resulting benefits, such as increased productivity and reduced healthcare costs, are appropriated by society at large. This demonstrates the creation of public value.

These differences between private and public values can be also illustrated through a hypothetical program of nutritional education for children and adolescents. In this case, even though the value created is privately appropriated by the children who benefit from the action through improvements in health indicators resulting from increased consumption of fruits and vegetables, public value is also created as society can benefit from the action, for example, through a decrease in healthcare costs.

These considerations lead us to a possible definition of the term "public value" based on strategy grounds. By expressing the relationship between benefits generated for a population and the costs associated with obtaining those benefits, public value can be understood *as the value created for both those who directly benefit from the policy and those who do not*. In other words, public value is created when the impact of an action extends beyond the immediate beneficiaries and positively affects the broader society. These beneficiaries may include both vulnerable and non-vulnerable stakeholders, as well as governments, firms, and other actors affected by the action.[7]

The Public Value Creation Dynamics

The creation of public value is not an exclusive task of public and nonprofit organizations. Private organizations can also generate benefits through their actions that have a positive impact on a broader segment of the population. This applies not only to private organizations involved in the delivery of public services but also to those that may not have direct interactions with governments.

Recognizing the potential of for-profit organizations to create public value is crucial for paving the bridges between the fields of strategy and public management. Such recognition provides valuable opportunities

[7] For a similar discussion focused on social firms pursuing both economic and financial goals, refer to Lazzarini (2020).

to enhance our understanding of how private firms can contribute to addressing social and environmental challenges, whether independently or in collaboration with public and nonprofit organizations.

In recent years, the world has witnessed the emergence of private organizations that, despite being profit-driven, seek to generate social impact. Examples include companies classified as Certified Corporations (B Corps) which consider the interests of various stakeholders in their decision-making processes, alongside the interests of shareholders. These organizations challenge the shareholder supremacy and advocate for more stringent regulations to constrain environmentally harmful activities and to mitigate wider social inequities. To showcase their commitment to sustainability causes, some B Corps not only advocate for changes in the external regulations but also promote changes in their internal structures to foster public value creation.[8]

Along these lines, firms acting in the consumer goods sectors, such as Danone and Natura have been actively developing pricing systems that consider the economic sustainability of their suppliers, especially small-scale producers. In parallel, they consider the environmental sustainability of their actions.[9] Further, organizations that are part of the so-called "fourth sector", like traditional cooperatives, social enterprises, and those with business models that promote the circular economy and solidarity economy organizations are also striving to crate public value by enhancing their social impact in their activities.[10]

The Importance of Mission for Public Value Creation

A common feature of organizations committed to public value creation initiatives is the incorporation of aspects related to social goals within the

[8] The B-Corp phenomena has been covered by the (strategic) management literature in the recent years. Kim and Schifeling (2022) and Lyon et al. (2018) provide a good account of this movement.

[9] McGahan and Pongeluppe (2023) identify a causal link between Natura's business policies and improvement on environmental outcomes. For the purpose-based role of Danone, see Durand (2023) and Durand and Huysentruyt (2022).

[10] A detailed description of the so-called Forth Sector is available here https://www.ie.edu/cgc/research/the-fourth-sector/.

organizational mission, or within the corporate purpose.[11] This element is fundamental in the formulation of a strategy that reflects the purpose of organizations and corporations, providing direction, meaning, and intensity to the decisions and actions undertaken. Governments may also design mission-oriented programs aimed at achieving public value, which can ultimately influence market conditions.[12] Therefore, the effective generation of public value is evidenced through the achievement of the organizational mission.

Aligning goals in contexts where the mission explicitly or implicitly comprises multiple objectives tends to be more complex than in settings characterized by single objectives. This challenge is particularly evident in the case of public organizations, characterized by diffuse control and numerous and often conflicting objectives. Taking prison services as an example, what would be the indicator of mission fulfillment? Is it improving security and order dimensions by preventing escapes and riots? Is it segregating individuals from society as punishment for the problems they purportedly caused? Or is it promoting the social reintegration of incarcerated individuals through dignified treatment that respects the principles of human rights?

While the aforementioned list is not exhaustive, it is evident that reconciling these various dimensions poses a significant challenge. Each dimension may represent the preferences of different segments of society. However, even if the organizational mission provides a clear roadmap for action, implementing the strategy in a specific direction is not without limitations. The pursuit of public value can become even more complex when the organizational mission is ambiguous, encompassing multiple dimensions that may often conflict with one another. Achieving these

[11] In recent years, organizations have increasingly embraced the concept of corporate purpose as a guiding principle to prioritize different stakeholders than shareholders (Ocasio et al., 2023). Fitzsimmons et al. (2022) make a distinction between mission and purpose, highlighting that while a mission statement informs what organizations do, a purpose statement refers to the principles that guide the organization towards achieving social impact. However, in practice, there is often overlap between these terms. For example, Danone, a purpose-driven B-Corp, does not explicitly use the term "purpose" to communicate its socially oriented intentions. Instead, Danone articulates its commitment through its mission statement: "Bringing health through food to as many people as possible." This illustrates that the terminology used to express corporate purpose may vary among organizations, but the underlying intention to create positive social impact remains consistent.

[12] See Mazzucato (2018).

multifaceted objectives through the actions of a single organization becomes inherently difficult.

Imagine the case of a non-governmental organization aiming to address the needs of patients with a specific health condition. The hypothetical organizational mission can be stated as follows: "*Our aim is to provide patients with a dignified life, which includes promoting their health, ensuring access to leisure activities, and facilitating their integration into society. We also aim to support the patient's family by equipping them with the necessary tools for coexistence both at home and in society. Finally, we also aim to actively promoting and encouraging research on the condition to contribute to the dissemination of accumulated knowledge*".

A careful examination of this noble (and hypothetical) mission raises doubts about the organization's capacity to fulfill all the objectives it sets out to achieve. Even if it had a tremendous munificence of resources to invest in all areas encompassed by this comprehensive mission, the diversity of actions, ranging from patient care to basic research on the specific condition, could lead to limited economies of scale and scope, components.

Having said that, the process of public value creation can include choices regarding organizational scope to ensure that efforts will be channeled in a specific direction. A clear focus mitigates conflicts between areas that compete for scarce resources. Yet, it is important to acknowledge that certain aspects outlined in the mission may be beyond the direct control of the organization's managers. These factors can thwart the organization's ability to effectively translate its efforts into tangible results. Notably, nonprofit organizations with broad missions often face skepticism due to the potential for "mission drift". This occurs when conflicting dimensions within the mission undermine the organization's ability to effectively execute its intended mission.[13]

The multiplicity of objectives in the organizational mission can generate behavioral distortions that not only impede the creation of public value but may even lead to its destruction. Consider the example of watchdog and audit bodies. For the sake of simplicity, suppose that these bodies are engaged in two primary activities: compliance audits and performance-based audits. Which activity may watchdog bodies employees choose? If these employees act as rational agents and prioritize

[13] See Jones (2007).

maximizing their personal utility, they are likely to choose compliance audits over performance-based audits. The reason behind this choice is straightforward: compliance audits are generally easier to carry out and produce outputs that are simpler to measure and evaluate. These efforts, however, come at the expense of performance-based audits, which are more complex, time-consuming, and technically challenging. As a result, the focus of auditors may shift toward activities that are easier to measure and evaluate, such as counting the number of instructional hours delivered by teachers or ensuring compliance with bureaucratic norms.

This emphasis on compliance audits often takes precedence over gaining a deeper understanding of factors like changes in students' learning outcomes or the long-term impact of public schools on students' future income growth. The complex nature of performance-based audits, which involve assessing the effectiveness and broader impact of educational institutions, requires additional resources, expertise, and time commitment, making them less attractive in comparison. Consequently, the tendency is to prioritize simpler and more quantifiable tasks, even if they may not fully capture the overall public value created by the organization or institution being audited. In addition, by not focusing on performance-based audits, the audit body fails to fully leverage its potential in assisting the audited organization in enhancing its capabilities.

Therefore, organizations must pay particular attention to the design of missions that successfully lead the organization to create public value. Indeed, poorly designed missions have the potential to destroy value, instead of creating it.

Public Value Creation: The Strategic Triangle

We observed that the creation of public value may be hampered by conflicting dimensions in excessively wide missions with objectives over which organizations have little control. The development of public value depends on focused organizational missions (or corporate purposes) that are dedicated to environmental and social issues as well as broad stakeholder concerns. Even with these commitments, there are still issues like how to achieve public value. What extra prerequisites must be met before public, nonprofit, and private organizations can create value for the public?

One of the most significant authors to examine the idea of public value, Mark Moore, suggests a model for understanding the conditions in which it is being created. Moore asserts that legitimacy and support along with operational capacity are additional factors that influence the creation of public value.[14]

According to the sociologist Mark Suchman, "*legitimacy is a generalized perception or assumption that the actions of an entity are desirable, proper, or appropriate within some socially constructed system of norms, values, beliefs, and definitions*".[15] Obtaining legitimacy is key to gain the support of stakeholders who provide financial and institutional backing for an organization's actions.

To ensure the sustainability of value-creating actions, organizations committed to the creation of public value must build relationships with a myriad of stakeholders. Besides building ties with suppliers and buyers/ beneficiaries/citizens, these organizations oftentimes build relationships outside the market arena, including regulators, policymakers, politicians, and civil society groups. The so-called nonmarket strategies are crucial for mobilizing external actors who are aligned with the organization's mission.[16]

Likewise, when an organization has clear objectives aligned with the public interest, the volume of material and immaterial resources provided by the support network can generate virtuous cycles of value creation within the scope of the organizational purpose. This, in turn, reinforces the structures of legitimacy and support, further enhancing the organization's ability to create public value.

Mark Moore also contends that operational capacity in terms of knowing how to carry out the organizational mission also affects pubic value creation.[17] In this regard, the organization may require internal and external resources. Organizations must develop skills to entice, keep, and motivate staff, and involve strategic stakeholders when the operational capacities are based on human capital resources. Routines, practices, and technologies that are not easily accessible at low costs in factor markets may also be necessary for achieving the mission and adding value to society at large.

[14] Moore (1995).

[15] See Suchman (1995, p. 574).

[16] Dorobantu et al. (2017).

[17] Refer to Moore (1995) for a general view of the model and to Moore (2000) for further connections between his model and firms and nonprofits.

However, merely having access to resources does not guarantee the creation of value. According to well-established theories in the field of strategy, such as the resource-based view,[18] enduring and sustainable positions of prominence, require valuable, rare, and difficult-to-imitate resources, along with an internal organizational structure that leverages these resources for optimal results. When an organization can easily acquire the necessary resources, its distinctive position may come under challenge. Possessing the human capital that aligns with its purpose along with the skills to develop collaboration networks and partnerships with external actors who possess unique competencies is crucial for creating virtuous dynamics of value creation. However, if the costs required to obtain necessary resources become disproportionately high, thee cost–benefit relationship is affected and value creation is challenged.[19]

Public Values and Public Value Creation

While the strategic triangle has been widely adopted by practitioners and supported by received support from serval empirical studies, it is not immune to criticisms. One of the primary critiques is the failure to address how value-creating programs should align with core public values, such as open public communication, equity, conservation of resources, democracy, and others.[20] The challenge lies in reconciling management-oriented contents, oftentimes centered on outcomes, with the broader societal-oriented public values, as these dimensions can sometimes collide. In fact, in countries, like Chile, under the government of Augusto Pinochet, and Singapore, public sector reforms aimed at enabling public value creation from a managerial standpoint occurred at the expense of civil liberties, and civil rights. A balanced approach that takes fundamental public values into account is essential for effective strategies for all types of organizations.

To call the attention of public managers beyond effectiveness, John Bryson, Barbara Crosby, and Laura Bloomberg provide a framework that highlights the role of public values in public value creation: the public

[18] See Barney (1991) and Peteraf (1993).

[19] It is not a coincidence that, in merger and acquisition processes within the private sector, the stock prices of the acquiring company frequently decline. This phenomenon occurs due to the market's perception that the value of the acquisition is more likely to lead to value destruction rather than value creation.

[20] Bozeman (2007).

value governance triangle (PGVT).[21] This framework connects traditional management-concerns and broader societal interests, particularly those related to the functioning of democracies.

Figure 3.2, adapted from the work of John Bryson and coauthors, exemplifies the virtuous relationships between legitimacy and support, operational capacity, public values, and public value creation in the light of conditional cash-transfer programs.

Many governments have implemented strategies to address poverty alleviation issues by allocating financial resources to targeted individuals in exchange for satisfying educational and health conditions, such as enrolling children in schools or attending official programs in health. Similar to the aforementioned Bolsa Familia program in Brazil, initiatives in several countries like Colombia,[22] Mexico,[23] Kenya,[24] and Pakistan[25]

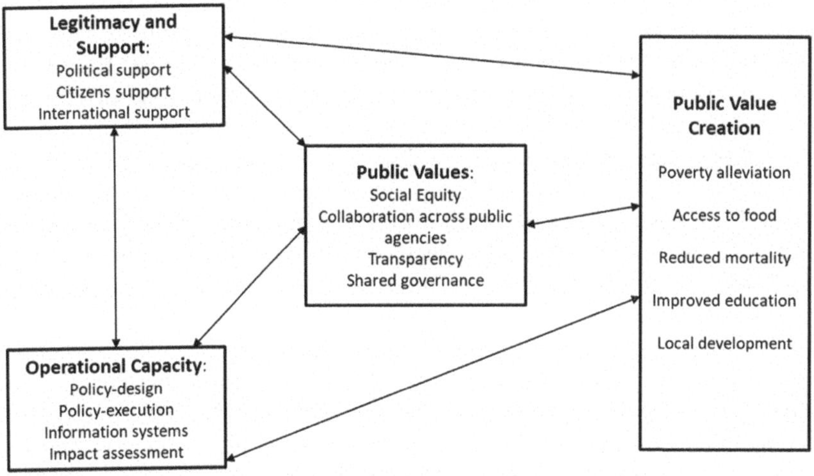

Fig. 3.2 The public value governance triangle (PGVT): Illustration from conditional cash-transfer programs

[21] Bryson et al. (2015).

[22] Lopez-Arana et al. (2016).

[23] De Brauw and Hoddinott (2011).

[24] Asfaw et al. (2014).

[25] Chaudhury and Parajuli (2010).

enabled public value creation by providing benefits beyond direct beneficiaries at a reasonable cost.

The creation of public value in conditional cash-transfer programs designed to alleviate poverty hinges on the presence of operational capacity. In fact, the capacities embedded within government agencies and multilateral agencies play a leading role in designing and implementing viable value-creating programs. These programs require capable staff to craft legal and institutional frameworks, and modern information systems for screening, selecting, registering, and paying program participants. In some countries, these programs enabled a culture of impact evaluation and fostered integration among several government departments to work in a collaborative fashion.[26]

Adequate operational capacity that reduces red tape and increases access to citizens can reinforce the legitimacy of the program as well as the support of the authorizing environment.[27] Indeed, successful conditional cash-transfer programs can significantly increase political support for incumbents who sponsor them. There is evidence to suggest that these programs play a crucial role in expanding the electoral base of incumbent politicians and provide political dividends at least in the short run.[28] The political support along with the support of citizens and other prominent actors, such as advocacy groups, is key to overcome the resistance of vocal groups against the program. Not surprisingly, even right-wing politicians, who may have been elected with a platform against poverty alleviation programs, hardly ever interrupt these programs to preserve their popularity.

Conditional cash-transfer programs can also spur public value. In addition to promoting social equity, one of the most fundamental "public values", successful programs are characterized by effective governance protocols that ensure collaborative efforts among all parties involved in the implementation process. In democratic societies where rival political parties occupy different government branches and the political power is divided among different political coalitions, fostering a collaborative mindset is key to ensure the continuity of value-creating programs over

[26] Cecchini (2023).

[27] Schoen et al. (2015).

[28] Zucco Jr. (2013).

time. In fact, collaborative efforts between bureaucrats overcome the hazardous effects of political turfs among rival groups.[29]

Conclusions

This chapter presents the strategy-based view of value creation, expressed by the difference between the buyer's willingness to pay and the supplier's opportunity costs, alongside the concept of public value creation inspired by the public and nonprofit literature. Departing from the idea that public value creation refers to the value created for both those who directly benefit from the policy and those who do not, the notion of public value aligns with cost–benefit perspectives. Public value is not exclusive to public and nonprofit organizations; it is likely to occur through strategies crafted by both profit-oriented and purpose-driven private organizations.

In a world of scarce resources and increased political polarization, aspects of value creation and value appropriation provide a common ground for discussions in designing and implementing business and public policies that can transform the reality of targeted communities, especially those who are more disenfranchised at the intersection between race, gender, and economic vulnerability.

However, discussions about public value creation must move beyond cost–benefit analysis and consider the systems of values and beliefs embedded in society, as well as processes for identifying legitimate stakeholders, their claims, ways to stimulate their engagement, and processes to ensure the appropriate distribution of the value created. In this vein, ensuring legitimacy for the actions taken and building operational capacity are key actions to create public value within established and commonly accepted public values, such as transparency, equity, social justice, or fairness.

References

Asfaw, S., Davis, B., Dewbre, J., Handa, S., & Winters, P. (2014). Cash transfer programme, productive activities and labour supply: Evidence from a randomised experiment in Kenya. *The Journal of Development Studies, 50*(8), 1172–1196.

[29] Cabral and Krane (2018).

Barney, J. B. (1991). Firm resources and sustained competitive advantage. *Journal of Management, 17*, 99–120.

Bozeman, B. (2007). *Public values and public interest: Counterbalancing economic individualism*. Georgetown University Press.

Brandenburger, A. M., & Stuart, H. W., Jr. (1996). Value-based business strategy. *Journal of Economics & Management Strategy, 5*(1), 5–24.

Bryson, J. M., Crosby, B. C., & Bloomberg, L. (2015). Discerning and assessing public value. In J. M. Bryson, B. C. Crosby, & L. Bloomberg (Eds.), *Public value and public administration* (pp. 1–21). Georgetown University Press.

Cabral, S., & Krane, D. (2018). Civic festivals and collaborative governance. *International Review of Administrative Sciences, 84*(1), 185–205.

Cecchini, S. (2023). The hidden impact of conditional cash transfer programs on state capacity. In K. J. Baehler (Ed.), *The Oxford handbook of governance and public management for social policy* (pp. Pages 983–999). Oxford University Press.

Chaudhury, N., & Parajuli, D. (2010). Conditional cash transfers and female schooling: The impact of the female school stipend programme on public school enrolments in Punjab, Pakistan. *Applied Economics, 42*(28), 3565–3583.

Chioda, L., De Mello, J. M., & Soares, R. R. (2016). Spillovers from conditional cash transfer programs: Bolsa Família and crime in urban Brazil. *Economics of Education Review, 54*, 306–320.

De Brauw, A., Gilligan, D. O., Hoddinott, J., & Roy, S. (2015). The impact of Bolsa Família on schooling. *World Development, 70*, 303–316.

De Brauw, A., & Hoddinott, J. (2011). Must conditional cash transfer programs be conditioned to be effective? The impact of conditioning transfers on school enrollment in Mexico. *Journal of Development Economics, 96*(2), 359–370.

Dorobantu, S., Kaul, A., & Zelner, B. (2017). Nonmarket strategy research through the lens of new institutional economics: An integrative review and future directions. *Strategic Management Journal, 38*(1), 114–140.

Durand, R. (2023). From the boardroom: Making purpose research relevant for practice. *Strategy Science, 8*(2), 149–158. https://doi.org/10.1287/stsc.2023.0182

Durand, R., & Huysentruyt, M. (2022). Communication frames and beneficiary engagement in corporate social initiatives: Evidence from a randomized controlled trial in France. *Strategic Management Journal, 43*(9), 1823–1853.

Fitzsimmons, A. B., Qin, Y. S., & Heffron, E. R. (2022). Purpose vs mission vs vision: Persuasive appeals and components in corporate statements. *Journal of Communication Management, 26*(2), 207–219.

Jones, M. B. (2007). The multiple sources of mission drift. *Nonprofit and Voluntary Sector Quarterly, 36*(2), 299–307.

Kim, S., & Schifeling, T. (2022). Good corp, bad corp, and the rise of B Corps: How market incumbents' diverse responses reinvigorate challengers. *Administrative Science Quarterly, 67*(3), 674–720.

Lazzarini, S. G. (2020). The nature of the social firm: Alternative organizational forms for social value creation and appropriation. *Academy of Management Review 45*(3), 620–645.

Lopez-Arana, S., Avendano, M., Van Lenthe, F. J., & Burdorf, A. (2016). The impact of a conditional cash transfer programme on determinants of child health: Evidence from Colombia. *Public Health Nutrition, 19*(14), 2629–2642.

Lyon, T. P., Delmas, M. A., Maxwell, J. W., Bansal, P., Chiroleu-Assouline, M., Crifo, P., ... & Lenox, M. (2018). CSR needs CPR: Corporate sustainability and politics. *California Management Review, 60*(4), 5–24.

Mazzucato, M. (2018). Mission-oriented innovation policies: challenges and opportunities. *Industrial and Corporate Change, 27*(5), 803–815. https://doi.org/10.1093/icc/dty034

McGahan, A., & Pongeluppe, L. S. (2023). There is no planet B: Aligning stakeholder interests to preserve the Amazon rainforest. *Management Science, 69*(12), 7860–7881. https://doi.org/10.1287/mnsc.2023.4884

McKevitt, D. (2015). Debate: Value for money—In search of a definition. *Public Money & Management, 35*(2), 99–100.

Moore, M. H. (1995). *Creating public value: Strategic management in government*. Harvard University Press.

Moore, M. H. (2000). Managing for value: Organizational strategy in for-profit, nonprofit, and governmental organizations. *Nonprofit and Voluntary Sector Quarterly, 29*(1_suppl), 183–204.

Ocasio, W., Kraatz, M., & Chandler, D. (2023). Making sense of corporate purpose. *Strategy Science, 8*, 123–138.

Olson, Z., Clark, R. G., & Reynolds, S. A. (2019). Can a conditional cash transfer reduce teen fertility? The case of Brazil's Bolsa Familia. *Journal of Health Economics, 63*, 128–144.

Peteraf, M. A. (1993). The cornerstones of competitive advantage: A resource-based view. *Strategic Management Journal, 14*(3), 179–191.

Rasella, D., Aquino, R., Santos, C. A., Paes-Sousa, R., & Barreto, M. L. (2013). Effect of a conditional cash transfer programme on childhood mortality: A nationwide analysis of Brazilian municipalities. *The Lancet, 382*(9886), 57–64.

Schoen, C., Buttorff, C., Andersen, M., & Davis, K. (2015). Policy options to expand Medicare's low-income provisions to improve access and affordability. *Health Affairs, 34*(12), 2086–2094.

Shei, A., Costa, F., Reis, M. G., & Ko, A. I. (2014). The impact of Brazil's Bolsa Família conditional cash transfer program on children's health care utilization and health outcomes. *BMC International Health and Human Rights, 14*, 1–9.

Suchman, M. C. (1995). Managing legitimacy: Strategic and institutional approaches. *Academy of Management Review, 20*(3), 571–610.

Zucco, C., Jr. (2013). When payouts pay off: Conditional cash transfers and voting behavior in Brazil 2002–10. *American Journal of Political Science, 57*(4), 810–822.

PART II

Inside the Organizational Boundaries

CHAPTER 4

Incentives in Public and Nonprofit Organizations

George Baker, a Harvard University scholar, coined an emblematic phrase: "*The problem is not that incentives can't work but that they work all too well*".[1]

When reading this phrase, we can recall the influence of variable compensations on the efforts of salespeople to persuade us to buy something we do not want. We also remember the extra and controversial efforts of some police officers to recover stolen vehicles in response to rewards offered by insurance companies. On the other hand, after the strengthening of control and accountability structures in the public sector, many agents responsible for public procurement processes think twice before accepting or proposing bribes to suppliers. Incentives also explain how the threat of severe punishment to individuals who break the silence of criminal organizations contributes to the perpetuation of illicit arrangements for years.

Incentive structures based on mechanisms of rewards and punishments are, therefore, essential elements to justify the success, failure, and survival of organizations. Adapting the phrase coined by James Carville, strategist of Bill Clinton's 1992 campaign, regarding the importance of the

[1] Baker et al. (1993).

S. Cabral, *Strategy for Public and Nonprofit Organizations*,
https://doi.org/10.1007/978-3-031-64969-1_4

economy in the lives of US citizens, we can say for the organizational context: "It's the incentives, stupid!".[2]

Principal-Agent Relationships[3]

Achieving results within an organization depends on some level of effort from the individuals comprising it. For instance, in a school setting, ensuring students' learning outcomes and reducing dropout rates requires efforts from the school's management, teachers, and staff.

Teachers must dedicate time to preparing their lessons according to the characteristics and needs of the students, while support staff need to ensure the necessary infrastructure for proper pedagogical activities. The school's management plays a crucial role in coordinating the flow of resources and information to facilitate the functions of teachers and support staff. Naturally, the likelihood of meeting the student's demands increases with the level of effort invested by those involved.

Therefore, the creation of value, privately appropriated by the direct beneficiaries of the educational service and publicly appropriated by other stakeholders who benefit from a better-educated and more productive population, largely depends on how individuals fulfill what is expected of them and, eventually, exceed the expectations of those responsible for financing the activities. In other words, the satisfaction or utility of the principal, who delegates a task to someone (the agent), requires efforts from the individuals to whom the activity was delegated (Fig. 4.1).

Here, one can perceive a chain of relationships between agents and principals. In our example in the field of education, from the perspective of teachers and staff (agents), the person responsible for the school's management assumes the role of the principal. In turn, from the perspective of the educational authority responsible for the schools in the region, the school management is the agent in the relationship. This chain reaches its limit with the citizen, the ultimate principal, who through voting

[2] The original phrase in Clinton's campaign bunker was indeed "The economy, stupid". Over time, it evolved and came to be used in the form "It's the economy, stupid!"

[3] This chapter somewhat reflects the teaching notes I have employed in my undergraduate and graduate courses at the Federal University of Bahia and Insper. I owe a debt of gratitude to my colleagues Sergio Lazzarini and Guilherme Fowler Monteiro, who previously developed some of the ideas in these notes. I also thank the hundreds of students who gave me the opportunity to test these contents on several occasions and helped me improve it. Errors and omissions are my own.

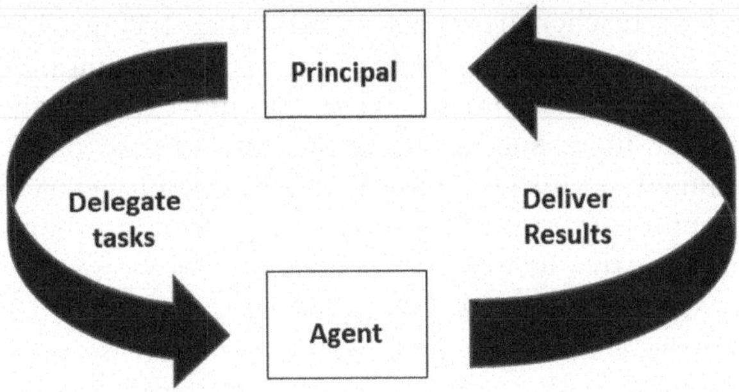

Fig. 4.1 Principal-agent model

chooses political agents responsible for governing a given territory, at least in democratic societies.

Based on the premise that individuals are rational and self-interested, meaning they consciously adjust their goals and means and prioritize what is best for themselves, and that observing efforts and results obtained is not always feasible, the relationship between agents and principals is not always harmonious. In fact, agents and principals may have conflicting interests in the appropriation of available resources and generated outcomes. Indeed, given the finite nature of resources, one party's utility can come at the expense of the other's utility.

The sources of conflicts between principals and agents are multiple. Agents may wish higher salaries and benefits for performing the same level of effort, but such additional expenses reduce the surplus that could be allocated to other areas and the value to be appropriated by the principal. For example, the coveted increase in salaries, benefits, and advantages by the elite of the public sector, who has job stability, can lead to lower investments in activities capable of creating public value, such as healthcare, education, and research and development.

The principal's utility depends on the agent's efforts, and since there are costs involved, rational agents avoid excessive exertion. In fact, being rational, agents focus on the value they will receive from their efforts minus the costs associated with undertaking such efforts, especially if these costs increase marginally and exponentially. After all, the higher the level of effort exerted, the greater the opportunity costs associated with alternative activities.

For example, a teacher incurs extra costs when trying to individualize teaching plans and implement new teaching methods, among other activities that will benefit the students. Rational and extrinsically motivated teachers will only incur such costs if they are rewarded for doing so. The rewards aimed at satisfying their utility can be monetary or symbolic (awards, recognition from peers and superiors, among others), and their choice depends on the agent's preferences. In both cases, however, the agent's utility will be affected based on whether they obtain the rewards resulting from the additional effort, which can decrease or increase the appropriation of the value created by the principal. Less effort from teachers will result in lower learning outcomes and reduced possibilities of future income gains for the students.

Agency Costs

Conflicts between agents and principals can also arise due to the parties' risk preferences. Risk-averse agents may hesitate to exert efforts intensely and vigorously in activities with uncertain returns, preferring fixed payments and avoiding variable ones as much as possible. They may also refrain from assuming the costs and the risks associated with supervising colleagues and subordinates, as they internalize these costs privately and do not capture the benefits, which in this case are captured by the principals.

Hence, the misalignment of interests between the agent and principal exacerbates agency costs, which arise from measures taken to prevent suboptimal actions by the agent. The utility of the principal is impacted when such suboptimal actions occur, or even when the mere potential for them exists. In situations where the actions and outcomes of an agent's conduct remain unobservable, the principal may face monitoring costs. These costs involve deploying supervisors to verify conduct, investing time in tracking activity reports, establishing monitoring and control structures, and more. Such expenses are integrated into the principal's utility function, diminishing their value appropriation. In the context of the public sector, these outlays can lead to reduced investments in alternative activities or make it unfeasible to alleviate tax burdens.[4]

[4] Fama and Jensen (1983) provide a comprehensive depiction of agency costs in principal-agent relationships.

Agents, in addition to incurring the costs of their efforts, also bear *costs related to demonstrating the activities* they have undertaken, such as preparing activity reports and providing evidence of their efforts. Anyone who has spent days and nights preparing reports for review by superiors and/or auditing bodies is aware of the challenges involved.

Moreover, beyond the costs of verification and demonstration, agency costs also encompass *residual costs* that emerge from inefficiencies generated and missed opportunities for innovation due to the attention allocated to demonstrating and verifying conduct.

Finally, agency costs can also arise due to *monitoring and measurement errors* and biases. Activities measured by inadequate methods or based on inappropriate performance indicators may not accurately reflect the agents' real contribution to observed performance.[5] Some agents may also refrain from implementing innovations in the public sector out of fear of facing sanctions, especially following the movement to strengthen control bodies, also known as the "audit explosion".[6] While, on one hand, this movement improves transparency and accountability levels of public agents, on the other hand, it has been criticized for its discretion and uncertainties, sometimes resulting in public value destruction.

The situations described above clearly enable inefficiencies that can hinder the creation of value. In fact, any resemblance to the reality of civil servants expending efforts on activities related to monitoring their conduct, to the detriment of focusing on their main activities, is not mere coincidence. To try to mitigate inefficiencies resulting from agency costs, policy-making professionals can consider establishing incentive contracts to align interests between principals and agents.

Incentive Contracts with Complete Information

Let us first analyze the situation where the efforts of the agent and the corresponding result obtained are observable by the principal.

For illustrative purposes, let us consider the case of Matthew, the tax collector of the Roman Empire in ancient times, later chosen for the noble role of an apostle of Jesus Christ. In the name of Herod (principal), the representative of the Roman Empire in Galilee, Matthew (agent)

[5] See Jensen and Meckling (1976).

[6] Power (2003).

collected taxes resulting from the economic activities of his fellows in Capernaum. In the eyes of the people of those times, tax collectors were not well-regarded as they were seen as collaborating with the invaders of the territory and enriching the foreign rulers at the expense of their compatriots.

One way for Matthew to reduce the rejection among his fellow compatriots would be to avoid antagonizing them by exerting lower levels of effort and collecting fewer taxes from the taxpayers of that time. For example, Matthew could ignore the income generated from merchandise sold by a certain merchant or simply refrain from visiting fishing and agricultural areas. However, by choosing to exert lower levels of effort and not collecting taxes as a deliberate option, Matthew could impact the wealth of the Roman Empire, something certainly undesirable by the Roman emperors.

Knowing this possibility and to reduce the chances of Matthew ignoring the activities carried out in the region, strategically, Herod could propose an incentive contract to Matthew to induce the maximum effort from the tax collector and maximize the income collected for the local government. Ignoring the potential ethical constraints of his conduct and focusing solely on pecuniary motivations, from Matthew's perspective, such a contract could be appealing, as it would allow him to appropriate a portion of the product of his efforts, which, in theory, could motivate him to work even more vigorously and aligned with Herod's interests.[7]

Suppose that Matthew's utility is given by:

$$U = w - e^2 \tag{4.1}$$

In the equation above, w is the remuneration offered by Herod to Matthew. In turn, e corresponds to the effort exerted. As we discussed earlier, the cost of effort increases exponentially. For simplicity, we assume a quadratic function to denote this relationship.

Note that in this case, Herod delegates the activity of tax collection entirely to Matthew, who in turn must choose an effort level $e > 0$. A high value of e indicates that Matthew would be closely and attentively monitoring the region's economic activities to ensure the taxes owed

[7] The mathematical demonstrations are inspired by the works of Milgrom and Roberts (1992), Brickley et al. (2001), and Bolton and Dewatripont (2004) and on teaching notes developed by Sergio Lazzarini, Guilherme Fowler Monteiro, and I.

are collected. Low values of e would imply negligence on Matthew's part in his duties, either by ignoring the activities of the taxpayers or by engaging in unrelated tasks (I leave it to the reader's imagination to picture what Matthew could do to distract himself from work in a time when WhatsApp, Instagram, and YouTube did not exist).

Now, suppose that Matthew has a reservation utility (R) corresponding to 1000 denarii (the Roman Empire currency at that time). In practice, this value would represent the minimum remuneration that Matthew would accept to exert any effort above zero. In other words, if Matthew stayed at home sleeping and, in his free time, enjoyed the sunset in the Middle East, he would still earn 1000 denarii from, for example, rental income from his family's properties.

Once the parameters on the agent's side are established, it is necessary to look at the situation from the principal's perspective. In this case, Herod's profit (Π) is given by:

$$\Pi = Q - w \tag{4.2}$$

where Q is the quantity produced (taxes collected) by Matthew. To collect the taxes, Matthew needs to exert some level of effort greater than zero, according to the expression below:

$$Q = \alpha e + \mu \tag{4.3}$$

In Eq. (4.3), α represents the marginal productivity of the agent, which is a conversion factor of efforts into results. It indicates how much the tax collection will increase with each unit increment of Matthew's effort. On the other hand, μ corresponds to an uncontrolled random shock that affects the amount of taxes collected and is not under Matthew's control. For example, a severe drought could prevent wheat harvest and bread production, disrupting exchanges between people and, consequently, affecting the tax collection. Assuming a value of $\alpha = 100$, we have:

$$\Pi = 100e - w \tag{4.4}$$

Assuming Matthew's effort is observable and measurable, we assume a complete contract signed with Herod, where the remuneration is based on the observed effort (e).

For simplification, we assume that the expected value of the random shock is zero, $E(\mu) = 0$, meaning that Matthew, by disregarding the role of external causes in his decision to make an effort, can be classified as a *risk-neutral* agent. In other words, Matthew agrees to absorb the risk of the random shock that may affect him positively or negatively.

The expression $w - e^2 \geq 1000$ refers to the agent's incentive compatibility constraint and can be rewritten as $w = 1000 + e^2$. Therefore, the profit maximization function is given by:

$$\text{Max}\,\Pi = 100e - w$$

$$s.t.\, w - e^2 \geq 1000$$

$$\text{Replacing}\, w :$$

$$\text{Max}\,\Pi = 100e - 1000 - e^2 \tag{4.5}$$

We can solve Herod's profit maximization problem by anticipating the choice of an optimal effort level e^*. To do this, we need to obtain the derivative of the profit with respect to effort. The first-order condition for Eq. (4.5) is:

$$\frac{\mathrm{d}\Pi}{\mathrm{d}e} = 100 - 2e = 0$$

$$e* = 50$$

Replacing, we have $w* = 1000+50^2 = 3500$; and $\Pi = 100*50-3500 = 1500$.

Thus, Matthew receives \$3500 in exchange for an optimal effort (e^*) of 50 units of effort.

Incentive Contracts with Asymmetric Information

Above, we discussed a scenario where the parties have information symmetry. However, how would the parties behave in a situation marked by asymmetric information, where, for example, Herod cannot observe the level of effort exerted by Matthew? After all, Matthew could promise to exert high efforts.

Indeed, in an environment characterized by asymmetric information, there is no way to guarantee that the agent will exert effort. Besides not observing e, Herod also does not observe the random component, μ, which complicates matters further. Therefore, Matthew could claim that the level of taxes collected was below expectations due to a decrease in economic activity in the region, excessive rainfall, locust plagues, or any other reason unrelated to low effort. In this case, Herod would hardly know what was really happening and would have no way to explain to his superiors the reasons for the impact on tax collection.

One possibility for Herod to address this problem and ensure high effort from the agent would be to reduce the degree of information asymmetry by increasing the level of supervision over Matthew. To do so, the ruler could personally conduct the supervision or hire someone to do the job. In the first case, Herod would need to consider his opportunity costs when performing such a task, which, given the volume of activities he had to deal with, would not be feasible. The second alternative, investing in supervision/monitoring, would imply costs to select, compensate, and oversee the person responsible for the supervision. Since the hired supervisor could collude with Matthew or not exert supervision diligently to reduce their own costs, Herod might have to hire a supervisor for the supervisor, giving rise to the philosophical/organizational problem formulated centuries earlier by Plato: "*But who will guard the guardians*?" Further, monitoring technologies like GPS or surveillance cameras were not available at that time. Overall, the option of hiring a supervisor would probably be unfeasible due to the prohibitive costs involved.

However, all hope is not lost. The Roman representative, despite not being able to observe the agent's efforts, can observe the outcome of Matthew's actions: the quantity of taxes collected, expressed as Q. In this case, to induce the agent's effort, Herod could propose a contract with payments tied to the results obtained (*outcome-based contract*), where Matthew would receive a fraction of the collected taxes as shown below:

$$W = Wo + \beta Q, \tag{4.6}$$

Wo would be Matthew's fixed monthly salary (regardless of the level of taxes collected). $\beta Q (0 \leq \beta \leq 1)$ corresponds to Matthew's variable compensation for the period, similar to a commission of β% on the taxes collected. As the agent appropriates part of the generated surplus, it is expected that Matthew will be motivated to choose an elevated level of effort, benefiting both himself and the principal.

According to Fig. 4.2, at the first level, Herod could propose the fixed salary *Wo* and the variable portion β to Matthew, who in turn would decide whether to accept the proposal (see 2nd level). If accepted, in the

3rd level, Matthew chooses an optimal effort level e^* capable of maximizing his utility, according to Eq. (4.1). To solve this problem, one can use the backward induction approach, as Herod, by acting rationally, should propose a contract based on Matthew's expected behavior. In other words, Herod can anticipate the choices to be made by the agent, following a sequential game with interdependent actions. The choice of effort is a new game that starts after Matthew's decision to accept the contract. To find the perfect equilibrium of the game between the agent and the principal, the process begins with the definition of the optimal effort (e^*) on Matthew's part.

Substituting (4.3) into (4.1), we can rewrite Matthew's utility function in the following terms: $U = Wo + \beta Q - e^2$.

Let us remember that Q has a random component, μ, so it is necessary to consider how Matthew tends to act in the presence of risks. In fact, it is possible that Matthew exerts maximum effort, but several factors in the external environment that he cannot control may lead to a decrease in the collected taxes. For example, a drought could reduce the variable component and, consequently, the total remuneration. For simplification, we

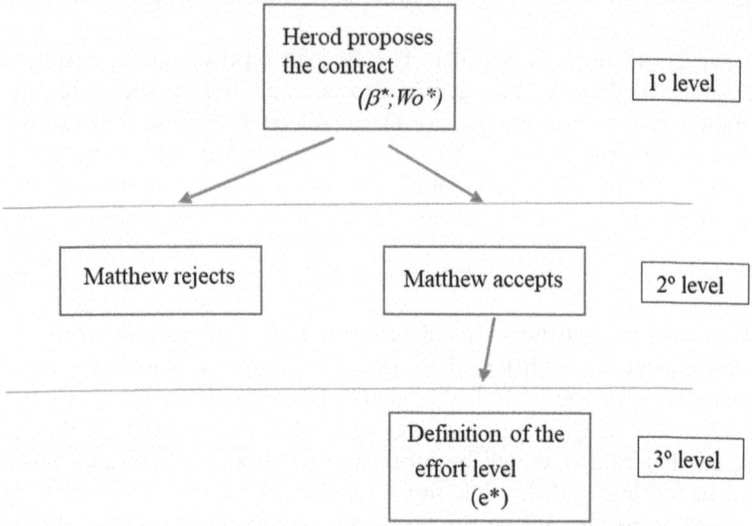

Fig. 4.2 Sequence of decisions in the incentive contract between Herod and Matthew

assume that Matthew *is risk-neutral* and will seek to choose the optimal effort level to maximize the expected value of his remuneration. Formally, Matthew's expected utility can be written using the following equation: $E(U) = E(Wo + \beta Q - e^2) = Wo + \beta E(Q) - e^2$.

As $E(\mu) = 0$, due to the assumption of risk neutrality of the agent, the expected value of taxes to be collected takes the following form: $E(Q) = \beta\alpha e + E(\mu) = \beta\alpha e$. Therefore, Matthew's expected utility can be simplified according to the expression below:

$$E(U) = Wo + \beta\alpha e - e^2 \tag{4.7}$$

Matthew chooses an optimal effort level e^* to maximize the expression above. Thus, by taking the derivative of his utility with respect to effort, we have:

$$\frac{dE(U)}{de} = \beta\alpha - 2e = 0 \tag{4.8}$$

Therefore, resulting in an optimal effort level of:

$$e* = \frac{\beta\alpha}{2} \tag{4.9}$$

The passages above allow for some interpretations. For example, expression (4.8) reflects a point of maximum of the function since the second derivative, −2, is negative. Expression (4.9) shows the optimal effort level to be chosen by Matthew in response to the intensity of incentives proposed by Herod. This intensity reflects the pattern of variation in the agent's remuneration according to the observed performance, in this case, tax collection. Note that higher values of β indicate higher levels of incentive intensity, suggesting that the agent's responses are based on what is proposed by the principal. The response in terms of effort tends to be amplified in situations of high levels of marginal productivity (α), meaning that the greater the possibility for Matthew to increase the conversion rate of efforts into results, for example, due to an extended knowledge of the region where taxes will be collected or the strategies used by taxpayers to evade taxes, the higher his level of effort.

Note that the agent's efforts are not influenced by the fixed salary (*Wo*) offered by the principal. Why does this happen? Remember that the fixed salary is not affected by the observed performance and is independent of the effort exerted by the agent, so in this case, Matthew would receive *Wo* even if he exerts zero effort ($e = 0$). Therefore, disregarding relational aspects or other implicit factors related to maintaining the agent's reputation or even any psychological cost for not making high efforts, Herod must offer some type of variable compensation based on the agent's performance so that Matthew exerts some effort. Such a situation is not uncommon in public organizations where civil servants enjoy job stability and are hardly ever subject to any sanction for insufficient efforts (or performance). Under these conditions, it is rational not to make an effort! The consequences are evident: decreased productivity, lower quality of services provided, public expenditures above what is delivered, dissatisfaction of the population with the services provided, demotivation of professionals committed to the public cause, and stigmatization of the public service in general. In other words, *it's the incentives, stupid*!

One way to try to overcome the problems above is to establish a package that motivates the agent to make an effort. Returning to our case and within the strategy of backward induction, it is now necessary to know under what conditions the agent will accept the proposed contract (2nd level). Considering Matthew's rational nature, he will only accept the eventual remuneration proposed by Herod if the package is greater than his reservation utility (R) discussed earlier.

We assume that $R \geq 0$ because if Matthew does not work for Herod, he does not receive any payment, but also does not incur any cost related to the effort exerted. He will accept a payment W (sum of fixed and variable components) if the expected value of his utility when working is greater than or equal to his reservation utility. Formally, the agent's participation constraint can be written as follows:

$$E(U) \geq R$$

$$Wo + \beta\alpha e - e^2 \geq R \tag{4.10}$$

It is time to address the first level of Fig. 4.2, that is, determine the optimal package composed of the optimal sharing level of results ($\beta*$) and the optimal fixed salary (Wo) offered by Herod to Matthew. This involves solving the principal's problem (Profit Maximization – Π), considering the agent's possible choices that are foreseeable by the principal. The problem to be solved can be seen below.

$$\text{Max}\,\Pi => E(\Pi) = E(Q - W)$$
$$\text{s.t. } Wo + \beta\alpha e - e^2 \geq R$$

Making the necessary substitutions parsimoniously, the expected value of the profit can be written as follows:

$$E(\Pi) = E(\alpha e + \mu) - (Wo + \beta(\alpha e + \mu))$$
$$\boxed{Q} \qquad \boxed{\quad W \quad}$$

Setting $\mu = 0$, due to the risk neutrality of the principal, just like the agent, we have:

$$E(\Pi) = \alpha e - Wo - \beta\alpha e$$

Manipulating (4.10) to substitute *Wo*, we get: $Wo = R - \beta\alpha e + e^2$. Hence:

$$E(\Pi) = \alpha e - (R - \beta\alpha e + e^2) - \beta\alpha e;$$

$$E(\Pi) = \alpha e - R - e^2 \tag{4.11}$$

Substituting (4.9) into (4.11) to incorporate the optimal effort level, $e*$, we obtain:

$$E(\Pi) = \alpha\frac{\beta\alpha}{2} - \left(\frac{\beta\alpha}{2}\right)^2 - R \tag{4.12}$$

The principal (Herod) tends to choose an optimal level of β to transfer the maximum variable compensation to the agent. Taking the derivative of the expected profit with respect to the commission β in expression (4.12), we get:

$$\frac{d\Pi}{d\beta} = \frac{\alpha^2}{2} - \frac{2\beta\alpha^2}{4} = 0 \tag{4.13}$$

Solving (4.13), we have:

$$\beta * = 1 \tag{4.14}$$

The above value corresponds to the optimal intensity of incentives to be offered to the agent. Let us now calculate the fixed salary to be proposed. Recalling:

$$Wo = R - \beta \alpha e + e^2 \tag{4.15}$$

With risk neutrality ($\mu = 0$) and replacing Eqs. (4.9) and (4.14) into Eq. (4.15), we have:

$$Wo = R - \frac{\alpha^2}{2} + \frac{\alpha^2}{4}$$

$$Wo* = R - \frac{\alpha^2}{4} \tag{4.16}$$

Hence, the optimal contract offered by Herod to Matthew is $(\beta*;\ Wo*) = (1;\ R - \frac{\alpha^2}{4})$.

Indeed, the optimal contract proposed to the agent suggests that Herod allows Matthew to appropriate 100% of the collected tax revenue, which would be equivalent to a 100% commission for a salesperson at a store. In this case, one may infer that tax collection would be "privatized" and Matthew would have the authority to allocate the collected taxes according to his goals. On the one hand, this makes sense as it is always advisable to increase the intensity of incentives for agents to exert high levels of effort and thereby increase the principal's utility. However, with such a high intensity of incentives, how does the principal, Herod, get rewarded? Would Herod be in trouble with the Roman Empire for allowing a tax collector to appropriate all the surplus? Could his neck, literally, be on the line for renouncing the empire's revenues? How can Herod and the empire be rewarded in a contract like this?

The observation of the second term in Eq. (4.16) provides clues that help determine what Herod's remuneration would be. Notice that there is no condition that requires $\frac{\alpha^2}{4}$ to be smaller than R. In fact, the reservation utility (R) could be close to zero! A more attentive reader, when analyzing Eq. (4.16), might ask: Could Matthew receive a negative fixed salary (*Wo*)? Would Matthew be paying to work for the empire? In this case, the fixed salary would represent a payment from the agent to the principal as permission to work and collect taxes for the empire. Is this possible? Would such subservience of Matthew to the empire be reasonable? Similarly, could a salesperson pay to work?

The answer is yes! The situation described above is quite common in the public sector. Surprised? This is exactly what happens when someone gains the right to exploit revenues from a public service. When granted, governments forego the receipt of service revenues (along with associated costs) and, in return, receive compensations from the private sector. To maximize their benefits from their efforts, private actors may pay the government a concession fee for the right to exploit a specific activity. This occurs when a company wins the bid to operate a power transmission line, the telecommunications spectrum, a park, an existing road, or when taxi drivers purchase licenses from municipalities. However, in public services, public supervision and regulation are essential to preserve public value creation and prevent subpar provision by financially driven private providers. These providers, aiming to boost profits, may compromise quality standards. Unfortunately, intense public supervision and regulation are not always effective in curbing rent-seeking and self-interest among providers.[8]

In the private sector, this is a characteristic of franchising contracts, where the franchisee pays a fee to the franchisor for the right to associate with the chain and economically exploit its benefits. In return, the franchisee receives a high variable compensation, entirely comprising the revenues, minus costs and any royalties paid to the franchisor, if applicable. In summary, even in the public sector, it is possible to conceive situations where high incentive intensity is beneficial for both agents and principals.

Up until now, however, we have discussed a situation in which the agent exhibits risk neutrality, meaning they absorb the random component of the activity ($E(\mu) = 0$). But what happens when the agent is risk-averse and does not tolerate external shocks ($E(\mu \neq 0)$)?

In this case, agents will demand higher fixed payments to compensate for the potential loss of utility resulting from external factors beyond their control. The perceived values would be a kind of "certainty equivalent" to offset the risk they would be assuming and no longer neglecting. Such values tend to be higher if the agent has higher levels of reservation utility. In this case, the agents have outside options that allow them to obtain higher remuneration through their abilities and efforts.

[8] See Cabral et al. (2010). We will further discuss this dilemma in Chapter 9.

To conclude, incentive contracts are important tools for aligning interests between the agent and principal by inducing additional efforts that would not occur in the absence of incentives. The inclusion of incentive structures, based on mechanisms of rewards and punishments, is often invoked to mitigate contractual problems related to incomplete information. Since agents are in a better position to know whether their actions are efficient or not, incentive contracts can address adverse selection problems that arise from information asymmetry. Aware of this possibility, the principal introduces a series of safeguards that may negatively impact all agents, even those who are less likely to act opportunistically.

Furthermore, incentive contracts can efficiently deal with moral hazard problems that occur when agents engage in hidden actions that are not aligned with the interests of the principal and other stakeholders. The likelihood of being punished in case of misbehavior can induce higher efforts, provided that the contractually specified punishment is credible, has a reasonable probability of being implemented, and significantly affects the agent's utility. Along these lines, the absence of incentive structures helps explain the elevated levels of corruption and the low quality of services in various public and nonprofit organizations.

Group-Based Incentives and Relational Contracts in Public and Nonprofit Organizations

By establishing a structure composed of fixed and variable payments, principals can induce greater efforts from agents, thus promoting the best cost–benefit relationship for the parties involved according to different risk preferences. However, models based on individual incentives are not able to address situations where the outcomes are the result of collective efforts from a group of agents working in an interdependent fashion. In such cases, it becomes challenging to observe and measure the individual contributions of each agent to the final performance.

Consider the following situation. To keep the city clean and prevent the transmission of diseases, the mayor of a certain municipality launches a crusade. Besides placing garbage bins in various locations throughout the city, she implements a strict program to combat littering on the streets and starts fining citizens caught throwing trash on the ground. The campaign begins to take effect. The presence of municipal guards on the streets, authorized to issue fines, deters such behavior and makes people think twice before disposing of their waste in public areas.

Everything was going well until the day after a local football game (soccer for the US citizens), when the streets around the stadium became filthy, filled with beer cans and barbecue skewers. In response, the following week, the mayor increased the number of inspectors and municipal guards. Despite the intensified monitoring and the fact that the crowd around the stadium remains the same, the actions do not have the desired effect: the cleanliness indicators, measured by the amount of trash collected out of garbage bins, show insignificant variation.

Now imagine a second hypothetical situation. A high school teacher in a public school decides to implement a group project as part of the student evaluation. The teacher aims to develop teamwork and collaboration skills among the students and sets a maximum group size of three people. Two days later, eight students, all members of the school's volleyball team, asked to be in the same group because they already knew each other. Also, they argue that being in the same group would facilitate the project's progress due to their shared training schedule. The teacher accepts the request for the eight students to be in the same group. Later, the teacher realizes that the only project that did not reach the minimum required quality level was precisely the project of the volleyball team members, which he found strange because individually, they were all diligent students with good grades.

To understand the reasons why the observed performance in the two cases diverged, not increasing in the first case, and decreasing in the second case, we resort to a simple model.

Let us consider the case of the municipal guards tasked with combating litter and denote each guard as (i).

In the municipal force, we would have N guards present in the enforcement action (*i.e.*, $i = 1, 2, \ldots, N$). Each guard i chooses a certain level of effort (qi), which reflects their contribution to the amount of litter collected, so that $qi > 0$. A high value of qi indicates that the guard undertakes exemplary surveillance work, does not turn a blind eye, and issues fines to offenders on a professional basis. On the other hand, a low value of qi indicates that the guards do not take their duties seriously and spend most of their time engrossed in social media, ignoring their surroundings.

For simplicity, assume there is no random factor affecting the relationship between individual effort and the amount of litter collected. In other words, there is no rain or climatic factors that alter people's propensity to litter on the streets.

However, the mayor does not directly observe the individual effort *qi* of each guard, but rather observes only the final work produced by the group of guards, which results in the quantity *Q* of litter collected in the trash bins. This litter is then weighed and sold, generating revenue for the municipality. Ideally, the litter should be disposed of into the trash bins, as litter on the ground is more prone to contamination and leads to sweeping costs.[9] Thus:

$$Q = q_1 + q_2 + \cdots + q_N = \sum_{i=1}^{N} q_i \tag{4.17}$$

Suppose now that the municipality's profit is a function of the quantity of litter collected in the trash bins and the salary paid to the guards for their efforts. Considering that the litter on the ground cannot be recycled and sold, we have:

$$\Pi = vQ - \sum_{i=1}^{N} P_i \tag{4.18}$$

where (v) is the unit value of the litter in each trash bin and (Pi) is the payment that the mayor offers to each guard for their work in the municipality.

As the mayor can only observe the total quantity produced, she will reward the guards as a group. Suppose the mayor pays a group variable salary, involving a fraction $\beta > 0$ of the total value collected from the litter, resulting from the surveillance efforts of each guard (vQ), divided by the total number of guards (N). For simplification purposes, assume there is no fixed salary, and all payment is based on the quantity of litter collected in the trash bins. The total payment that each guard will receive is given by:

$$P_i = \frac{\beta(vQ)}{N} \tag{4.19}$$

The utility function of each guard is:

$$U = Pi - qi^2 \tag{4.20}$$

[9] The mathematical demonstrations are inspired by the work of Kandel and Lazear (1992) and on teaching notes developed by Sergio Lazzarini, Guilherme Fowler Monteiro, and I.

In Eq. (4.20), ${q_i}^2$ refers to the amount of garbage collected in the trash bins and, therefore, to the personal cost that the guard incurs to prevent people from littering. We assume the convention that the personal effort cost increases exponentially and in a marginally increasing way.

Now let us analyze how the guards will choose their optimal level of individual output, considering the payment set by the mayor. Substituting (4.19) into (4.20), the utility of each guard will be:

$$U_i = \frac{\beta(vQ)}{N} - q_i^2,$$

Substituting (4.17):

$$U_i = \frac{\beta v(q_1 + \cdots + q_i + \cdots + q_N)}{N} - q_i^2 \tag{4.21}$$

Each guard will maximize (4.21) to determine their optimal level of individual output, *qi*. Note that since there is no random shock affecting the production, we can consider the utility function directly in the maximization problem instead of its expected value. The first-order condition for maximizing the utility with respect to the effort of each guard is given by:

$$\frac{\mathrm{d}U}{\mathrm{d}q} = \frac{\beta v}{N} - 2q_i = 0,$$

Hence, the optimal output of each guard is:

$$q_i* = \frac{\beta v}{2N} \tag{4.22}$$

Observe that the individual output *decreases* with the number of guards in the group, N. Let us go back to Eq. (4.21) to understand the reason behind this. By increasing their individual output *qi*, guard i incurs the entire personal cost given by $-{q_i}^2$ but only receives marginally a fraction $(\beta v/N)$ of what is produced collectively. In this context, it is more beneficial for the guard to reduce their effort and benefit from what other colleagues are producing. In other words, reducing effort, given the current incentive structure, is a rational choice.

The Free-Rriding Problem

The example above illustrates a critical issue in collective action: the *free-riding* problem, where a member benefits from being part of the group but does not contribute to the provision of benefits in the same proportion as others.[10] In our case, each guard will "free ride" on the production efforts of their peers and tend to rely on the efforts of others. Notice that as the number of individuals in the group increases, it becomes more difficult to determine each one's individual contribution to the result, and the smaller the group, the larger the proportion of the created value that each member receives. These factors help explain the lower performance when there are many people involved in the collaborative process. This also helps us understand why the performance of the group of volleyball players was lower than the other groups in the class.

How can we solve this issue? The problem of free riding could indeed be mitigated if the mayor could observe the individual production, qi, of each guard, for example, by dividing each area into sectors and setting production targets to maximize the quantity and penalize guards who do not make adequate efforts. However, it is much easier to measure the total amount of collected garbage than to individually weigh each bin to assess the individual contribution of each guard, especially considering the multiple tasks these employees perform. The costs of measuring individual effort tend to be high, making group incentives a non-trivial matter.

Indeed, *innovative technologies* can play a crucial role in reducing the costs associated with measuring individual contributions and, at the same time, shift the burden of low effort to individuals themselves. Improved measurement techniques can more accurately reward individuals who make greater efforts or penalize those whose behaviors do not align with the collective interest. A notable example is the installation of individual water consumption meters in residential units. In older buildings (and some still today), water usage was divided equally among all residents, regardless of their individual consumption. The sense of injustice, where a single person would pay the same amount as a large family, coupled with the inability to verify individual behaviors, often led to various forms of waste, which harmed a broad group of people beyond just the building's

[10] See Olson (1965), Albanese and Van Fleet (1985), and Kandel and Lazear (1992) to know more about free riding and the dilemmas associated to group-based incentives.

inhabitants. The installation of individual meters, while adding an extra cost, can correct such distortions.

The same dilemma of measuring individual contributions also arises in the collection of taxes for residential waste disposal, considering the high costs of weighing daily (or weekly) produced waste. In this case, a solution is to charge based on the property's area: property owners with larger properties pay more compared to those with smaller properties. Although this method of charging is not perfect, as a single individual may live alone in a larger property and pay more than those living in smaller properties but producing more waste, the approach of charging based on property size is superior to the alternative of flat rate charging for all individuals indiscriminately.

Ultimately, the development of measures to improve the measurement of individual contributions to the production of goods and services in group settings tends to be beneficial.

Peer pressure is one of the most traditional ways to reduce the problem of free riding. Basically, peers can use coercive and subtle mechanisms to induce free riders to exert more effort. In our hypothetical case, although the mayor does not directly observe the individual efforts (qi) of the guards, the guards themselves can observe whether their colleagues are working diligently or simply free riding on the efforts of others. Since the payment depends on the efforts of their colleagues, the guards have an incentive to hold their peers accountable if they are not making sufficient effort, especially if qi is observable among the guards. By noticing that a particular guard i is choosing a low qi, the colleagues could socially isolate them within the group or report the situation to higher authorities, provided that the internal culture does not impose extra costs for such behavior. Initiatives to reduce the group size can also increase the possibility of peers' effort observation. This is one of the reasons why teachers tend to avoid, even intuitively, forming large groups for school assignments, to try to maximize the level of effort.

The free-riding behavior can also be inhibited through *increased effort by the principal*. If the principal is the residual claimant, she can appropriate the surplus produced. Hence, there are incentives to incur extra monitoring costs, provided that the potential to be appropriated outweighs the personal costs. In fact, some principals may avoid the cost of confronting the agents, either due to the incurred cost or the fear of future reprisals if they become agents themselves. This is quite common in the public sector, where executing agents switch roles with monitoring agents, such as police officers alternating between street duties and internal affairs, or educators moving between teaching and administrative roles.[11]

In our case, the mayor can signal credible punishments and increase the sense of surveillance over the guards to make them weigh their inclination to exert low efforts. In practice, corporatist structures that limit the punishment of public officials with inappropriate conduct, combined with constraints on hiring, make monitoring efforts by the principal more difficult, especially when their position of command is temporary, and the possibilities of future retaliation are not negligible. Nevertheless, the commitment of the principal is a key condition for the effectiveness of group (and individual) incentives to induce agent efforts; in fact, *there is nothing more favorable for malicious agents than having uninterested or uninformed principals.*

Informal ties between principals and agents can be leveraged to address these potential problems.

Relational Contracts

In the real world, many contractual relationships are not formalized and do not involve performance-based payments. Further, these relationships often do not establish clear expectations for performance. In fact, in many activities, defining what constitutes satisfactory performance can be challenging, making the measurement of results even more complicated. Take, for example, hiring a painting service. How can one determine if the service was performed with decent quality? What are the parameters to define what quality means? Beauty? Esthetics? Absence of blemishes? How can measurement criteria be established for dimensions that are not straightforward? The parties involved could engage in lengthy negotiations for months to reach an agreement on the level of service provided, but this would require meetings, drafts, and often lead to friction and tension, whose costs could outweigh the perceived benefits for the parties, making the existence of the contractual relationship unfeasible.

[11] The issue of monitoring in the public sector is addressed in Cabral and Lazzarini (2015).

Contractual Incompleteness

Knowing these costs and the difficulty of anticipating all possible contractual contingencies, the parties prefer to leave the terms open based on tacit understandings and negotiate later in case of different perceptions regarding expectations. Such situations, quite common in our daily lives, reveal that contracts are incomplete, meaning they cannot account for all specificities and possibilities of future developments. Complete contracts, in fact, are mere abstractions found in some economics manuals and academic exercises. The real world, therefore, is marked by incomplete contracts in which it is difficult and/or costly to establish detailed clauses for all courses of action. The difficulty in observing the efforts made and the ambiguity related to the results obtained means that the presence of external actors to mediate conflicts is not free from subjectivities and biases.[12]

Economic theory predicts three sources of contractual incompleteness. The first one is bounded rationality.[13] Unlike the assumptions of rationality present in neoclassical economics, bounded rationality models admit that actors have cognitive limits that prevent them from processing all available information, leading to decisions that are not optimal but rather satisfactory. Secondly, *information is not available without costs*, meaning that even if agents could process all information, it may simply not be available. Thirdly, parties perceive costs related to the process of contractual design and adaptation in the face of unforeseen contingencies, as well as costs associated with specification, search, negotiation, monitoring, and contract enforcement, which parties may find prohibitive and prefer not to incur—these are known as *transaction costs*. This leads the parties to deliberately leave contractual gaps.[14]

Consequently, incomplete contracts are rarely overseen by third parties, such as courts and external arbitrators. It is also challenging to incorporate environmental factors and aspects that are difficult to specify ex-ante, as well as to include explicit incentives that link efforts to performance.

[12] Advances in the incomplete contract theories granted the 2016 Nobel Prize in Economics to Bengt Holmström and Oliver Hart. See Hart (2003) and Hölmstrom (1979).

[13] See Simon (1991).

[14] See Williamson (1985).

What to do in these situations? Should we include clauses and establish obligations even if they are inefficient? Should we avoid engaging in relationships under these conditions?

In response to the above questions, an answer is the introduction of relational mechanisms based on implicit understandings of obligations and rights of each party, and the use of contracts that are self-enforcing, i.e., without the need for third parties.[15] Unlike contracts with a single interaction, the effectiveness of relational contracts relies on the expectation of continued relationships that repeat over time, if the parties perceive such continuity as beneficial and superior to existing alternatives. Similarly, aspects grounded in reputation, honor, trust, and, in some cases, commitment to one's word have become prominent in many contractual relationships in both the public and private sectors. These aspects are increasingly being formalized to provide explanations for why such arrangements are enduring and sustainable, even if they are informal and lack contracts that can be scrutinized by third parties.

Reputational effects can foster the flow of information about the parties' conduct during their interactions, shaping both the pattern of decisions made by the parties and how external actors perceive the actions (and omissions) of those involved on aspects that are not formally codified. Below, we show how such interactions can be analytically understood through repeated interactions between mutually dependent parties.

Relational (or Implicit) Contracts: A Simple Game

The relationship between agents and principals in an environment of contractual incompleteness can be addressed through a simple game,[16] where the principal may or may not trust the intentions expressed by the agent, who, in turn, can act opportunistically, either considering or not considering only their own utility.

For illustrative purposes, let us consider the following hypothetical situation within the public sector. Anaelia is a professor and researcher at a management school within a large public university. With tenure and devotion to serious and cutting-edge research, she also ensures to care

[15] For a discussion on the use of relational contracts in general, refer to Bull (1987). For a discussion on the use of relational mechanisms in public and nonprofit organizations, see Bertelli and Smith (2009).

[16] See Bull (1987) and Kreps (1990).

for and prioritize the learning of her students. Over the past few years, Anaelia has accumulated several teaching and research awards.

Given such success, her peers unanimously elected her to lead the graduate department of the school, which entails the responsibility of managing research budgets and devising the overall teaching strategy for the offered master's and doctoral programs. Despite Anaelia's reluctance, as this position involves little financial gain and demands considerable effort that does not align with her teaching and research activities, she does not want to give up, and she accepts the task.

Despite being intrinsically motivated, the workload becomes unbearable, and Anaelia begins to show signs of exhaustion due to the accumulation of tasks. Seeing Anaelia struggling with bureaucratic obligations, a colleague suggests that she use part of her department's budget to hire an assistant who can handle reports and administrative tasks related to her role, thus reducing her burden of bureaucratic work. As it is not possible to conduct a public hiring process due to budget cuts announced by the Department of Education, Anaelia will have to hire an outsourced assistant, subject to more flexible labor regulations that allow for dismissal and hiring without significant costs.

Anaelia's life is very hectic, and she truly needs help, being willing to use the budget, she must hire someone. Assuming, for the sake of simplicity, that the costs of hiring, training, and dismissal are zero, at the end of each period (e.g., one month), Anaelia can decide whether to rehire the assistant for another period or dismiss him before the start of the new cycle.

Suppose that if Anaelia does not hire the assistant, her result will be zero, and naturally, the assistant will also receive zero if the hiring does not occur. If the decision is to hire, the assistant will receive a salary of 5 monetary units at the end of each period. Upon being hired, the assistant decides the effort to be employed. For simplicity, let us assume that the effort function is not continuous but rather discrete, reflecting two patterns: low effort and high effort.

On the one hand, the assistant can work hard (high effort) and incur a personal cost equivalent to 4 monetary units. In this case, their high effort yields a benefit of 6 monetary units to Anaelia. On the other hand, the assistant can choose to slack off, meaning he spends time on Instagram, WhatsApp, and continues working on side projects during his working hours (low effort). In this low dedication scenario, the effort cost incurred by the assistant is zero, and the benefit obtained by Anaelia is also zero.

In a situation like the one described above, what should Anaelia do? Hire an assistant or not?

The answer to this dilemma can be outlined through a diagram that represents a decision tree of the game between Anaelia and the potential hired assistant, as shown below (Fig. 4.3).

It is evident that without explicit incentives, such as the impossibility of enforcing penalties for the assistant's low effort and considering a one-shot game, Anaelia will choose not to hire the assistant. In fact, this happens because, in situations of interdependence, parties choose the best option for themselves based on the possible actions of the other party. Therefore, in equilibrium, this is an undesirable outcome, where neither party is satisfied.

It is possible, however, to reverse this situation if the relationship repeats over time. In the case of repeated interactions, the equilibrium can shift to the upper-right quadrant (hire; high effort). Reputational mechanisms and social norms can be particularly useful to change this undesirable situation.

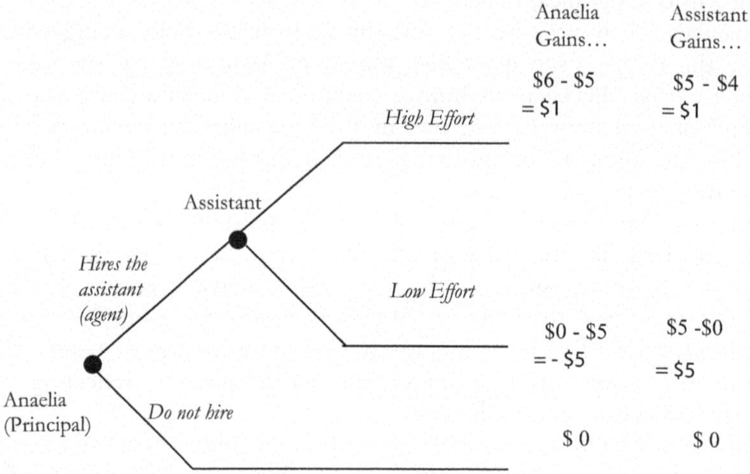

Fig. 4.3 Example of a principal-agent decision tree

Reputational mechanisms

Suppose that if the situation repeats over time. Let us incorporate into the decision-making process in each period the probability that Anaelia and the assistant will meet again. Such probability is denoted by δ ($0 < \delta < 1$), and its existence can affect the utility of both. In this case, as δ approaches 1, there is a greater chance of the parties interacting again, and as δ gets closer to 0, the chances are lower (think of a situation where the assistant will move to another country after the end of the first hiring period).[17]

Remember that if the agent always chooses to exert high effort, he will always profit $1. Since the probability of meeting again in the next period is conditioned on the assistant's past behavior, if he exerts low effort, he tends to be punished and not rehired.[18] Thus, his income flow (R) can be written as follows:

$$R = 1 + \delta\,1 + \delta^2\,1 + \delta^3\,1 + \cdots + \delta^n\,1$$

We have a time series, which corresponds to a geometric progression (GP). By the formula for the sum of terms in a GP that we learned in high school, the income flow can be expressed as follows:

$$R = \frac{1}{1-d}$$

For the assistant, it will only make sense to always exert high effort if the option of consistently making high effort over time results in higher gains than deviating from it. Going back to the numerical example, if the assistant deviates in period 1, the remuneration is 5, but since their behavior is detected, their remuneration in the following period is zero, as they are never hired again. Thus, if Anaelia's retaliation is credible, and if she has alternative suppliers in the market, the assistant will choose to make an effort under the following conditions:

$$\frac{1}{1-d} \geq 5 + 0$$

[17] Please refer to Abreu (1988) for a formalized treatment of infinitely repeated games with discounting.

[18] Terminating the contract and not rehiring the agent represents the most rigorous punishment possible. However, there are several other sanctions that can be implemented, such as temporarily freezing the hiring of the agent after some time and imposing fines. The choice of sanctions depends on the formal and informal institutions within which the contracting parties are embedded (Miller, 1992).

Hence, $\delta \geq 0{,}8$.

The above result shows that the option to exert high effort depends on a high probability of future encounters. In this case, a collaborative dynamic can occur, and it will be rational for both parties to cooperate and fulfill their part of the agreement, meaning the assistant exerting high effort and Anaelia paying as agreed and rehiring them in the next period. This dynamic will only be broken when one of the parties fails to fulfill the agreement.

Notice that this collaborative arrangement is similar to cartels and other forms of relationships in closed networks where the gains from collaboration outweigh the probabilities of retaliation, which are credible. Such structures also prevail in supplier networks in the automotive industry (***keiretsu***), in immigrant communities or ethnic groups that transact with each other, and even in organized crime organizations such as the Mafia. In these conditions, it is rational to collaborate because behavior and outcomes can be observable, albeit with imperfections, making retaliation easier to exercise. Therefore, concerns about reputation tend to prevail among the parties involved.

From the agent's point of view, reputational mechanisms can explain collaborative behavior. In this case, agents, eager to maintain a positive reputation, exert significant effort to increase their chances of being rehired or obtaining recommendations for being hired by other principals. This helps to explain why, in the public sector, when explicit incentives cannot be provided, managers often prefer to work with outsourced employees or individuals in commissioned positions rather than choosing career employees with job stability, where the threat of retaliation and dismissal is almost nonexistent. This undermines the reputational channel for the exertion of superior efforts that would benefit the utility of the principal.

The possibility of termination also helps to understand situations where tenured civil servants exert greater effort in the presence of extra payments for performing specific tasks. Depending on the magnitude of the additional benefits compared to the base salary, agents may experience a type of efficiency wage and exert effort in the direction desired by the principal to continue holding their positions and not lose the benefits. If the principal's objectives are aligned with the broader interests of society, this is excellent, as efforts will be converted into public value. This is one of the reasons that explain why the appointment of civil servants as wardens of privately managed prison units helps to achieve superior performance. If there are credible mechanisms for retaliation against misconduct, the appointed professionals will make efforts to oversee the actions of the private sector on behalf of the public interest to maintain their extra payments.[19]

From the principal's point of view, if she wants to continue benefiting from the agent's collaboration or attract agents with high potential, she will need to keep making payments. Notice that credibility is a fundamental element for collaborative and value-creating dynamics. Therefore, budgetary problems and opportunism by public managers or political actors can compromise the efficiency of the relational contract. Similarly, the lack of credibility in the sanctioning structure, whether due to the principal's lack of criteria to terminate the contractual relationship or due to barriers imposed on deliberating sanctions for those who exert low effort, also undermines the feasibility of self-enforcing agreements.

The lack of credibility in governments and its adverse effects is not limited to a single contractual transaction; on the contrary, information flows about the lack of reliability spread to networks of suppliers. Knowing the possibility of such conduct, suppliers may reduce their efforts or collude with self-interested and corrupt public agents who selectively address situations of low effort or non-compliance with agreed terms.

Overall, the lack of credibility leads to socially undesirable effects in relational contracts, making reputation an ineffective instrument for dealing with scenarios of contractual incompleteness. In other words, not fulfilling agreements is one of the keys to failure.

The Role of Social Norms in Relational Contracts

In addition to reputation, a utilitarian-biased mechanism where agents choose greater effort in the hope of obtaining monetary rewards over time, the presence of social norms rooted in cultural elements also induces effort. In this case, the personal cost resulting from exerting high effort would not be conditioned by the existence of future rewards, but rather by the voluntary adherence to a set of implicitly accepted rules by the parties interacting with each other. Altruistic behaviors deeply rooted in individuals, such as "*doing the right thing*", "*not harming the other party*"

[19] This argument is developed in Cabral (2006) and Cabral et al. (2010).

or "*always helping those in need*" can explain the collaborative propensity of the agents.

Such behaviors may be present in broader cultural elements found in certain territories.[20] Various societies have incorporated routines based on reciprocity into their behavioral patterns. For example, in the United States, it is socially accepted to reward waiters and taxi drivers with tips as a sign of gratitude for their service, even though it is not explicitly written in any formal norm. However, the same type of conduct may be rejected in other countries. Certain localities show respect for others' space and, for example, avoid occupying the entire width of an escalator, leaving room for those in a hurry to pass. Even individuals who originally do not share such values quickly adapt to the prevailing collective mental models, either because they come to understand such behaviors as legitimate or to avoid disapproving looks and potential retaliation from those accustomed to the local rules.

The parties involved can also condition their behavior independently of any threat of retaliation. Behaviors can be guided, for example, by values related to public spirit, so that agents may exert high efforts regardless of the nature of their employment relationship or potential gains at stake. Tenured civil servants having a low probability of being punished for low efforts may be intrinsically motivated to exert high efforts. These individuals may even incur personal costs if they do not put in earnest effort. For example, we can consider the existence of a factor equivalent to a "psychological cost" to be incurred in situations of low effort, something that individuals associate with a feeling of guilt for not having done their best. If such psychological costs are extremely high, the tendency is for the individual not to deviate and fulfill what is expected of them.

The question that arises is: how to select individuals who have a low propensity for deviation? The observation and measurement of this characteristic in the real world is not trivial. In practice, managers can rely on other factors to select individuals based on known expected behavior. For example, the hiring of individuals belonging to certain ethnic and religious groups is a path adopted by many organizations, despite potential concerns about the discriminatory bias of such conduct. In this case, the psychological cost of exerting low effort may be reinforced by the combined effect of reputation and social norms.

[20] For a comparison of the cultural factors in different countries, please refer to Hofstede (1997).

Likewise, there are organizations with strong organizational cultures that allow for the identification of individuals during interviews or initial stages of training. In the public sector, this can be seen in the armed forces. In the private sector, companies with well-defined cultural values can attract candidates inclined to work within the organization based on the signals emitted by the culture. In nonprofits, adherence to organizational culture is key for the organizational performance and the welfare of paid workers and volunteers. These organizations can swiftly remove individuals who do not align with the informal aspects ingrained in the organization.

While on one hand, such processes reinforce alignment, on the other hand, they undermine organizational diversity and the recycling of ideas and knowledge necessary for the organization to stay attuned to the external environment and the needs of new stakeholders, which were previously absent and now prominent.[21]

In summary, social norms and reputation can be complementary or substitutes in terms of their effect on alignment and interests between principal and agent in relational contracts used as a response to contractual incompleteness. They can even serve as inducements for efforts in incentive contracts involving groups of individuals whose individual contributions to the results achieved are not easily observed.

Although public and nonprofit organizations have limited leeway compared to those in the private sector, understanding the principles that foster collaboration among individuals through formal and informal mechanisms is extremely useful for establishing practices associated with superior performance or, at worst, routines and patterns of conduct that at least mitigate relative performance losses. While incentives are key elements in this regard, they can also be potential sources of behavioral distortion if designed inadequately and misaligned with the performance measurement. As we will explore in the following chapter, successful performance management is intricately connected to the design of both implicit and explicit incentives. Successful performance management also hinges on how organizations address incentive distortions exacerbated by multitasking, social comparison, and moral erosion, all discussed in the next chapter.

[21] See Uzzi (1996).

Conclusion

As firms, much of the success of public and nonprofit organizations relies heavily on efforts of employees and suppliers aligning with the goals devised by strategists. Yet, obtaining such alignment is not trivial, and conflicts may arise between those who delegate tasks in an organization (principals) and those who perform the tasks and must deliver results (agents). This is because actors tend to prioritize actions that address their own utility functions. Consequently, the conflict between agents and principals gives rise to a series of costs with the potential to destroy value rather than create it.

To promote alignment and mitigate conflicts, incentive contracts are often employed. These contracts are structured to involve rewards and/or sanctions contingent on the attainment of expected outcomes. The idea is to create a setting that encourages agents to act in the best interest of the principal while simultaneously maximizing the overall value created by their actions and achieving their own interests. For example, the Department of Education could implement a pay-for-performance contract for teachers and school managers, with variable compensation based on the reduction of dropouts. This approach anticipates that increased efforts by agents will enhance the school's efficiency, benefiting targeted students who, by remaining in school, can expect better employment opportunities in the future. If these goals are met, teachers and managers could then capture a portion of the value they have created in the form of financial bonuses.

However, when organizational outcomes hinge on collective efforts, additional challenges arise for organizations in ensuring effective coordination and addressing issues stemming from collective action, such as free-riding behavior. These challenges stem from the difficulty of observing, rewarding, and retaliating against individual conduct by rational agents not aligned with the principal's best interests, particularly when agents are part of teams with many members. To address these challenges, this chapter explores several remedies, including harnessing peer pressure, offering additional incentives for principals who intensify monitoring efforts, and integrating innovative technologies to reduce monitoring costs. An example of this technological approach is the use of body cameras worn by police officers in various countries.

This chapter also highlights that, in various situations, the use of detailed and formal contracts to align incentives is not always feasible.

To overcome these limitations, individuals, and organizations of all types (public, private, and nonprofits) resort to employing informal agreements. These informal arrangements serve to induce efforts from agents and ensure value creation through recurring interactions over time. Relational contracts, which balance extrinsic and intrinsic motivation, have found applications in collaborative networks within the private sector, cross-sector collaborations involving multiple types of organizations, and regular principal-agent relationships, serving as platforms for enhanced value creation.

References

Abreu, D. (1988). On the theory of infinitely repeated games with discounting. *Econometrica: Journal of the Econometric Society, 56*, 383–396.

Albanese, R., & Van Fleet, D. D. (1985). Rational behavior in groups: The free-riding tendency. *Academy of Management Review, 10*(2), 244–255.

Baker, G., Stewart, B., Appelbaum, E., & Beer, M. (1993). Rethinking rewards. *Harvard Business Review, 71*(6), 37–49.

Bertelli, A. M., & Smith, C. R. (2009). Relational contracting and network management. *Journal of Public Administration Research and Theory, 20*(suppl_1), i21-i40.

Bolton, P., & Dewatripont, M. (2004). *Contract theory*: MIT Press.

Brickley, J. A., Smith, C. W., & Zimmerman, J. L. (2001). *Managerial economics and organizational architecture* (2nd ed.): McGraw-Hill.

Bull, C. (1987). The existence of self-enforcing implicit contracts. *The Quarterly Journal of Economics, 102*(1), 147–159.

Cabral, S. (2006). *Além das grades: uma análise comparada das modalidades de gestão do sistema prisional. Salvador: , (Tese de Doutorado), 292 p.* (PhD in Management), Universidade Federal da Bahia, Salvador.

Cabral, S., & Lazzarini, S. G. (2015). The 'guarding the guardians' problem: An analysis of the organizational performance of an Internal Affairs Division. *Journal of Public Administration Research and Theory, 25*(3), 797–829.

Cabral, S., Lazzarini, S. G., & Azevedo, P. F. (2010). Private operation with public supervision: Evidence of hybrid modes of governance in prisons. *Public Choice, 145*(1–2), 281–293.

Fama, E. F., & Jensen, M. C. (1983). Separation of ownership and control. *The Journal of Law and Economics, 26*(2), 301–325.

Hart, O. (2003). Incomplete contracts and public ownership: Remarks, and an application to public-private partnerships. *The Economic Journal, 113*(486), C69–C76.

Hofstede, G. (1997). *Culture and organizations: Softwares of the mind*. McGraw Hill.

Hölmstrom, B. (1979). Moral hazard and observability. *The Bell journal of economics*, 74–91.

Jensen, M. C., & Meckling, W. H. (1976). Theory of the firm: Managerial behavior, agency costs and ownership structure. *Journal of Financial Economics, 3*, 305–360.

Kandel, E., & Lazear, E. (1992). Peer pressure and partnerships. *Journal of Political Economy, 100*, 801–816.

Kreps, D. M. (1990). Corporate culture and economic theory. In J. Alt & K. Shepsle (Eds.), *Perspectives on positive political economy* (pp. 90–143). Cambridge University Press.

Milgrom, P. R., & Roberts, J. (1992). *Economics, organization and management*. Prentice-Hall.

Miller, G. J. (1992). *Managerial dilemmas: The political economy of hierarchy*. Cambridge University Press.

Olson, M. (1965). *The logic of collective action*. Harvard University Press.

Power, M. (2003). Evaluating the Audit Explosion. *Law & Policy, 25*(3), 185–202. https://doi.org/10.1111/j.1467-9930.2003.00147.x

Simon, H. A. (1991). Bounded rationality and organizational learning. *Organization Science, 2*(1), 125–134.

Uzzi, B. (1996). The sources and consequences of embeddedness for the economic performance of organizations: The network effect. *American Sociological Review*, 674–698.

Williamson, O. E. (1985). *The economic institutions of capitalism*. The Free Press.

CHAPTER 5

Performance Management in Public and Nonprofit Organizations

Consider a hypothetical scenario where a politician, boasting a record of accomplishment of success in business management, ascends to power with a market-oriented platform. Among his significant commitments is the introduction of performance management systems including payment systems designed to incentivize civil servants through the recognition of accomplished performance objectives. According to his logic, teachers would invest greater effort in preparing classes, motivating students to work diligently both in the classroom and at home, creating exams and evaluation activities to gauge student progress, and collaborating on activities with teachers from other disciplines, all for the benefit of the students. In a similar vein, police officers under his command, with the prospect of increased salaries, would also collaborate to patrol the streets, preempt criminal strategies, expedite investigative processes, solve crimes, and enhance the sense of safety within their local communities.

The recently elected politician also envisions an extension of pay-for-performance (PFP) programs to nonprofit organizations that offer social services to the local government. Drawing on his business astuteness, he believes that implementing performance-based payments would not just incentivize nonprofit managers to enhance their efforts for the citizens' benefit but would also aid in refining their operational practices. Introducing performance management systems, in fact, could foster a more professional approach within nonprofits, thereby enhancing

S. Cabral, *Strategy for Public and Nonprofit Organizations*,
https://doi.org/10.1007/978-3-031-64969-1_5

their decision-making process on behalf of the communities they serve. The politician also holds the belief that outcome-oriented sponsors would value a results-driven focus from the nonprofit organizations they endorse. In line with this perspective, rather than disbursing funds solely for philanthropic activities lacking concrete evidence of performance enhancement, certain nonprofit sponsors may favor supporting organizations that actively contribute to improving social and/or environmental outcomes. Certain donors draw inspiration from W. Edwards Deming, a distinguished management professor and a key figure in spearheading the quality movement after World War II. They adopt a mantra that echoes one of Deming's most renowned quotes: "*In God, we trust; all others, please bring the data*".

The euphoria of the political campaign has faded away. "*The party is over, and it is time to uphold the promises I have made*", the elected politician says to himself as he stands in front of the mirror, while shaving in the morning. However, after weeks in the office, he realized that implementing PFP programs in the public and nonprofit sectors is not as uncomplicated as he had thought. Numerous unforeseen barriers emerged, leading the politician to acknowledge his naivety in assuming that public and private organizations operated similarly. He not only underestimated the challenges of managing public entities but also overlooked certain principles of management theories.

For instance, he overlooked the fact that civil servants, acting as rational individuals, also aim to maximize their utility and income while minimizing personal costs. These servants could either advocate for the implementation of PFP programs with easily attainable bonus thresholds or refrain from exerting extra effort if they already receive efficiency wages—payments that exceed the market average—and are protected from contract termination by the government, even in instances of subpar performance. The situation can become more challenging when it involves civil servants with higher levels of risk aversion compared to workers in the private sector.[1] Given that risk-averse individuals typically require higher fixed wages to exert greater efforts in PFP programs, in such cases, the combined fixed and variable wages provided to civil servants might not adequately offset the associated costs.

[1] Hartog et al. (2002).

Another factor that could limit the meaningful involvement of civil servants in PFP programs is the presence of uncertainty in the connection between efforts and outcomes. According to the informativeness principle,[2] it is valuable for the chosen indicator to be impacted by the agent's actions in a manner that elucidates these relationships and motivates the direction of agent efforts toward the principal's interests. Considering this, the politician also came to realize that the task of selecting suitable performance indicators was far more intricate than initially perceived. Setting performance indicators that accurately capture the impact of civil servants' actions on factors facilitating public value creation, while remaining easily measurable and resistant to manipulation, is a complex challenge. Furthermore, outcome-based initiatives encounter opposition from civil servant unions, which advocate for elevated (and guaranteed) fixed wages rather than combinations of modest fixed wages paired with ambitious yet uncertain variable compensations.

The elected politician also did not anticipate the adverse responses from nonprofit organizations. Even though there is evidence suggesting that the implementation of performance management systems can enhance the effectiveness of nonprofit organizations and bolster their credibility with sponsors and funders, some critics might argue that a heightened market orientation driven by performance management systems could potentially undermine the community-building aspect of nonprofits and their ability to address the needs of citizens.[3] Nonprofits may also resist pressure to gather evidence of their social impact when receiving public funds, as it is challenging to link their efforts to observable outcomes. Given that identifying pertinent outcomes is a time-consuming and resource-intensive task, it is reasonable that a preference might arise for measures of outputs that are simpler to define and measure.[4] Common sense, supported by existing research, also suggests that some nonprofit managers resist due to a fundamental principle of human behavior: nobody enjoys being under constant supervision![5]

[2] Holmström (2017).

[3] See Suykens et al. (2022).

[4] For an assessment of the arguments influencing politicians and public managers to persist with output measures rather than outcomes in performance measurement systems within public organizations, please refer to Rajala et al. (2018).

[5] Arvidson and Lyon (2014).

Certainly, the scenario depicted above is hypothetical. Nevertheless, it provides a concise overview of the primary challenges inherent in implementing performance management systems. Incorporating performance-based methodologies into public, nonprofit, and private organizations necessitates a series of crucial decisions. These encompass determinations about the foundation for performance evaluation (whether objective or subjective standards are utilized), the establishment of key performance indicators, the strategies for performance assessment, and the recognition of potential incentive distortions that could emerge while implementing performance management systems incorporating pay-for-performance initiatives.

Objective Versus Subjective Performance Indicators

Performance appraisals serve as essential tools to guide individuals and teams in their endeavors, establishing benchmarks against which rewards and sanctions can be applied. The challenge lies in achieving equitable assessments when individual and collective efforts remain unobserved. What types of performance measures should be employed to assess the contributions of agents in alignment with the objectives set by the organization's top managers or its most significant stakeholders?

According to the principles of managerial economics, objective measures are typically embraced when outputs can be precisely defined, measured, and outlined in a contract. However, while governments worldwide have favored objective measures to steer the management of public organizations, and despite the endorsement of these measures within the scientific community due to their collection by individuals independent of the focal phenomena, they are not exempt from criticisms.

Indeed, certain measures do not inherently capture dimensions associated with (public) value creation and may not be linked to actions controlled by the individuals being assessed. For example, consider a scenario where a government aims to provide variable compensations through a PFP program to internal revenue agents based on the total tax amount collected across the entire country. The reasoning to justify the program is quite simple: the efforts of agents to perform inspections to verify if taxpayers are compliant with the fiscal requirements and enforce the payments of due taxes would benefit the entire society.

Yet, some individuals, such as the hypothetical politician portrayed at the beginning of this chapter, would consider it fair to share with internal revenue agents a portion of the taxes collected above an established threshold. However, one may argue, would not the taxes collected depend on other factors that are not influenced by agents? Indeed, an increase in economic activity in the country, stimulated by improvements in external conditions, would increase the amount of taxes collected regardless of the efforts made by revenue agents. In this case, payments that are contingent on performance established by objective and quantifiable measures would not be a promising idea.

Performance management systems based on objective measures are also subject to problems related to the establishment of performance standards, measurement costs, and incentive distortions. In addition to these aspects, which will be further discussed in this chapter, objective measures have their own limitations.

Often, objective measures cannot fully encompass the value-creating activities performed by individuals and teams. For example, while it is expected that police forces reduce the number of homicides, street robberies, and other quantifiable crimes, it is also expected that police officers treat citizens with courtesy, respect, and within the bounds of the law. Indeed, a sizable portion of citizens tends to prioritize aspects related to fair treatment over criminal records published months later. This is not only because they observe the behavior of the civil servants who are supposed to serve them but also because they can become victims of abuse and misconduct at the hands of police officers. In this case, subjective measures based on the perceptions and judgments of citizens and superiors can be used to assess the extent to which police officers adhere to the required standards of fair treatment.

Subjective measures are also utilized when objective measures for assessing certain activities do not exist. Consider a scenario where the chief of a police department wishes to evaluate whether the police officers under her authority are effectively collaborating in their policing activities. In fact, the effectiveness of police forces in reducing crimes hinges on coordinated actions that involve planning, sharing information about criminal activities within the territory, as well as the dissemination of managerial practices and routines that are not easily codified and are tacitly transmitted. To achieve this, senior officers are expected to allocate some of their time to mentor less experienced officers. However, even though the police chief can use output measures like the number of hours spent in planning meetings and mentoring sessions, it is challenging to believe that these objective measures will be effective in assessing the collaborative aspects that the organization values. As a result, a compelling argument can be put forth in favor of employing subjective measures when individuals and teams engage in activities that are not easily quantified using objective output or outcome measures.

Usually, subjective measures are rooted in perceptions and are gathered through surveys or other instruments that employ rating scales to evaluate individuals based on the attributes of interest. These measures are extensively utilized to gauge citizens' perceptions of public programs and the performance of both public and nonprofit organizations. While citizens' perceptions of the quality of a particular public service may not always align with actual records derived from administrative data, managing citizens' perceptions becomes increasingly vital in the age of social media. For instance, official and reliable data may indicate a decreasing crime rate in a region, but a single isolated crime incident can significantly increase the sense of insecurity within the local community. Managers responsible for public security should closely monitor citizens' perceptions to address their feelings of fear and insecurity.

Nonprofit organizations can find value in citizens' perceptions, particularly when objective measures are either unavailable or controversial, as is often the case in cultural services. A noteworthy example is the Bahia State Symphonic Orchestra (OSBA), based in Salvador, Brazil, and operated by the nonprofit organization *Associação Amigos do Teatro Castro Alves*. Over the past decade, 92% of the orchestra's performances featured classical music. However, the orchestra adopted a strategic approach to engage citizens and boost concert attendance by organizing periodic concerts featuring popular music, including movie soundtracks and folk music played by the full orchestra. These concerts consistently sold out in advance, and those initially attracted by these popular events began attending regular concerts more frequently. The orchestra and the nonprofit organization responsible for its management gained immense popularity to the extent that citizens reacted strongly when a competing nonprofit won a competitive bid to manage the orchestra. Despite the bidding process being technically oriented, watchdog agencies, influenced by public opinion, argued that citizen input should be considered, resulting in a demand for a new bidding process.[6]

Public and nonprofit organizations often rely on subjective measures to assess individuals and establish a foundation for rewards and sanctions. Typically, after the evaluation based on instruments that rate individuals on a scale, the result is an ordered ranking. Subsequently, the ranking is accompanied by comments summarizing the strengths of the evaluated individual as well as areas for improvement and further development. Organizations may also assess their employees by setting goals for a given period and conducting periodic checks to determine whether these goals have been achieved or not. While some goals are easy to check and resemble objective measures, subjectivity comes into play in certain dimensions (e.g., "Has the employee acted as a team player?").

Distortions and Problems in Objective and Subjective Measures

Certainly, both objective and subjective measures can introduce incentive distortions that may compromise the effectiveness of performance evaluation systems and the relevance of pay-for-performance programs. Let us begin by discussing the issues that most affect objective measures.

Multitask

In many roles, individuals are often responsible for performing multiple tasks simultaneously. For example, a traffic officer's duties encompass not only directing traffic to ensure the smooth flow of vehicles but also enforcing traffic laws by issuing fines to violators. Similarly, an auditor working within a watchdog agency must effectively allocate her time among tasks such as selecting investigation targets, coordinating investigations with other agents and government agencies, conducting the investigations, and compiling detailed reports. Furthermore, employees

[6] See more in https://www.correio24horas.com.br/minha-bahia/nao-acho-que-vou-sair-diz-carlos-prazeres-sobre-futuro-na-osba-0823. This video illustrates the successful strategy employed by this Brazilian nonprofit organization to engage citizens with the local orchestra. Particular attention should be given to the attire of the conductor, Mr. Carlos Prazeres, and the other musicians. https://youtu.be/c4ah-gIMGSk.

of nonprofit organizations dedicated to serving disenfranchised communities frequently find themselves balancing their time between fundraising efforts, maintaining public relations with communities of interest, and carrying out mission-related activities.

All the tasks listed above are important and essential for the respective organizations' objectives. However, assigning multiple activities to individuals can lead to multitask issues, which pose challenges for managers in these organizations. Motivating employees to excel in all these activities is not a straightforward endeavor. Rational agents tend to exert more effort in activities that yield greater personal rewards and are easier to assess. This challenge becomes even more pronounced when performance-based payments are involved. On the one hand, managers want their employees to excel in all these tasks. On the other hand, employees tend to prioritize tasks that offer superior rewards and are more easily quantifiable.[7]

Examples of multitasking are abundant in both public and nonprofit organizations. For instance, Hee-Je Bak and Do Han Kim show that Korean faculty members who were provided with stronger financial incentives to focus on research experienced an increase in their research output, but this was accompanied by lower scores in teaching evaluations.[8] In a recent study, Gustavo Tavares, Antonio Cesar Marcolino, and I have examined the impacts of Body-Worn Cameras (BWCs) on the incidence of fatalities arising from police interventions within the largest Brazilian police force. While BWCs have led to a notable decrease in the number of deaths involving police officers, our research has identified diminished rates of firearm seizures in specific police units. This observation implies that officers in these less productive units may be responding to BWC implementation by scaling back their efforts in street patrols, as a strategy to evade potential sanctions for violent conduct.[9]

Multitask also manifests itself in the realm of nonprofits. In this context, Sara Stühlinger and Sophie E. Hersberger-Lang conducted an analysis of 544 Swiss nonprofit organizations and found that organizations focusing on fundraising from private and impact-oriented sponsors

[7] Holmstrom and Milgrom (1991) explores the challenges associated with multitasking in incentive contracts, organizational design, and performance management.

[8] Bak and Kim (2015).

[9] Tavares et al. (2024).

tend to allocate fewer resources toward providing information to public authorities.[10]

There are potential solutions to the multitask problem, although all of them come with their own imperfections. Managers, when assigning tasks to subordinates, can encourage greater specialization, and minimize conflicting responsibilities. While this approach may prevent the substitution of effort, reducing the number of activities assigned to individuals can also hinder value-creating complementarities. Certainly, a university professor who is at the forefront of research in her field cannot effectively transmit innovative knowledge to her students in her classes if she solely concentrates on research activities.

Managers may opt to reduce pecuniary incentives and rely on the assumption that subordinates will exert the necessary efforts driven by their intrinsic motivation. Nevertheless, while personal values and a sense of mission accomplishment can discourage the overuse of strong monetary incentives, some subordinates might still experience demotivation. Balancing subjective and objective measures and integrating them into the assessment process can serve as an intriguing alternative for reconciling tasks. This approach accommodates tasks where outputs and outcomes are observable and measurable alongside measures that, although more challenging to observe, hold significant importance in the value creation process.[11]

Ratchet Effect

Objective measures typically depend on administrative records derived from past performance. While managers (principals) do gain insights over time into the past performance of subordinates and contractors (agents), which aids organizations in setting future performance targets, it is important to note that agents possess privileged information regarding the connection between their efforts and the resulting outcomes. Agents are aware that managers have an imperfect view of their efforts and lack complete awareness of the relationship between the efforts exerted by the agents and the actual outcomes achieved. Furthermore, agents can

[10] Stühlinger and Hersberger-Langloh (2021).

[11] John Roberts (2010) provides an intriguing and succinct overview of how weak incentives, not totally reliant on monetary rewards, can assist organizations in addressing incentive challenges like multitask.

anticipate that managers tend to raise performance targets in the future, which increases the agents' future effort costs. Consequently, agents can be inclined to moderate their present efforts to prevent a significant increase in performance standards in the future. This incentive distortion is referred to as the "*ratchet effect*".[12]

The ratchet effect is dysfunctional for all types of organizations that incentivize agents' efforts through output or outcome-based measures. Agents can diminish their potential for value creation by either barely meeting the current targets or by reducing their efforts in the present, anticipating the next year. For example, salespersons and supply chain managers who surpass their quotas for a given period may choose to delay deliveries until the next fiscal year, when economic conditions may not be as favorable as in the current fiscal year. This allows them to achieve a steady stream of revenues from performance-based payments.

In the public sector, firefighters, who receive partial compensation based on their response times to assist the population, may moderate their efforts in the present, foreseeing that the upcoming year will bring a season more susceptible to fires due to climate cycles. The ratchet effect can have even more far-reaching consequences when strategists establish rewards and penalties tied to the achievement of performance goals based on past records. The case of the Soviet Union illustrates how the ratchet effect contributed to the country's economic stagnation: individuals anticipating longer job tenures pursued efforts they could sustain in case performance goals were raised in the future. As job continuity depended on meeting these targets, the expectation of job retention led workers to shirk, resulting in reduced productivity and the destruction of public value.[13]

James Brickley and colleagues[14] propose some solutions to mitigate the consequences of agents' strategic behavior and reduce the impact of the ratchet effect. One such solution is to carefully define the piecework rate and refrain from changing it until a new study is conducted, even when agents are performing exceptionally well. Promoting job rotation can also

[12] The propensity to underproduce in the present to avoid more stringent demands in the future has been a central concern of economics scholars for decades. To learn more about the ratchet effect, refer to: Freixas et al. (1985) and Litwack (1993).

[13] Litwack (1993) provides an account of the problems associated with the under fulfillment of targets in the Soviet Union throughout the twentieth century.

[14] Brickley et al. (2001).

help limit manipulation efforts, although it may have a potential negative impact on productivity rates. Additionally, initiatives aimed at capturing random errors that influence the relationship between efforts and performance are essential for establishing performance targets that align more closely with what evaluated individuals and groups can realistically deliver, thus mitigating the effects of the ratchet effect.

Using performance evaluation data from Korean state-owned enterprises, Ahn and colleagues have found that taking actions to acquire more information about the capabilities of an organization's employees, coupled with involving subordinates in the target-setting process, can mitigate the unintended consequences of the ratchet effect. The combination of efforts to gather comprehensive information about employees' traits beyond their past performance, along with strengthening connections with employees, can reduce detrimental and value-destroying behaviors.[15]

Gaming

As highlighted in the previous chapter, the problem with incentives is that they can work too well. In addition to moderating their efforts, individuals and groups exposed to robust pecuniary incentives and/or credible punishments in the event of goal non-achievement often resort to cheating and manipulating their efforts and performance outcomes.

Examples of manipulation are abundant. The manipulation of balance sheets, as witnessed in the well-documented Enron case,[16] is not limited to private firms. There is consistent evidence that several nonprofit organizations manipulate their financial reports by bunching the contributions they receive from donors. This practice is often employed to bolster their balance sheets and appear solvent to donors, particularly when these nonprofits rely heavily on charitable contributions for their revenues.[17]

[15] Ahn et al. (2018).

[16] Healy and Palepu (2003).

[17] Homonoff et al. (2020).

Nonprofits that rely on donations from sponsors, who consider financial solvency when allocating their charitable funds, as well as government funding, appear to respond to incentives and adapt their behavior according to the preferences of their donors.[18]

Individuals and organizations can also manipulate the system and engage in activities that diminish rather than create public value. A notable case is that of teachers who are incentivized with financial bonuses tied to students' test scores. Using an algorithm to detect cheating patterns, Brian Jacob and Steven Levitt demonstrated an elevated incidence of cheating in Chicago public schools following the implementation of a pay-for-performance program. According to the authors, teachers and school administrators aiming to boost student scores resorted to illicit practices by tampering with students' test papers. Fortunately, there are simple measures that can help prevent illicit behaviors and deter cheating, such as engaging independent organizations to prepare, administer, monitor, and grade the tests. Alternatively, using teachers and administrators from different schools where the test is being conducted to manage the tests can also be effective in maintaining integrity.[19]

Individuals with a short-term orientation often jeopardize long-term outcomes by prioritizing actions that yield immediate personal gains. For instance, a manager may impose an excessive workload on subordinates in the present to maximize their chances of achieving positive results, securing bonuses, and enhancing their opportunities both within and outside the organization, potentially at the expense of the overall organizational climate. Individuals and groups can also engage in collusion when organizations set performance standards based on internal benchmarks to account for random components affecting the effort-performance relationship. It is common for peers to discourage individuals who consistently exert superior efforts, pressuring top-performers to limit their output. In the end, this collective behavior results in an overall reduction in performance, and value creation is hindered.

There are several remedies that can be employed to mitigate the consequences of opportunistic actions by agents, but it is important to recognize that these solutions are not perfect. One approach is to leverage compliance and accountability standards to raise the costs of

[18] Calabrese (2013).

[19] Jacob and Levitt (2003).

cheating and engaging in illicit activities, thereby increasing the likelihood of punishing at least the individuals engaging in such behavior. However, in many countries, especially where civil servants are granted tenure after a probationary period, threats of severe punishment may lack credibility.

Even if a serious and unequivocal violation is detected, investigations typically adhere to the standards of judicial procedures, involving the collection of evidence, scheduling hearings for accused individuals and witnesses, and making efforts to document the entire process. Consequently, these procedures can be time-consuming, and there is a risk that the statutes of limitations may expire before a resolution is reached.

In addition to enhancing the efficiency of oversight bodies responsible for monitoring the conduct of civil servants, such as Internal Affairs Divisions for police officers, one potential solution to mitigate misconduct is to extend the probationary period before granting tenure. In a collaborative research Sergio Lazzarini and I have discovered that police officers investigated for misconduct are more likely to face disciplinary action when they have less than five years of experience in the police force.[20] However, it is crucial to acknowledge that while improved accountability standards are essential, they may also introduce inflexibility and place greater emphasis on strict rule and procedure adherence, potentially at the expense of factors that contribute to enhanced value creation.[21]

Another potential solution to prevent moral erosion in the pursuit of financial bonuses within PFP programs is the implementation of weak, non-pecuniary incentives. John Roberts argues that weak incentives, in the form of non-pecuniary rewards, are optimal under various conditions, including situations where there are poor effort or performance measures, multitask is prevalent and good measures are not accessible for all value-creating tasks, agents need to collaborate and work interdependently, organizations require agents to innovate, and agents need to follow the courses of action chosen by the principal.[22]

[20] Please refer to Cabral and Lazzarini (2015).

[21] Power (2021) offers a compelling overview of both the intended and, notably, the unintended consequences stemming from the widespread proliferation and empowerment of audit bodies in the society.

[22] Roberts (2010).

Social Comparison

Social scientists have long recognized that individuals often compare their own earnings to those of their peers. When individuals perceive inequities in comparison to others within their reference group, it can lead to frustration and trigger various unintended behaviors. These behaviors may include reducing their level of effort, leaving the organization, and even engaging in acts of sabotage because of *social comparison*.[23]

Perceptions of inequity are exacerbated by inflated self-assessments of performance. In research involving individuals engaged in Research and Development activities, Todd Zenger found that individuals tend to overstate their perceived performance in comparison to their peers: more than 60% of the individuals assessed rate themselves as being among the top 10% of performers.[24] The level of frustration can easily intensify when the organization ranks these individuals based on actual performance standards, and they are not deemed eligible for receiving higher financial rewards.

Certainly, the costs incurred by organizations due to "*better-than-average effect*" are significant and manifest in many ways, including reduced productivity, increased transaction costs, and a depletion of investments in human capital. To mitigate the widespread effects of social comparison, organizations can opt to compress rewards and minimize the differentiation between top- and low-performers. By doing so, organizations can have individuals and teams with closer performance scores, thereby mitigating the consequences of social comparison and reducing the likelihood of sabotage from lower-performing individuals who might not receive bonuses in a setting with higher differentiation. Consequently, organizations must carefully weigh the social comparison costs against the benefits of increased incentive intensity before deciding to compress the rewards they offer.[25]

[23] See Festinger (1954).

[24] Zenger (1994).

[25] Nickerson and Zenger (2008) analysis of the implications of social comparison costs for various organizational decisions and their corresponding consequences for organizational failure underscores the consequences of how organizations address incentive distortions. Their study illustrates how organizational responses to these distortions can either foster value creation or lead to value destruction. While the authors' focus is primarily on private organizations, their insights hold value and can be extended to public and nonprofit organizations as well.

Distortions in Subjective Measures

While subjective performance measures can complement objective measures, their use is not without limitations. Subjective measures rely on the perceptions of managers or peers, and organizations often do not employ structured instruments to address internal validity issues. Consequently, the views of those conducting assessments can be significantly biased, resulting in either overrating or underrating the individuals and groups being evaluated. In fact, evaluators are not always fully aware of the actual relationships between the efforts of individuals and groups and their actual performance outcomes.

In the case of public organizations, where numerous and often conflicting dimensions coexist, achieving consensus is even more challenging than in private organizations. Although validity issues are not exclusive to subjective measures, biased judgments can lead to a sense of inequity and unfairness among those who believe they deserve better scores, potentially sparking social comparison problems.[26]

Another concern related to the use of subjective performance measures is the cost associated with the evaluation process. Conducting evaluations entails various personal costs for evaluators, including the effort required to gather and analyze relevant information, time allocation for evaluation and committee meetings, and the management of tensions arising from dissatisfied individuals and groups who receive unfavorable scores. Since evaluators typically internalize these costs and are not always compensated for their efforts, some may shirk their responsibilities and provide imprecise assessments to minimize these evaluation-related costs. In some cases, in the context of 360-degree evaluations some may even collude with evaluated individuals and groups, offering favorable reviews with positive ratings to peers and subordinates.[27]

This situation can be further complicated in public organizations where tenured civil servants often rotate and change their supervisor-subordinate roles. For instance, police officers in the Internal Affairs Division today may find themselves in patrolling streets tomorrow, or a schoolteacher

[26] Andrews et al. (2006) work offers a compelling review of the challenges associated with subjective performance measures in the public and nonprofit realm.

[27] Prendergast and Topel (1996).

may temporarily assume the role of principal before returning to the classroom. As a result, the fear of potential retaliation in future evaluations may discourage evaluators from providing tough assessments in the present.[28]

Subjective measures can also lead evaluated individuals to incur influence costs and exert unproductive efforts to please the evaluators and obtain positive evaluations. In a randomized field experiment conducted with civil servants in China, Alain de Janvry and colleagues noted that employees tend to prioritize efforts that are valued by evaluators. However, the presence of uncertainty regarding who will be the evaluator not only decreases the tendency of civil servants to invest in activities to please the evaluators, but also enhances performance.[29]

Defining Relevant Performance Indicators: The Importance of Theory of Change

Subjective and objective measures have both pros and cons. This makes the task of defining relevant performance indicators even more challenging. Which criteria should guide decision-makers' choices when there are several conflicting measures? How should performance indicators for complex and interdependent activities with impacts beyond the focal area of assessment be defined?

One possibility is the use of multicriteria decision analysis (MCDA) to assess and compare several options. MCDA typically relies on pre-established goals to facilitate decision-making. It is a complex process that considers the opinions and judgments of decision-makers and informed actors familiar with the project or public activity under scrutiny. MCDA has been used in environmental issues to address socioenvironmental costs, public benefits, citizen preferences, and provide valuable performance indicators for decision-making. Decision matrices help summarize the relevant information, facilitate the ordering of alternatives, and enable a more structured and analytical approach with the support of methods such as Analytic Hierarchy Process (AHP), Preference Ranking Organization Method for Enrichment Evaluation (PROMETHEE), Technique for

[28] Cabral and Lazzarini (2015).

[29] De Janvry et al. (2023).

Order Preference by Similarity to Ideal Solution (TOPSIS), Multicriteria Satisfaction Analysis (MUSA), among others.[30]

However, the subjective aspects involved in selecting the relevant criteria and defining the criterion weights, the mathematical complexity of the available methods, and the need for computational resources contribute to making methods based on multicriteria tools not entirely actionable for managers.

More recently, practitioners in public, nonprofit, and multilateral organizations, such as the World Bank, have widely used the theory of change approach to address complex public policies, programs, or projects involving many stakeholders. A theory of change outlines the landscape of change by connecting the necessary actions to the expected results. Achieving enhanced public value creation in the form of superior social and environmental outcomes necessitates the presence of preceding intermediate results that are logically interconnected.

Theories of change can be applied in the design, monitoring, and evaluation of programs, including the definition of relevant performance indicators for both new and existing intervention programs. A standard theory of change typically consists of the following components[31]:

- Inputs (physical, monetary, and human resources)
- Activities (actions and interventions that are necessary for fulfilling the objectives)
- Outputs (what is created by the program/policy for the targeted populations)
- Activity Outcomes (changes in relevant dimensions valued by targeted populations)
- Societal outcomes (impacts and long-term societal changes influenced by outcomes and other factors)

[30] Manolitzas and Yannacopoulos (2013) and Bortoluzzi et al. (2021) offer valid examples of multicriteria analysis in relevant public performance indicators.

[31] For further information on the components of the theory of change, the reader can refer to Insper Metricis (2022) and McLaughlin and Jordan (2015). More recently, strategy scholars have proposed a simplified version of the theory of change by introducing a causal chain that links resources, practices, and performance, extending beyond the realm of public management (Lazzarini & Zenger, 2023).

Figure 5.1 illustrates a theory of change for an education intervention. While the example below is purely illustrative, it can be used to demonstrate a program implemented by an education department to enhance the quality of education in secondary schools by addressing two key issues in education: improving learning outcomes and reducing dropout rates. Also, consider that by improving these two outcomes, public value is created as the cost–benefit relationship is altered. In fact, by boosting students' learning and reducing dropout rates, the students who benefit not only increase their chances of earning higher salaries in the future but are also more likely to be more productive, leading to productivity gains that benefit society. Additionally, reducing dropouts reduces the cost per student for the education department.[32] The program may also help to address three United Nations Sustainable Development Goals (SDGs): improving quality education (SDG #4), fostering decent work and economic growth (SDG #8), and reducing inequalities (SDG #10). The connections between inputs, activities, outputs, activity outcomes, and societal outcomes are established based on evidence from similar documented interventions. Previous studies play a crucial role in ensuring the relationship between these dimensions and the intended outcomes. Additionally, previous works that provide insights into the magnitude of effect sizes are valuable in constructing valid and practical theories of change. It is essential to understand cause-and-effect relationships in this context.

In the example above, we observe that resources are necessary to implement a series of pedagogical actions that will result in measurable and quantifiable outputs. While these outputs are straightforward to assess, their attainment alone does not guarantee the achievement of the ultimate goals. Given that activity outcomes closely align with the project

[32] This example draws inspiration from a project conducted by the Department of Education of the State of São Paulo, Brazil. The project aimed to launch the first social impact bond initiative in Brazil and was managed by Insper Metricis, a Brazilian research group, in collaboration with Social Finance, a leading consulting organization based in the United Kingdom specializing in impact investment projects. The initiative received support from multilateral organizations such as the Inter-American Development Bank (IDB) and the International Finance Corporation (IFC). It underwent public hearings in 2017 but was canceled by public authorities in 2018 due to pressure from teacher's unions. It is worth noting that the author of this book is one of the founding members of Insper Metricis and was actively involved in this project. For more information, see Lazzarini (2020).

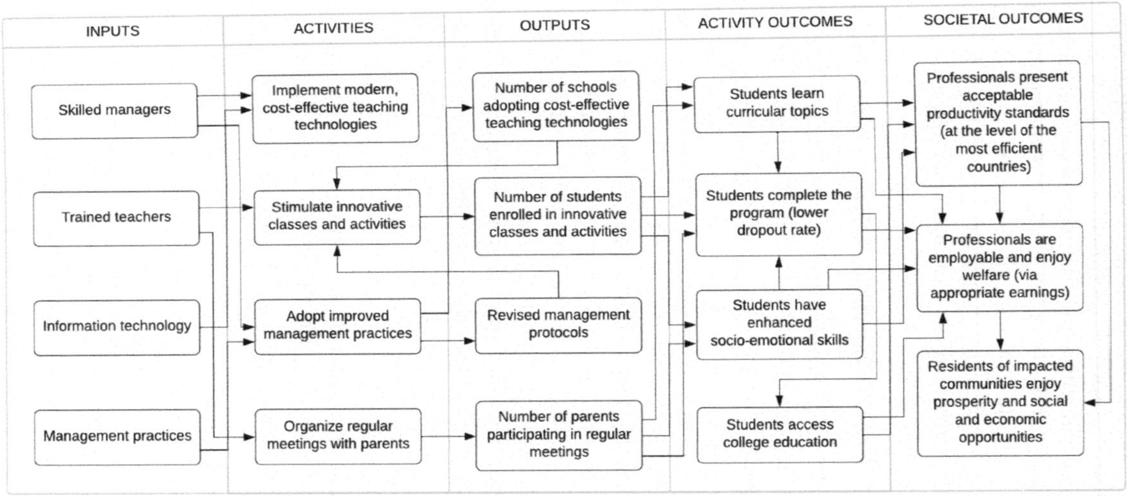

Fig. 5.1 Theory of change: an illustrative example in education[33]

[33] See Metricis (2022).

goals, it is advisable for performance management systems to prioritize the assessment of outcome measures, preferably with the support of counterfactual assessment methods. Experimental and quasi-experimental methods are indispensable in ensuring that the observed outcomes are a result of the intervention and not influenced by other random factors unrelated to the efforts of the evaluated groups and individuals. These methods are also crucial for determining what would have happened to the targeted groups if the intervention had never occurred.

Selecting Key Performance Indicators (KPIs)

Within a theory of change, various inputs, activities, outputs, and outcome measures may be identified. While some of these measures may require monitoring, others should take a more prominent role as key performance indicators (KPIs) and receive closer management attention. When it comes to performance-contingent rewards (or sanctions), it is crucial to select KPIs that genuinely reflect meaningful improvements in the conditions of the target groups affected by the intervention. But the question remains: how do we choose the most relevant measures?

The "Insper Metricis guide to the assessment of socio-environmental impact for use in impact-oriented projects and investments"[34] suggests a straightforward criterion for selecting effective measures, whether they are subjective or objective. Regardless of whether the choice is output or outcome measures, these selected metrics should possess four key attributes: relevance, actionability, precision, and low cost measurement.

First, the measure must be relevant and characterize (public) value creation while providing information on dimensions that benefit not only the targeted populations but also the public more generally. In the example above, the three measures meet the relevance criteria.

Second, the measure must be actionable, meaning it is affected by individuals and groups that are part of the intervention and are to be evaluated based on this measure. Following the informativeness principle mentioned earlier, the measure must reflect a clear relationship between actions and results and should avoid factors that evaluated individuals cannot control. Normally, output measures are more influenced by individuals' impact and societal outcomes. In our example,

[34] Insper Metricis (2022).

dropouts, learning, and socioemotional skills can be influenced by activities performed by individuals in charge of the program.

Third, the measures must be as precise as possible. In other words, they should not be subject to manipulation (gaming) and should have a low potential to present measurement errors. Along these lines, data recorded and collected by external actors who are not part of the project, as well as objective measures based on administrative data, tend to be more precise than measures originating from internal sources and/or based on perceptual measures. While dropouts are not easy to manipulate and easy to measure, learning and socioemotional outcomes must be assessed with appropriate methods and preferably by third parties to become reliable and valid KPIs.

Fourth, good measures should be assessed at low cost. If the costs of collecting data, performing analysis, and convincing relevant stakeholders about the assessment method are high, then a case can be made against the possible KPIs. Public organizations are a fruitful terrain for performance management systems when administrative data are available. However, data structures built specifically to assess the performance of the focal project increase the measurement costs and must be viewed with caution. In the example, while dropout rates are collected at a low cost, the other two measures require specific measurement plans.

Conclusion

This chapter discussed the importance of performance management systems for successful strategies in public and nonprofit organizations. Public, and nonprofit researchers and managers, as well as politicians seeking to instill a strategic management approach within the organizations they oversee, must carefully consider the fundamental principles of performance management systems outlined in this chapter.

This involves recognizing the distinctions between subjective and objective measures, along with their respective pros and cons, particularly the various incentive distortions that may arise. Furthermore, the development of a theory of change is essential for organizations aiming to clarify their ultimate objectives, establish causal links between inputs and activities, and predict outcomes and impacts. This not only forms the basis for defining reliable and meaningful Key Performance Indicators (KPIs) but also guides performance management strategies. In this context, KPIs based on criteria such as relevance, the relationship between actions and results, precision, and evaluation costs can assist public and nonprofit organizations in formulating and implementing strategies conducive to enhanced public value creation.

To ensure confidence in achieving public value creation, the measurement of performance should integrate the use of the most advanced and appropriate techniques available. Prioritizing the employment of counterfactual assessment methods whenever feasible, alongside protocols designed to refine the evaluation process, is pivotal—especially for subjective measures. These efforts play a crucial role in legitimizing performance management systems, ensuring transparency, and promoting the fair allocation of rewards and penalties to individuals, groups, and organizations that contribute, either directly or indirectly, to the betterment of society.

Last, but not least, it is imperative to recognize that effective management relies heavily on data. In an era where relevant stakeholders value evidence-based decision-making, meticulous attention must be given to formulating rules and procedures for data collection. Additionally, establishing robust data management structures is crucial, as they underpin performance management systems.

References

Ahn, T.-S., Choi, Y.-S., Hwang, I., & Hyeon, J. (2018). The effect of information asymmetry and participative target setting on target ratcheting and incentives. *Public Performance & Management Review, 41*(3), 439–468.

Andrews, R., Boyne, G. A., & Walker, R. M. (2006). Subjective and objective measures of organizational performance: An empirical exploration. In K. J. M. George A. Boyne, Laurence J. O'Toole Jr., & Richard M. Walker (Eds.), *Public service performance: Perspectives on measurement and management* (pp. 14–34). Cambridge University Press.

Arvidson, M., & Lyon, F. (2014). Social impact measurement and non-profit organisations: Compliance, resistance, and promotion. *VOLUNTAS: International Journal of Voluntary and Nonprofit Organizations, 25*, 869–886.

Bak, H.-J., & Kim, D. H. (2015). Too much emphasis on research? An empirical examination of the relationship between research and teaching in multitasking environments. *Research in Higher Education, 56*, 843–860.

Bortoluzzi, M., de Souza, C. C., & Furlan, M. (2021). Bibliometric analysis of renewable energy types using key performance indicators and multicriteria decision models. *Renewable and Sustainable Energy Reviews, 143*, 110958.

Brickley, J. A., Smith, C. W., & Zimmerman, J. L. (2001). *Managerial economics and organizational architecture* (2nd ed.). McGraw-Hill.

Cabral, S., & Lazzarini, S. G. (2015). The "guarding the guardians" problem: An analysis of the organizational performance of an internal affairs division. *Journal of Public Administration Research and Theory, 25*(3), 797–829.

Calabrese, T. (2013). Running on empty: The operating reserves of US nonprofit organizations. *Nonprofit Management and Leadership, 23*(3), 281–302.

De Janvry, A., He, G., Sadoulet, E., Wang, S., & Zhang, Q. (2023). Subjective performance evaluation, influence activities, and bureaucratic work behavior: Evidence from China. *American Economic Review, 113*(3), 766–799.

Festinger, L. (1954). A theory of social comparison processes. *Human Relations, 7*(2), 117–140.

Freixas, X., Guesnerie, R., & Tirole, J. (1985). Planning under incomplete information and the ratchet effect. *The Review of Economic Studies, 52*(2), 173–191.

Hartog, J., Ferrer-i-Carbonell, A., & Jonker, N. (2002). Linking measured risk aversion to individual characteristics. *Kyklos, 55*(1), 3–26.

Healy, P. M., & Palepu, K. G. (2003). The fall of Enron. *Journal of Economic Perspectives, 17*(2), 3–26.

Holmström, B. (2017). Pay for performance and beyond. *American Economic Review, 107*(7), 1753–1777.

Holmstrom, B., & Milgrom, P. (1991). Multitask principal–agent analyses: Incentive contracts, asset ownership, and job design. *The Journal of Law, Economics, and Organization, 7*(special_issue), 24–52.

Homonoff, T., Spreen, T. L., & Clair, T. S. (2020). Balance sheet insolvency and contribution revenue in public charities. *Journal of Public Economics, 186*, 104177.

Jacob, B. A., & Levitt, S. D. (2003). Rotten apples: An investigation of the prevalence and predictors of teacher cheating. *The Quarterly Journal of Economics, 118*(3), 843–877.

Lazzarini, S. G. (2020). Social impact bonds in São Paulo's state public school system: New modality of public-private partnership in Brazil: Commentary. *Education Policy Analysis Archives, 28*, 112. https://doi.org/10.14507/epaa.28.5148

Lazzarini, S. G., & Zenger, T. (2023). Strategy as (a causal) theory of change. *Academy of Management Proceedings, 2023*(1), 11924. https://doi.org/10.5465/AMPROC.2023.11924abstract

Litwack, J. M. (1993). Coordination, incentives, and the ratchet effect. *The RAND Journal of Economics, 24*, 271–285.

Manolitzas, P., & Yannacopoulos, D. (2013). Citizen satisfaction: A multicriteria satisfaction analysis. *International Journal of Public Administration, 36*(9), 614–621.

McLaughlin, J. A., & Jordan, G. B. (2015). Using logic models. In H. P. H. Kathryn, E. Newcomer, & J. S. Wholey (Eds.), *Handbook of practical program evaluation* (4th ed., pp. 62–87). Wiley.

Metricis, I. (2022). *Guide to the assessment of socio-environmental impact for use in impact-oriented projects and investments: general guide focused on and verification of additionality.*

Nickerson, J. A., & Zenger, T. R. (2008). Envy, comparison costs, and the economic theory of the firm. *Strategic Management Journal, 29*(13), 1429–1449.

Power, M. (2021). Modelling the micro-foundations of the audit society: Organizations and the logic of the audit trail. *Academy of Management Review, 46*(1), 6–32.

Prendergast, C., & Topel, R. H. (1996). Favoritism in organizations. *Journal of Political Economy, 104*(5), 958–978.

Rajala, T., Laihonen, H., & Vakkuri, J. (2018). Shifting from output to outcome measurement in public administration-arguments revisited. In E.A.-P.E. Borgonovi & C. Bianchi (Eds.), *Outcome-based performance management in the public sector* (pp. 3–23). Springer.

Roberts, J. (2010). Designing incentives in organizations. *Journal of Institutional Economics, 6*(1), 125–132.

Stühlinger, S., & Hersberger-Langloh, S. E. (2021). Multitasking NPOs: An analysis of the relationship between funding intentions and nonprofit capacities. *VOLUNTAS: International Journal of Voluntary and Nonprofit Organizations, 32*(5), 1042–1053.

Suykens, B., Meyfroodt, K., Desmidt, S., & Verschuere, B. (2022). Does performance-based accountability impact how non-profit directors perceive organizational performance? Insights from rational planning. *Public Management Review, 24*(9), 1355–1382.

Tavares, G. M., Marcolino, A. C., & Cabral, S. (2024). Câmeras nos Uniformes Reduzem Mortes Decorrentes de Intervenção Policial? Avaliando Potenciais Mecanismos Explicativos. *Administração Pública e Gestão Social*. https://doi.org/10.21118/apgs.v16i1.15774

Zenger, T. R. (1994). Explaining organizational diseconomies of scale in R&D: Agency problems and the allocation of engineering talent, ideas, and effort by firm size. *Management Science, 40*(6), 708–729.

CHAPTER 6

Centralization Versus Decentralization in Public and Nonprofit Organizations

A portion of this book was written during a sabbatical leave at the Robert Wagner Graduate School of Public Service at New York University from August 2023 to January 2024. Accompanying me on this journey was my 14-year-old daughter, which worked out quite well. While I was focused on writing this book, she had the unique opportunity to attend a New York City high school as a 9th grader. Since we were not residents of New York City during her 8th grade, she was unable to take the necessary exams to apply for a NYC high school. However, finding an available seat for her was not an issue, thanks to the Family Welcome Center (FWC), a facility designed to assist NYC families whose children are without a school, precisely our situation. The FWC has access to information on all schools with available seats, and due to this centralization, guardians do not need to visit multiple schools in search of a spot. Instead, the FWC can identify an available seat and enroll the child, provided the guardian accepts the offer. Thanks to the centralized and well-coordinated enrollment system of the NYC Public Schools, we were able to enroll my daughter on the very same day we arrived in town.

The benefits of centralized enrolment in the NYC high schools were described by Atila Abdulkadiroğlu, Nikhil Agarwal, and Parahg Pathak.[1] They found that under the centralized and coordinated enrollment system

[1] Abdulkadiroğlu et al. (2017).

S. Cabral, *Strategy for Public and Nonprofit Organizations*,
https://doi.org/10.1007/978-3-031-64969-1_6

implemented after 2003, NYC students, on average, received more preferred assignments. The gains were more pronounced for students who were more likely to be poorly assisted by the previously more decentralized system. They also demonstrated that students who were more likely to benefit from the old system exhibited increased test scores and graduation rates. In a similar vein, Ursula Melo[2] has demonstrated that centralized applications in Brazilian public universities increased enrollments of disenfranchised students, especially non-white and low-income individuals. The transparency induced by the centralized system reduced barriers to entry in public universities, fostered a more competitive process, and enabled affirmative action programs.

Although these cases illustrate that enhanced centralization improves coordination, decreases misallocation, and enables public value creation by improving the overall conditions of large populations, there is also evidence that more decentralized structures can be beneficial.

Take the example of government responses to the COVID-19 crisis. Even though successful strategies were associated with centralization in communication and decision-making at the national level, as well as a coordinating role in vaccination campaigns, as seen in the cases of Australia, Taiwan, and New Zealand, decentralization at the regional or municipal level also proved successful.[3] After failures in central coordination in Brazil, the Supreme Court allowed states and municipalities to decide on social distancing policies, mask mandates, school operations, and business closures. This autonomy to implement strict non-pharmaceutical interventions helped some regions achieve reduced rates of infection and lethality per 100,000 inhabitants.[4] These measures served to counteract the effects of denialism at the central government level, particularly in states and municipalities where the incumbent president between 2019 and 2022, Mr. Jair Bolsonaro, did not secure more than 50% of the valid votes in the 2018 presidential election.[5] In Italy, the decentralization allowed the Emilia-Romagna and Veneto regions to exploit the existing financial, material, and human capital resources and implement contention measures, purchasing the necessary goods

[2] Mello (2022).

[3] Moloney and Moloney (2020).

[4] Touchton et al. (2021).

[5] Cabral et al. (2021).

and services, engaging relevant stakeholders, thus providing effective responses to the pandemic.[6]

The importance of allocation of decision rights, i.e., the authority and responsibility to decide and make choices, establish who has the right to decide, and the limits of decision-making,[7] for organizational success is evident. In fact, decisions regarding the concentration of decision-making rights at higher hierarchical levels or the delegation of decision-making rights to lower levels, including frontline workers, are inherently strategic.

A decision is considered strategic if it is interdependent with other decisions and has the potential to influence subsequent choices. A strategic decision not only pertains to other internal choices and decisions in the present, but it can also shape future decisions and those made by other actors. These characteristics distinguish strategic decisions from important decisions, which do not necessarily meet the same criteria.[8] Indeed, the allocation of decision rights is a strategic decision in public and nonprofit organizations, as it significantly influences public service performance, as documented by previous works in the field.[9]

The allocation of decision-making authority also has implications for both current and future resource allocation needed to execute a strategy. For instance, a more decentralized structure may necessitate the implementation of performance management systems to align organizational incentives. Additionally, the way organizations allocate decision rights can elicit varied responses from a wide range of stakeholders, including competitors, clients, suppliers, sponsors, donors, and citizens. Consider how regulated firms would formulate their strategies to navigate highly centralized bureaucratic procedures.

[6] Capano and Lippi (2021).

[7] Brickley et al. (2001).

[8] In this work Leiblein et al. (2018) distinguish what sets a strategic decision apart from other decisions. They highlight three unique characteristics: interdependence across contemporaneous decisions, across the decisions of other economic actors, and across time.

[9] Andrews et al. (2009) conducted a study testing the effects of centralization on public service organizations in the United Kingdom. They found that the relationship between the structure of decision rights (centralized or decentralized) and organizational performance is contingent on the type of organizational strategy adopted by each entity. Similarly, Altamimi et al. (2022) found that the outcomes of centralized or decentralized decision-making depend on environmental and strategic contingencies.

The Canadian Cannabis Act, enacted in 2018,[10] regulates the production, use, and commercialization of cannabis (marijuana) for recreational, medical, and scientifical purposes. It serves as an interesting example of how the degree of concentration of decision rights can be a strategic choice. In Canada, the personal use of cannabis is allowed in accordance with the guidelines set by provinces and territories. The central government determined how decision rights were distributed among various levels of government. In this case, the central government advocated for a form of political decentralization, where authority is exercised by territorial units with significant decision-making powers.[11]

By specifying how cannabis can be sold, where stores are located and operated, who is authorized to commercialize cannabis, and establishing possession limits, minimum consumption age, and designated consumption spaces, local government decisions affect the decisions of myriad of stakeholders. This extends to decisions made by regional offices overseeing regulation, budget, and personnel determinations by departments responsible for health, education, public security, and social care. Moreover, the operationalization of these regulations also influences the strategies of incumbents and potential entrants in the cannabis supply chain, including suppliers, retailers, and users.

Naturally, the structure chosen to allocate decision rights has implications for the performance of both public and private organizations. For instance, the centralized regulation of cannabis activities can influence a range of factors including hospitalization rates, criminal records, economic growth, public spending on rehabilitation programs, increased tax collection, as well as firm performance. In other words, by shaping social and economic outcomes, the dynamic chosen by the Canadian government to allocate decision rights for regulating the cannabis industry directly affects public value creation. Along these lines, early evidence suggests the Canadian Cannabis Act is associated with a substantial reduction (between 55 and 65%) in cannabis-related crimes among adolescents.[12] Yet, further studies with comprehensive cost–benefit analysis are still needed to know whether the allocation of decision rights to subnational governments effectively created (or destroyed) public value.

[10] See https://www.canada.ca/en/services/health/campaigns/cannabis.html.

[11] Porter and Olsen (1976).

[12] Callaghan et al. (2021).

For all these reasons, the decision of the Canadian central government is strategic.

Centralization Versus Decentralization of Decision Rights: Pros and Cons

The issue of centralization and decentralization in government is not a new one. For centuries, governments have entrusted external actors with critical tasks such as tax collection, education, and healthcare provision. In recent decades, public service reforms, inspired by the principles of New Public Management, have once again brought decentralization decisions to the forefront. The aim was to empower private and nonprofit organizations in the delivery of public services, as well as lower-level managers, with the belief that this would enhance flexibility and enable governments not only to enhance performance, but also to address citizens' needs more effectively. In this context, governments have advocated for decentralized structures to enhance decision-making and strengthen their customer orientation.[13]

Grosso modo, decentralization has gained legitimacy as a countermeasure to the concentrated decision-making of a few individuals with limited insight into the genuine needs of citizens. The dispersal of decision-making authority to a broader range of actors is a concept that holds significant appeal, and it is challenging to argue against decentralization in democratic societies. This concept has been widely debated and put into practice in various countries under two major forms: political decentralization and administrative decentralization. Political decentralization occurs when central governments delegate authority to regional or provincial units, or when regional governments delegate to local authorities. Administrative decentralization occurs when a politically independent unit delegates authorities to subordinates within public organizations or to private and nonprofit organizations legally separate from the state. Both forms have been extensively discussed and implemented in several countries.[14]

[13] Andrews et al. (2009).

[14] See Porter and Olsen (1976) and Pollitt (2007) for detailed accounts of centralization and decentralization in governments.

However, despite the apparent consensus in favor of decentralized forms, centralized decision-making is still present in several organizations and coexists with structures in which frontline workers and low-end managers accumulate decision rights and are key players in the participative decision-making process. The quest for centralizing or decentralizing decision rights in organizations requires an analysis of the relative benefits and costs of each form. As these forms are polar and are two sides of the same coin, sometimes benefits and costs are symmetrical. In other words, the benefits of decentralization mirror the costs of centralization, and vice versa.

Benefits of Decentralization

Supporters of decentralization decisions argue that the delegation of authority to other political and administrative actors creates several benefits to organizations. In general, political and administrative decentralization compared with centralized forms are associated with the advantages below.

Adaptation to Local Conditions

The delegation of decision-making authority to political powers, organizations, managers, and frontline employees who are closer to citizens enables the development of solutions that better align with the needs of local populations. Close engagement with local contexts facilitates the design of policies and the provision of goods and services that are more aligned with citizens' preferences. Similarly, proximity to local contexts allows for the identification of needs that are often difficult to anticipate from a distance. In fact, local managers and frontline workers are more likely to gather relevant information on local needs and make decisions regarding the portfolio of services offered. In some cases, local managers can be better equipped to make pricing decisions because they know more about the local context. These decisions are often more effective and difficult to make by upper echelons who may be unaware of the specific local conditions. Enhanced local knowledge allows agents to make more informed decisions and increases responsiveness. Moreover, a more effective utilization of local knowledge can facilitate the transfer of pertinent information to superiors, thus supporting subsequent decisions that require coordination across different territories.

Consider the case of training centers sponsored by central governments to assist disenfranchised populations in enhancing their employability and future economic prospects. Compared with centralized structures, decentralized training centers can tailor programs to better align with the specific characteristics of local populations. For instance, offering a program that instructs unemployed individuals on how to program in modern computational languages like Python[15] in regions where most citizens are not computer-savvy may not yield the desired results. Providing instruction on text processors and spreadsheet programs could potentially be more beneficial. Decentralized management plays a crucial role in pinpointing the need for more fundamental training programs that are better aligned with the local context. In the same vein, local managers, armed with an in-depth understanding of the local conditions, are better equipped to identify citizens who would benefit from more advanced programs.

Agility in the Decision-Making

Strategy literature has long recognized the positive association between agility in decision-making and superior performance. While centralized structures can enable faster decisions, especially when appropriate information systems allow for bottom-up information flows that support concentrated authority in decision-making, the decentralization of operational decisions, including hiring, promotion, and control of the production process, improves the extent of information available to frontline workers and speeds up the decision-making process.[16] Decentralization is conducive to improved agility in decision-making, especially in uncertain environments.[17]

More informed and empowered managers can make faster and more accurate decisions without waiting for authorization from upper echelons, which is often time-consuming. This, in turn, improves responsiveness to citizens. Evidence from a public health organization responsible for providing healthcare to over 2 million citizens (about the population of

[15] This chapter was written in 2023. At that time, Python was one of the most advanced computational languages. The author is aware that a reader in 2035 will probably find bizarre classifying Python as an innovative tool.

[16] Baum and Wally (2003).

[17] Capano and Toth (2023).

Nebraska) in Sweden suggests that decentralization during the COVID-19 pandemic was associated with improved agility. In the face of such an unprecedented emergency, the decentralized structure, with decision-making delegated to frontline health workers, demonstrated the necessary flexibility to quickly adapt operational structures to cope with new challenges. Swedish workers exercised their delegated decision-making authority to address issues that could not be handled by higher levels in a timely manner. This decentralized decision-making structure allowed frontline workers to identify, use, and manage the necessary resources to respond to the emergency in an agile manner.[18] Similarly, nonprofit organizations working in a decentralized but coordinated fashion with public organizations delivered rapid responses after the September 11 event in New York. They played a crucial role in preventing the escalation of the disaster, reinforcing the importance of decentralized structures in situations of uncertainty.[19]

More Efficient Use of Top-Management Time

By delegating authority to subordinates or other organizations, decision-makers in upper echelons can free up their time to take other decisions that cannot be transferred. In the training center's example, rather than allocating time to discuss and decide on the courses offered in each unit, top-management teams can focus their efforts on conceiving new strategies and working on more important and critical decisions. Decentralization can assist managers to avoid the expenditure of their most scarce resource—their time—on analyzing different courses of action and assessing the associated advantages and disadvantages to solve problems that subordinates or contractors can address more quickly and more efficiently. From a public policy perspective centralization can overwhelm decision-makers at higher hierarchical levels with abundant information, creating distraction and diverting their attention from other priorities. In other words, decentralization decisions can allow top-management teams to use their time more efficiently.[20]

Better management of public managers' time through improved allocation of decision rights can enable public value creation. Some years ago,

[18] Ohrling et al. (2022).

[19] Kapucu (2006).

[20] See Jones and Baumgartner (2005) and Wong et al. (2011).

while conducting field research with prison managers, I had the opportunity to interact with a professional who had experience as a warden in both public and privately operated prisons in Brazil. When asked to explain the main difference between the two modes, he pointed to the conservation of management time. The following quote, obtained in a personal communication, illustrates his reasoning:

> When I oversaw Prison X, a publicly operated prison, a major issue was the maintenance of the facility. One day, I became frustrated because the prison department's maintenance service was unable to replace the fluorescent lamps. I had been asking them to address this issue for weeks, but with no response. I got my car, drove to a hardware store, and purchased the required lamps with my personal funds. Upon returning to the prison, I enlisted the help of some inmates to replace the lamps. By the end of day, before returning home, I reflected on my actions: 'What did I accomplish today? Instead of managing the prison and devising strategies to improve its conditions, I found myself replacing light bulbs.' This experience was markedly different from at Prison Y, a privately operated facility where I served as warden appointed by the state prison department. At Prison Y, all I had to do was request the private operator to handle such tasks. They have a contract for that! Without these concerns, I was free to set my sights on more strategic aspects of prison management, and the results were evident in the performance.[21]

Overall, allocating decision rights to subordinates can be an effective way for high-ranking managers to have more time to devote to strategic decisions. Given that the opportunity costs for top-management teams tend to be high, managing them effectively can be crucial for (public) value creation.

Improving Behavioral Traits

The act of decentralizing decision-making authority can also serve as a catalyst for improving organizational behavior. Delegating authority to subordinates can empower and motivate individuals and teams to make decisions on behalf of their organizations, especially when decentralization is coupled with changes in incentive structures and performance management systems. Empowered employees may experience an

[21] For more information on authority delegation in prison systems, see Cabral et al. (2010).

enhanced sense of belonging and ownership, feeling that they play a significant role in achieving organizational goals. Encouraging individuals to make decisions can also serve as a means of preparing them for future leadership roles and facilitating the succession planning process for their superiors.[22]

Findings from a study conducted by Alan Zarychta, Tara Grillos, and Krister Andersson with Honduran health workers strongly support the relationship between decentralization and improved motivation. When comparing bureaucrats in decentralized municipalities with those in centrally administered municipalities, they found that motivation is higher in decentralized settings. The results are primarily driven by decentralized systems managed by non-governmental organizations, which are more likely to attract and select highly motivated bureaucrats compared to those decentralized led by municipal governments or associations of municipalities. Nonprofit organizations, apparently, are better equipped to harness the advantages of increased authority.[23]

Assigning additional responsibilities to frontline employees and citizens can motivate them to exert even greater efforts and stimulate organizational innovation. In highly decentralized arrangements, employee ideas stemming from local observations do not necessarily require authorization from superiors. This can catalyze the search for solutions and the generation of ideas that are more suitable for local contexts. Evidence from decentralization reforms in India has indicated that efforts to increase citizen involvement in budgeting and planning have spurred institutional innovations, leading to enhanced citizen participation and innovative responses to the COVID-19 pandemic.[24] Decentralized structures that facilitate information sharing can also foster innovation in nonprofit organizations.[25]

[22] Brickley et al. (2001) and Pollitt (2007) provide compelling arguments regarding the relationship between decentralization and motivational aspects.

[23] Zarychta et al. (2020).

[24] See Heller et al. (2007) and Benny et al. (2023).

[25] Shin and Choi (2019).

Problems of Decentralization

While the decentralization of decision-making can lead to significant contributions in improving performance and creating public value by addressing some of the dysfunctions associated with centralized structures, such as rigidity and a lack of adaptation to local contexts, certain issues may arise when delegating authority to subordinates or other organizations. Decentralized structures that involve participatory forums may, at times, necessitate lengthy discussions that can slow down the decision-making process. Additionally, dispersed structures can hinder the development of a clear and aligned organizational vision.

Below, I outline some challenges that can undermine the effectiveness of decentralization and, at the same time, provide reasons to consider centralized decision-making.

Coordination Issues

Individuals, teams, and organizations with decision-making authority may take actions without considering the existing interdependence with other units. They might overlook the consequences of their decisions on other units and at the aggregated level. Coordination challenges arising from highly decentralized activities can produce adverse spillover effects beyond the focal unit and potentially lessen the effectiveness of the entire organization.

Imagine a hypothetical, empowered dean of a business school within a public university system. This dean possesses significant autonomy to make decisions on various aspects, including setting tuition fees, determining which courses students under their authority can or cannot take, and establishing faculty salaries. Due to insufficient allocations from the university to cover current expenses, the dean has both the incentive and the authority to maximize the school's earnings. In pursuit of this goal, the dean can take actions to differentiate the school's programs and charge tuition fees that exceed those of main competitors. The dean can also foster executive education programs and weekend executive MBAs to expand revenue sources. Since tuition revenue is distributed among the school's units based on the number of students enrolled in their respective courses, the dean is motivated to encourage students to enroll in courses offered by the business school as much as possible. Further, the dean may discourage students from enrolling in courses from other units, either by imposing extensive bureaucratic procedures to grant students the right to take classes in other schools within the university or by offering similar courses within the business school itself.

While these actions enhance the school's revenues, it is easy to anticipate adverse effects. By charging tuition fees higher than those of other units, the dean can widen the gap with other schools. If other deans follow suit, the average tuition of the university's average tuition rates will rise, potentially discouraging applications from economically disenfranchised students. The imposition of barriers to students enrolling in courses offered by other units can spark the retaliation of other deans, erecting additional obstacles to cross-disciplinary collaborations among different schools. Offering an excessive number of courses can hinder the efficient allocation of university resources, as similar courses may be duplicated across different units. With fewer students enrolled in each course, inefficient resource allocation can lead to higher costs and impede the university's ability to benefit from economies of scale.

Evidence regarding the relationship between decentralization and coordination issues is extensive. C. Simon Fan, Chen Lin, and Daniel Tresman analyzed how political decentralization influenced perceptions of corruption. Using data from a firm-level survey conducted in 80 countries, they found that decentralization, as proxied by the presence of many government tiers, led to an increase in the number of reported bribery cases. This finding underscores the challenges associated with uncoordinated rent-seeking. Furthermore, the presence of additional decentralized layers may create more opportunities for corruption, as it increases the number of "pockets to fill" and raises the likelihood of nurturing corrupt practices.[26] In their analysis of the impact of fiscal decentralization on Brazilian municipalities' efforts to combat the COVID-19 pandemic, Ricardo Cardoso and his coauthors highlight that unconditional transfers—allocations of financial resources that did not consider the actual vulnerability of municipalities—created incentives for municipalities to reduce health investments. This reduction in health investments did not yield any noticeable effects on death rates.[27] In the same vein, robust evidence also suggests the decentralization of environmental authority

[26] Fan et al. (2009).

[27] Cardoso et al. (2023).

is linked to increased pollution levels. This association arises from the heightened costs of coordinating actions across multiple jurisdictions.[28]

Economies of Scale and Uniformization

While decentralization, with its focus on addressing local demands, can enhance adaptability and responsiveness, an excessive emphasis on local contexts can lead empowered managers to overlook the broader implications of their decisions. Typically, in decentralized settings, local managers lack incentives to consider the interdependence with other units in their decision-making process. Furthermore, local managers often lack the necessary and relevant information to make decisions that optimize the entire organization, extending beyond their focal unit. Often, they do not have visibility into the conditions under which decisions are made by their peers in similar units. Consequently, achieving improved efficiency through economies of scale becomes challenging under these circumstances.

Consider the case of hospitals under the authority of elected politicians that opt to decentralize the management of these healthcare facilities to local managers. In this scenario, Chief Executive Officers (CEOs) and the local top-management teams of each hospital are granted autonomy to make all relevant decisions necessary for running the hospital, including matters related to procurement. Italian scholars Simona Baldi and Davide Vannoni conducted an analysis to compare centralized and decentralized structures in terms of pharmaceutical drug prices. Their research revealed that decentralized procurement officers tended to pay higher prices compared to their centralized counterparts, who could leverage bulk purchasing to negotiate discounts from suppliers. The lack of coordination in decentralized procurement also hindered hospitals from benefiting from increased volumes of standardized products. In fact, the standardization of acquired products allows suppliers to reduce production costs and offer discounts to their customers. Additionally, they have also demonstrated that decentralized structures are even less desirable in regions characterized by higher corruption standards.[29]

[28] Sigman (2005) and Lipscomb and Mobarak (2016) have both identified that decentralization in pollution control can result in negative externalities. One of the primary reasons cited for this phenomenon is the lack of coordination among different agencies.

[29] Baldi and Vannoni (2017).

Central management also plays a pivotal role in ensuring coordination and facilitating effective information flows among decentralized decision-makers, contributing to superior performance at the local level.[30] For example, the development of extensive datasets containing detailed information about the procurement processes of all decentralized units can help local procurement officers become aware of the prices paid by other units, along with information on payment conditions and suppliers' characteristics. These innovations enable public organizations to enhance communication channels, manage information flows, and achieve superior results within decentralized structures.

Incentives Issues

Beyond the coordination processes facilitated by communication, delegating authority to individuals and teams can potentially lead to adverse consequences driven by incentive issues. As discussed in earlier chapters, it is presumed that task delegation occurs among self-interested individuals who make decisions based on their personal preferences. The issue at hand is that what may be advantageous for individuals is not necessarily in the best interest of the organization, thereby giving rise to a range of challenges.

In practice, managers operating in decentralized settings may choose to disregard the impact of their actions on other units, particularly if they are solely held accountable for the outcomes within their own units. Assessing the ramifications of one unit manager's decisions on other units is often complex, and since these inter-unit relationships are not always clear, rewards and sanctions tend to be confined to the decentralized units themselves. For example, prison managers overseeing individual correctional units may be eventually more inclined to prioritize law and order goals to prevent events like escapes, assaults, and lethal violence, as these can be more directly attributed to their leadership. If this is the case, consequently, they may overlook the potential adverse effects of a leadership style that emphasizes discipline and stricter rules on an inmate's prospects for successful reintegration into society. Wardens might even discourage rehabilitation programs to minimize inmate interactions that could lead to disruptions in internal order. Given that the broader consequences of recidivism across the entire prison system are challenging to

[30] Brickley et al. (2001).

attribute to individual managers, the delegation of authority without some degree of coordination tends to be a suboptimal solution due to inherent incentive issues.

Like managers operating in centralized structures, personnel working within decentralized settings may also engage in shirking and exhibit abusive behavior toward employees, suppliers, customers, and the public. This issue can become even more problematic when accountability standards are ineffective, and systems for rewarding appropriate behavior or penalizing misconduct are either absent or challenging to implement. Activities such as misreporting, gaming, deviating from established codes of conduct, and engaging in various hidden actions become more challenging to detect within decentralized structures where control systems are not effective. This further underscores the need for a balanced approach between centralization and decentralization to address incentive-related issues.

Balancing Centralization and Decentralization

Naturally, the advantages and disadvantages discussed above represent the outcomes of extreme scenarios of (de)centralization. It is apparent that both complete decentralization without any form of coordination and absolute centralization without delegating authority to frontline workers or contractors who are closer to citizens can hinder improved performance and the creation of enhanced public value. The existing trade-offs between centralized and decentralized structures emphasize the need to determine an optimal degree of decision rights allocation.

Precisely quantifying the ideal level of decision rights allocation is a complex task, as it depends on unique characteristics of both internal organizational dynamics and external environments. Nevertheless, there is a need for efforts to provide a simplified framework illustrating the costs and benefits of (de)centralization. Such a framework can aid in identifying whether a specific decision is more suited to centralized or decentralized decision-making processes.

Brickley and colleagues have developed a simple model for illustrating price decisions in private firms, which can be readily adapted to the public and nonprofit contexts.[31] The idea is quite simple, calculating an optimal

[31] Brickley et al. (2001).

level of decentralization (or centralization) of the decision-making based on the correspondent benefits and costs associated with the decision.

Suppose that the level of decentralization in a decision is denoted as Δ, where $\Delta = 1$ represents maximum decentralization, $\Delta = 0$ represents maximum centralization, and $0 < \Delta < 1$ represents varying levels of decentralization. In this context, low levels of Δ indicate that decision authority is concentrated at the upper echelons, while higher levels of Δ indicate that decision-making is delegated to local managers or other organizations.

The benefits of decentralization are given by $B = b\Delta$, where $b > 0$. These benefits encompass various advantages associated to the decentralization of decision-making, including adaptation to local conditions, increased agility in the decision-making processes, more efficient utilization of top-management time, and opportunities for improving behavioral traits among subordinates in terms of empowerment and motivation aspects.

The costs of decentralization are represented as $C = (a\Delta + c\Delta^2)$, with $a > 0$, $c > 0$. The first term, $a\Delta$, refers to costs associated with addressing incentives issues, while the second term, $c\Delta^2$, corresponds to costs associated with coordination issues and information issues that hamper the organization benefitting from economies of scale. It is noteworthy that coordination costs increase at a faster rate than incentive costs. This is because these coordination costs extend beyond the focal decentralized unit where the decision was made and affect other organizational units. For instance, if police officers in a specific territory opt to promote violent actions against citizens, the negative externalities and reputational costs tend to impact all other units, irrespective of their actions. Similarly, the costs arising from missed opportunities due to the mismanagement of information flow and economies of scale affect the entire organization.[32]

The process of choosing Δ is based on the maximization of net benefits, which is determined by the difference between the benefits and costs associated with the decentralization decision: Net benefits $= b\Delta - a\Delta - c\Delta^2$

[32] According to Brickley et al. (2001), the quadratic representation of coordination and information costs serves as a convenient way to capture these negative spillover effects. Changing it to other polynomial functions or assuming nonlinearity in other benefits and costs does not alter the fundamental implications of the mode.

To find the values at which the difference between benefits and costs is maximized, it is necessary to optimize the function above.

Taking its first derivative with respect to Δ yields: $b - a - 2c\,\Delta^* = 0$. Hence:

$$\Delta * = (b - a)/2c$$

It is important to note that, as per the condition mentioned above, an increase in the benefits of decentralization leads to higher values of Δ^* and, consequently, higher costs associated with addressing incentive and coordination issues. For instance, in the context of research and development activities, substantial benefits (parameter "b") of decentralization may come from granting researchers greater autonomy to devise customized solutions for local challenges.

Likewise, organizations dealing with substantial coordination challenges, particularly those heavily influenced by the parameter "c", tend to operate in a more centralized manner, resulting in lower values of Δ^*. This is evident in the case of air traffic control, which is typically centralized in control centers equipped with information from local airports and traffic in established airways recommended for pilots. Through the coordination of departures and arrivals and the management of airways, centralized structures can effectively prevent collisions, enhance the operational efficiency of airports, and optimize the entire air network under their authority. Consequently, delegating decision rights over air traffic management to local airports would have potentially catastrophic consequences.

In the real world, organizations strive to strike a balance between centralization and decentralization by integrating a certain level of central coordination to ensure the availability of essential information, guidelines, and resources while also affording local units a degree of autonomy in decision-making. The allocation of decision rights to local managers can vary based on the internal and external contingencies that organizations encounter. Organizations under pressure from citizens to provide customized solutions tailored to specific target populations are more inclined to engage with frontline workers who possess a deeper understanding of the prevailing demands during the decision-making process. However, it is plausible for the same organization to simultaneously centralize other decisions, such as ethical guidelines and accountability standards.

Central coordination can facilitate the establishment of shared resource centers that could benefit all units and help prevent redundant efforts. This combination of centralization and decentralization is reflected in organizational structures that group various functions and activities, as discussed next.

Organizational Structures

The examination of the advantages and disadvantages of decentralized structures, coupled with an understanding of the significance of a well-balanced allocation of decision rights, underscores the continued importance of top management even within decentralized settings. Managers at higher echelons continue to play crucial roles in ensuring the smooth flow of information, coordinating decisions made by multiple decentralized decision-makers, and serving as stewards of the organization's mission, vision, core values, and major strategic objectives.

In this context, it is essential to recognize that decentralization does not equate to a relaxation of controls over subordinates. The right to decide often differs from the right to control the decisions made. Eugene Fama and Michael Jensen posit that the decision-making process comprises four distinct steps[33]:

- Initiation: This step involves the generation of proposals for the allocation of organizational resources.
- Ratification: It is related to the selection of decisions to be effectively pursued.
- Implementation: This step encompasses the execution of the ratified decisions.
- Monitoring: It involves the evaluation of the outcomes resulting from the decisions taken.

While the initiation and implementation steps fall under decision management, as they involve the same agents (agents in a principal-agent perspective), the ratification and monitoring phases fall under decision control (principals).

[33] Fama and Jensen (1983).

In essence, there exists a separation of roles between those responsible for making decisions and managing them, and those tasked with controlling and overseeing the decisions. Modern public and private organizations recognize this division by establishing mechanisms to ensure accountability and compliance with standards.

However, a significant organizational design distinction sets public organizations apart from their private and nonprofit counterparts. In the former, individuals responsible for controlling and monitoring are typically appointed by external actors, such as a board of directors representing the interests of shareholders or donors. In contrast, in public organizations, those entrusted with monitoring the behavior of other agents responsible for implementing policies are often appointed by their own peers. This uniqueness gives rise to an organizational design challenge, often referred to as the "*guarding the guardians problem*". In this scenario, "agent-monitors" may not have the strongest incentives to oversee "agent-executers" either because they are concerned about the potential consequences if they were to switch roles in the future or due to existing pressures from within the organization, such as corporatism.[34] Design problems can indeed be mitigated, and at the very least, better understood, through the development of appropriate organizational structures.

Organizational structures (or forms) provide a sense of how responsibilities and authority are granted, and how tasks are grouped and shared among individuals and teams. The way people work together within an organization, and at its boundaries, has a direct influence on information flow and communication channels to internal and external stakeholders. Organization forms also affect how activities are coordinated in a myriad of settings, ranging from mass production and large-scale production to customized contexts. Not surprisingly, organizational design issues have been at the core of economics and management scholarship for centuries since Adam Smith and his classic work, "The Wealth of Nations", and the use of interchangeable parts conceived by the French gunsmith Honoré Blanc, who is known for being one of the pioneers in the development of mass production systems.

[34] For discussions about the "guarding the guardians problem", refer to Hurwicz (2008) and Cabral and Lazzarini (2015).

Considering the implications of organizational design on performance and on how public and nonprofit organizations create public value, further examination of the most used organizational forms is crucial.

The Unitary Form (U-Form)

The *unitary form* (U-form) organization is one of the most employed structures for organizing economic and social activities, particularly when dealing with single or a few products or services that require specialization and economies of scale. In this form, strong coordination and control from centralized bodies are essential to maintain cohesiveness in terms of routines, managerial practices, procedures, communication, culture, and leadership characteristics.[35] The U-form organization comprises specialized functions such as operations, marketing, finance, and human resources, working under tight coordination, rigid rules, and hierarchical relationships. This structure aims to achieve economies of scale by maximizing output and minimizing costs, particularly in environments with low levels of uncertainty. In the U-form, different organizational functions operate under unified command chains and coordinate efforts to produce a narrow range of standardized products or services. Information flows horizontally among the heads of each function and vertically from top to bottom within the hierarchy. The key to the U-form's success lies in its enhanced coordination, which outweighs coordination costs across functions and allows for the realization of economies of scale.[36]

Figure 6.1 illustrates the example of a U-form organization within the context of healthcare, specifically focusing on a maternity hospital specializing exclusively in childbirth practices and procedures. Under this model, the maternity's CEO (Chief Executive Officers) assumes authority over various organizational functions necessary for providing comprehensive healthcare services throughout pregnancy, labor, and post-birth care. Each function requires specialized attention. For example, the Chief Medical Officer oversees obstetricians, neonatologists, anesthetists, nurses, physiotherapists, psychologists, and other specialized professionals. Meanwhile, the VP of infrastructure ensures that all physical facilities are prepared and maintained in excellent condition to support

[35] Burton et al. (2020).

[36] Fan et al. (2009).

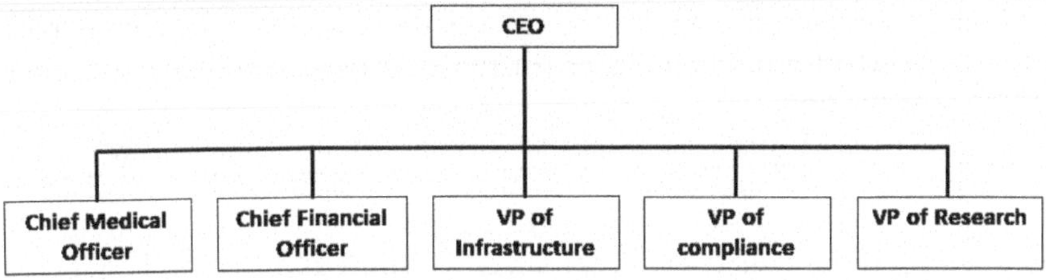

Fig. 6.1 U-form in public organizations—example of a maternity hospital

the childbirth process. Effective coordination among both core and non-core areas is essential to achieve economies of scale within this specialized healthcare unit.

Just as in private firms and corporations, the choices of organizational structures in public organizations and state-owned enterprises can either enhance or hinder performance.

However, as an organization expands and diversifies its services, the coordination costs of functions can increase significantly, challenging the effectiveness of U-form structures. Using the example above, if the maternity hospital decides to expand its services to other unrelated medical specialties beyond childbirth, the costs of managing the functional form will rise. Top management may struggle to coordinate and monitor the increased variety of specialties effectively. In more diversified environments, not only does coordination become costly, but the benefits of economies of scale diminish due to the increased allocation of resources that cannot be shared. The lack of complementarity among organizational functions hampers the realization of synergies in such diversified settings.

Multidivisional Forms (M-Form)

To address the limitations of U-form structures, organizations often adopt *multidivisional forms (M-forms)* when diversifying their activities. M-forms group tasks into more decentralized business units (BUs) or subunits and are considered more suitable for managing challenges related to geographic, product/service, or customer diversification. In M-forms, heads of subunits have greater autonomy in decision-making, with higher-level management primarily responsible for resource allocation across subunits, strategic corporate decisions (in the case of private conglomerates), or broader public policies (in the case of government and large public organizations).[37]

Managers in M-forms are closer to local demands, making them more informed about various citizen needs that can be addressed by specialized subunits. Compared to U-forms, there are lower information asymmetries between decision-makers in decentralized subunits and the local contexts. This reduced asymmetry allows for quicker responses and the development of more adaptable products and services. M-forms offer improved flexibility and autonomy in resource utilization, resulting in a less bureaucratic and rigid approach. Besides increasing the likelihood of innovation in uncertain settings, the semi-autonomous operation of subunits equips them to better address external demands.

Public and nonprofit organizations also utilize M-forms. Consider a police department within a specific jurisdiction as an example. While the overarching goal is to investigate all crimes, it is understood that crimes vary significantly in nature, requiring specialization. For instance, narcotics and drug trafficking cases differ from domestic violence crimes. Although police officers undergo similar entry-level training programs, the nuances of each type of crime demand additional training, specialized resources, and distinct investigation practices. To address these differences, police departments often establish specialized and semi-autonomous subdivisions with decision-making authority allocated by police leadership or by the rule of law. Figure 6.2 illustrates the utilization of M-form in police forces.

In Fig. 6.2, we see the hypothetical structure of a police force, where the police chief oversees several specialized subunits, such as narcotics and domestic violence. Each subunit's head enjoys an important level of autonomy and discretion in conducting investigations and policing activities. Note that M-forms do not necessarily entail complete decentralization. To prevent excessive duplication of functions, a common challenge in M-forms, they can include shared centers that handle functions common to all subunits and are not highly specific to the chosen segmentation, whether it is based on products/services, geography, or customer

[37] Alfred Chandler Jr (1962), one of the founders of the strategy field, has extensively studied the management structures of modern corporations and recognized the importance of multidivisional forms to successful strategies of large corporations such as General Motors, Dupont, Standard Oil, and Sears.

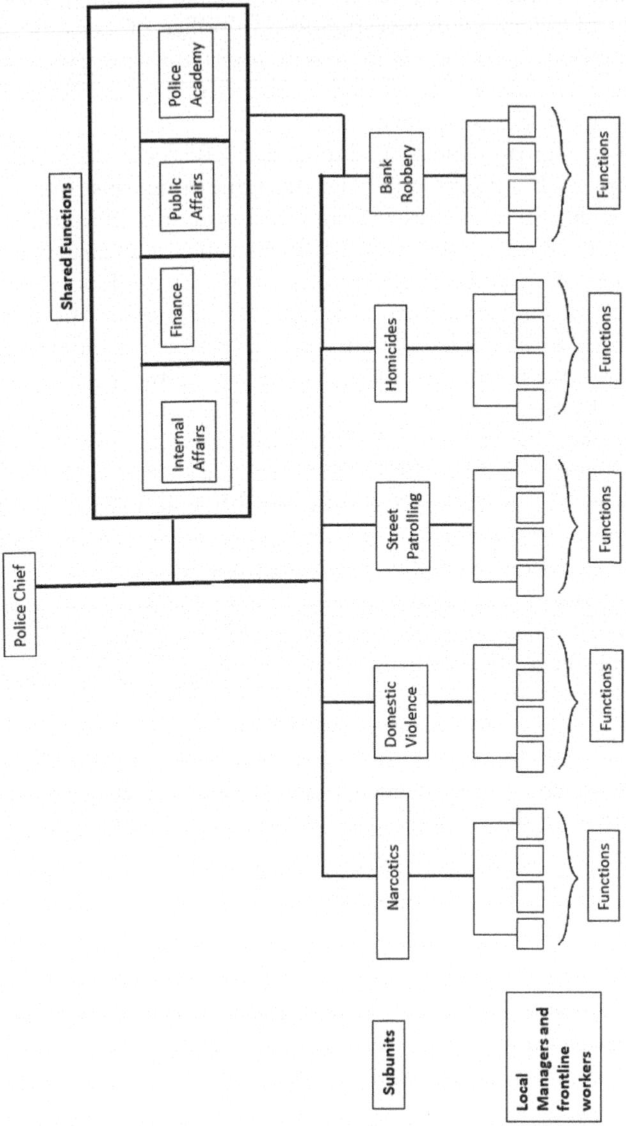

Fig. 6.2 M-form in public organizations—police department example

orientation. For instance, functions like Internal Affairs Divisions, responsible for policing the police, can be shared among all subunits, providing more efficient and independent investigations of police officer misconduct compared to alternative arrangements where internal investigation bodies are allocated to each subunit. In this case, the organizational form can be called a hybrid multidivisional form.

In addition to the possibility of duplicating efforts in M-form organizations, where each subunit can have the same functions and prevent economies of scale, there are other issues and potential limitations. The relative autonomy of each subunit in M-forms can hinder organizational cohesion. Heads of subunits may become overly focused on their own performance, promoting actions that negatively affect other subunits and the organization. For example, one subunit may prioritize media-friendly actions to boost the popularity of its personnel at the expense of the overall quality of policing activities. Of course, this can tarnish the image of the entire police department. Additionally, consolidating a common identity, organizational culture, and a clear sense of direction can be challenging in M-forms, especially when subunits differ significantly in terms of the communities they serve, environmental pressures they face, and the types of resources needed to fulfill their institutional mandates.[38]

Subunits may also invest their time in influential activities to persuade top management to allocate more resources and larger budgets to them, potentially resulting in inefficient resource allocation. While these problems can also occur in U-form organizations with distinct functions competing for prestige and resources within the organization, the larger size of organizations adopting M-forms may make it more difficult for top management to have an unobstructed vision of the actual needs of each subunit, exacerbating the consequences of influence activities in M-forms.

Matrix Forms

An alternative to combining the positive aspects of M-forms and U-forms and attenuating their negative aspects is the adoption of *matrix forms*. To harness the advantages of both U-form (efficiency from enhanced coordination and specialization) and M-forms (greater flexibility and heightened focus on local demands), organizations may appoint local managers to

[38] See Fan et al. (2009), Pollitt (2007), and Altamimi et al. (2022).

report to both a functional superior and a geography- or product-related superior. This setup can establish internal checks and balances, encouraging managers to consider both functional aspects and those closely tied to local demands. As depicted in Fig. 6.3, this matrix form is exemplified in a state university with four campuses distributed across the territory.

Local managers overseeing functions that cater to different student needs (e.g., facilities management and infrastructure) report to the head of their respective campus, who focuses on local demands. These managers are more likely to possess extensive knowledge about local suppliers in their regions compared to centralized managers at the headquarters.

By having a direct link to a superior responsible for consolidating information from all campuses, local managers can also leverage the advantages of economies of scale through improved coordination in matrix forms. For instance, instead of each local manager independently developing their information systems and procuring hardware and

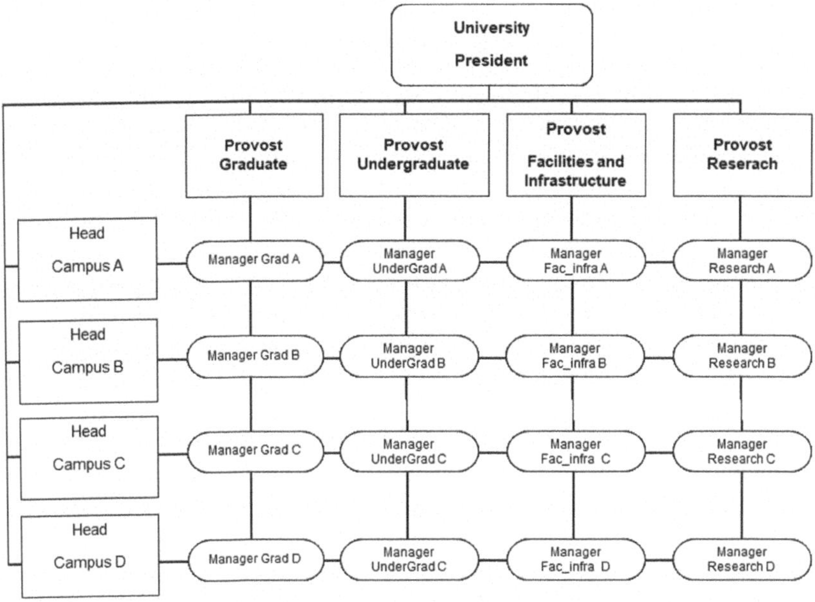

Fig. 6.3 Matrix organization—multicampus university example

software in a decentralized manner, a centralized functional office can facilitate a unified bidding process that encompasses all campuses. This coordinated effort ensures economies of scale that benefit all units and strengthens organizational cohesion through standardization, all while accommodating local needs.

While the double assignment can help balance centralized and decentralized powers in the organization, ensure information sharing, and improve information flows in a more flexible manner, matrix organizations are not without their problems. The dual chain of command can create tensions among the heads of subunits and functional heads, leading to internal turf wars and political maneuvering. Furthermore, the decision-making process can become more intricate and slower, reducing organizational responsiveness. With two different superiors who often have different objectives and goals, local managers in matrix forms can find it challenging to navigate internal power dynamics, potentially increasing the cost of exerting influence to survive in potential internal conflicts.

Conclusions

Centralization and decentralization decisions are strategic and can significantly impact the creation (or destruction) of public value. Allocating decision rights to agents in a decentralized manner can aid public and nonprofit organizations in adapting to local conditions, facilitating the development of goods and services that align with the specific demands of local populations. Empowering personnel with an enhanced understanding of local needs allows for faster responses to targeted populations, saving valuable time for managers who would otherwise need to perform concentrated decisions. Individuals with decision-making authority can also experience reinforced motivation and develop a stronger sense of ownership.

While decentralization can enhance the performance of public and nonprofit organizations, there are cases where centralized forms may be more appropriate. This is particularly true for activities where improper decentralized decisions can create negative externalities for other interdependent units, compromising the entire organization. For example, a remote office of an international NGO engaging in corruption with local public authorities could tarnish the image of the entire organization, even affecting units with a clean compliance record. In addition to mitigating coordination and incentive issues, centralization enables a more effective use of information by upper echelons. This, in turn, can promote economies of scale and improved efficiencies, as seen in the case of centralized public procurement in Italy.[39]

Building on the idea that organizations in practice often balance decentralized and centralized decision-making, the chapter introduced a straightforward contingency model to anticipate the conditions in which the allocation of decision rights is more or less suitable. Additionally, various types of organizational structures were explored, reflecting how information flows within the organization, how tasks and responsibilities are assigned, and the mechanisms in place to ensure appropriate checks and balances. This is particularly crucial in public and nonprofit organizations, which face heightened scrutiny from a myriad of stakeholders compared to private firms.

In summary, there is no one-size-fits-all solution for assigning decision rights in organizations. The choice between centralized and decentralized forms, along with the selection of organizational structures reflecting more concentrated or diffuse decision-making authority, should be determined based on the specific contingencies surrounding each organization. The capacity to adapt to changing external environments and evolving organizational and corporate strategies is crucial for the successful implementation of strategies, as we will delve into in the next chapter.

References

Abdulkadiroğlu, A., Agarwal, N., & Pathak, P. A. (2017). The welfare effects of coordinated assignment: Evidence from the New York City high school match. *American Economic Review, 107*(12), 3635–3689.

Altamimi, H., Liu, Q., & Jimenez, B. (2022). Not too much, not too little: Centralization, decentralization, and organizational change. *Journal of Public Administration Research and Theory, 33*(1), 170–185. https://doi.org/10.1093/jopart/muac016

Andrews, R., Boyne, G. A., Law, J., & Walker, R. M. (2009). Centralization, organizational strategy, and public service performance. *Journal of Public Administration Research and Theory, 19*(1), 57–80.

[39] See Baldi and Vannoni (2017).

Baldi, S., & Vannoni, D. (2017). The impact of centralization on pharmaceutical procurement prices: The role of institutional quality and corruption. *Regional Studies, 51*(3), 426–438.

Baum, J. R., & Wally, S. (2003). Strategic decision speed and firm performance. *Strategic Management Journal, 24*(11), 1107–1129.

Benny, G., Joseph, J., Surendran, S., & Nambiar, D. (2023). On the forms, contributions and impacts of community mobilisation involved with Kerala's COVID-19 response: Perspectives of health staff, Local Self Government institution and community leaders. *PLoS ONE, 18*(6), e0285999.

Brickley, J. A., Smith, C. W., & Zimmerman, J. L. (2001). *Managerial economics and organizational architecture* (2nd ed.). McGraw-Hill.

Burton, R., Håkonsson, D. D., Larsen, E. R., & Obel, B. (2020). New trends in organization design. *Journal of Organization Design, 9*, 1–2.

Cabral, S., Ito, N., & Pongeluppe, L. (2021). *The disastrous effects of leaders in denial: evidence from the COVID-19 crisis in Brazil*. Available at SSRN 3836147.

Cabral, S., & Lazzarini, S. G. (2015). The "guarding the guardians" problem: An analysis of the organizational performance of an internal affairs division. *Journal of Public Administration Research and Theory, 25*(3), 797–829.

Cabral, S., Lazzarini, S. G., & de Azevedo, P. F. (2010). Private operation with public supervision: Evidence of hybrid modes of governance in prisons. *Public Choice, 145*, 281–293.

Callaghan, R. C., Vander Heiden, J., Sanches, M., Asbridge, M., Hathaway, A., & Kish, S. J. (2021). Impacts of Canada's cannabis legalization on police-reported crime among youth: Early evidence. *Addiction, 116*(12), 3454–3462.

Capano, G., & Lippi, A. (2021). Decentralization, policy capacities, and varieties of first health response to the COVID-19 outbreak: Evidence from three regions in Italy. *Journal of European Public Policy, 28*(8), 1197–1218.

Capano, G., & Toth, F. (2023). Thinking outside the box, improvisation, and fast learning: Designing policy robustness to deal with what cannot be foreseen. *Public Administration, 101*(1), 90–105.

Cardoso, R. L., Azevedo, R. R. d., Pigatto, J. A. M., Fajardo, B. d. A. G., & Cunha, A. S. M. d. (2023). Lessons from Brazil's unsuccessful fiscal decentralization policy to fight COVID-19. *Public Administration and Development, 43*(2), 106–119.

Chandler Jr., A. D. (1962). *Strategy and structure: Chapters in the history of the American industrial enterprise* (1ed ed.). MIT press.

Fama, E. F., & Jensen, M. C. (1983). Separation of ownership and control. *The Journal of Law and Economics, 26*(2), 301–325.

Fan, C. S., Lin, C., & Treisman, D. (2009). Political decentralization and corruption: Evidence from around the world. *Journal of Public Economics, 93*(1–2), 14–34.

Heller, P., Harilal, K., & Chaudhuri, S. (2007). Building local democracy: Evaluating the impact of decentralization in Kerala, India. *World Development, 35*(4), 626–648.

Hurwicz, L. (2008). But who will guard the guardians? *American Economic Review, 98*(3), 577–585.

Jones, B. D., & Baumgartner, F. R. (2005). *The politics of attention: How government prioritizes problems*. University of Chicago Press.

Kapucu, N. (2006). Public-nonprofit partnerships for collective action in dynamic contexts of emergencies. *Public Administration, 84*(1), 205–220.

Leiblein, M. J., Reuer, J. J., & Zenger, T. (2018). What makes a decision strategic? *Strategy Science, 3*(4), 558–573.

Lipscomb, M., & Mobarak, A. M. (2016). Decentralization and pollution spillovers: Evidence from the re-drawing of county borders in Brazil. *The Review of Economic Studies, 84*(1), 464–502.

Mello, U. (2022). Centralized admissions, affirmative action, and access of low-income students to higher education. *American Economic Journal: Economic Policy, 14*(3), 166–197.

Moloney, K., & Moloney, S. (2020). Australian Quarantine Policy: From centralization to coordination with mid-Pandemic COVID-19 shifts. *Public Administration Review, 80*(4), 671–682.

Ohrling, M., Solberg Carlsson, K., & Brommels, M. (2022). No man is an island: Management of the emergency response to the SARS-CoV-2 (COVID-19) outbreak in a large public decentralised service delivery organisation. *BMC Health Services Research, 22*(1), 371. https://doi.org/10.1186/s12913-022-07716-w

Pollitt, C. (2007). Decentralization: A central concept in contemporary public management. In E. Ferlie, L. E. Lynn, & C. Pollitt (Eds.), *The Oxford handbook of public management* (pp. 371–397). Oxford University Press.

Porter, D. O., & Olsen, E. A. (1976). Some critical issues in government centralization and decentralization. *Public Administration Review, 36*, 72–84.

Shin, J., & Choi, Y. K. (2019). Organizational innovativeness and its determinants in South Korean nonprofit human service organizations. *Nonprofit Management and Leadership, 30*(1), 51–68.

Sigman, H. (2005). Transboundary spillovers and decentralization of environmental policies. *Journal of Environmental Economics and Management, 50*(1), 82–101.

Touchton, M., Knaul, F. M., Arreola-Ornelas, H., Porteny, T., Sánchez, M., Méndez, O., … & Rosado, J. A. (2021). A partisan pandemic: State government public health policies to combat COVID-19 in Brazil. *BMJ Global Health, 6*(6), e005223. https://doi.org/10.1136/bmjgh-2021-005223
Wong, E. M., Ormiston, M. E., & Tetlock, P. E. (2011). The effects of top management team integrative complexity and decentralized decision making on corporate social performance. *Academy of Management Journal, 54*(6), 1207–1228.
Zarychta, A., Grillos, T., & Andersson, K. P. (2020). Public sector governance reform and the motivation of street-level bureaucrats in developing countries. *Public Administration Review, 80*(1), 75–91.

CHAPTER 7

Strategy Implementation

Like many other countries in the 1990s, the Australian government introduced managerial reforms in public organizations following the principles of the New Public Management paradigm. Outsourcing to private and nonprofit organizations was among the primary policies implemented. Aligned with free-market principles, Australian authorities at the national, subnational, and local levels transferred several activities that were previously carried out by civil servants in government departments and public organizations to external parties. Outsourcing public services aimed to reduce costs, improve service quality, prioritize strategic functions, enhance flexibility, and instill a competitive mindset in the public sector, as opposed to in-house provision by public authorities.

In 1996, a major public health organization in an Australian state, overseeing six hospitals and dozens of healthcare units, outsourced various operational functions in the facilities management domain. This included services such as food provision, cleaning, security, waste management, and laundry. Additionally, the organization contracted out non-medical services provided to patients and their families, which were performed by patient services assistants. However, after a few years, the state government authorities came to realize that the anticipated cost savings did not materialize. Suzanne Young and Manuela Macinati demonstrated that the anticipated benefits from increased flexibility and reduced operational and transaction costs in managing relationships with contractors did not

S. Cabral, *Strategy for Public and Nonprofit Organizations*, https://doi.org/10.1007/978-3-031-64969-1_7

occur as expected. Consequently, the government decided to backsource some of these functions in 2004, and the remaining non-clinical services were brought back under state authorities in 2009. For similar reasons, in 2008, the Italian government chose to insource hospital maintenance services, which had previously been outsourced in 2003.[1]

In his analysis of the implementation of an innovative approach for treating patients with chest pain in nine public hospitals in Germany, Eric Piening discovered notable discrepancies in performance levels. Specifically, while three hospitals successfully reduced patient stays—a crucial performance metric in this context—two hospitals experienced an increase in this duration, measured as the difference between admission and discharge dates. These disparities among top-performing and underperforming hospitals suggest unequal standards of quality care for patients across regions. Furthermore, variations in cost-effectiveness indicate that the introduced innovations may not be fully realizing their efficiency potential. According to the author, the necessary routines, and managerial practices for the effective operation of specialized chest pain units were not uniformly implemented across all public hospitals.[2]

The two situations mentioned above illustrate that implementation problems can compromise the translation of strategic intentions into improved performance. Failing to execute strategies in a way that leads to the desired outcomes not only results in the wastage of organizational resources but also poses a significant threat to organizational survival. Recognizing the fundamental role of active engagement from both top and lower-level management in translating strategic plans into actionable initiatives, it is widely acknowledged that effective strategy implementation poses a persistent challenge for practitioners in both for-profit and nonprofit organizations.[3] Hence, the understanding of the drivers behind

[1] See Young and Macinati (2012) for a comparative analysis exploring the dynamics of outsourcing and backsourcing decisions in the context of health activities in both Australia and Italy.

[2] Piening (2011).

[3] Early contributions to the field of strategy underscore the significance of strategy implementation in shaping organizational and corporate objectives (Cohen & Cyert, 1973). For recent advances of strategy implementation in public and nonprofit literature, please refer to Andrews et al. (2011). For an account of strategy implementation in for-profit firms, see Friesl et al. (2021).

strategy implementation and their intricate relationships with the organizational change process becomes pivotal for organizations to successfully attain their intended objectives.

Defining the Concept of Strategy Implementation

One of the most recurrent challenges in academia is finding a unified conceptual definition for some phenomena. Epistemological, theoretical, methodological, and contextual diversity along with the evolving nature of scientific knowledge make it difficult to arrive at common definitions for certain concepts. On the contrary, it is much more prevalent to find several definitions that either complement or conflict with existing conceptualizations.

Naturally, the concept of strategy implementation (or strategy execution) is not an exception, and several definitions are available. Yet, the prevailing view in strategy literature is recognizing strategy implementation as a collection of decisions and processes to turn strategic intents into reality. Charles Hill and Gareth Jones posit that "*strategy implementation involves putting the strategies (or plan) into action*", which includes "*taking actions consistent with the selected strategies*".[4] Complementary, Paul Nutt conceives strategy implementation as a "… *series of steps taken by responsible organizational agents in planned change to elicit compliance needed to install changes*",[5] while Charles Noble defines strategy implementation as "*the communication, interpretation, adoption, and enactment of strategic plans*".[6] Assuming that strategy implementation is an adaptive process, Ann-Kristin Weiser, Paula Jarzabkowski, and Tomi Laamanen define strategy implementation as "*the continuous interplay of three interrelated activities — conceptualizing, enacting, and coordinating — that enable an organization to realize strategies through collective actions by organizational stakeholders*".[7] Similarly, by acknowledging that strategy implementation involves a bundle of functions working in a coherent and coordinated fashion, Carla Albuquerque de Oliveira, Jorge Carneiro, and

[4] Hill and Jones (2011, p. 8).

[5] Nutt (1986, p. 230).

[6] Noble (1999, p. 119).

[7] Weiser et al. (2020, p. 973).

Felipe Esteves identify that key components in the strategic implementation process include translating the strategy into action plans, keeping managers and employees informed about organizational challenges, and ensuring consistency in resource-allocation decisions.[8]

All these definitions converge toward the idea that implementing strategies involves a set of integrated decisions and coordinated actions to bring formulated strategies to fruition. Another common observation for someone interested in investigating strategy implementation is the recurring statement found in most published materials on the subject: that strategy implementation receives far less attention than strategy formulation.

Lawrence Hrebiniak, a former professor at The Wharton School of the University of Pennsylvania and one of the most prolific scholars on strategy implementation, echoed this sentiment. He noted that while formulating strategy is difficult, making strategy work was even more, but "*unfortunately, most managers know far more about developing strategy than they do about executing it*".[9] Hrebiniak also suggested that a significant extent of the several problems faced during the implementation phase occur because managers are just not prepared because they were trained to plan, not execute plans. In fact, strategy implementation is hardly ever a core course in master's in business administration (MBA) or master's in public administration (MPA) programs that train managers to act in public, private, and nonprofit organizations. Further, the separation between an elite who thinks, according to Hrebiniak, the "smart" people, who develop plans and those who follow and execute the work conceived by the others, creates a wrong impression that executing requires less abilities and intelligence than planning, and this devalues the implementation process. Not surprisingly, reports that implemented strategies do not deliver what was promised during the formulation process are common.[10] Understanding the drivers of successful implementation of strategies becomes crucial.

[8] Oliveira et al. (2019).

[9] Hrebiniak (2006, p. 12).

[10] See Mankins and Steele (2005) and Higgins (2005).

Drivers of Successful Implementation

While the previous chapters emphasized the role of the three components of the organizational architecture (incentives, performance management, and decision rights) in organizational performance,[11] they can also significantly influence the dynamics of strategy implementation.

First, *incentives* can drive distinct levels of effort in individuals and groups compared to a scenario where incentives do not exist, and they can guide the organization toward achieving the chosen strategy. Organizations can elevate the standards of strategy implementation by implementing measures that boost the motivation of those responsible for carrying out the strategies. This can be achieved through the establishment of monetary bonuses and/or non-pecuniary awards contingent on the achievement of intermediate goals related to the implementation process. In public and nonprofit organizations facing cultural or economic challenges in implementing PFP programs, finding the right balance between extrinsic and intrinsic motivation is crucial. For example, in Lebanon, the presence of incentives provided by the government was instrumental in encouraging local organizations to adopt regulatory standards in the food industry. These incentives included tax exemptions, funding for capacity building, and the provision of loans.[12]

Effective strategy implementation also requires *performance management* systems to monitor the progress of implementation efforts. The use of dashboards or approaches like balanced scorecards can help organizations in controlling and adjusting the implementation process, allowing the (re)alignment of resources and structures crucial for ensuring a successful strategy implementation. Conversely, a lack of control can hinder the implementation process.[13] Appropriate performance management systems can accelerate the implementation process, track implementation milestones, and at the same time maintain a heightened focus on the ultimate strategic choices.[14]

In their analysis of the implementation of different strategies in Spanish hospitals, David Naranjo-Gil and Frank Hartmann found that performance management systems were valuable in supporting cost-reduction

[11] Brickley et al. (2001).

[12] Massoud et al. (2010).

[13] Friesl et al. (2021).

[14] Kaplan (2001).

strategies by CEOs with a predominant administrative background. They also demonstrate that CEOs with a medical background are more inclined to employ performance management systems to bolster quality-focused strategies, aligning more with the quality of care provided to patients and less with financial aspects. This suggests that performance management systems are not only pivotal for the implementation process but also must be aligned with the intended or emergent strategies pursued by the organization.[15]

Third, the *allocation of decision rights* is also recognized as a key aspect for successful strategy implementation. Ensuring clarity regarding who has the authority to make decisions and appropriately assigning roles in the decision-making can enhance the speed and accuracy of strategy implementation. For instance, the role of recommending a decision differs from the roles of saying yes or no, providing inputs, deciding, and implementing a decision. Therefore, it is imperative that everyone in the organization is aware of who is responsible for each decision to ensure a smooth implementation process.[16]

Besides holding accountable those managers responsible for the implementation, the assignment of decision rights can facilitate the coordination of information flows across different layers of the organization. This ensures that top-management teams, who are sponsoring the strategy implementation efforts, and the various individuals and teams executing the strategies, have a shared understanding of the implementation milestones and access to the highest level of information possible to support decision-making in the implementation process. The improved information flows resulting from the clear assignment of decision rights may also encourage the participation of various stakeholders in the implementation process, which is often crucial in the context of public and nonprofit organizations. Taha Hameduddin, Sergio Fernandez, and Mehmet Akif Demircioglu analyzed the implementation of Challenge.gov, an innovation platform in the US federal government aimed at enhancing citizen engagement and public participation. They noted that specific configurations in the distribution of decision rights, such as empowering employees, are linked to a heightened utilization of the platform by

[15] Naranjo-Gil and Hartmann (2007).

[16] Rogers and Blenko (2006).

federal agencies. This increased usage stands as one of the intended outcomes stemming from the implementation process.[17]

The next driver of successful implementation relates to the formulation process. Indeed, strategy formulation and strategy implementation are inherently connected. These two phases can occur either sequentially, where formulation precedes implementation, or interactively, with bottom-up strategies emerging from the organization and co-existing with deliberately formulated top-down strategies. While it is intuitive to assume a positive relationship between the mere existence of formulated strategies and successful strategy implementation, the *quality of strategy formulation* is, in fact, one of the most critical factors in ensuring the success of what was originally planned. Bert George analyzed the relationships between strategic planning and successful plan implementation in Belgian municipalities. He has found that high-quality plans covering topics that are found to be strategically relevant and conceived in an integrated manner with the participation of skilled and motivated people are key to successful strategy implementation. In other words, the quality of formulated strategies hinges on an interplay between people involved in the strategic planning and processes combining informativeness and the creation of constructive solutions.[18]

In a world where public and nonprofit organizations face mounting pressure from a broader and more diversified array of stakeholders for improved services, all while contending with decreased budgets and public resistance to tax increases, the approach to strategic formulation (planning) becomes pivotal for successful strategy implementation. In the case of public and nonprofit organizations, the combination of deliberate and emergent formulation becomes crucial. Given the multitude of stakeholders involved in public policies and cross-sector collaborations spanning public, private, and nonprofit realms, harmonizing formal processes—with a clear definition of vision, mission, values, and expected goals—and emergent approaches that can incorporate diverse perspectives from the network of affected stakeholders, becomes key to

[17] Hameduddin et al. (2020).

[18] George (2021).

formulation efforts that are not only adaptable but, most importantly, implementable.[19]

Another factor driving successful implementation is the availability of adequate *resources and capabilities* to implement the strategies accordingly. Understood as the assets an organization uses to choose and implement its strategies,[20] tangible (e.g., human capital, financial resources, technologies) and intangible resources (e.g., patents, brands, reputation) can help organizations in the strategy implementation by enabling decision-making, facilitating allocation decisions, and supporting organizational members to put into practice their leadership styles. Jay Barney, one of the most prominent authors of the so-called resource-based view of strategy, posits that resources that are valuable, rare, difficult to imitate, and organized in a way that allows its effective use are sources of sustained competitive advantage, basically because they allow the organizational create and sustain barriers to rivals in the long-run. Conceiving capabilities as the result of resources and accumulated experience overtime that allow the implementation of strategies, it is possible to argue that the ability of implementing strategies is a source of improved performance.[21] For instance, some organizations are known for their ability to implement buyer–supplier strategies and manage their alliance portfolio because of a unique combination of skilled human resources and appropriate technology.[22]

In the public management context, resources and capabilities can also be used to attenuate the negative consequences of policies. In analyzing the effects of a policy designed to favor small and medium enterprises (SMEs) in the Brazilian public procurement system, I found that the formulated strategy did not lead improved government and firm-level outcomes in general. However, I also found that auctions with the participation with more capable procurement officers resulted in improved costs, and government responsiveness in terms of reduced contracting lead-times, thus attenuating the negative outcomes resulting from the policy

[19] For a more comprehensive understanding of strategic formulation in public and nonprofit organizations, refer to Bryson (1988, 2018).

[20] Barney (2001).

[21] See Barney and Zajac (1994) and Barney (2001, 2012).

[22] Vasudeva and Anand (2011).

implementation.[23] Capabilities can also facilitate the implementation of organizational structure innovations as in the German's public hospitals specialized chest units described in the beginning of this chapter.[24]

Appropriate *managerial practices* are also deemed key to successful strategy implementation. Understood as a set of activities that organizations execute attempting to obtain the desired outcomes,[25] practices include diverse managerial technologies such as goal setting, Total Quality Management, Six-Sigma, among others. These approaches are widely adopted by organizations to formulate and implement strategies and directly influencing organizational performance. Managerial practices and resources are intertwined. While resources are assets reflecting what organizations can potentially do, and capabilities reflect the ability of an organization to do something, practices reflect what the organization does. Furthermore, the availability of resources can influence the adoption of performance-enhancing practices, but unlike resources that organizations tend to protect to differentiate themselves from others, successful practices can be imitated and transferred across organizations. This helps managers understand what and how they need to do.

Thomaz Teodorovicz, Sergio Lazzarini, Leandro Nardi, and I have analyzed the propensity of public and private schools implementing practices related to human resources management and planning. Although the results show that the implementation practices are conducive to superior performance in terms of improved student outcomes in standardized tests, private schools are less likely to adopt performance-enhancing practices, giving rise to a performance gap between the two modes. Yet, the presence of enhanced level of human capital resources (more skilled teachers) in public schools is associated with an increased likelihood of implementing managerial practices, reducing the public–private performance gap.[26] In other words, practices either in isolation or in tandem with resources are important vehicles to public organizations to implement strategies that are conducive to improved performance.

Leadership styles are also recognized as a major aspect influencing the strategy implementation. Leaders can infuse in the organization the set

[23] Cabral (2017).

[24] Piening (2011).

[25] Bromiley and Rau (2014).

[26] Teodorovicz et al. (2023).

of values, the vision, and envisaged goals and support the implementation process by demonstrating with actions their commitment with the new aspired settings. Strategic leadership is also needed to orchestrate all other drivers of successful implementation, such as establishing rewards contingent to the attainment of implementation milestones in tandem with the adoption of appropriate performance management systems.[27] Victoria Crittenden and William Crittenden examined Battered Women Fighting Back! (BWFB), a Boston-based nonprofit organization focused on combatting domestic violence. They concluded that the leadership style of the executive director shaped an organizational culture that was a critical implementation lever for building a capable organization.[28] Likewise, when analyzing the implementation of a total quality management (TQM) initiative in the Malaysian government, Teddy Fei and Hal Rainey have found that successful implementation was linked to a strong commitment from top-management teams. Committed leaders exhibited a sharp vision for the future, provided encouragement and recognition to staff responsible for program implementation, and fostered collaboration among team members.[29]

Overall, the presence of adequate incentives, performance management systems, strategic plans, resources, practices, and leadership styles are important features for successful strategy implementation. However, the existing interdependencies between the organization and its external environments as well as among the drivers of successful implementation call for further examination of the influence of external and internal fit in the strategy implementation process.

The Importance of External and Internal Fit in Strategy Implementation

US Gymnastics is a nonprofit organization responsible for promoting gymnastics in the United States. Serving approximately 200,000 individuals in the country, US Gymnastics' efforts range from beginners to elite levels. Affiliated with the US Olympic and Paralympic Committee, this nonprofit supports the US teams for major international tournaments,

[27] See Higgins (2005) and O'Reilly et al. (2010).

[28] Crittenden and Crittenden (2008).

[29] Fei and Rainey (2003).

including the Olympic Games. The results achieved by US Gymnastics are impressive: besides fostering the practice of a healthy sport in six disciplines (acrobatic, artistic, gymnastics for all, parkour, rhythmic, and trampoline and tumbling) all over the country, the achievements of US elite athletes in the most international events are remarkable. Athletes like Simone Biles, Bart Conner, and Shawn Johnson, to name a few, have collected medals and served as sources of inspiration for other athletes and the public in general beyond the US borders. In addition to the innate abilities and supreme athleticism of leading gymnasts, the accomplishment of US Gymnastics' mission also relies on successfully formulating and implementing strategies that involve the articulation of several organizational elements, including decision rights, incentives, resources, capabilities, along with performance-enhancing practices that shape world-class gymnasts.[30]

However, after the astonishing performance of Simone Biles in the 2016 Summer Olympic Games in Rio de Janeiro, Brazil, an unprecedent scandal involving the US Gymnastics shocked the world. On September 12, 2016 Marisa Kwiatkowski, Mark Alesia, and, Tim Evans, three reporters of the Indianapolis Star, have published an article reporting that two former US gymnasts were victims of sexual abuse perpetrated by a member of the US Gymnastics. The article provided visibility to omissions from US Gymnastics' executives in terms of failing to report the cases and to alert law enforcement authorities of allegations of sexual abuse by coaches.[31] These denounces encouraged other women to report abuses during gymnastics practices in the United States and helped to make the public aware that the sport's national government body had already received complaints of sexual misconduct and took no serious action.

Naturally, the impact of the scandal on US Gymnastics was huge and made some major corporations such as ATT, Kellogg's, and Procter & Gamble suspend their sponsorship agreements. Besides complicating the financial situation of US Gymnastics as well as the organizational reputation, the resulting underfunding caused by the losses of marketing

[30] See https://usagym.org/about/mission/.

[31] See https://www.indystar.com/story/news/2016/09/12/former-usa-gymnastics-doctor-accused-abuse/89995734/ and https://www.indystar.com/story/news/investigations/2016/08/04/usa-gymnastics-sex-abuse-protected-coaches/85829732/.

revenue negatively impacted athletes in their preparations for the subsequent competitions.[32] The pressure from external and internal stakeholders provoked strong turbulence in US Gymnastics triggering lawsuits, forcing several top executives and board members to resign, and making the organization close to insolvency. These problems associate with a negative sportive performance following the scandals: the US gymnastics team has collected only 6 medals in the 2020 Tokyo Olympic Games, which represents a 50% slump compared to 2016 Rio Olympic Games, when the team reaped 12 medals, four of them gold medals. Simone Biles, one of the greatest gymnasts of all time and a victim of abuse, withdrew from participating in several competitions, including the 2020 Olympics Games held in 2021.

These events sparked changes in US Gymnastics that altered the way strategies are executed in the organization. After four CEOs in less than two years, in 2019, Li Li Leung an experienced executive with experience in the sports management industry, became President and CEO of US Gymnastics and focused on redesigning the governance to improve transparency and provide safety to athletes. The organization implemented actions to make the organization more visible, and managers and coaches more accountable. Organizational structures were redesigned to improve the information flows and assure that the demands of athletes, families, and staff are heard. Along these lines, the US Gymnastics has created whistleblower systems and platforms for athletes reporting problems without threats of retaliation and created several councils to increase the athletes' voices in the decision-making, nurturing an internal environment for the enforcement of the existing safety and protection policies.[33]

After seven years from the major scandal and after losing several sponsors, in August 2023, USAG signed a five-year sponsorship contract with Nike that would support the US teams for the 2024 and 2028 Olympic Games.[34] In October 2023, the US women's gymnastics team won the gold medal at the 2023 Artistic Gymnastics World Championships in Antwerp, Belgium. This victory served as an unequivocal sign of successful strategy implementation following poor results in previous

[32] See https://apnews.com/92a93c3fabb142179680f33dfde8275d.

[33] https://abcnews.go.com/Sports/usa-gymnastics-changed-larry-nassar-scandal/story?id=78839442.

[34] https://www.sportsbusinessjournal.com/Articles/2023/08/04/usa-gymnastics.aspx.

important tournaments. Additionally, Simone Biles secured the all-around title at the gymnastics world championships for the sixth time, solidifying her status as the greatest woman of all time in the sport.

External Fit and Strategy Implementation

The example above shows that the processes of formulating and implementing strategies are dynamic and require adaptation to unforeseen events that cannot be anticipated. The capacity of public and nonprofit organizations to adapt to changes in their external environments is key to their own survival, as the US Gymnastics scandal suggests. The fit between the mode of organizing activities and external forces helps organizations to support the strategic decision during the implementation (execution) process as suggested by the contingency perspective.[35]

Organizational theorists and strategy scholars have long relied on a contingency approach to understand the dynamics of adaptations and changes in organizations.[36] Essentially, the contingency approach posits that fitting the internal characteristics of the organization, such as structures, incentives, systems, resources, practices with contingencies, including the external environment, organizational size, and organizational strategy can lead to enhanced performance.

Given the inherent interplay between organizational changes and strategy implementation, where the pursuit of a new strategy often requires changes in both the formal and informal organizational elements, achieving synergies between these elements and the contingencies faced by the organization is crucial for successful strategy implementation.[37] Furthermore, while striving for alignment between the organization and its external contingencies (*external fit*) is a paramount goal, it is even more critical to avoid the adverse consequences stemming from a misalignment caused by shifts in external contingencies. Indeed, the failure to adapt the organization promptly to emergent contingencies, whether in terms of altering the nature of proposed changes or responding belatedly to performance crises resulting from external misfit,

[35] For more information on the contingency approach in strategy implementation see Govindarajan (1988) and Friesl et al. (2021).

[36] Lawrence and Lorsch (1967).

[37] Lynch and Mors (2019).

can have catastrophic repercussions and pose a serious challenge to the organization's long-term survival and to the organization's legitimacy.

Figure 7.1 uses the model conceived by Lex Donaldson[38] to illustrate how shifts in contingencies lead to organizational changes in the context of the US Gymnastics scandal. While the horizontal axis reflects the contingencies faced by the national governing sports body, for simplicity, low and higher pressure from stakeholders for improved accountability standards, the vertical axis refers to the internal organizational structures characterized by the presence of low and high transparency standards. The NW quadrant exhibits the initial situation of US Gymnastics where an internal structure with low transparent standards to report abuses and other types of misbehavior fits with external environments that do not demand improved accountability.

The breakthrough denunciations made by the Indianapolis Star reporters sparked a change in the environmental contingencies. In the new scenario, most of US Gymnastics' stakeholders, including athletes, sponsors, public authorities, and the public, are much more concerned with accountability standards and exert pressure on the organization. The

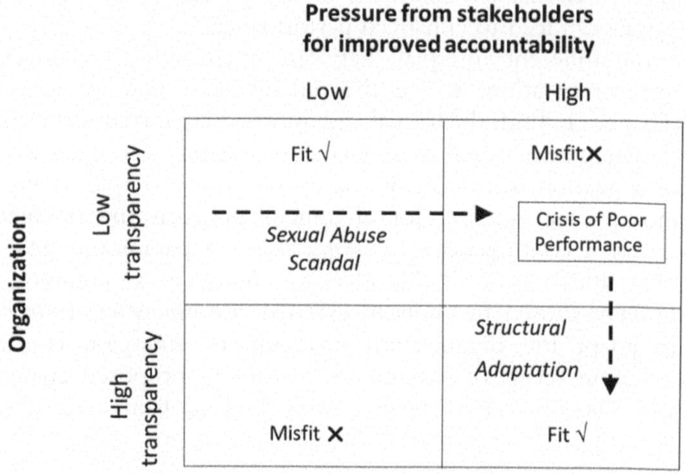

Fig. 7.1 External fit and strategy implementation at US gymnastics

[38] L. Donaldson (2001).

misfit between internal structures and contingencies resulted in a structural maladaptation and consequent crisis of poor performance, which in the case of US Gymnastics almost led the organization to bankruptcy. Structural adaptation in the form of changes in the information flows to ensure that complaints from victims are heard, registered, and seriously investigated both internally and by law enforcement agencies helped the organization to move from misfit into fit, as shown in the SE quadrant.

Overall, adapting the organization to the new contingencies was essential for US Gymnastics reinforcing the implementation of the necessary strategies to promote the sport in the country and at the same time accomplish its mission (*to build community and culture of health, safety, and excellence, where athletes can thrive in sport and life)* within the limits of its core values: safety, integrity, accountability, transparency, and listening.[39]

The example of the US Gymnastics is illustrative about the importance of recognizing environmental forces in the processes of formulating and implementing strategies. *Environmental changes* affecting organizations can be influenced by stakeholders that are close to the focal public or nonprofit organization, such as suppliers, users, customers, regulators, labor unions, competing organizations, and political rivals.

Consider a government-owned airport with the operation franchised out to private agents. In response to the inauguration of a new airport, intensifying competition, the airport can establish incentive systems and adjust its implementation strategies. For instance, the airport can encourage employees to treat passengers with enhanced respect and courtesy. Environmental contingencies can also manifest at a macro level, originating from shifts in politics, demographics, cultural, social, economy, or technology. Returning to the airport example, the private operator could reevaluate their internal structures and strategies to meet the surging demand for ridesharing services fostered from environmental changes in the technological landscape. These responses can involve delineating spaces and redistributing decision-making authority to engage with pertinent stakeholders. This process also encompasses assigning managers to liaise with stakeholders impacted by the innovative technology. They must adeptly manage any tensions that may emerge among ridesharing

[39] See https://usagym.org/about/mission/.

drivers, taxi drivers currently serving the airport, users, transit agencies, and law enforcement organizations. As one can see, changes in the external environment are major contingencies that can propel internal structures in the organization to readapt.

Another contingency source that may cause changes in the way strategies are implemented is the *organization's size*. Indeed, organizations experiencing fast growth tend to face challenges in the structure of decision rights. Smaller organizations tend to concentrate on several decisions with few managers, but as the organization grows the centralization process becomes ineffective as both the quality and the speed in the decision-making process are thwarted. The lack of clarity about who is responsible and accountable for the decision-making in fast-growing organizations can induce a crisis of poor performance.

Equally, contingencies can arise from *changes in the organizational and corporate strategies*. Strategic decisions associated with improvement in the quality of the services delivered via increased customization may conflict with the currently rigid structures. Imagine how difficult it is for hospitals to deal with an increase in the scope of services offered and the same dealing with a growing number of patients looking for medical services. However, in this case, the absence of structural changes in the internal organization is problematic and can cause a serious crisis of poor performance.

The various combinations of contingencies and the multitude of components unique to each organization lead to different responses. These responses are often shaped by an organization's preferences, values, and constraints, making it clear that "one-size-fits-all" solutions are not feasible. In essence, it is improbable to find silver bullets or universal solutions that can be universally applied. Good or bad outcomes may hinge on the articulation of several dimensions in the internal organization and in its external environments that, when combined, result in unique configurations that are highly context-dependent. All in all, organizations at large tend to adopt context-specific approaches in their implementation endeavors to adjust their structures according to external contingencies.[40]

[40] Shenhar (2001).

Internal Fit and Complementarities During Strategy Implementation

One of the primary changes implemented by US Gymnastics was the redesign of its internal structures to facilitate communication flows and ensure that any potential abuses would be reported and investigated. To implement this strategy, changes were made to the way this nonprofit organization allocates decision rights. This took the form of assigning specific roles for handling received allegations, creating committees, and establishing procedures to ensure the necessary transparency to align the organization with the new contingency and overcome the crisis of poor performance. Yet, the achievement of sustainable results does not necessarily stem from single decisions and actions, but it results from the combination of complementary and integrated decisions affecting the effectiveness of implemented strategies.[41] Successful strategy implementation requires internal alignment among organizational elements and organizational functions.[42]

Along these lines, in the case of US Gymnastics, changes in the allocation of decision rights were accompanied by adjustments in the way incentives are set (e.g., sanctions against perpetrators must be credible to inhibit misconduct), in human capital policies (e.g., actions to increase diversity in the top management, in the executive boards, and advisory councils), and in performance management systems to assure the effectiveness of the implemented strategies. Hence, enhanced performance stemming from successful implementation not only relies on the ability of the organization to reconfigure its activities in response to contingencies (*external fit*), but also on the pursuit of mutually reinforcing and complementary actions that are coherently aligned (*internal fit*).

Both economics and strategic management scholars have debated the importance of consistent choices and their synergistic effects on organizational outcomes. Paul Milgrom and John Roberts argue that complementarities among various elements of an organization's strategies—whether between pairs of inputs or among groups of activities, decisions, or other organizational elements—can enhance aggregated marginal returns when some of the elements are increased.[43] If the

[41] Hrebiniak (2006).

[42] See Higgins (2005) and Neilson et al. (2008).

[43] P. Milgrom and Roberts (1990).

marginal costs of these complementary activities decrease, the organization also benefits from an increased level of all other activities. Despite the complex mathematics used to demonstrate the effects of internal fit, the underlying principle is straightforward: when certain elements work together, they provide superior results compared to when they operate in isolation.[44] For instance, the introduction of computer-aided designs in manufacturing helped to reduce the time to market for developing new products, facilitated flexibility on the shop floor, and enabled an increased variety of products offered to customers.[45] An improvement in one element reinforces the other elements and the system as a whole. In the US Gymnastics example, increased diversity in the internal organization tends to change the internal incentive structures by increasing the likelihood of reporting misbehavior from potential victims and raising the perceived costs for potential perpetrators. This, in turn, helps to mitigate, and hopefully eliminate, future cases of abuse.

However, failing to alter one element without changing other complementary elements may lead organizations to achieve suboptimal performance. For instance, several public, private, and nonprofit organizations experienced unsuccessful implementation of total quality management (TQM) systems because they did not ensure consistency among organizational elements. While most TQM implementations focused on changes in the assignment of decision rights, enabling cross-functional teams, encouraging teamwork, and using group-based performance measures instead of individual measures, several implementations of this quality-driven strategy overlooked the use of pay-for-performance incentives. This omission was due to potential incentive distortions such as multitasking (with agents focusing only on dimensions that are measured), or because pay-for-performance might be detrimental to the necessary intrinsic motivation. Consequently, by neglecting the power of incentives to change the behavior of individuals and groups, most TQM implementations initially failed to exploit the potential of complementarities and achieved suboptimal results. On the other hand, once organizations realized that TQM results fell below expectations, some of them engaged in complementary

[44] See Aral et al. (2012), Bresnahan et al. (2002), and Zenger (2002).

[45] Siggelkow (2001).

changes to pursue internal fit and began to promote payments contingent on the achievement of quality goals.[46]

Innovative technologies, such as those enabling ridesharing services, have brought about significant changes not only in the taxi services industry but also in public transportation agencies. This has led to new business practices, regulations, and public policies, necessitating major adjustments in incentives, decision rights, performance management systems, and resources and capabilities to adapt to the new landscape. Organizations facing such conditions encounter fit-destroying changes and are highly motivated to promptly realign their structures to counteract the performance decline resulting from these severe misalignments across various organizational elements.[47]

Yet, changes do not occur in a vacuum, and resistance to change may impede the necessary organizational changes required to implement the desired strategies.

Strategy Implementation and Organizational Inertia

Organizational changes during strategy implementation can involve modifications in a few or many elements at the same time. Changes can also occur in a parsimonious or more hurried way, and they may involve structural changes in the formal organization and cultural changes affecting the informal organization. When implementing strategies, organizations must define which dimensions must be changed, at which pace, and consider the pros and cons associated with the possible courses of action. On the one hand, drastic changes in several organizational dimensions can paralyze the organization and put the daily routines at risk while the new strategy is not completely absorbed and implemented by relevant stakeholders. On the other hand, not implementing the necessary changes promptly may inhibit the organization from reaping the benefits stemming from complementary elements that, once aligned, can move the organization from a suboptimal to a satisfying performance standard.

[46] See Wageman (1995), Hackman and Wageman (1995), and Zenger (2002).

[47] Refer to Siggelkow (2001) for an insightful discussion on the relationships between internal activities' alignment and the capability to effectively respond to environmental changes.

Although underperforming organizations have strong incentives to implement changes in relevant organizational elements rapidly to obtain the best possible results with the set of available resources and practices, managers in charge of the implementation efforts cannot neglect the change management process as well as the barriers to implementation. In a survey with managers responsible for implementing strategies, Lawrence Hrebiniak found that the inability to successfully manage the change process and overcome resistance to change was the main obstacle to strategy implementation. Another significant challenge is related to the conflicts between the implemented strategies and the existing power structures within the organization.[48] While these results have been observed in managers within private organizations, it is worth noting that resistance to change is also a significant issue in public and nonprofit organizations. In the public sector, for instance, the initial expenditures associated with the implementation process, coupled with the anticipated short-term dip in performance, along with resistance to top-down, imposed policy decisions, can all contribute to increased resistance to change.[49]

In a seminal contribution, Michael Hannan and John Freeman acknowledge that organizations, to a greater or lesser extent, may exhibit *structural inertia*. This can limit the inclination of organizations to alter their formal organizational elements—such as structures, incentives, and procedures—in response to environmental conditions or other contingencies, like shifts in organizational size. The degree of structural inertia tends to be higher when the pace of organizational responses lags significantly behind the rates of change in these contingencies. Additionally, inertia increases when organizational elements are highly complementary. This is because alterations in one element necessitate corresponding changes in other dimensions to yield the desired results. However, as the number of elements involved increases, so does the likelihood of conflicts, as decision-makers may prioritize changes that serve their own interests. Achieving alignment in preferences is not straightforward, and consequently, change becomes challenging when multiple actors hold distinct views. Finally, the authors posit that both organizational size and age contribute to higher levels of structural inertia. This is because

[48] Hrebiniak (2006).

[49] See Guth and MacMillan (1986) and Andrews and Boyne (2012).

organizational reliability and accountability necessitate structures that are highly replicable. The reproducibility of a given structure increases with age because, compared to new ventures, it is easier to continue existing routines than to create them from scratch in established organizations. Accumulated learning over time and path dependency, respectively, decrease the costs associated with using existing routines and increase the costs associated with replacing them. As a result, more stable structures are less likely to undergo significant changes.[50]

It is interesting to note that the very features that contribute to making organizations more stable can also generate resistance to change within the formal structure. In order to preserve the status quo, some managers may obstruct changes through acts of sabotage, by refraining from taking action during the implementation process, or by assigning low priority to implementation activities.[51] These (in)actions can prolong the implementation process and hinder the long-term benefits of a new set of changes in formal elements—provided that these elements are aligned both externally and internally.

In addition, inertia can extend beyond formal organization and become ingrained in the norms, codes, and taboos of informal organization. The collective beliefs held by members of the organization can influence how they perceive their reality, approach solutions to existing problems, and process the information they receive. This *cultural inertia* can present challenges for managers seeking to depart from established practices and embrace novel approaches—particularly when those practices have proven successful in the past. This is especially true as organizations age and managers accumulate more experience. Much like structural inertia, cultural inertia tends to grow with the age of the organization. It also strengthens in the presence of cultural uniformity—organizations are less inclined to implement new strategies when the resulting changes conflict with the prevailing cultural norms. In such cases, there is a strong commitment to maintaining the status quo, resisting change.[52]

Altering the culture to facilitate the implementation of new strategies is a major challenge faced by organizations of all types. Informal dimensions are not easily adjusted, and this process requires time. Hence, adapting or

50 Hannan and Freeman (1984).

51 Guth and MacMillan (1986) and Siggelkow (2001).

52 Carrillo and Gromb (2007).

changing the organizational culture to overcome cultural inertia is significantly more complex than addressing the aspects that influence structural inertia.

The consequences of organizational inertia, stemming from its two components—structural and cultural, are straightforward: the presence of organizational inertia can prolong the strategic implementation process and affect the effectiveness of the implementation itself, particularly when combined with internal misfit.

Paulo Reis, Paulo Arvate, and I collaborated on a study examining the implementation process of a new procurement regulation aimed at streamlining and making the procurement process in Brazil less bureaucratic and more agile. In Brazil, procurement officers were, and to a large extent still are, accustomed to a culture focused on achieving price savings and meticulously adhering to bureaucratic procedures throughout the procurement process. The procurement officers' concerns about accountability and potential sanctions were further heightened by the increased powers of oversight agencies. The new procurement regime introduced novel and flexible procedures to reduce red tape, increase competition among bidders, and prevent collusion. The findings indicate that, on average, the new procurement regime successfully decreased contracting lead-times. However, auctions managed by procurement officers with longer tenure tended to take longer, possibly due to conflicts with their established mental models. The existing tensions between flexibility and accountability standards, as well as between the incentive structures and the new allocation of decision rights, appear to hinder more experienced managers from fully leveraging the potential of the new policies. This case serves as an illustration of how the interplay between internal misfit and cultural inertia can impede the effectiveness of strategy implementation.[53]

However, organizational inertia is not inherently bad. While the presence of ossified structures in the formal and informal organization can pose difficulties to strategy implementation by creating obstacles to fitting between organizational elements with environmental conditions and to an enhanced internal fit, organizational inertia can also inhibit the implementation of value-destroying policies. Indeed, organizational changes do not occur automatically. Instead, they face a delay due to the influence of both structural and cultural inertia, creating a gap between strategy

[53] Reis et al. (2023).

implementation and its ensuing impacts. During this time, elements of the former and of the new strategy coexist, thus allowing the organization to experience the pros and cons of each choice. If the new strategy entails undesired features, resistance from organization members can impede the implementation of these strategies in case they conflict with the formal and informal elements.[54]

For instance, civil servants in the United States during Donald Trump's presidential mandate resisted to attempts of implementing value-destroying programs or discontinuing value-creating programs. While senior executive officers resisted to the dismantlement of programs that thwarted civil rights programs benefiting disenfranchised populations and did not endorse actions of political appointees by refusing to sign some documents, civil servants in environmental protection agencies preserved climate change efforts by reframing their communications and using vague euphemisms to underemphasize the focus on climate change.[55] In the same vein, some Hungarian judges resisted to endorse and implement discriminatory policies of the authoritarian regime led by Viktor Orbán after 2010. The way the judicial careers are organized in Hungary along with the embedded culture of following the rule of law were sources of organizational inertia that prevented widespread implementation of discriminatory policies.[56]

Therefore, while resistance to change may hinder the implementation of strategies that organizations need to improve their performance, sometimes organizational inertia can be a blessing, instead of a curse.

Conclusion

This chapter highlighted the crucial role of strategy implementation in accomplishing organizational objectives. Factors such as incentives, performance management systems, well-crafted strategic plans, resources, practices, and leadership styles are key to the successful execution of strategies. These elements are paramount considerations for public and nonprofit organizations in their strategic endeavors. Yet, since strategy

[54] Nickerson and Zenger (2002).

[55] Kucinskas and Zylan (2023).

[56] Bencze (2021).

implementation necessitates a shift from an initial state to an envisioned outcome, observing change management dynamics is imperative.

In this regard, organizations must carefully assess the intricate interplay between internal structures and their external environments (external fit), as well as the synergy, and coherence among the drivers of successful implementation (internal fit). Additionally, the chapter explored how strategy implementation may grapple with organizational inertia, which acts as a two-edged sword. It can either impede the smooth transition of plans into enhanced performance or serve as a protective barrier against the adverse effects of poorly conceived policies that may endanger the organizational capacity to create public value.

References

Andrews, R., & Boyne, G. (2012). Structural change and public service performance: The impact of the reorganization process in English local government. *Public Administration, 90*(2), 297–312.

Andrews, R., Boyne, G. A., Law, J., & Walker, R. M. (2011). Strategy implementation and public service performance. *Administration & Society, 43*(6), 643–671.

Aral, S., Brynjolfsson, E., & Wu, L. (2012). Three-way complementarities: Performance pay, human resource analytics, and information technology. *Management Science, 58*(5), 913–931.

Barney, J. B. (2001). Is the resource-based "view" a useful perspective for strategic management research? Yes. *Academy of Management Review, 26*(1), 41–56.

Barney, J. B. (2012). Purchasing, supply chain management and sustained competitive advantage: The relevance of resource-based theory. *Journal of Supply Chain Management, 48*(2), 3–6.

Barney, J. B., & Zajac, E. J. (1994). Competitive organizational behavior: Toward an organizationally-based theory of competitive advantage. *Strategic Management Journal, 15*(S1), 5–9.

Bencze, M. (2021). Judicial populism and the weberian judge—The strength of judicial resistance against governmental influence in Hungary. *German Law Journal, 22*(7), 1282–1297.

Bresnahan, T. F., Brynjolfsson, E., & Hitt, L. M. (2002). Information technology, workplace organization, and the demand for skilled labor: Firm-level evidence. *The Quarterly Journal of Economics, 117*(1), 339–376.

Brickley, J. A., Smith, C. W., & Zimmerman, J. L. (2001). *Managerial economics and organizational architecture* (2nd ed.). McGraw-Hill.

Bromiley, P., & Rau, D. (2014). Towards a practice-based view of strategy. *Strategic Management Journal, 35*(8), 1249–1256.
Bryson, J. M. (1988). A strategic planning process for public and non-profit organizations. *Long Range Planning, 21*(1), 73–81.
Bryson, J. M. (2018). *Strategic planning for public and nonprofit organizations: A guide to strengthening and sustaining organizational achievement*. Wiley.
Cabral, S. (2017). Reconciling conflicting policy objectives in public contracting: The enabling role of capabilities. *Journal of Management Studies, 54*(6), 823–853.
Carrillo, J. D., & Gromb, D. (2007). Cultural inertia and uniformity in organizations. *The Journal of Law, Economics, & Organization, 23*(3), 743–771.
Cohen, K. J., & Cyert, R. M. (1973). Strategy: Formulation, implementation, and monitoring. *The Journal of Business, 46*(3), 349–367.
Crittenden, V. L., & Crittenden, W. F. (2008). Building a capable organization: The eight levers of strategy implementation. *Business Horizons, 51*(4), 301–309.
Donaldson, L. (2001). *The contingency theory of organizations*: Sage.
Fei, T., & Rainey, H. G. (2003). Total quality management in Malaysian government agencies: Conditions for successful implementation of organizational change. *International Public Management Journal, 6*(2), 145–172.
Friesl, M., Stensaker, I., & Colman, H. L. (2021). Strategy implementation: Taking stock and moving forward. *Long Range Planning, 54*(4), 102064.
George, B. (2021). Successful strategic plan implementation in public organizations: Connecting people, process, and plan (3Ps). *Public Administration Review, 81*(4), 793–798.
Govindarajan, V. (1988). A contingency approach to strategy implementation at the business-unit level: Integrating administrative mechanisms with strategy. *Academy of Management Journal, 31*(4), 828–853.
Guth, W. D., & MacMillan, I. C. (1986). Strategy implementation versus middle management self-interest. *Strategic Management Journal, 7*(4), 313–327.
Hackman, J. R., & Wageman, R. (1995). Total quality management: Empirical, conceptual, and practical issues. *Administrative Science Quarterly, 40*, 309–342.
Hameduddin, T., Fernandez, S., & Demircioglu, M. A. (2020). Conditions for open innovation in public organizations: Evidence from Challenge. gov. *Asia Pacific Journal of Public Administration, 42*(2), 111–131.
Hannan, M. T., & Freeman, J. (1984). Structural inertia and organizational change. *American Sociological Review, 49*(2), 149–164. https://doi.org/10.2307/2095567
Higgins, J. M. (2005). The eight 'S's of successful strategy execution. *Journal of Change Management, 5*(1), 3–13.

Hill, C. W., & Jones, G. R. (2011). *Essentials of strategic management*. Cengage Learning.

Hrebiniak, L. G. (2006). Obstacles to effective strategy implementation. *Organizational Dynamics, 35*(1), 12–31. https://doi.org/10.1016/j.orgdyn.2005.12.001

Kaplan, R. S. (2001). Strategic performance measurement and management in nonprofit organizations. *Nonprofit Management and Leadership, 11*(3), 353–370.

Kucinskas, J., & Zylan, Y. (2023). Walking the Moral Tightrope: Federal civil servants' loyalties, caution, and resistance under the Trump administration. *American Journal of Sociology, 128*(6), 1761–1808.

Lawrence, P. R., & Lorsch, J. W. (1967). *Organization and environment: Managing differentiation and integration*. Richard D. Irwin.

Lynch, S. E., & Mors, M. L. (2019). Strategy implementation and organizational change: How formal reorganization affects professional networks. *Long Range Planning, 52*(2), 255–270. https://doi.org/10.1016/j.lrp.2018.02.003

Mankins, M. C., & Steele, R. (2005). Turning great strategy into great performance. *Harvard Business Review*, p. 2607.

Massoud, M. A., Fayad, R., El-Fadel, M., & Kamleh, R. (2010). Drivers, barriers and incentives to implementing environmental management systems in the food industry: A case of Lebanon. *Journal of Cleaner Production, 18*(3), 200–209.

Milgrom, P., & Roberts, J. (1990). The economics of modern manufacturing: Technology, strategy, and organization. *The American Economic Review*, pp. 511–528.

Naranjo-Gil, D., & Hartmann, F. (2007). How CEOs use management information systems for strategy implementation in hospitals. *Health Policy, 81*(1), 29–41.

Neilson, G. L., Martin, K. L., & Powers, E. (2008). The secrets to successful strategy execution. *Harvard Business Review, 86*(6).

Nickerson, J. A., & Zenger, T. R. (2002). Being efficiently fickle: A dynamic theory of organizational choice. *Organization Science, 13*(5), 547–566.

Noble, C. H. (1999). The eclectic roots of strategy implementation research. *Journal of Business Research, 45*(2), 119–134.

Nutt, P. C. (1986). Tactics of implementation. *Academy of Management Journal, 29*(2), 230–261.

O'Reilly, C. A., Caldwell, D. F., Chatman, J. A., Lapiz, M., & Self, W. (2010). How leadership matters: The effects of leaders' alignment on strategy implementation. *The Leadership Quarterly, 21*(1), 104–113.

Oliveira, C. A., Carneiro, J., & Esteves, F. (2019). Conceptualizing and measuring the "strategy execution" construct. *Journal of Business Research, 105*, 333–344.

Piening, E. P. (2011). Insights into the process dynamics of innovation implementation: The case of public hospitals in Germany. *Public Management Review, 13*(1), 127–157.

Reis, P. R. C., Cabral, S., & Arvate, P. (2023). Fostering agility through public procurement reforms: The role of experienced procurement officers. *International Journal of Public Administration*, 1–12. https://doi.org/10.1080/01900692.2023.2205048

Rogers, P., & Blenko, M. (2006). Who has the D. *Harvard Business Review, 84*(1), 52–61.

Shenhar, A. J. (2001). One size does not fit all projects: Exploring classical contingency domains. *Management Science, 47*(3), 394–414.

Siggelkow, N. (2001). Change in the presence of fit: The rise, the fall, and the renaissance of Liz Claiborne. *The Academy of Management Journal, 44*(4), 838–857. https://doi.org/10.2307/3069418

Teodorovicz, T., Lazzarini, S., Cabral, S., & Nardi, L. (2023). Can public organizations perform like private firms? The role of heterogeneous resources and practices. *Organization Science, 34*(4), 1527–1553.

Vasudeva, G., & Anand, J. (2011). Unpacking absorptive capacity: A study of knowledge utilization from alliance portfolios. *Academy of Management Journal, 54*(3), 611–623.

Wageman, R. (1995). Interdependence and group effectiveness. *Administrative Science Quarterly, 40*, 145–180.

Weiser, A.-K., Jarzabkowski, P., & Laamanen, T. (2020). Completing the adaptive turn: An integrative view of strategy implementation. *Academy of Management Annals, 14*(2), 969–1031.

Young, S., & Macinati, M. S. (2012). Health outsourcing/backsourcing: Case STUDIES in the Australian and Italian health sector. *Public Management Review, 14*(6), 771–794.

Zenger, T. R. (2002). Crafting internal hybrids: Complementarities, common change initiatives, and the team-based organization. *International Journal of the Economics of Business, 9*(1), 79–95.

PART III

Outside the Organizational Boundaries

CHAPTER 8

Stakeholder Management in the Public Interest

For millennia, fishing, collecting, and hunting activities have been central to human existence on this planet. They were essential for providing nutrients crucial to the evolutionary process of humans, particularly during times when agriculture was neither available nor feasible, ensuring survival and adaptation to the environment. In addition to assuring necessary nourishment and the continuity of life in various parts of the planet, these activities remain embedded in the cultural traditions of certain populations. They form an integral part of rituals and celebrations, imparting meaning and influencing the cohesiveness of groups. Even in contemporary times, fishing and hunting continue to serve as sources of revenue for individuals and organizations engaged in profit-oriented activities exploiting natural resources, as well as for governments and other entities integrated into existing supply chains. Furthermore, these activities hold significance for leisure and recreation purposes.

However, the exploitation of fishing, collecting, and hunting activities poses a challenge to ecosystem conservation and threatens the survival of wildlife. The extinction of species, coupled with other irreversible ecological changes resulting from the misuse of natural resources, can impact the well-being of both those directly benefiting from these activities and those residing in regions more distant from the communities surrounding the wildlife.

S. Cabral, *Strategy for Public and Nonprofit Organizations*,
https://doi.org/10.1007/978-3-031-64969-1_8

Typically, the policy and decision-making related to such environmental issues are coordinated by public bodies in the form of departments, commissions, boards, and other arrangements, wherein relevant parties affected by the implemented policies are represented. In theory, these bodies should consist of actors primarily affected by the decisions and individuals with scientific knowledge and technical expertise in wildlife management issues, aiming to balance the interests of groups benefiting from fishing, hunting, and collecting with environmental conservation principles. In practice, however, the problem is more complicated.

In his exploration of agencies responsible for wildlife policy and management organizations in the United States, Martin Nie suggests that conflicts may arise when interested parties are not proportionally represented or when these bodies are influenced by members with clear conflicts of interest. Typically, these members include ranchers, hunters, tourist guides, taxidermists, and other self-oriented actors, who may impede a balanced emphasis on natural resource conservation in decision-making processes. To address issues related to capture, some states have resorted to ballot initiatives to prohibit abusive hunting practices. However, these initiatives have faced criticism as the plebiscitarian atmosphere has heightened adversarial relationships and polarization. Moreover, it has amplified the voices of actors not directly impacted by wildlife decisions, such as urban populations, while potentially neglecting the necessary input from scientists and professionals with expertise in wildlife management. The incorporation of underrepresented yet significant actors is crucial in finding actionable solutions to complex problems involving conflicting demands, as seen in the case of wildlife management. Balancing cultural, economic, and environmental perspectives is essential in informed decision-making.[1]

Like environmental management, healthcare, especially for those in greater need, is a global challenge requiring coordinated efforts from public, private, nonprofit, and multilateral entities. These efforts span across the entire spectrum, encompassing research and development of drugs and vaccines to the delivery of care services through hospitals, clinics, and laboratories. Nonprofit organizations play a leading role in health provision, operating in both developed and developing countries.

[1] Nie (2004).

While these organizations encounter various structural and operational challenges, they can also identify successful configurations to fulfill their mission. Their involvement underscores the interconnected and collaborative nature required to address the complex challenges associated with healthcare on a global scale.

The North Star Alliance, a nonprofit organization dedicated to providing health services to combat the spread of HIV/AIDS in Sub-Saharan Africa, stands as an exemplary model of how nonprofits can effectively contribute to addressing global challenges with the collaboration of diverse stakeholders. HIV/AIDS in Africa disproportionately affects long-distance truck drivers due to their frequent engagement with multiple sexual partners across various locations. Given the nature of their sexual encounters, often involving commercial sex workers, and the limited dissemination of safe sexual practices in the region, curtailing the spread of the disease proves challenging given the mobile nature of both truck drivers and sex workers. In response, North Star Alliance has pioneered an innovative solution by establishing numerous health centers along major roads in countries such as Botswana, the Democratic Republic of the Congo, Eswatini, Kenya, Lesotho, Malawi, Mozambique, South Africa, Tanzania, Uganda, Zambia, and Zimbabwe. These health centers, housed in adapted shipping containers, operate during convenient hours, typically in the afternoons and evenings, to maximize interaction with the targeted populations, offering both preventive and treatment care. Integrated information technology systems enable the seamless transmission of patients' medical records between clinics, facilitating proper treatment and enhancing internal efficiency. Research conducted by Aline Gatignon and colleagues highlights that high-performing North Star clinics, measured by the number of visits, prioritize building relationships with local communities, donors, managers of other clinics, and local civil servants in health bodies. The emphasis on fostering further engagement with relevant actors emerges as a crucial factor contributing to North Star's positive outcomes. This underscores the importance of collaborative efforts and community involvement in achieving impactful results in health interventions on a global scale.[2]

[2] See Gatignon et al. (2023). For further information on North Star and other nonprofit initiatives in the healthcare in Africa, see also Mossman et al. (2017).

The examples provided in environmental management and healthcare underscore the significance of established routines and procedures in navigating relationships with stakeholders who can either positively or negatively impact the achievement of defined objectives. These stakeholders, leveraging their resources and accumulated scientific and technical knowledge, play a pivotal role in contributing to the creation of public value. Effectively managing relationships with various actors, often connected to the focal organization through informal and relational mechanisms rather than formal agreements, is crucial. Additionally, ensuring that relevant parties have a voice becomes imperative in obtaining public democratic values, even when these voices may not align with the preferences of certain organizational members. The two cases highlight the importance of stakeholder management approaches in the pursuit of the public interest.

The stakeholder management movement, originating in the United States in the 1980s, has progressively gained popularity among academics and practitioners in public and nonprofit organizations. Despite its roots in business schools and its initial focus on issues affecting private organizations, the concept has evolved to address the complexities inherent in the public and nonprofit sectors. An in-depth examination of stakeholder management, encompassing its meaning, the diverse attributes within stakeholder theory, the intricate interdependencies among stakeholders, and the processes of recognizing, empowering, and managing relevant stakeholders, proves exceptionally valuable. This exploration is particularly useful for managers interested in formulating effective strategies for public and nonprofit organizations. Moreover, it holds broader relevance for those grappling with solutions to intricate and wicked problems involving multiple actors with distinct preferences and aspirations.

Stakeholder Management: What Is?

For an extended period, the focus of strategic management scholars was predominantly on private for-profit organizations. The primary goal was the achievement of financial gains, addressing the needs of organizational financiers, or shareholders. With shareholders being the main residual claimants of the created value, executives were traditionally directed toward decisions that aimed at maximizing value for the benefit of shareholders. This perspective of shareholder supremacy prevailed among executives without significant challenge until the early 1980s. A pivotal shift occurred when R. Edward Freeman, a philosopher with a keen interest in moral principles in business, challenged this prevailing view. Freeman argued that firms could enhance their overall well-being by broadening their focus beyond shareholders to include stakeholders. In this alternative approach, attention is given not only to those who invest in the organization but also to a wider range of stakeholders, acknowledging their interests and contributions. According to Freeman, in his classical 1984 book[3]: "*a stakeholder in an organization is (by definition) any group or individual who can affect or is affected by the achievement of the organization's objectives*".

Stakeholder theories draw upon several disciplines, including management, economics, law, philosophy, organizational behavior, and ethics. In general, these theories posit that employees, suppliers, customers, governments, and civil society organizations are part of the stakeholder ecosystem and can serve as sources of both value creation and value destruction. This is contingent on how relationships with parties that can affect or be affected by the organization are managed. This is particularly critical in an era where social media can amplify or distort details about stakeholder relationships, potentially leading to scandals with catastrophic consequences or fostering a positive reputation for the implicated organizations. Along these lines, Sinziana Dorobantu, Witold Henisz, and Lite Nartey[4] conducted an analysis of how various social and political stakeholders—such as politicians, NGOs (non-governmental organizations), religious organizations, scientific associations, and artists—responded to critical events involving gold-mining companies operating in developing countries. They found that while influential and visible stakeholders have the capacity to mobilize others and impact shareholder value, negative news about an organization tends to be less amplified when there are stakeholders who were supportive of the organization prior to the negative events. In fact, stakeholders with previously positive beliefs about the focal organization may even endorse the firm's actions and provide context for the accusations against the firm.

While the prevailing perspective of managers as fiduciaries solely responsible for shareholders' interests, rooted in mainstream economics,

[3] With more than 55,000 citations on Google Scholar as of October 2023, his 1984 book, entitled 'Strategic Management: A Stakeholder Approach,' serves as the cornerstone of stakeholder theory. See Freeman (1984).

[4] Dorobantu et al. (2017).

still holds sway, and guides a profit maximization focus on many organizations, there is a growing consensus that investing in stakeholder relationships is essential for safeguarding shareholder interests. This does not mean discarding financial goals or other instrumental objectives; instead, addressing stakeholders is seen as crucial to making profit maximization sustainable. According to the stakeholder approach, value creation for shareholders is achievable by offering goods and services that clients appreciate, establishing robust relationships with suppliers to ensure inputs with the required quality and reasonable costs, managing human resources effectively to keep employees creative and motivated, and paying attention to environmental and social aspects that impact communities and society at large.

The strategic management literature provides compelling evidence that heightened managerial attention to the interests of stakeholders during policy- and decision-making is consistently linked to increased financial performance and other strategic outcomes. Caroline Flammer has uncovered a causal relationship between stakeholder-oriented actions, such as the adoption of Corporate Social Responsibility (CSR) practices, and various financial performance indicators, including return on assets, net profit margin, and return on equity. Her research also shows that increased engagement with stakeholders can resonate with key stakeholders. For instance, employees respond to CSR practices with heightened labor productivity, while clients tend to express appreciation for stakeholder-oriented actions by increasing their purchases. Consequently, these actions contribute to firms achieving sales growth.[5]

Emanuele Bettinazzi and Emilie Feldman's research reveals that organizations with a stakeholder orientation exhibit different responses in managing stakeholder conflicts compared to their shareholder-oriented counterparts. Analyzing a sample of publicly listed firms in the United States, they discovered that a stakeholder orientation assists firms in avoiding the use of divestitures as a mechanism to eliminate contentious activities. In contrast, organizations with lower stakeholder orientation demonstrate a higher rate of divestitures, indicating that the nature of the relationship with stakeholders can indeed influence corporate

[5] Flammer (2015).

strategies.[6] The inclination of managers to consider the interests of stakeholders in decision-making also has implications for innovation-related outcomes. Companies with a robust stakeholder orientation tend to generate a higher number of patents and citations per patent. Strengthening connections with key stakeholders, such as customers, may enable stakeholder-oriented organizations to garner additional support and foster an innovative environment.[7]

The sentences above suggest that organizations can adopt a stakeholder orientation for instrumental reasons: organizations can satisfy their financial objectives by simply paying more attention to other actors than shareholders who have a stake and are affected by the organization's decisions or have the power to affect, positively or negatively, the focal organization. Briefly, the instrumental view posits that creating value for stakeholders who are not shareholders is a crucial condition for overall value creation that benefits stakeholders.[8] This perspective brought stakeholder theories closer to the business community. Indeed, by linking stakeholder relationships with economic performance, this instrumental approach to stakeholder management aligns with the strategic management tradition that emphasizes financial considerations. To a significant extent, these connections have played a role in strengthening the influence of stakeholders not only in strategy but also in corporate finance.[9]

However, in addition to the economic and instrumental dimensions and their corresponding value creation concerns, stakeholder theories also incorporate social and moral dimensions that determine what managers must and must not do. The emphasis on the management of relationships and on fairness in decision-making is central to stakeholder theories.[10] In fact, with stakeholder relationships as the unit of analysis, classic stakeholder theory departs from the idea that moral and normative ethics should guide managerial action. Instead of beginning with canonical questions such as "*where are going*" or "*which business should we be in*,"

[6] Bettinazzi and Feldman (2021).

[7] Flammer and Kacperczyk (2016).

[8] Donaldson and Preston (1995).

[9] Recent works in corporate finance have been examining the effects of the enactment of constituency statutes that incorporate stakeholder-oriented policies on financial indicators. See Ni et al. (2020) and Chowdhury et al. (2021).

[10] Bridoux and Stoelhorst (2022).

the primary question to be responded by managers should be "*what do we stand for?*".[11]

This normative question allows the organization to examine the moral grounds guiding managers in decision-making. Within such a normative framework, business and ethics are not seen as separate but rather as a set of jointly integrated decisions. In this context, both business and ethics coexist, and decision-makers are accountable for the consequences of their actions. In this sense, the achievement of organizational purpose and the value created would result from the capacity to manage and balance the diverse set of stakeholder relationships.[12] As proposed by Thomas Jones and Andrew Wicks, convergence between instrumental and normative approaches is possible by anchoring instrumental interests in moral principles.[13] This combination is helpful in the efforts to make stakeholder reasoning applicable beyond for-profit organizations. It is particularly relevant for public, nonprofit, or dual mission organizations that aim to address financial and social outcomes.

Stakeholder Management Beyond Profit-Oriented Organizations

Stakeholder theory was originally developed to tackle significant challenges faced by for-profit firms and to redefine the relationships between business and society within the capitalist system by incorporating the interests of stakeholders into decision-making. It is a managerial theory primarily focused on value creation for businesses, with financial performance indicators serving as the dependent variables.

While instrumentalism, which focuses on identifying connections between stakeholder relationships and economic objectives, plays a leading role in the stakeholder approach,[14] according to the original stakeholder theory developed by Edward Freeman and coauthors, stakeholder-related activities are understood as normative. In this view,

[11] Freeman (1984).

[12] See Freeman (1994). In this paper, Ed Freeman argues for the integration of business and ethics, rejecting the notion that these concepts are distinct. He challenges the so-called "Separation Thesis": the idea that business decisions lack moral content and those moral decisions have no business implications.

[13] Jones and Wicks (1999).

[14] Donaldson and Preston (1995).

there is no separation between ethical and business decisions; managers must pay attention to stakeholder relationships because it is an integral part of the moral principles guiding managerial action. Therefore, the coercive action of government bodies to enforce something considered a moral obligation does not make sense because managing stakeholder relationships is the right thing to do for free managers who act responsibly. While the original stakeholder theory has libertarian foundations and is explicitly intended to address issues in business and for-profit firms, the application of stakeholder principles extends widely beyond the for-profit context.[15]

Along these lines, two major streams distinct from original stakeholder theories have emerged. The first stream involves studies of stakeholder management in the context of public and nonprofit organizations, originating from the fields of public administration and public management scholarships. The second stream encompasses the efforts of strategic management researchers dedicated to reconciling financial, social, and environmental goals through improved stakeholder relationships. These efforts are orchestrated by various organizational arrangements, including firms, nonprofits, and cross-sector collaborations, aimed at addressing the so-called grand challenges defined by the United Nations. In both cases, the dependent variables affected by stakeholder relationships involve aspects that are not constrained to financial and economic objectives.

[15] Edward Freeman and Robert Philips (2002) argue that the original stakeholder management theory, as conceived by Freeman in his seminal book, is essentially libertarian and is grounded in the principles of freedom, property rights, and positive obligation. They express a preference for a more circumscribed domain for stakeholder management, particularly within the context of capitalism based on Westernized moral grounds, thus limiting the scope of their theorizing to a specific set of business environments. However, conceptions of property rights and individualism vary substantially across the globe. For example, even in Canada, a developed nation, some indigenous communities have a different conception of the meaning of property rights and view themselves as land stewards rather than landowners (Murphy & Arenas, 2010). Stakeholder relationships failing to incorporate these different cultural traits can be problematic. The so-called "New Stakeholder Theory" is an attempt to broaden the scope of stakeholder theories by considering different moral stances that shape stakeholder relationships (McGahan, 2023).

Stakeholder Approaches and Public Management

Although the original works on stakeholder management were part of the strategic management field, its assimilation into the strategy mainstream was not automatic. In the 1980s and the first half of the 1990s, strategy research evolved toward economic grounds, with market competition and shareholder maximization as central aspects for social and economic growth. Simultaneously, stakeholder theories challenged the Gordon Gekko's "greed is good" way of thinking and advocated those managers' duties were about nurturing relationships with stakeholders in a balanced way.[16] The social and moral dimensions explicitly present in stakeholder theories, along with their descriptive and normative orientation, were not aligned with the positive and empirically oriented trends in strategic management research during the decades of 1980 and 1990.[17]

Coincidentally, stakeholder approaches were received with enthusiasm and gained popularity among public management scholars and policymakers. During the same period when strategy scholars and their students were focused on financial and economically oriented topics, several governments have implemented to infuse private-sector principles into the public sector under the umbrella of the New Public Management (NPM) movement. By emphasizing the role of public managers in addressing citizens' needs through the implementation of managerial practices designed to improve the delivery of public services, these reforms were supposed to make governments more responsive to the demands of a broader range of constituencies.[18]

The managerial orientation of stakeholder theory aligned well with NPM principles and facilitated the dissemination of stakeholder management ideas in public organizations, even though stakeholder theories

[16] The 1987 movie 'Wall Street,' directed by Oliver Stone, portrays the 1980s era when free market ideas were central. The expression "greed, for lack of a better word, is good", said by Gordon Gekko (interpreted by Michael Douglas, who won the Academy Award for Best Actor), encapsulates the profit-centered and shareholder orientation prevailing in the year 1980 and still present today in corporate finance and also in some streams of the strategic management field.

[17] Wicks and Harrison (2017) and Bridoux and Stoelhorst (2022) offer valuable contributions that informs the points of divergence, convergence, and reconvergence between the strategic management and stakeholder theory literatures.

[18] For a further understanding of New Public Management principles, see Osborne and Gaebler (1992) and Hood (1991).

were originally conceived to focus on private firms' problems. Another point of convergence is related to the fact that most public problems affecting different populations require an understanding of the different parties (or stakeholders) that affect and are affected by the decision-making process. John Bryson, one of the pioneers in establishing bridges between strategy and public management, posits that stakeholder principles were always central in public policies, as it is widely documented that failures in addressing stakeholder concerns tend to result in lower performance in public services. He also emphasizes that taking stakeholders into account in problem-solving efforts, managing stakeholders and their networks is crucial for public organizations to find politically and technically acceptable solutions for problems that affect large populations and to avoid the opportunity costs of inadequate performance or the disasters that follow when public organizations fail to address the interests of key stakeholders.[19] Similarly, Lazzarini and his coauthors find that stakeholder orientation, characterized by the degree to which public managers establish communication channels to solicit input from various actors influencing or influenced by government-led initiatives, holds particular significance for governments aiming to carry out public activities internally, with minimal involvement of external actors. This is contingent upon public units fostering internal collaborations within the public bureaucracy.[20]

Stakeholder management approaches have proven particularly useful in addressing complex issues such as water management. Analyzing the case of a severe drought in Australia that led to ecological devastation and water shortages for agriculture and human consumption, Rob Skinner illustrated the importance of engaging stakeholders, including affected communities, scientists, and environmentalists. This engagement was crucial in developing a government plan to return a significant amount of water to the Murray-Darling Basin River system, the largest interconnected system of rivers in Australia, covering important regions like Queensland, New South Wales, and Victoria. To address the problem, public authorities proposed a technically informed solution involving the construction of a large desalination plant, upgrades in the water systems to save water, and an interregional pipeline. However, despite the proposal

[19] John M. Bryson (2004).

[20] Lazzarini et al. (2020).

being technically and scientifically sound, it did not receive ample support due to the lack of a massive and timely community engagement process. Despite the importance of evidence-based solutions for dealing with complex problems, such as water governance in the context of climate change, establishing collaborative arenas for discussion and deliberation with relevant stakeholders is crucial in democratic societies, especially when trade-offs exist.[21]

The support of stakeholders is also crucial for the successful implementation of public policies. Existing stakeholders can have distinct roles during the implementation phase, and their importance varies according to the type of strategic initiative. For instance, evidence from US municipalities[22] suggests that the successful implementation of polices with high complexity and high priority requires the support of communities in all project phases from planning, execution, and integration, while elected officials' support is restricted to the initial phases. In these initiatives, the support of senior executives of municipalities is key when new practices become incorporated into the municipality's routines. The support of top executives is also relevant to sustaining the new initiatives over time. The engagement of affected employees is relevant for initiatives related to internal innovation, with high complexity but low priority.

Likewise, stakeholder approaches have also been useful for nonprofit organizations delivering public services. Managing stakeholders with multiple objectives is key to these organizations achieving improved performance and demonstrating to broader audiences their ability to create public value. Bernadette Best, Sandra Moffett, and Rodney McAdam conducted an in-depth analysis of a nonprofit consortium comprising seven organizations contracted by a UK (United Kingdom) government unit to deliver employability services to individuals with disabilities and help them secure or retain employment. The authors offer compelling evidence that efforts to manage stakeholder relationships were crucial for improved value creation in terms of support to service users, monetary gains, and alignment with government strategy. Evolved relationships with stakeholders with utilitarian and symbolic power helped the consortium members secure the necessary resources and support to implement the strategies. These relationships also helped nonprofits

[21] Skinner (2017).

[22] Mitchell (2022).

achieve instrumental goals, like contract extensions and reputational gains.[23]

Firms and Collective Action Problems: A New Stakeholder Orientation

Besides their dissemination among public and nonprofit scholars to address problems affecting communities, stakeholder theories have also been invoked by strategic management scholars to further investigate questions related to value creation and value appropriation in the public interest. Departing from organizational economics arguments that place stakeholder claims as central in the value creation process, this emergent literature, coined as new stakeholder theory (NST),[24] evolves from the original stakeholder theories focused on morally and instrumentally based relationships among groups possessing stakes in organizations, as early developed by Edward Freeman and coauthors[25] and subsequent works, such as those from Thomas Donaldson and Lee Preston,[26] Ronald Mitchell, Bradley Agle, and Donna Wood,[27] among others.

Like original stakeholder theories, NST shares the idea that stakeholders are heterogeneous and must be managed according to their salience, specifically in terms of power, legitimacy, and urgency attributes (see more about stakeholder identification and salience in the subsequent sections). Both conceptions also converge on the importance of organizational purpose. The question of "what an organization stands for" a steppingstone of original stakeholder theories, is like a major concern of NST, that the essence, aspirations, and core values of the organization should guide stakeholder relationships and value creation actions for the organization's stakeholders.

A major divergence between the two fields is related to the centrality of social and environmental issues. Aligned with a perspective that views

[23] Best et al. (2019).

[24] For further details about new stakeholder theory please refer to McGahan (2021, 2023) and George et al. (2023).

[25] See Edward Freeman (1984, 1994) and Freeman and Phillips (2002).

[26] Donaldson and Preston (1995).

[27] Mitchell et al. (1997).

strategic management as a domain focused on investigating issues pertinent to firms and their managers, the libertarian leanings of certain proponents of the original stakeholder theory, such as Edward Freeman and Robert Philips, restrict the applicability of this theory to contexts beyond business firms.[28] Government is explicitly seen by original stakeholder theories and as an entity that offers unwanted advice (kibitzer).[29] In the prospects for future developments and extensions of original stakeholder theories, public policy challenges are restricted to normative propositions advocating changes in the role of government toward a facilitator of value creation, focusing on tasks that save taxpayers money, such as campaigns on preventing smoking and actions to spur innovation and encourage infrastructure development. To address public distrust of business activities and their disconnections from morality, firms could propose policies that attach executive compensation to "stake options", contingent on the results reflecting how firms impact their major stakeholders.[30]

By assuming that value appropriation is endogenously determined by the value created by stakeholders and the organization orchestrates the distribution of the value that is produced along with enfranchised stakeholders, NST enlarges the scope of original stakeholder theories by moving the focus of strategy theory and practice beyond firms and their managers. In light of the recent advancements in strategy and public management, which have shown a growing reliance on evidence-based recommendations, testing hypothesized relationships using experimental and quasi-experimental methods is crucial. This evidence-based approach helps to comprehend the potential outcomes for stakeholders in the absence of stakeholder-oriented actions by the focal organization, as well as the potential consequences of actions taken by stakeholders that could influence not only the responses of focal organizations but also the perceptions of these organizations by other stakeholders. Such endeavors enable a more robust understanding of the conditions under which value is generated (and captured) through stakeholder relationships. This concern with rigorous empirical tests and enhanced analytical efforts highlights an important distinctive feature between works built upon this

[28] Edward Freeman and Phillips (2002).

[29] Edward Freeman (1984, p. 60).

[30] Edward Freeman (2017).

research stream and those developed by original stakeholders and public and nonprofit scholars.[31]

Some recent works align well with the current trends toward more rigorous management of stakeholder relationships. With the support of quasi-experimental methods (regression discontinuity design) and in-depth fieldwork, Leandro Pongeluppe analyzed the context of Brazilian favelas (slums) to understand how the accumulated knowledge about settings inhabited by socially- and economically disenfranchised individuals help firms develop stakeholder relationships that enfranchise these communities. He demonstrated that while, on average, e-commerce firms are more likely to refuse orders and charge higher prices for delivering goods to consumers inside favelas, firms with a stronger stakeholder orientation treat disenfranchised customers more equitably. In fact, e-commerce firms with physical stores that cultivate relationships with their employees and consumers living in favelas are less likely to refuse an order from favela customers and charge less for delivering goods, aligning with the idea that firm strategies can help, at least at the micro-level, address some of the United Nations' Sustainable Development Goals (SDGs).[32]

The way firms govern stakeholder relationships with local communities can also influence reactions from shareholders. Understanding under which circumstances financiers positively evaluate firms' actions to gain the support of stakeholders with the potential of triggering social conflicts and media scandals are important for better understanding value creation drivers for both shareholders and stakeholders. Sinziana Dorobantu and Kate Odziemkowska examined abnormal returns of mining firms in Canada after signing community benefits agreements (CBA) with indigenous communities to find mutually acceptable solutions between firms and communities on the appropriation of the value created by mining activities. These agreements allow original inhabitants from Canada to be compensated for both the natural resources they provide, and social and environmental problems related to mining activities. The authors found that short-term cumulative abnormal returns are higher when firms sign contracts with communities exhibiting stronger property rights and with communities with a record of previous mobilization that may

[31] McGahan (2023).

[32] Pongeluppe (2022).

increase the costs of conflict. While the firm's efforts to sign an agreement with communities in these conditions are appreciated by investors, investors react negatively to agreements signed with communities that initiated legal actions against governments and firms in the past, probably because these communities can initiate legal actions in the future or even renegotiate the agreements ex-post, eventually imposing value losses to shareholders.[33]

Other works highlight the importance of considering different stakeholder claims when designing policies. In a joint work with Paulo Arvate, Anita McGahan, and Paulo Reis, I have noted that effective policies to reduce lethality against women require intersectional approaches that are able to capture the specific needs of even groups that are more disenfranchised. While women police stations with institutional mandates, routines, and women representation can reduce homicides against women on average, these results are concentrated on women who self-identified as white. Women self-identified as black or brown only benefit from these stakeholder-oriented organizations when living in cities with higher educational standards and urban infrastructures.[34] These results reinforce the importance of anticipating the needs of disenfranchised stakeholders and the conditions under which these needs are met at the initial stages of policymaking.

In the same vein, Carlos Inoue finds that elected officials strategically manipulate state-owned enterprises in the water sector before elections by increasing employment levels at the expense of financial performance in election years to obtain votes. These effects are stronger for organizations serving economically disenfranchised communities and attenuated for organizations with private investors, showing that actions to benefit a group of stakeholders can have consequences on other groups and are moderated by organizational and community attributes.[35]

A still pending and critical issue in the literature is the definition of which stakeholders must be enfranchised, i.e., which stakeholders have a formal (or informal) mandate or voice to influence the decisions and the outcomes of the decisions taken. Should all stakeholders be included irrespective of their contributions to value creation? Whose and when

[33] Dorobantu and Odziemkowska (2017).

[34] Arvate et al. (2022).

[35] Inoue (2020).

should stakeholders be enfranchised? Is it possible to allocate more voice or power to some stakeholders and less to others? These questions are critical for some sectors, like mega infrastructure projects in which the enfranchisement of stakeholders like communities, watchdog agencies, politicians, and prosecutors is one of the main sources of cost overrun and project delays. The timing in which stakeholders will be enfranchised in these projects is a double-edged sword. On one hand, anticipating the enfranchisement for the initial stages before project approval and securing funding can inflate project costs and thwart the project viability. On the other hand, enfranchisement of stakeholders at a later stage can lead to unforeseen costs that can jeopardize the legitimacy of the initiative.[36] These facts reinforce the importance of managing stakeholders for instrumental performance as well as for normative aspects related to probity concerns, both significant issues in public procurement and in cross-sector collaborations designed to deliver public services.[37]

Stakeholder Analysis: The Identification Issue

The first step for organizations aiming to adequately manage stakeholder relationships is the identification of the boundaries on stakeholder claims. This requires the identification of who are the relevant stakeholders, their stakes, interests, relative power, the legitimacy of their relationships with the organization, and the extent to which they can affect the organization or be affected by the organization's decisions.[38] The ability to identify stakeholders becomes even more crucial considering the moral components on which stakeholder theories are grounded. In this case, choices are not between illegitimate and legitimate claims but normally between legitimate and legitimate claims.

[36] Nuno Gil (2023) offers a pertinent reflection on the importance of stakeholder relationships for mega infrastructure projects. His analysis moves beyond crystallized ideas that insufficient performance is either due to deficient management or corruption. Rather, he points out the importance of considering the role of the institutional environment and stakeholder enfranchisement decisions on project outcomes.

[37] Refer to Williamson (1999), Baum and McGahan (2013), and Cabral et al. (2013) for a detailed discussion on probity concerns related to the involvement of nongovernmental stakeholders in the provision of public services.

[38] See McGahan (2020).

The existing trade-offs between claims that may both be legitimate make it more difficult to accommodate tensions in settings where resources to be allocated are scarce, as well as the attention of executives. This complicates the decision-making process. Given the several possible courses of action and the subsequent strategic implications, the establishment of routines to identify who the relevant stakeholders are and the type of correspondent strategies for the diverse types of stakeholders is critical for effective stakeholder management.

The Power-Grid Model

Original stakeholder theories emphasize the importance of mapping stakeholders based on their ability to transform reality (power) and their interests (stakes). In his seminal book, Edward Freeman divides power into three dimensions (formal, economic, and political) and stakes into equity, economic, and influencing stakes. In this view, shareholders are considered stakeholders with formal power and equity stakes, while unions can be perceived as stakeholders with economic power, as a strike can disrupt operations and impede the value creation process, and with economic stakes because union members are affected by the organization's decisions on their salaries.[39]

Building upon Freeman's "Power-Interest Grid", Fran Eden and Colin Ackerman provide a tool to move beyond understanding the stakeholder environment and assist managers in proactively managing their stakeholders.[40]

They propose a 2 × 2 matrix that combines high and low levels of power and interest. In the NE corner (high interest and high power) are the stakeholders labeled as "players", deserving sustained management attention as they can either support or frustrate strategic intents. In the NW corner, it features the group of "subjects", referring to stakeholders that require management action to either increase their power to make them players or neutralize them to prevent actions that undermine organizational goals. In the SW corner are the "context-setters" (high power and low interest) who can influence the organization's future. These stakeholders need management actions to make them aware of the

[39] See Edward Freeman (1984), Chapter 3.

[40] Ackermann and Eden (2011, p. 182).

organization and potentially increase their interest, converting them into players. Lastly, the SE corner holds the "crowd", comprised of actors with low power and low interest in the strategy outcomes. They can be seen as potential stakeholders or even as non-stakeholders. In this case, managers must analyze the feasibility of actions to increase their power to influence the strategy or their interest in the organization.[41]

Figure 8.1, adapted from the work of Ackermann and Eden, illustrates the stakeholder power-interest grid concerning the decision to open (or not) local schools during the COVID-19 pandemic.[42] This decision, critical for various governments worldwide, requires a delicate balance among the interests of numerous stakeholders, including students, families, education departments, health authorities, faculty, staff, and other entities. Although the decision to reopen schools for the continuity of safe educational activities was, to a significant extent, a technical matter informed by health authorities, decision-makers endowed with the power to decide and influence the diverse and competing outcomes of this decision must not only map the relevant stakeholders but also determine their relative positions to guide future managerial actions.

In this example, public authorities in the executive branch (e.g., mayors) and heads of education and health departments emerge as powerful and interested actors, categorizing them as players. Conversely, students, faculty, staff, families, and owners of private schools, while highly interested, are subjects with limited power to influence decisions. Context-setters, such as other public authorities (state governors, the president, or prime minister), judges, and the media, have the potential to shape the decisions of players and empower (or disempower) subjects, thereby increasing the likelihood of having their voices heard. There were instances where mayors advocated for reopening schools despite uncertainties about the pandemic, but they were constrained by context-setters who presented arguments to subjects opposing the idea of reopening schools in unsafe conditions. Context-setters also heightened the interest

[41] While Ackerman and Eden's model is particularly useful for stakeholder analysis involving a single decision, it offers limited insights when multiple decisions are at stake (pun unintended). In such cases, John Bryson (2004) recommends the stakeholder-issue diagram. After mapping the stakeholders and their interests in specific issues, managers can identify stakeholders with similar or dissimilar interests on various issues. This enables the identification of potential areas of alignment (and misalignment) among stakeholders, allowing managers to pinpoint potential areas for cooperation or conflict.

[42] I thank Marcelo Marchesini for this example.

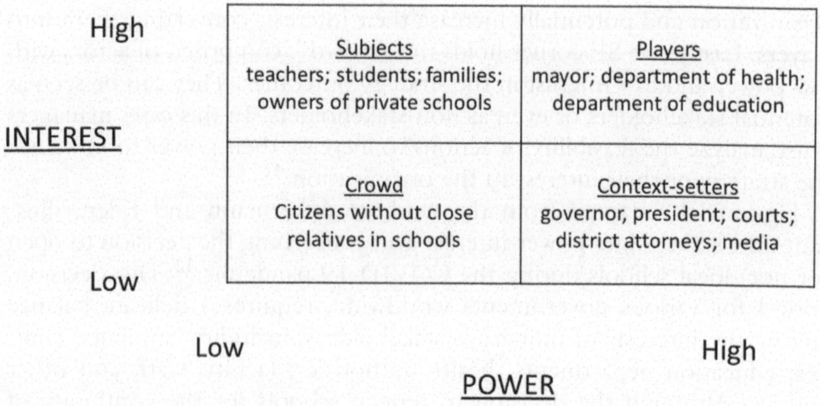

Fig. 8.1 Power-interest grid—example of the decision of reopening schools during the COVID-19 pandemic

of stakeholders with initially low interest and power, transforming these non-stakeholders into advocates prioritizing public health and sanitary aspects in decision-making.

The Stakeholder Identification and Salience Model

While power-grid models are valuable for classifying and prioritizing stakeholders along with their corresponding claims, these models do not consider the dynamic nature of stakeholders' roles over time. They also ignore how urgent the claims of stakeholders are.

Ronald Mitchell, Bradley Agle, and Donna Wood advance the theory of stakeholder identification by incorporating dynamic aspects to discern "who and what really counts", thereby influencing both managerial attention and responses to stakeholder claims. An extensive understanding of who the relevant stakeholders are and why they matter is crucial for reacting to or anticipating actions that could potentially challenge organizational performance and survival. According to their model, stakeholder salience should be assessed beyond the power and interest dimensions.

Instead, the salience of a stakeholder results from the combination of three attributes: power, legitimacy, and urgency.[43]

Stakeholders that are powerful (those who can impose their will in the relationship), legitimated (those who have a socially accepted claim on the organization), and with time-sensitive and critical claims (urgency) are considered *decisive* stakeholders and part of the dominant coalition, requiring full priority from managers to address their claims. Similarly, stakeholders possessing one or two of these attributes are also important and must be identified and managed accordingly. Latent stakeholders, those who possess one of these attributes, can be *dormant* (with power but without legitimate and urgent claims), *discretionary* (with legitimate claims but without power and urgency), or *demanding* (with an urgent claim but without power and legitimacy attributes), and they require different actions.[44] Equally, expectant stakeholders, such as those who can have a potential relationship with the organization because they possess two out of the three attributes, require special attention. For instance, a powerful and legitimate stakeholder (*dominant*), such as the corporate board of directors, may have formal mechanisms to make their claims heard, while their demands are not urgent. Likewise, *dependent* stakeholders with urgency and legitimacy attributes but without the power to impose their will, like communities affected by environmental disasters, differ from *dangerous* stakeholders with power and urgent attributes but with claims that are not legitimate, like employees who can promote sabotage in the firm's operations for illegitimate reasons. Identifying

[43] With almost 20,000 citations on google scholar as of November 2023, the paper by Mitchell et al. (1997) is a landmark in the stakeholder management literature. It explains in detail how managers can identify stakeholders and assess their salience, serving as the foundation for subsequent theoretical and empirical efforts in the field.

[44] Mitchell et al. (1997) provide an interesting example highlighting the differences among the different groups of stakeholders they propose and the potential consequences of their actions. A picketer standing in the organization's headquarters (a demanding stakeholder) requires a different degree of attention and different actions than a dormant stakeholder who can use latent power to promote actions that may challenge the organizational reputation (e.g., a fired employee making public denouncements in the media about moral and sexual harassment in the organization). The capacity for stakeholder management in terms of anticipating these possibilities is crucial for organizations aiming to manage stakeholders effectively. For further discussions about stakeholder management for private firms, refer to Freeman (1984). For insights into the importance of stakeholder management in the context of public and nonprofit organizations, see Cabral et al. (2019).

stakeholders according to attributes of power, legitimacy, and urgency becomes even more critical when stakeholders can change their status and acquire a missing attribute—a dependent stakeholder can transform into a definitive stakeholder if powers are granted to them by external entities such as courts and government bodies.

Table 8.1 provides a summary of the stakeholder identification and salience model proposed by Ronald Mitchell and his colleagues. This model serves as a guide for managers, aiding in the allocation of both resources and attention, and assisting them in prioritizing the various, and oftentimes competing, stakeholder claims.

The dynamism inherent in the model proposed by Mitchell and colleagues is unique. The model serves as a valuable tool to enhance our understanding of how the stakeholder landscape is shaped and how managers can effectively respond to and anticipate stakeholder claims, ensuring the attainment of strategic objectives and organizational survival. Despite these advancements, the model faces criticism for its lack of a moral stance and its omission of normative aspects, which are central to original stakeholder theories. In a recent statement, the authors contend that, despite their intention to provide a descriptive rather than normative model to help managers dynamically identify various stakeholders, they refute the critique suggesting that their approach may discourage managers from considering disenfranchised or illegitimate

Table 8.1 Stakeholder typology based on power, legitimacy, and urgency attributes

Stakeholder Attributes				
Power	Legitimacy	Urgency	Type of Stakeholder	
X	X	X	Highly salient stakeholders	Definitive stakeholders
X	–	–	Latent stakeholders (low saliency)	Dormant Stakeholders
–	X	–		Dominant Stakeholders
–	–	X		Demanding Stakeholders
X	X	–	Latent stakeholders (moderate salience)	Dominant Stakeholders
–	X	X		Dependent Stakeholders
X	–	X		Dangerous Stakeholders
–	–	–	Non-stakeholders	

stakeholders.[45] Efforts are required to integrate normative approaches into future stakeholder theorizing, with performance-oriented perspectives. This integration is essential to prevent illegitimate behavior and to refine the identification of stakeholders that should be included or excluded. Normative and instrumental approaches in stakeholder management should be seen as complementary, rather than as substitutes for each other.[46]

Conclusion

The notion that organizations should consider stakeholder claims, either as a crucial condition for achieving their strategic objectives or as the morally right course of action, is well-established in the field of strategic management. Despite the initial intentions of original stakeholder theories, which limited their scope to for-profit firms, mapping stakeholders and categorizing them based on specific attributes has also become fundamental for practitioners in public and nonprofit organizations.

While debates about 'who and what really counts' and the challenges of stakeholder enfranchisement are still ongoing, there is a consensus that value creation is directly associated with appropriate stakeholder management processes. These processes include actions to identify stakeholders, respond to their claims, enfranchise those aligned with the organizational purpose, and eventually neutralize actors that thwart the attainment of strategic goals. Returning to the example at the beginning of this chapter: Are urban populations that are distant from wildlife conservation units more legitimate stakeholders than ranchers and tourist guides directly affected by conservation policies or their absence? Which interests should policies be responsive to—economic, socioenvironmental? Is it possible to balance these existing claims and find a scientifically informed account for conflicting interests?

Answers to these questions are attainable with the support of stakeholder management theories. However, providing effective responses necessitates an understanding of both the boundary conditions and the causal mechanisms under which claims can be balanced. It also requires

[45] See Wood et al. (2021) for an overview of the progress made and challenges posed by the original model of stakeholder identification and salience.

[46] There are efforts to integrate normative and instrumental perspectives in stakeholder management theories, as explored in Lazzarini (2022).

knowledge of how stakeholders can be engaged and respond in line with organizational goals. These are still pending issues that can be addressed by the theoretical and empirical efforts of strategic management and public administration scholars in future research, with the hope of reconciling normative and performance-oriented approaches.

References

Ackermann, F., & Eden, C. (2011). Strategic management of stakeholders: Theory and practice. *Long Range Planning, 44*(3), 179–196.

Arvate, P., Cabral, S., Mcgahan, A. M., & Reis, P. R. (2022). Structural advocacy organizations and intersectional outcomes: Effects of women's police stations on female homicides. *Public Administration Review, 82*(3), 503–521. https://doi.org/10.1111/puar.13478

Baum, J. A., & McGahan, A. M. (2013). The reorganization of legitimate violence: The contested terrain of the private military and security industry during the post-cold war era. *Research in Organizational Behavior, 33*, 3–37.

Best, B., Moffett, S., & McAdam, R. (2019). Stakeholder salience in public sector value co-creation. *Public Management Review, 21*(11), 1707–1732.

Bettinazzi, E. L., & Feldman, E. R. (2021). Stakeholder orientation and divestiture activity. *Academy of Management Journal, 64*(4), 1078–1096.

Bridoux, F., & Stoelhorst, J. (2022). Stakeholder theory, strategy, and organization: Past, present, and future. *Strategic Organization, 20*(4), 797–809.

Bryson, J. M. (2004). What to do when stakeholders matter: Stakeholder identification and analysis techniques. *Public Management Review, 6*(1), 21–53.

Cabral, S., Lazzarini, S. G., & De Azevedo, P. F. (2013). Private entrepreneurs in public services: A longitudinal examination of outsourcing and statization of prisons. *Strategic Entrepreneurship Journal, 7*(1), 6–25.

Cabral, S., Mahoney, J. T., McGahan, A. M., & Potoski, M. (2019). Value creation and value appropriation in public and nonprofit organizations. *Strategic Management Journal, 40*(4), 465–475. https://doi.org/10.1002/smj.3008

Chowdhury, R., Doukas, J. A., & Park, J. C. (2021). Stakeholder orientation and the value of cash holdings: Evidence from a natural experiment. *Journal of Corporate Finance, 69*, 102029.

Donaldson, T., & Preston, L. E. (1995). The stakeholder theory of the corporation: Concepts, evidence, and implications. *Academy of Management Review, 20*(1), 65–91.

Dorobantu, S., Henisz, W. J., & Nartey, L. (2017). Not all sparks light a fire: Stakeholder and shareholder reactions to critical events in contested markets. *Administrative Science Quarterly, 62*(3), 561–597.

Dorobantu, S., & Odziemkowska, K. (2017). Valuing stakeholder governance: Property rights, community mobilization, and firm value. *Strategic Management Journal, 38*(13), 2682–2703. https://doi.org/10.1002/smj.2675

Flammer, C. (2015). Does corporate social responsibility lead to superior financial performance? A regression discontinuity approach. *Management Science, 61*(11), 2549–2568.

Flammer, C., & Kacperczyk, A. (2016). The impact of stakeholder orientation on innovation: Evidence from a natural experiment. *Management Science, 62*(7), 1982–2001.

Freeman, R. E. (1984). *Strategic management: A stakeholder approach*. Pitman.

Freeman, R. E. (1994). The politics of stakeholder theory: Some future directions. *Business Ethics Quarterly, 4*(4), 409–421. https://doi.org/10.2307/3857340

Freeman, R. E. (2017). Five challenges to stakeholder theory: A report on research in progress. In *Stakeholder management* (pp. 1–20). Emerald Publishing Limited.

Freeman, R. E., & Phillips, R. A. (2002). Stakeholder theory: A libertarian defense. *Business Ethics Quarterly, 12*(3), 331–349.

Gatignon, A., Clement, J., Pongeluppe, L. S., & Wassenhove, L. V. (2023). *Resource-poor but network-rich: A configurational approach to stakeholder engagement for scaling social inovvation*. Working paper.

George, G., Haas, M. R., McGahan, A. M., Schillebeeckx, S. J., & Tracey, P. (2023). Purpose in the for-profit firm: A review and framework for management research. *Journal of Management, 49*(6), 1841–1869.

Gil, N. A. (2023). Cracking the megaproject puzzle: A stakeholder perspective? *International Journal of Project Management, 41*(3), 102455.

Hood, C. (1991). A public management for all seasons? *Public Administration, 69*(1), 3–19.

Inoue, C. (2020). Election cycles and organizations: How politics shapes the performance of state-owned enterprises over time. *Administrative Science Quarterly, 65*(3), 677–709.

Jones, T. M., & Wicks, A. C. (1999). Convergent stakeholder theory. *The Academy of Management Review, 24*(2), 206–221. https://doi.org/10.2307/259075

Lazzarini, S. G. (2022). The strategic imperative: Do we need moral considerations in strategic theories of stakeholder engagement? Available at SSRN.

Lazzarini, S. G., Pongeluppe, L. S., Ito, N. C., Oliveira, F. d. M., & Ovanessoff, A. (2020). Public capacity, plural forms of collaboration, and the performance of public initiatives: A configurational approach. *Journal of Public Administration Research and Theory, 30*(4), 579–595.

McGahan, A. M. (2020). Where does an organization's responsibility end? Identifying the boundaries on stakeholder claims. *Academy of Management Discoveries, 6*(1), 8–11.

McGahan, A. M. (2021). Integrating insights from the resource-based view of the firm into the new stakeholder theory. *Journal of Management, 47*(7), 1734–1756.

McGahan, A. M. (2023). The new stakeholder theory on organizational purpose. *Strategy Science, 8*, 245.

Mitchell, D. (2022). Bought in? The contingent effect of stakeholder support upon strategic implementation success in American municipalities. *Public Management Review, 24*(5), 773–798.

Mitchell, R. K., Agle, B. R., & Wood, D. J. (1997). Toward a theory of stakeholder identification and salience: Defining the principle of who and what really counts. *Academy of Management Review, 22*(4), 853–886.

Mossman, K., Onil Bhattacharyya, M., McGahan, A., & Mitchell, W. (2017). Expanding the reach of primary care in developing Countries. *Harvard Business Review*.

Murphy, M., & Arenas, D. (2010). Through indigenous lenses: Cross-sector collaborations with fringe stakeholders. *Journal of Business Ethics, 94*, 103–121.

Ni, X., Song, W., & Yao, J. (2020). Stakeholder orientation and corporate payout policy: Insights from state legal shocks. *Journal of Banking & Finance, 121*, 105970.

Nie, M. (2004). State wildlife policy and management: The scope and bias of political conflict. *Public Administration Review, 64*(2), 221–233.

Osborne, D., & Gaebler, T. (1992). *Reinventing government: How the entrepreneurial spirit is transforming the public sector*. Addison-Welsey.

Pongeluppe, L. S. (2022). The favela effect: Spatial inequalities and firm strategies in disadvantaged urban communities. *Strategic Management Journal, 43*(13), 2777–2808. https://doi.org/10.1002/smj.3414

Skinner, R. M. (2017). Water policy in a time of climate change: Coping with complexity. *Public Administration Review, 77*(1), 13–16.

Wicks, A. C., & Harrison, J. S. (2017). Toward a more productive dialogue between stakeholder theory and strategic management. In *Stakeholder management* (Vol. 1, pp. 249–273): Emerald Publishing Limited.

Williamson, O. E. (1999). Public and private bureaucracies: A transaction cost economics perspectives. *Journal of Law, Economics, and Organization, 15*(1), 306–342.

Wood, D. J., Mitchell, R. K., Agle, B. R., & Bryan, L. M. (2021). Stakeholder identification and salience after 20 years: Progress, problems, and prospects. *Business & Society, 60*(1), 196–245.

CHAPTER 9

On the Government Boundaries

Probation services play a pivotal role in ensuring the reintegration and rehabilitation of individuals sentenced by courts. Beyond their immediate impact, these services are instrumental in preventing future crimes and reducing recidivism rates, making them a cornerstone for the creation of public value. This contribution extends to enhancing societal benefits while concurrently diminishing the costs associated with the criminal justice system. To fulfill this role effectively, probation officers engage in a range of activities, including monitoring individuals on parole and under court supervision, helping in finding employment, implementing programs to prevent substance abuse, facilitating community reintegration, and overseeing the involvement of offenders in community-oriented services, among other responsibilities.

In 2013, Chris Grayling, the former Secretary of Justice in the United Kingdom from 2012 to 2015, advocated for significant reforms in probation services across England and Wales to address the issue of high recidivism rates. To lower reconviction numbers, the UK government proposed the outsourcing of probation services for low and medium-risk offenders to private companies. As per the proposal, high-risk offenders would continue to be supervised by the state through a streamlined national probation service. By June 2014, the responsibility for probation services had been divided between the National Probation Service

S. Cabral, *Strategy for Public and Nonprofit Organizations*,
https://doi.org/10.1007/978-3-031-64969-1_9

(NPS) and 21 community rehabilitation companies, overseeing 31,000 and 236,000 offenders, respectively.[1]

However, after some years, evidence of malfunction in the probation services provided by private companies emerged. The reoffending rates among adult offenders increased from 25% prior to partial privatization to 29.2%.[2] While this rise does not reveal the outcome had the privatization policy not been implemented, there has been mounting pressure to bring these services back in-house due to concerns about the subpar quality of services delivered by private organizations. Various reports from the HM Inspectorate of Probation, the official and independent watchdog agency responsible for reporting to the government on the effectiveness of probation services for offenders, have identified signs of cost-cutting and declining quality in services provided by for-profit organizations. For example, instead of personal interactions, some companies have opted for remote supervision via telephone every six weeks. Additionally, there is evidence of reduced staff levels, leading to an increase in the number of offenders supervised by each probation officer, often staffed by early-career professionals with lower salaries and insufficient experience. Failures in probation services are also linked to unintended consequences, including major crimes committed by offenders that might not have occurred with adequate services in place.[3]

In response to these criticisms, the UK government, in 2019, declared its intention to reintegrate the services that were previously outsourced to private organizations. Immediate reintegration was hindered by existing contracts, but by 2023, a revamped structure had been established. Eleven

[1] The decision to partially privatize probation services in UK is well-documented by official sources and by the press. See: https://researchbriefings.files.parliament.uk/documents/SN06974/SN06974.pdf https://consult.justice.gov.uk/digital-communications/transforming-rehabilitation/results/transforming-rehabilitation-response.pdf and https://www.independent.co.uk/news/uk/crime/privatisation-of-probation-service-will-put-public-at-risk-8825106.html.

[2] See official records in https://assets.publishing.service.gov.uk/government/uploads/system/uploads/attachment_data/file/519643/proven-reoffending-2014Q2.pdf and https://assets.publishing.service.gov.uk/government/uploads/system/uploads/attachment_data/file/797439/proven_reoffending_bulletin_April_to_June_17.pdf.

[3] There is abundant evidence in both public documents as well as in the independent press about the problems related to deficient provision of probation services. Please, refer to https://www.justiceinspectorates.gov.uk/hmiprobation/media/press-releases/2019/03/reportofthechiefinspectorofprobation/ and https://www.theguardian.com/society/2017/dec/14/private-probation-firms-criticised-supervising-offenders-phone.

new probation regions in England and Wales are now under the direct responsibility of the National Probation Service (NPS). The NPS, in collaboration with private or nonprofit organizations, provides support for the implementation of unpaid work (community services) and accredited programs.[4]

Similarly, between 1999 and 2002, six new prisons were constructed in the state of Paraná, located in the south of Brazil, and their operations were outsourced to private operators. Unlike the US model, where prisons can be entirely privately owned and managed, the Brazilian example adopted the French hybrid model. In this approach, certain functions were delegated to for-profit firms, while others remained under the purview of civil servants and the control of public authorities. In this specific case, the state department of corrections outsourced all essential functions required to operate the new prisons. This included providing unarmed correctional officers, food services, health, and rehabilitation services, and facilities management. Beyond the physical construction of the correctional facilities, the state government appointed a warden, a deputy-warden, and a head of security in each outsourced prison. These individuals were tasked with both overseeing the private provider's operations and making strategic decisions related to prison security. External vigilance, conducted by armed personnel, was provided by the state military police.

In 2006, the state government made the decision to cease the outsourcing of prisons and fully bring their management back under state control. Unlike the situation with probation services in the UK, this decision in Brazil was not influenced by the performance of private organizations. Instead, it was grounded in moral considerations and the premise that prison management is a core function that should not be delegated to private actors. The decision was made without the support of any study comparing the public and private arrangements. In fact, studies conducted after the government opted to bring the activities in-house demonstrated that privately operated prisons underperformed their public counterparts in the state.[5]

[4] See https://researchbriefings.files.parliament.uk/documents/CBP-9252/CBP-9252.pdf and https://blog.govnet.co.uk/justice/probation-services-are-returning-in-house.

[5] I had the opportunity to investigate the outsourcing experience of prisons in the state of Parana in Brazil, as well as in other correctional systems across various countries. From my observations, decisions regarding insourcing or outsourcing are intricate and necessitate

Both cases illustrate decisions regarding the appropriate role of the government, initially driven by the belief that private provision is inherently superior to government in-house provision. However, while the privatization decision in the UK involved a function that should not be outsourced to for-profit firms without strong public supervision to align private efforts with the public interest, the decision to terminate the successful private operation with public supervision of prisons in Brazil must also be approached with caution.

Certainly, political aspects play a crucial role in the decision-making processes of organizations, particularly those that prioritize stakeholder relationships. This significance is even more pronounced in public organizations, which are often subjected to conflicting demands and goal ambiguity. However, akin to diversification decisions in the private sector, strategic scope-related decisions in government also require the integration of other elements. Identifying the pros and cons of each alternative is essential to create configurations that are most conducive to enhancing public value.

It is important to note that both the formulation and the implementation of decisions related to changes in organizational boundaries are not trivial in any type of organization. Whether the organization decides to expand its scope through organic growth, acquisitions, or alliances with other organizations, or to refocus its role through downsizing, divestitures, outsourcing, or, in the case of public organizations, through processes of privatization, concessions, or public–private partnerships, formulating and implementing these decisions are not only time and attention-consuming—two factors that are in short supply—but also demand the allocation of capable personnel and financial resources.

In addition to carefully considering the economic and social implications of expanding or reducing their scope, organizations must keep in mind the opportunity costs before engaging in scope decisions. Managers involved in these decisions can divert their attention from daily routines, leading to disturbances in operational outcomes. Apart from the increased

a thorough examination of the capacity of governments to establish appropriate incentives for encouraging the efforts of private actors while mitigating opportunistic behavior that may run counter to the public interest. For econometric assessments comparing public versus public–private operations in Parana state prisons, please refer to Cabral et al. (2010, 2013). A cross-country comparison of public, private, and hybrid modes of provision in prisons can be found in Cabral and Saussier (2013).

demands on existing employees, the mere idea of shifting organizational boundaries can introduce a sense of insecurity, especially among employees who might be affected by decisions that reduce the organizational scope. Organizations opting for scope reduction decisions, only to later reverse these decisions by bringing delegated functions back in-house, face several additional costs. These include transaction costs of terminating contracts and expenses associated with rebuilding capabilities previously transferred to external actors. It is important to note that the process of reintegration is not automatic and can pose significant challenges.[6] This appears to be the case in the UK probation services, where failures in tracking offenders after their release have resulted in violent crimes that would not have occurred if capable probation officers were implementing customized approaches to individuals with the potential to threaten citizen safety.[7]

The process of reintegrating activities formerly transferred to external providers can also lead to increased costs when external providers prioritize cost reduction at the expense of quality, often by decreasing the salaries of personnel, as is common in both public and private organizations.[8] Costs can also rise when organizations succumb to pressure from unionized employees, forcing them to pay salaries above market prices, as observed in the prison's reintegration process in Brazil mentioned earlier. Following the reintegration, the number of civil servants available to manage the reintegrated prisons was insufficient, prompting the state government to temporarily hire former employees of the private companies. Subsequently, the state government conducted competitive public examinations to hire new civil servants, who now receive, on average, 300% more than their former outsourced counterparts.[9]

All these considerations underscore the importance of exercising caution in decisions related to organizational boundaries, whether they involve diversification and divestiture decisions in firms or increased integration or privatization decisions in the public realm. With decision-makers increasingly influenced by a growing number of stakeholders, the

[6] For a detailed account of the problems related to reintegration of activities formerly transferred to external actors, see Berlin et al. (2023), Cabral et al. (2014), and Dachs et al. (2019).

[7] https://www.ft.com/content/0185c7a7-f210-4cfc-bf0a-377a51ef36dd.

[8] Cabral et al. (2014).

[9] Cabral et al. (2013).

task of balancing the pros and cons of different organizational boundary choices becomes even more challenging, particularly in governments where moral and ideological aspects may prevail over efficiency and value creation reasoning. An informed and careful examination of the different scenarios regarding the scope of the government is crucial to address the interests of the public, especially those who are disenfranchised and in greater need of effective public policies.

Setting the Boundaries: Drivers of Scope Choices

Recognizing the various discrete choices available for providing goods and services with value creation potential is crucial for a strategic orientation centered on addressing stakeholder claims. It also facilitates a deeper understanding of the conditions under which each mode of provision aligns with the organizational purpose. Such assessments become particularly relevant when activities can be executed by public, private, and nonprofit organizations independently or collaboratively through many contractual arrangements. Equally important is the examination of established frameworks used in both the strategy and public administration fields to comprehend the configurations of organizational boundaries.

Organizational Boundaries: The Contributions of Property Rights Theory and Transaction Cost Economics

The literature on strategic boundary choices is heavily shaped by economic reasoning. Decisions regarding internal provision (making), external provision (buying), or forming alliances arise from a comparative assessment across a range of discrete alternatives. Two major theoretical streams analyze these choices through distinct lenses: property rights theory and transaction costs economics.

The property rights approach departs from the idea that contracts are incomplete. As discussed in Chapter 4, in an incomplete contract setting, it is assumed that the costs of negotiation can be excessively high because self-interested actors will try to impose their preferences. Additionally, it is difficult to anticipate future contractual contingencies, especially in settings with information asymmetries, as obtaining relevant information is also costly. Central questions in the property rights perspective are: How should one own the assets? Should the focal firm be in a vertically integrated fashion, or should external suppliers be involved? Sanford

Grossman and Oliver Hart argue that the party possessing the residual control rights, i.e., those rights that are not explicitly assigned to any party, should own the asset. By allowing the free use of an asset within the limits of the law and the contract, residual control rights are noncontractible rights that enable the capture of the value created after the ex-ante investments have already been made. The ownership of residual control rights significantly affects the incentives of parties investing in a relationship, as it influences the potential losses of those who own the asset.[10] For instance, the owner of an estate has superior incentives to invest in major repairs and significant improvements than tenants renting the estate. In general, the allocation of property rights complements the existing gaps when contracts are incomplete. It is up to the holder of residual control rights to make decisions.

However, since investments and actions of contracting parties are not always observable and contractible underinvestment or socially undesired investment may occur and this can be particularly problematic in public services. In a seminal paper, Oliver Hart and other two colleagues, Andrei Shleifer, and Robert Vishny, analyzed the example of private prisons to develop a property rights approach to the scope of government. Building upon the idea that the desired quality of some services is difficult to specify (e.g., how to define in the contract the level of physical coercion that a correctional officer can employ against an offender in case of a riot or a fight among offenders), as are the actions performed by prison staff, whether private managers or civil servants, the authors posit that existing contractual incompleteness can lead to a serious cost-versus-quality tradeoff. This tradeoff can challenge the effectiveness of private management in prisons. The willingness to reduce costs at the expense of quality is particularly worrisome because innovations in quality improvements are not in the interest of private firms unless these investments lead to cost reductions. The inherent contractual incompleteness costs efforts that deteriorate quality, which are not easily identified. For instance, a firm can employ staff with lower salaries and insufficient skills and provide second-grade food to inmates to preserve their profit margins,

[10] Grossman and Hart (1986).

with limited odds of being sanctioned by public authorities. This skepticism leads the authors to question the effectiveness of a reduced scope of government in the provision of prison services.[11]

Transaction Cost Economics (TCE) developed by Oliver Williamson is the more influential theory to inform make, buy, or ally decisions in both for-profit, nonprofit, and public organizations.[12] Building upon the idea of Ronald Coase who defined transaction costs as the costs of using the price mechanism,[13] TCE is grounded in two assumptions: bounded rationality and opportunism. Organizational decisions, including scope choices, are based on the premise that self-interested decision-makers evaluate options through logical reasoning with the information they have, but within certain limits.

Asset specificity, i.e., the extent to which an asset can be used for other alternatives without significant losses, is a crucial consideration in TCE. For instance, a truck adapted with special tanks to transport orange juice cannot be adapted to transport gasoline without incurring meaningful costs. A cargo supplier interested in providing services to the sole orange juice firm in a territory will incur costs for this transaction, making them vulnerable if the firm uses its market power to negotiate lower freight prices. Similarly, the supplier firm can influence the contract by increasing freight prices, exploiting the absence of available alternative suppliers. Since the presence of asset specificity imposes a situation of bilateral dependency, the higher the level of asset specificity in a particular transaction, the higher the likelihood of vertical integration. Consequently, the probability of using the market to supply the firm's needs decreases. In a similar vein, a private firm would be hesitant to invest in building a prison facility for high-risk offenders requiring adapted buildings and customized managerial practices without a long-term contract ensuring a return on their investments.[14]

[11] Hart et al. (1997) posits that prison management would be inadequate in the context of privatization. Yet their model does not account for the possibility of other hybrid arrangements involving private operation under intense public supervision, which, under certain conditions, can be superior to public provision (Cabral et al., 2010, 2013).

[12] Williamson (1985, 1991, 1999).

[13] Coase (1937).

[14] More about the role of transaction cost economics (TCE) in make or buy decisions in public services can be seen in Williamson (1999). Applications of TCE and new institutional economics to prisons can be seen in Cabral (2006, 2007).

Organizational Boundaries: The Contributions of Public Eonomics and Policy Analysis

While property rights and transactional approaches are useful for informing decision-making on organizational boundaries, additional elements are necessary to understand the peculiarities of public services. Market failures can obliterate the participation of private entities in public service provision, thereby stimulating government provision. Recognizing the sources of market failures and understanding the conditions under which these failures can be relaxed to allow governments to delegate some functions to external actors is crucial for making boundary choices in public organizations.

The inability of market forces, the so-called invisible hand, to promote collective well-being without any form of government intervention has been viewed with skepticism since the origins of economic thought. In fact, Adam Smith advocated in his work "The Wealth of Nations" in 1776 for the need for government investments in goods that are not attractive to individual economic agents due to the high investments required for their viability.[15] A similar argument is made by Arthur Pigou about the need for state intervention in the economy. While recognizing that governmental action could bring various inconveniences, such as corruption and political favoritism, he argued that the participation of government agents in the direct provision or regulation of public services provided by private actors could be beneficial for the development of society in the presence of market failures.[16]

Market failures arise from the presence of natural monopolies, externalities, and collective goods. Some goods and services are natural monopolies when it is socially optimal to have only one producer. This occurs when both fixed installation and sunk costs are high, decreasing marginal production costs. These barriers may impede the entry of potential entrants making governments opt for the direct provision. Government can be the provider to protect served communities from the opportunistic behavior of private monopolists. Examples of natural monopolies include the supply of water, sanitation, and electricity. Externalities occur when the outcomes resulting from actions of a particular agent impact in some way the utility or production functions of other agents. Environmental

[15] Smith (1999 [1776]).

[16] Pigou (1920).

and noise pollution serve as examples of negative externalities that also require the interference of regulatory bodies to assure the public's interests by curbing inadequate actions of providers. Collective goods and services involve activities in which is not feasible to enforce users to pay for the provision, and the resulting benefits are widely shared among communities, as in the case of conservation parks, defense systems, and street lightening.

Although goods and services that benefit large populations and meet the criteria above are provided by governments in its various levels around the world, there is also abundant evidence of private and nonprofit organizations providing these goods, including services that are natural monopolies and services in which the enforcement of the services provided is not straightforward. The 1991 Nobel Prize in Economics winner, Ronald Coase, illustrates the private provision of public services meeting the conditions above with a historic example that of lighthouse services. Opposing to the claims of reputed scholars, like John Stuart Mill, Arthur Pigou, and Paul Samuelson, he shows that private organizations effectively provided lighthouse services for a long time by charging fees from ship-owners. In this private provision of public services, ships paid tolls at ports, and authorities calculated them based on the size of vessels for each lighthouse they passed.[17] Similarly, Joel Baum and Anita McGahan show that private military companies have been supplying military services to several governments around the world for a long time, replacing sworn officers.[18]

Complicating matters further, there are numerous examples of goods and services traditionally considered private and more likely to be provided by for-profit organizations, now being supplied by governments. This repertoire is extensive and includes metallurgic mills, hotels, leisure services, and plantations.[19] Determining government boundaries is not easy.

To shed light on the role of for-profit firms in the provision of public services and the government response regarding the delineation of their boundaries, public administration, political science, and policy analysis scholars like Elinor Ostrom, Vincent Ostrom, Emanuel Savas, Aidan R.

[17] Coase (1974).

[18] Baum and McGahan (2013).

[19] Shirley (1999).

Vining, and David Weimer have proposed the identification of differences between public and private goods in two dimensions: excludability and rivalry in consumption.[20] *Excludability* refers to the feasibility to deprive individuals of enjoying the benefits of a particular good or service[21] if they do not agree or cannot accept the terms proposed by the provider, which includes the unwillingness or the incapacity to pay for the service. However, exclusion is not always feasible. In fact, at an outdoor concert, even if tickets are charged, it is not easy to prevent people from the neighborhood, who did not pay for the benefit of enjoying the show by hearing the music. The feasibility of exclusion depends on the cost of enforcing payments. The higher the likelihood of free riders, the more difficult it becomes to convince people to pay. This may lead to a reduced likelihood of private investments given the difficulty of obtaining financial returns, thus increasing the propensity for either government provision or under-provision.

The second dimension, *rivalry in consumption*, is also crucial in this analysis. It pertains to the idea that the consumption of certain goods by one individual may lead to a decrease in quantity and quality of consumption for another individual. The availability of a good for one person may mean its unavailability for another, as seen in the consumption of a cup of coffee. Conversely, the fact that several people make use of a good often does not imply its decrease or depreciation, as exemplified by the broadcast of a television program, which represents a situation of low rivalry in consumption. There are situations of moderate rivalry in consumption; for instance, a beach does not see its resources significantly diminished due to the use by a group of people. However, as the number of individuals enjoying its use increases, natural resources can be depleted, and the quality of the benefits individually obtained decreases. The combination between excludability and rivalry in consumption leads to a 2×2 matrix containing in each quadrant a different type of good. See Fig. 9.1, present in the works of Ostrom and Ostrom (2019), Savas (2000), and Weimer and Vining (2017).

The upper-left corner represents a scenario characterized by high rivalry in consumption and the feasibility of exclusion by those holding corresponding property rights. This mirrors the situation of private goods

[20] See Ostrom and Ostrom (2019), Savas (2000), and Weimer and Vining (2017).

[21] Eventually I will use the terms goods and services interchangeably.

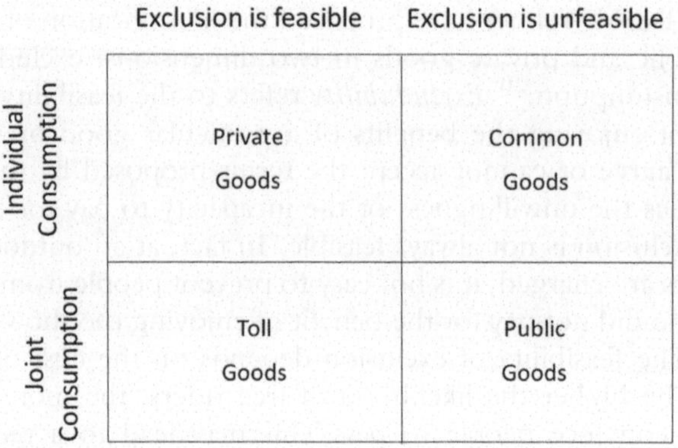

Fig. 9.1 Types of goods

typically distributed by organizations through market mechanisms. Take, for instance, the shirt I am currently wearing: my use of it prevents someone else from using it, and I have the discretion to permit or deny others the use of it. In this context, education, and health—two services often offered by governments in various countries—can be typified as private goods, based on the exclusion versus rivalry conceptualization. Consider a hospital bed occupied by a patient; this occupation not only limits access to that service for another patient but also implies a rivalry in consumption, whether patients are paying or not for the service. The potential for exclusion is also evident, as seen in the case of a public university in the United States that charges tuition fees for its services. The decision to implement exclusion or offer health and education systems for free rests with the owners of the right to exclude.

Toll goods are characterized by collective consumption and feasible exclusion, as seen in the lower-left corner. Examples of toll goods include those with collective use, such as roads. The construction, operation, and maintenance costs of the infrastructure can be shared among road users, who may contribute to covering these expenses by paying tolls for roads. While the costs of provision can decrease as the number of users increases, the level of congestion can affect the benefits of collective consumption. In the case of roads, congestion can be influenced by both the demand of users and the capacity of the road. Toll goods may also exhibit characteristics of natural monopolies, as in the case of roads, bridges, water distribution, and electricity distribution. While there is potential for market provision of toll goods, it is common for governments to undertake these activities. This may be due to elevated costs deterring private participation or governments aiming to safeguard the population from rent-seeking or incapable providers. As an alternative, some governments utilize regulation to enable capable providers to create public value while concurrently addressing the inherent issues of private opportunism that can undermine the public interest.

Goods exhibiting characteristics of individual consumption and unfeasible exclusion are classified as common goods (upper-right corner). In this scenario, demanding payment for use is nearly impossible due to the ease of consumption and the difficulty in enforcing the requirements necessary for the maintenance or improvement of the good. A poignant example is the fishing industry, where, in the absence of entities capable of regulating the activity, fishers may opt to catch as many fish as possible, often aware that such behavior contributes to the depletion of the stock, harming their own interests in the future. When the residual returns of an asset are dispersed, individual agents lack sufficient interest in bearing the costs of maintaining and improving the common good.[22] The absence of incentives for supplying and conserving common goods, coupled with strong incentives for their indiscriminate use, can lead to depletion—a situation famously termed "the tragedy of the commons" by Garrett Hardin.[23] To address this issue, Elinor Ostrom proposed an alternative to direct government provision. She suggested that the introduction of collective action mechanisms, achieved through the allocation of property rights to groups or individuals interested in preserving these goods, can be an effective way to conserve common goods.[24]

Finally, in the lower right quadrant, we encounter public goods, utilized by numerous individuals with minimal possibilities of exclusion. Like common goods, there is a tendency to access public goods without individual efforts toward their provision. In terms of externalities, prisons fall into this category, as the outcomes resulting from their operation are collectively appropriated by the population regardless of individual contributions. Attempts to impose fees or exclude non-contributing users

[22] Milgrom and Roberts (1992).

[23] Hardin (1968).

[24] Ostrom (1990).

for public goods are economically and politically unfeasible. Nonetheless, while Weimer and Vining argue that "*pure public goods will not be supplied at all by markets because of the inability of private providers to exclude those who do not pay for them*"[25] as seen earlier, there are instances of private provision of public goods globally, including lighthouses, prisons, defense, and street lighting.

In fact, public, private, and nonprofit organizations can all offer goods and services in each of the four quadrants. Decisions to define the proper scope of government should consider both the varying degrees of public involvement and the conditions under which each mode is preferred to ensure the creation of public value. These aspects will be discussed in the next sections.

The Different Modes of Provision

The centrality of governments in the provision of goods and services that benefit society at large is a fact irrespective of the ideological inclination of political leaders in power or the societal beliefs about which tasks are better performed by public, private, and nonprofit organizations.

Governments can either exhibit an enhanced scope by directly providing goods and services through specialized departments and state-owned companies, establish arm-length contracts with external suppliers for goods and services in which obligations are contractible or regulate activities presenting collective consumption, unfeasible exclusion or potential to generate positive and negative externalities, as in privatized services like water, electricity, and urban transportation.

Besides its role on polar modes, governments may also have a leading role in hybrid arrangements in which management is shared to a greater or lesser extent with private or nonprofit organizations. This can include contracts to manage hospitals originally built by the government, outsourcing to external actors of some activities in state-owned organizations, like billing functions in a publicly provided water service, or even more complex contracts where public and private organizations can share functions of designing, building, financing, operating, and maintaining the assets, as in the case of concessions and public–private partnerships (PPP).

[25] Weimer and Vining (2017, p. 83).

The role of governments extends beyond scope decisions toward increased or decreased assignments of property, decision, and control rights to public authorities. Governments are central not only because they can provide goods and services but also because they can take a leading position in efforts to attract and retain capable private and nonprofit organizations—either to provide or co-produce goods and services, contributing to enhanced public value creation. In the same vein, government also plays, or should play, a leading role in curbing opportunism of external organizations and protecting citizens from actions against the public interest by regulating and closely supervising private and nonprofit actors to assure that the value created is appropriated by a larger number of stakeholders.

Even in privatization settings where private organizations retain substantial property rights, governments can influence the decision-making process. For instance, former state-owned organizations that were privatized often see governments preserving equity stakes and having veto power over strategic decisions, using the so-called golden shares. This is exemplified by the Italian government's power over decisions in Telecom Italia, a major telecommunications conglomerate. In Brazil, the federal government retained veto power in Embraer, a leading commercial and military firm, particularly in decisions related to changes in organizational purpose and aspects related to military programs.

Figure 9.2 exemplifies the different modes of provision of public services, ranging from full public provision to full private provision.[26]

Full Government Provision

With the proliferation of elections after the mid-nineteenth century and the growing demands of societies for essential services such as education, transportation, and healthcare—at that time typically provided by private and religious entities—governments faced the challenge of meeting these needs for the collective welfare. In a period where scalable service providers were scarce, and private provision often seemed unattractive due to the absence or fragility of regulatory structures, several governments responded by enlarging their scope and expanding their roles to ensure

[26] The examples of PPP configurations in this figure are merely illustrative and not exhaustive. See Cabral (2006, 2023).

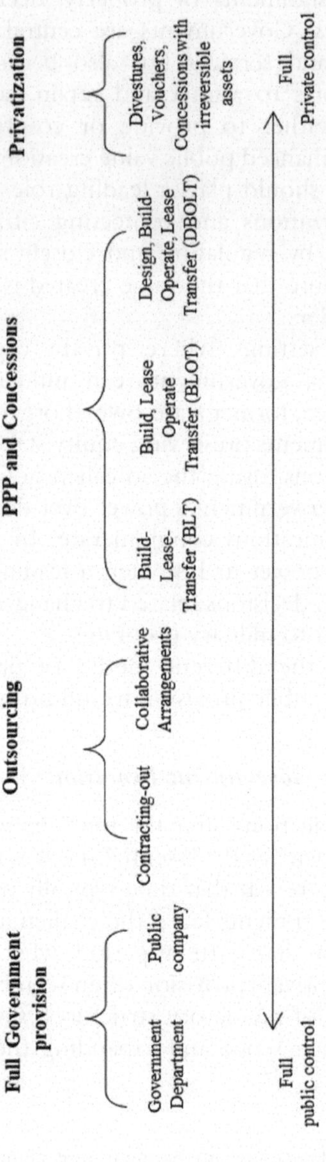

Fig. 9.2 Modes of provision of public services

the delivery of goods and services deemed necessary for both economic and social development.

Through state-owned enterprises or departments in public bureaucracies, public provision, in addition to potentially allowing greater societal control over service delivery, served to enhance the legitimacy of governments in the eyes of citizens. Government provision, facilitated by massive public investments, also allowed the expansion of infrastructure, thereby improving citizens' living standards and fostering development. To address disparities between prices and production costs, government provision often involves offering tariff subsidies, benefiting low-income citizens and specific societal groups. For example, students in New York City are not charged for their bus and subway rides during school days.

However, the inherent imbalances in government accounts resulting from subsidies can lead to diminished investments in expanding infrastructure and maintaining existing assets. This, in turn, fosters dissatisfaction in society due to a decline in the quality of services offered. In addition, the control exerted by state-owned entities also creates conditions for rent-seeking behavior by political actors and groups seeking privileged relationships with governments, thereby facilitating the emergence of corruption in government-controlled services. These challenges open the door to discussions about the potential replacement of direct government provision with alternative arrangements involving private and nonprofit organizations, either wholly or partially, as in the case of hybrid arrangements involving public and private participation.

Outsourcing

To circumvent the limitations of public provision in terms of lack of expertise, low-powered incentives, and rigidity[27] can promote an increased participation of private entities in a cautious manner, without fully delegating responsibilities to private and nonprofit organizations.

At times, governments may be unwilling and unable, either from an ideological or political perspective, or due to legal constraints, to encourage the widespread involvement of private and nonprofit organizations in the provision of services provided by public authorities. Maintaining control over activities and retaining ownership of assets,

[27] See Chapter 1 for an account of the problems that public organizations face.

while also permitting partial entry of private actors, prompts governments to explore various possibilities in terms of management models and contractual arrangements. This approach enables governments to preserve the advantage of control, preventing assertions about a potential abandonment of their historical responsibilities, while minimizing the burden imposed by the limited flexibility dictated by rigid statutes and regulations characteristic of public bureaucracies. At the same time, it involves sharing some of the risks associated with the provision with external organizations.

According to Fig. 9.2, the most elementary form of private or nonprofit participation in the provision of public services occurs through outsourcing activities. In this case, the involvement of external actors in the entire operation is not high, and the duration of the property rights of the supplier is limited to the contract period, typically not exceeding 5 years. The extent of services delegated to private actors varies from specific functions, such as the supply of maintenance services in schools, to activities with a broader scope, like the management of a hospital by a public or nonprofit entity. In both cases, when outsourcing activities, public authorities can reap economic advantages by transforming fixed costs into variable costs and making financial resources available for acquiring and renewing resources for other priorities. Outsourcing also allows organizations to focus on their core competencies and improve efficiency. This can be achieved through accessing differentiated technologies do not present in the public organization but provided by the supplier, or through increased flexibility resulting from the transfer of activities and the distinctive technical capabilities of external suppliers. Finally, organizations may benefit from a reduction in transaction costs compared to internal provision.

To reduce its scope through outsourcing, governments can utilize arms-length contracts or collaborative arrangements in which public, private, and nonprofit partners pool resources, capabilities, and share knowledge that was previously dispersed. These collaborative relationships can be used to run public services or specific initiatives in various areas, ranging from the development of vaccines to defense projects.[28] Arms-length contracts are used in situations where the features of the provision are contractible. This occurs when the buyer can specify their needs, when

[28] The next chapter provides a more detailed discussion of cross-sector collaborations, their multiple extensions, and contractual forms.

the parties have strong incentives to be efficient, when bilateral dependency is not an issue, and when courts are effective instruments to solve conflicts.[29]

Public–Private Partnerships and Concessions

Governments can reduce their scope through concessions and public–private partnerships (PPP). In these forms, private actors replace public authorities in making the necessary investments to build, revamp, and operate the assets. Consequently, governments can allocate public funds to other investments or address fiscal imbalances. When opting for concessions and PPP, governments also expect that the expertise brought by private organizations enables *value for money*, signifying a better relationship between incurred costs and obtained outcomes. Furthermore, the possibility of sharing responsibilities through improved risk allocation processes is a hallmark in these arrangements, which is particularly important in areas requiring massive investments and subject to a myriad of contingencies. In fact, several risks, including technical, demand, and political risks, can thwart the effectiveness of complex projects. PPP and concessions are particularly suitable for these situations.

While the distinctions between concessions and PPP vary according to the country and its legal regime, in general, concessions differ from PPP in the extent of the required public investments. Some services involve assets in which it is possible to generate revenues over time sufficient to cover construction and operation costs and assure profits for private entrepreneurs who incurred major risks to provide the service. Toll goods such as roads and bridges exemplify this, with revenues stemming from fees paid by users and/or from ancillary sources, such as the exploitation of complementary commercial activities and advertising. On the other hand, public–private partnerships demand government investments to cover the costs and risks involved. For some services, like subway lines, fees paid by users do not suffice, and governments can either reimburse private operators for their investments or assume certain responsibilities in the project, such as the construction of tunnels or the acquisition of trains. In other services where it is not possible to obtain revenues from assets, like prisons, where inmates and their families cannot be charged for

[29] See Williamson (1991).

the services provided, governments provide payments to private operators to cover the incurred costs.[30]

Both concessions and PPP can involve a myriad of configurations where private actors can take different degrees of responsibilities. In some cases, the government may be responsible for financing and building the assets, subsequently transferring their operation to private organizations. In other cases, private operators can bundle the construction, financing, and operation of the project, often transferring back to the state the assets at the end of the contract. The more tasks the private operator integrates, the less scope of the government.[31]

Privatization

Among the options for reducing the scope of governments, privatization is the extreme alternative. It involves the transfer of assets and functions, previously under the responsibility of public authorities, to private organizations. These responsibilities encompass strategic and operational decisions necessary for value creation purposes.

Governments have various motivations for privatization. Ideological beliefs, rooted in the notion that a reduction in government intervention is necessary to enable individuals to fully exercise their initiatives and enjoy their fundamental right to freedom, serve as a major steppingstone in privatization decisions. Additionally, privatization may be driven by political motivations, including the possibility of dismantling opposition strongholds, such as workers' unions, and the construction of new political alliances with economic actors affected by these decisions.[32] The reasons for privatization also include reducing government deficits by reviving deficit-prone companies and securing credits for the treasury through their sale. There are also intentions to enhance the coverage and quality of services provided through private investment, achieving greater operational flexibility as companies would no longer be constrained by the bounds that characterize public bureaucracies.

[30] Cabral (2023).

[31] To gain a deeper understanding of the preferences and motivations of private organizations in concessions and PPP, refer to the work of Quelin et al. (2019).

[32] In his book, Nicholas Spulber (1997) provides a historical view of the process of reducing government boundaries in both developed and developing countries.

Nevertheless, privatization requires control mechanisms to ensure the attainment of public interest. It demands regulatory frameworks and regulatory agencies to coordinate tariffs, establish, and ensure the levels of services provided to users. In this matter, regulations are supposed to protect all parties involved—society, government, and private operators—from opportunistic behavior. From the citizens' perspective, clear rules that preserve the public interest and their effective enforcement are crucial when public monopolies are transformed into private monopolies. Since regulations have not been able to deliver on their promises to impose limits on profit-maximizing behavior of private operators, privatization is viewed with skepticism by users experiencing increased tariffs without the corresponding quality improvements. Not surprisingly, both resistance against new privatization processes and claims for statization are common in both developed and developing countries, despite the evidence that, on average, state-owned enterprises underperform comparable private organizations.[33]

Governments may also employ market forces to provide services by issuing vouchers to citizens. Aligned with free-market principles, citizens can use these allowances to choose their preferred suppliers for services such as education. While the existing evidence on the adoption of vouchers in education fails to demonstrate consistently positive results and, in some cases, even shows negative outcomes when compared to traditional public provision, their use is supported by think tanks and advocates of market-based solutions for public services provision.[34]

[33] See Megginson and Netter (2001), Galiani et al. (2005), and Brown et al. (2006).

[34] Schwerdt et al. (2012) analyzed vouchers for adult education in Switzerland and could not find evidence of relevant labor market outcomes, such as earnings, employment, and subsequent education. Abdulkadiroğlu et al. (2018) when analyzing voucher plans providing public funds for low-income students to enroll in private schools in the state of Louisiana, United States, found that students enrolled in the program exhibited lower scores in math, reading, science, and social studies. Lazzarini (2022) argues that voucher programs tend to be ineffective for several reasons, including supply constraints and increasing prices, low-quality private providers, and the exclusion of citizens who are more in need from voucher programs that present superior quality. Fixing these failures would demand increased public supervision over the voucher program, which contradicts the free-market principles that ground voucher programs.

Choosing the Mode of Provision

This section delves into the underlying factors that can guide governments in choosing one of these forms and determining the size of their boundaries.

Anecdotal evidence and ideological considerations often fuel debates regarding the scope of decisions of governments and the selected modes of provision. Given the multitude of provision modes, the various contingencies influencing boundary decisions, and the costs associated with both altering and potentially reverting scope choices, decision-makers involved in boundary choices within the government realm need to pay special attention to the conditions that render one alternative more attractive than another. In this context, certain dimensions are particularly relevant for guiding decision-makers in scope decisions: probity, capabilities of suppliers, and required private investments and property rights over the assets.

Probity Concerns

The literature in organizational economics and strategy heavily relies on transaction costs to inform make-or-buy decisions. According to this view, the presence of asset specificity increases the odds of bilateral dependency and conflicts between buyers and suppliers, causing the costs of contracting-out to escalate and influencing organizations to vertically integrate some activities. While assets with limited value in the best alternative employment are also present in public services and may influence governments to opt for in-house provision instead of delegation to external partners, some functions normally performed by public authorities require the examination of other aspects that are not central in boundary decisions in private organizations. Integrity-related features, or *probity* concerns, are particularly important in the decision between in-house provision or delegation to external actors.

Oliver Williamson refers to probity as loyalty and rectitude, implying high standards of integrity that involve abiding respect for the organizational mission and reliable responsiveness to superiors and other relevant stakeholders.[35] In functions like defense, prisons, or foreign affairs, probity hazards can undermine the confidence of society in the

[35] Williamson (1999).

service providers and in the government itself. A prison franchised out to private operators lacking probity can become a breeding ground for privileges to certain inmates and all sorts of illegalities, putting the legitimacy of private provision into perspective.

The degree of contractual incompleteness can also exacerbate probity problems. Oliver Hart and colleagues, in their seminal work on the proper scope of government, caution that the difficulty in specifying quality requirements in contracts, the non-observability of actions by private operators, and the catastrophic consequences of holdup arising from private opportunism recommend caution in the decision to delegate functions subject to probity concerns to private actors. Hence, a case against private participation is made when functions where honesty, morality, and righteousness are crucial.[36]

However, in some cases, effective public supervision can mitigate probity concerns and allow governments to benefit from the flexibility and innovation brought by private actors while simultaneously mitigating the pervasive effects of private opportunism to preserve the public interest. In previous works with outsourced prisons, we have demonstrated that state-appointed supervisors (wardens) working in prisons run by private entrepreneurs can prevent the occurrence of quality deterioration at the expense of cost reductions. Assigning decision rights to these public supervisors that allow them to impose credible sanctions against non-compliant private operators, along with the implementation of accountability systems that impose burdens on civil servants colluding with firms, are some of the mechanisms that can ensure private operation under public supervision when probity aspects are worrisome.[37]

Capable Suppliers

The availability of capable suppliers in the market is a hallmark in "*make-or-buy?*" decisions. Oftentimes, organizations vertically integrate some activities simply because the market offers no viable options. Indeed, suppliers cannot be attracted because the existing demand does not sufficiently compensate entrepreneurs' efforts to make the necessary investments in physical and capital resources required to address the needs

[36] Hart et al. (1997).

[37] See Cabral et al., (2010, 2013) and Cabral and Santos (2018).

of potential buyers. In these settings, outside options may seem more promising. Structural market imperfections can also contribute to the lack of suppliers. For instance, in the presence of buyers with increased market power, suppliers may refrain from investing, fearing exploitation by monopolists or oligopolists. Environments with institutional voids, characterized by information asymmetries, nonexistent or deficient regulatory frameworks, courts with limited capacity to enforce property rights, and preferred treatment for individuals and organizations with privileged connections, may also create barriers for suppliers and stimulate in-house provision.[38]

However, in settings with reduced market frictions, suppliers can be valuable to organizations attempting to use the market to address their needs instead of relying on internal organization, provided they are capable—meaning they have the required abilities to increase the value created in a transaction compared to in-house provision. In tandem with transaction cost perspectives, capability-based theories have been central to explaining the conditions under which organizations reduce or increase their scope and the investments that both buyers and suppliers make in an existing relationship.[39]

Capabilities resulting from the combination of resources, accumulated knowledge, and experience are widely recognized as sources of value creation. In buyer–supplier relationships, execution capabilities on the supplier side allow the delivery of goods and services according to customer requirements, thereby enhancing the efficiency and/or differentiation of value chains.[40] Enabling suppliers to earn a living,[41] execution capabilities on the supplier side encompass both the ability to deliver a given service and the ability to manage contracts with buyers, cultivating sophisticated buyer–supplier relationships. These contract-management capabilities are crucial in relationships where the government is the buyer, given the inherent peculiarities of public organizations. An adequate supplier for public organizations must be able to understand how government operates its procurement process, how decision-making in public

[38] Khanna and Palepu (1997).

[39] Argyres and Zenger (2012).

[40] See Teece et al. (1997) and Helfat (2000).

[41] Winter (2003).

organizations is shaped, how contract disputes are resolved, and how to deal with the myriad stakeholders in public organizations.[42]

Hence, the existence of suppliers acquainted with public–private interactions and able to understand both the requirements and constraints of public bureaucracies is crucial for scope decisions in the government realm. Enhanced knowledge of how government works allows for incentive alignment, fosters trust-based relationships, and facilitates adaptability, even when contracts are incomplete.[43]

Private Investments and Ownership

While crucial, the presence of capable suppliers is not the only aspect to be considered by governments in scope decisions, even when probity is not a major issue. Inherent characteristics of the goods and services that are candidates for private provision, along with the intrinsic characteristics of the assets involved, the feasibility of private providers investing both their financial resources and their accumulated knowledge in the pursuit of public value creation, and the level of property rights assigned to public and private entities over time, are also relevant aspects in the choice for the adequate mode of provision.

Goods and services can be attractive to private organizations based on their economic sustainability. The capacity of assets to generate revenues, as well as the ability of governments to provide funds to cover both the costs of constructing the assets and the costs of operation when user fees are insufficient to cover all the expenses, are key features that must be considered by decision-makers involved in scope decisions. When assets for providing goods and services can be built, operated, and funded by user fees or other revenues, scope choices can be made through comparative assessments between public or private provision, with the mode that creates the greatest public value being chosen. This is evident in electricity provision for urban areas, where revenues from users and ancillary sources, such as leasing existing networks for cable TV and telephony providers, are sufficient to attract capable private firms.

[42] For a comprehensive view on capabilities perspectives in public organizations, see Brown and Potoski (2003), Bruce et al. (2019), and Cabral (2017).

[43] See Cabral (2017).

When revenue streams from users and other sources are not sufficient to ensure the economic sustainability of the initiative, some degree of government intervention is required to attract private entrepreneurs for the provision. Governments can build the facilities and outsource the operation to private organizations with the necessary expertise or even allow private entrepreneurs to bundle construction and operation phases to enable incentive alignment and the exploitation of synergies.[44]

An Integrative Model for Selecting the Mode of Delivery

Having described the different modes of provision and once demonstrated the contributions of strategic management theories for scope choices in public, private, and nonprofit organizations, Fig. 9.3 portrays a flow of decisions that can help decision-makers in the selection of the different modes of delivery: public provision, outsourcing/contracting-out, PPP, concession without public investment, and privatization.

Before considering the provision of a hypothetical good or service, decision-makers must first address the question of whether relevant probity concerns are present in the potential delegation to external actors. These concerns can pose challenges to upholding the social dimensions of performance and ensuring the observance of the public interest, including the interests of disenfranchised populations. If problems with integrity and rectitude are significant and can not only damage the government's reputation and legitimacy but also generate extremely negative consequences for society, a second question must be asked: can public supervision address or attenuate probity hazards? While a negative response to this question may suggest that public provision must be chosen, a positive response can prompt managers to ask themselves: "Okay, if probity is not an issue, do we have capable suppliers to deliver these goods and services should we want to reduce the government scope?".

Although the absence of capable suppliers is a necessary and sufficient condition for organizations to vertically integrate activities, even when decision-makers prefer to use the market through external providers, the presence of capable suppliers is not a guarantee that goods and services

[44] See Cabral (2006) and Hart (2003).

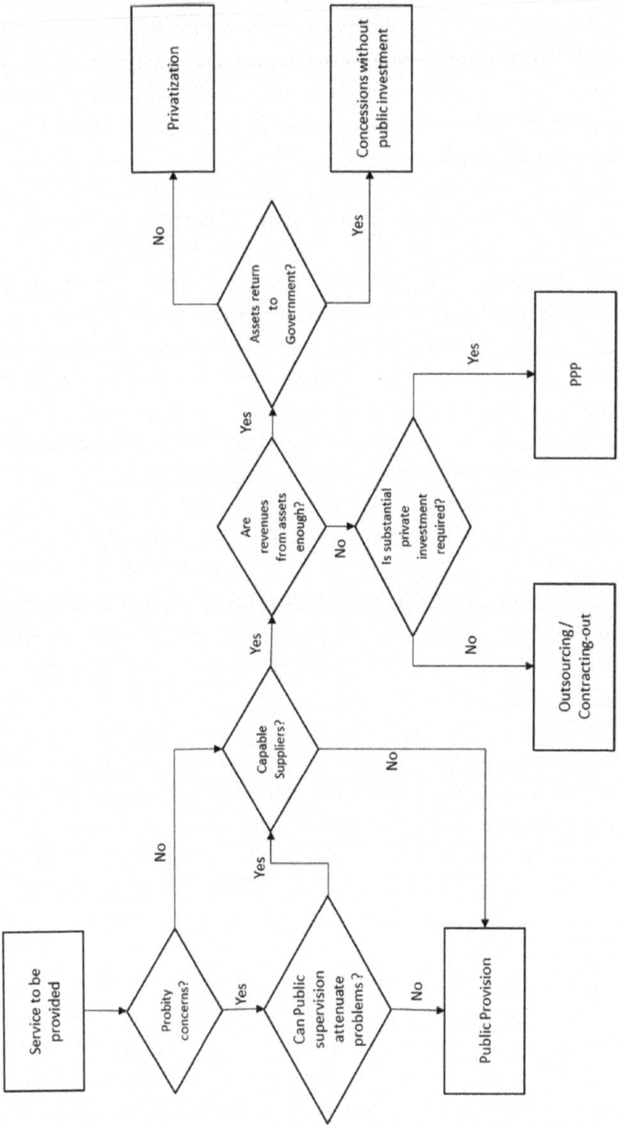

Fig. 9.3 Choosing the mode of delivery

must be delegated. Besides the comparative efficiency between public provision and other modes of delivery, both the attractiveness to private providers and the extent of government co-participation in terms of resource allocation to make initiatives with external partners are key even when capable suppliers exist. If the revenues of assets are not enough to cover construction and operation costs, some degree of government participation will be required.

For goods and services requiring high investments from the government along with low investments from private investors in specific assets, outsourcing or contracting-out tends to be the preferred choice, as in the case of prisons or sports facilities. In these cases, the facilities are normally built by public authorities and later franchised out to private or nonprofit organizations using arms-length contracts, in which governments specify, within the bounds of the cognitive capacities of public managers and watchdog agencies, the tasks to be performed by external organizations.

However, in settings where substantive short-term investments from external actors are required, and capable suppliers can allocate both their financial resources and accumulated expertise in the construction and execution phases, but investments from governments are needed, decision-makers can opt for public–private partnerships (PPPs). For instance, a private operator in charge of building and operating a prison facility will have strong incentives to avoid cost savings during the construction phase to improve the management of the prison ex-post. More specifically, choosing high-quality pipes or adequate cement can decrease the occurrences of water leakages, impede inmate escapes, and prevent the firm from having to refurbish the facilities and receive contractual penalties for its misbehavior. Taking the example of sports facilities, governments can also delegate to private operators the right to build and operate the facilities under PPPs. Using their expertise in entertainment activities, private operators can design facilities that can combine sports and cultural events without major disruptions, thus maximizing the utilization of the assets.

Finally, when private or nonprofit organizations can deploy their capabilities in the pursuit of the public interest in activities that do not need financial support from the government and can be mostly sustained by users, decision-makers can opt for privatization or concessions without public investment. While, in the latter case, assets return to governments as the contract is finished, in privatization, the assets are transferred to external providers, normally at cost, and do not return to the government, thus granting private and nonprofits the highest levels of property and decision control rights over the assets.

Conclusion

This chapter discussed the importance of scope decisions, the diverse types of goods and services, the various existing modes of provision, and the factors that can influence governments to opt for in-house or external provision through private and nonprofit organizations. Interestingly, the chapter demonstrated several instances of private participation in services with low rivalry in consumption and unfeasible exclusion, such as prisons, street lighting, and defense, which are normally provided by public authorities. By highlighting these nuances, the chapter offers instruments to decision-makers for identifying the conditions under which each mode of provision can be invoked.

While the extent of public intervention can range from full control over decisions with zero participation of external actors to extreme privatization, it is important to note that regardless of the mode of provision, public value creation is dependent on capabilities present in the government side. Governments have a significant role in specifying the requirements of the service to be provided and devising and maintaining monitoring or regulation structures to address citizens' needs. Indeed, the presence of contractual incompleteness may exacerbate the cost-versus-quality trade-offs that can arise from profit-oriented organizations, as portrayed in the examples of prisons at the beginning of this chapter.

Governments also play a key role in articulating and orchestrating relationships with private, nonprofit, and multilateral organizations to make major initiatives viable. Besides possessing capabilities to deal with external actors, public officers engaged with scope decisions must be able to navigate internal structures and establish collaborative arrangements with several government agencies in the executive, legislative, and judicial branches. Overall, effective public–private relationships need capable governments to build effective public-public relationships.

References

Abdulkadiroğlu, A., Pathak, P. A., & Walters, C. R. (2018). Free to choose: Can school choice reduce student achievement? *American Economic Journal: Applied Economics, 10*(1), 175–206.

Argyres, N. S., & Zenger, T. R. (2012). Capabilities, transaction costs, and firm boundaries. *Organization Science, 23*(6), 1643–1657.

Baum, J. A., & McGahan, A. M. (2013). The reorganization of legitimate violence: The contested terrain of the private military and security industry during the post-cold war era. *Research in Organizational Behavior, 33*, 3–37.

Berlin, J., Carlström, E., & Karlsson, D. (2023). Backsourcing in the private and public sectors—A systematic review. *Financial Accountability & Management, 39*, 636–687.

Brown, J. D., Earle, J. S., & Telegdy, A. (2006). The productivity effects of privatization: Longitudinal estimates from Hungary, Romania, Russia, and Ukraine. *Journal of Political Economy, 114*(1), 61–99.

Brown, T. L., & Potoski, M. (2003). Contract–management capacity in municipal and county governments. *Public Administration Review, 63*(2), 153–164.

Bruce, J. R., de Figueiredo, J. M., & Silverman, B. S. (2019). Public contracting for private innovation: Government capabilities, decision rights, and performance outcomes. *Strategic Management Journal, 40*(4), 533–555.

Cabral, S. (2006). *"Além das grades": uma análise comparada das modalidades de gestão do sistema prisional* (Doctoral Dissertation [Phd in Management]), Federal University of Bahia, Salvador, Bahia, Brazil.

Cabral, S. (2007). Sobre a participação privada na gestão e operação de prisões no Brasil: uma análise à luz da nova economia institucional. *Organizações & Sociedade, 14*, 29–47.

Cabral, S. (2017). Reconciling conflicting policy objectives in public contracting: The enabling role of capabilities. *Journal of Management Studies, 54*(6), 823–853.

Cabral, S. (2023). Public–Private Partnerships. In *The Brazilian way of doing public administration: Brazil with an's'* (pp. 97–106): Emerald Publishing Limited.

Cabral, S., Lazzarini, S. G., & de Azevedo, P. F. (2010). Private operation with public supervision: Evidence of hybrid modes of governance in prisons. *Public Choice, 145*, 281–293.

Cabral, S., Lazzarini, S. G., & De Azevedo, P. F. (2013). Private entrepreneurs in public services: A longitudinal examination of outsourcing and statization of prisons. *Strategic Entrepreneurship Journal, 7*(1), 6–25.

Cabral, S., Quelin, B., & Maia, W. (2014). Outsourcing failure and reintegration: The influence of contractual and external factors. *Long Range Planning, 47*(6), 365–378.

Cabral, S., & Santos, M.-F. (2018). Accountability mechanisms in public services: Activating new dynamics in a prison system. *International Public Management Journal, 21*(5), 795–821.

Cabral, S., & Saussier, S. (2013). Organizing prisons through public-private partnerships: A cross-country investigation. *BAR-Brazilian Administration Review, 10*, 100–120.

Coase, R. (1937). The nature of the firm. *Economica, 4*, 386–405.

Coase, R. (1974). The lighthouse in economics. *The Journal of Law and Economics, 17*(2), 357–376.

Dachs, B., Kinkel, S., & Jäger, A. (2019). Bringing it all back home? Backshoring of manufacturing activities and the adoption of Industry 4.0 technologies. *Journal of World Business, 54*(6), 101017.

Galiani, S., Gertler, P., & Schargrodsky, E. (2005). Water for life: The impact of the privatization of water services on child mortality. *Journal of Political Economy, 113*(1), 83–120.

Grossman, S. J., & Hart, O. D. (1986). The costs and benefits of ownership: A theory of vertical and lateral integration. *Journal of Political Economy, 94*(4), 691–719.

Hardin, G. (1968). The tragedy of the common. *Science, 162*, 1243–1248.

Hart, O. (2003). Incomplete contracts and public ownership: Remarks, and an application to public-private partnerships. *The Economic Journal, 113*(486), C69–C76.

Hart, O., Shleifer, A., & Vishny, R. W. (1997). The proper scope of government: Theory and an application to prisons. *The Quarterly Journal of Economics, 112*(4), 1127–1161.

Helfat, C. E. (2000). *Guest editor's introduction to the special issue: The evolution of firm capabilities* (Vol. 21, pp. 955–959). Wiley Online Library.

Khanna, T., & Palepu, K. (1997). Why focused strategies. *Harvard Business Review, 75*(4), 41–51.

Lazzarini, S. G. (2022). *The right privatization: Why private firms in public initiatives need capable governments*. Cambridge University Press.

Megginson, W. L., & Netter, J. M. (2001). From state to market: A survey of empirical studies on privatization. *Journal of Economic Literature, 39*(2), 321–389.

Milgrom, P. R., & Roberts, J. (1992). *Economics, organization and management*. Prentice-hall.

Ostrom, E. (1990). *Governing the commons: The evolution of institutions for collective action*. Cambridge University Press.

Ostrom, V., & Ostrom, E. (2019). Public goods and public choices. In *Alternatives for delivering public services* (pp. 7–49). Routledge.

Pigou, A. C. (1920). *The economics of welfare*. Macmillan.

Quelin, B. V., Cabral, S., Lazzarini, S., & Kivleniece, I. (2019). The private scope in public–private collaborations: An institutional and capability-based perspective. *Organization Science, 30*(4), 831–846.
Savas, E. S. (2000). *Privatization and public-private partnerships*. Seven Bridges Press.
Schwerdt, G., Messer, D., Woessmann, L., & Wolter, S. C. (2012). The impact of an adult education voucher program: Evidence from a randomized field experiment. *Journal of Public Economics, 96*(7–8), 569–583.
Shirley, M. M. (1999). Bureaucrats in business: The roles of privatization versus corporatization in state-owned enterprise reform. *World Development, 27*(1), 115–136.
Smith, A. (1999 [1776]). *The wealth of nations*. Penguin.
Spulber, N. (1997). *Redefining the state: Privatization and welfare reform in industrial and transitional economics*. Cambridge University Press.
Teece, D. J., Pisano, G., & Shuen, A. (1997). Dynamic capabilities and strategic management. *Strategic Management Journal, 18*(7), 509–533.
Weimer, D., & Vining, A. (2017). *Policy analysis: Concepts and practice*. Routledge.
Williamson, O. (1985). *The economic institutions of capitalism*. Free Press.
Williamson, O. (1991). Comparative economic organization: The analysis of discrete structural alternatives. *Administrative Science Quarterly, 36*, 269–296.
Williamson, O. (1999). Public and private bureaucracies: A transaction cost economics perspectives. *Journal of Law, Economics, and Organization, 15*(1), 306–342.
Winter, S. G. (2003). Understanding dynamic capabilities. *Strategic Management Journal, 24*(10), 991–995.

CHAPTER 10

Cross-Sector and Public-Public Collaborations

High-quality care during the primary infant stage is widely recognized as one of the main predictors of individual socioemotional skills. It enables the nurturing of children with appropriate mental and physical health, language, motor, and cultural skills that contribute to improved educational and labor market outcomes. In addition to ensuring access to adequate education and health services, actions to promote and preserve family bonds, ensure stable environments for children, prevent traumatic situations, and avoid children entering out-of-home care are crucial to providing value for affected children. These efforts increase their chances of enjoying a better life. Moreover, appropriate care during the primary infancy stage serves as an engine for leveraging public value by enhancing societal benefits. This leads to a population with higher education, increased productivity, and lower rates of trauma. Simultaneously, it helps to reduce public spending on out-of-home care services.[1]

To prevent children from entering out-of-home care, in 2013, the New South Wales state government in Australia launched an innovative program aimed at improving family functioning and promoting a safer environment for children in at-risk families. The "Resilient Families" program encompassed several actions, including in-house interventions

[1] For further details on the consequences of interventions in the primary infant stage, see Engle et al. (2011), Rocha and Soares (2010), and Almond et al. (2018).

S. Cabral, *Strategy for Public and Nonprofit Organizations*,
https://doi.org/10.1007/978-3-031-64969-1_10

with families whose children were at risk of being placed in out-of-home care. The targeted populations included families dealing with challenges related to domestic violence, substance abuse, and mental health conditions.[2]

Public authorities in Australia partnered with a nonprofit organization, The Benevolent Society, to execute their public value-creating strategy through a unique form of outcome-based contract called Social Impact Bonds (SIB).[3] Under this arrangement, private investors injected around AU$ 10 million into a five-year contract (2013–2018). With the guidance of the Department of Communities and Justice (the government agency that set the targets and oversaw the contract), and with financial intermediation by both the Westpac Banking Corporation and the Commonwealth Bank of Australia, the contract aimed to reduce entries of targeted children into out-of-home care by providing services for families that have reached the risk of significant harm (ROSH) threshold and enabling the creation of safer home environments.

Using measurement techniques with the support of matched treatment and comparison groups, the evaluation compared 303 similar families, totaling 816 children when all siblings are included in the measurement. The results recorded 32% fewer children entering out-of-home care compared to the matched control group. In other words, children assisted by this collaborative arrangement involving public, private, and nonprofit organizations are less likely to be placed in out-of-home facilities when compared to children who received business as usual services provided by the local authorities. Furthermore, the private investors who funded the nonprofit at risk reaped an overall weighted return on their investment across five years of 16%.[4] In this case, the government shared part of the savings generated by the nonprofit intervention with investors. This is a stylized win–win-win situation in which the benefits are shared with the citizens, the investors, and the political actors who sponsored the initiative.

[2] https://www.nsw.gov.au/osii/social-impact-investments/resilient-families-program.

[3] In a social impact bond, private investors fund initiatives in specific target areas, engage specialized organizations to deliver services, and receive compensation upon the achievement of prespecified goals. For more on social impact bonds and other types of outcome-based contracts, see Lazzarini et al. (2022), Nardi et al. (2022), and Economy et al. (2023).

[4] https://www.benevolent.org.au/about-us/innovative-approaches/social-benefit-bond.

In addition to stimulating the provision of classical social services like education and health, governments often rely on cross-sector collaborations for other activities with both social meaning and economic implications for the communities they serve. One of these activities is the organization of sporting, cultural, and civic events, which requires interactions among public, private, and nonprofit organizations to attain successful outcomes. Based on the multiple preferences, goals, incentives, and moral beliefs of the entities involved, conflict and alignment can arise and alternate, requiring policies and actions to orchestrate interactions among a myriad of stakeholders. The Carnival of Salvador in Brazil offers an interesting example of this dynamic.

With a population of 2.4 million inhabitants as of the end of 2023, Salvador stands as the fifth-largest municipality in Brazil. Serving as the capital of the state of Bahia in northeast Brazil, Salvador held the status of the Brazilian capital between 1549 and 1763 during Portuguese colonization. Boasting approximately 81% of its citizens self-identifying as Black or Brown, Salvador is renowned as one of the world's hubs of Black culture. The city has attracted global attention, with myriad world-class artists such as Beyoncé, Jimmy Cliff, Michael Jackson, Quincy Jones, Paul Simon, and Bono Vox expressing admiration for the local culture, music, and iconic artists such as Gilberto Gil and Caetano Veloso.

Salvador is particularly recognized for its distinctive Carnival, where festivities unfold on the streets. During the official six days of festivities around 700,000 people at the same time go to the streets to follow musical groups, mostly playing in huge cargo trucks with stages and powerful sound (*trio elétrico*).[5] The activation of local supply chains and their economic and political implications, along with the intangible sentiment of pride and esteem to local citizens, are some of the benefits of the carnival. However, organizing a major event such as this is far from evident. For that, the municipality of Salvador. Indeed, massive

[5] While most trios are free for revelers with costs supported by both public authorities and private sponsors, other trios charge from revelers the right of staying in a cordoned area close to trucks. The paid trios do not preclude people outside of the ropes following the parade and enjoying the music without bearing any cost. Wealthy citizens may also watch the parades in paid stands (balconies or camarotes) in structures built by private entrepreneurs with entry fees ranging from US$50 to US$500 per day. Taxes charged from private entrepreneurs and sponsorships of major brands, especially beer, banking, and consumer goods companies, subsidize non-paying masses and allow them to watch their preferred artists free of charge.

investments in public security, healthcare, health, city transit, mass transportation, and sanitation control are needed to ensure successful operation. These investments can be made by distinct levels of government at the federal, state, and city levels, thus requiring coordination to both secure funds and assure the participation of myriad public agencies and public departments. In addition to coordinating several agencies, often involved in political turfs, the municipality must involve representatives of entrepreneurs, street vendors, artists, and civil society organizations, among other groups whose interests often conflict.

In joint research with Dale Krane, I have found that collaborative governance, especially among public agencies, is a key factor for the perpetuity of the successful model of Salvador's Carnival. The establishment of an official collaborative arena in which relevant stakeholders have a voice to express their claims, despite existing power-knowledge asymmetries, is an important feature to discuss and deal with tensions between profit-oriented, culture-oriented, and power-oriented stakeholders. While trust among participants was not identified in this arrangement, its absence seems not to preclude stakeholders from acting in a collaborative fashion. In fact, collaboration, even among rivals, can occur because an unsuccessful event does not interest anybody: an eventual failure could trigger political, economic, social, and symbolic implications for all involved. Along these lines, informal connections and networks built over time can foster stakeholders to collaborate and lead to cooperating in this unusual example of cross-sector collaboration.[6] As in the Australian case, this is also a triple-win situation benefiting society, entrepreneurs, and politicians, either for succeeding or not failing.

Both cases illustrate the importance of cross-sector collaboration in areas in which neither public agencies, private organizations, nor nonprofits acting in isolation can attain the expected social outcomes. These two cases also highlight the importance of further exploring under which conditions cross-sector collaborations are needed and create public value. They also stimulate reflections about the leading role of governments in terms of orchestrating different stakeholders and myriad organizations from different sectors with competing interests. Most importantly, as mentioned in the previous chapter on organizational boundaries and the proper scope of the government, public-public collaborations among

[6] Cabral and Krane (2018).

myriad public bureaus are a necessary condition for effective public–private collaborations. They can also be crucial for the development of some novel and value-creating arrangements to deliver public services through providers from different sectors.

Cross-Sector Collaborations: Definition and Forms

If you want to go fast, go alone; if you want to go far, go together.

Sometimes, we encounter the saying above with variations in political speeches, in business meetings with emotional content, and more recently in short communications on social media. Despite the controversy around the origins of the saying above—some attributes originate from Africa in a loose and imprecise way—this proverb allows some reflections for those who are interested in exploring the relationship between strategy and public policies. It challenges an ossified individualistic view present in Westernized societies and calls attention to a communal and collective way of addressing these problems. It also sheds light on the fact that problems characterized by complexity, with multiple stakeholders with conflicting views involved, massive interdependencies, and trade-offs with solutions benefiting some groups, sometimes at the expense of other groups, and with a nonobvious solution are rarely solved by a single actor acting alone.

In other words, the complexity inherent in significant problems affecting businesses and society at large demands the collaboration of multiple actors, especially when the issues lack a clear definition and the required resources to address the situation are uncertain. Addressing wicked problems, such as climate change, poverty alleviation, reduction of social inequalities, affordable healthcare, public security, and malnutrition, among others, requires collaborative efforts due to the ineffectiveness of individual actions and the difficulty of reaching a consensus among collaborating partners. Despite the challenges, collaborative actions among diverse stakeholders with different resources, knowledge, and perspectives are crucial for obtaining partial solutions to these persistent issues.

After the surge of the so-called "new public management", existing arrangements involving public, private, nonprofits, and citizens aimed at delivering services with social implications gained the attention of practitioners and scholars from public administration and (strategic) management fields, bearing different labels such as cross-sector partnerships to address social issues, multi-sectoral collaborations, cross-sector partnerships, tri-sector collaborations, cross-sector collaborations, among others. For the sake of consistency, I adopt the term "cross-sector collaborations" (CSC) to describe voluntary or contractual relationships involving two or more actors from different sectors. These collaborations entail joint efforts to address a wicked problem by collectively understanding, framing, and designing viable solutions. Additionally, CSCs involve implementing the necessary activities to achieve outcomes that would not be attainable by single-sector actors working in isolation.[7]

In an influential paper, John Selsky and Barbara Parker identify four arenas where CSC can be invoked to address wicked problems: public–private, business-nonprofit, government-nonprofit, and tri-sectoral collaborations.[8]

First, as mentioned in the previous chapter, *public–private collaborations* involve joint action between governments and firms to address societal goals. Although the combination of financial resources, human capital, technologies, managerial expertise, and legitimacy dispersed between governments and firms is largely invoked to address infrastructure and logistic projects, the menu of sectors is vast and, in practice, includes almost all services provided by public authorities, such as education, health, leisure, rehabilitation activities, defense, urban services, and so on. The degree of involvement of governments varies according to the capacity of the private sector to fund and deliver the goods and services, as well as according to the existing probity concerns arising from a further involvement of external actors in the provision of services normally provided by public authorities. Public–Private Partnerships (PPP) can be included in this category.

Second, *collaborations between business firms and nonprofit organizations* can be formed to address social issues in several areas and in diverse ways. Frequently, firms engage with nonprofit organizations based on

[7] While the literature on cross-sector collaborations is vast, in general, existing works in public administration (Agranoff, 2012; Bryson et al., 2006, 2015), strategy (Gatignon & Capron, 2023; Quélin et al., 2017), and general management (Dentoni et al., 2016; Selsky & Parker, 2005) adopt similar definitions for CSC.

[8] Selsky and Parker (2005).

instrumental grounds to address the needs of surrounding communities and reap the benefits of improved relational ties that allow firms to conduct business as usual. Corporate Social Responsibility (CSR) activities, with nonprofit organizations' support, have been largely invoked by firms whose activities involve negative externalities, as seen in the mining and oil and gas industries. Nonprofits are particularly useful to firms in deploying projects in areas with material implications for firm performance, as well as actions that can reduce future liability for firms and eventually uncover poor environmental performance.[9] Firms may also engage with nonprofits to fill existing institutional voids and provide access to education and training in areas that will benefit both the firm and society. This type of collaboration aids firms in maintaining continuous operations and achieving their financial objectives.[10] Firms also collaborate with nonprofits to develop products and services for disenfranchised populations, as seen in the case of vaccines and medicines for infectious and neglected diseases. Major pharmaceutical companies often partner with nonprofits, such as the Bill & Melinda Gates Foundation, to address critical health issues and ensure broader access to essential medical solutions.[11] Finally, firms may collaborate with nonprofits to address voids in market-based institutions, align the interests of citizens, firms, and society, and achieve public value creation. Aline Gatignon and Laurence Capron illustrate this case by showing how Natura, a worldwide cosmetic company, was able to initiate collective action efforts with the support of nonprofit organizations. This collaboration helped the firm establish financially sustainable supply chains while simultaneously preserving natural resources and improving the conditions of disenfranchised stakeholders.[12]

Third, *collaborations between government and nonprofit organizations*, whether through charitable, religious, or other government-induced nonprofits, have been extensively utilized for decades in providing social services such as education, health, research, development, and innovation, among others. In a study on government-nonprofit relationships,

[9] An excellent discussion about the drivers of greenwashing can be seen in Delmas and Burbano (2011).

[10] Khanna and Palepu (1997) provide several examples of corporate and competitive strategies to address institutional voids in both developed and developing countries.

[11] George et al. (2012).

[12] Gatignon and Capron (2023).

Dennis Young posits that nonprofits play three major roles when interacting with governments. First, they can supplement the government by filling voids left by public authorities and supplying services funded by sources other than government expenditures. Second, they can complement government functions by bringing different capabilities, engaging citizens and other relevant stakeholders, providing flexibility lacking in public structures, and legitimizing some government policies. Third, government-nonprofit relationships can be adversarial, with nonprofits opposing and creating barriers to government intents, as seen in movements advocating for minority rights or self-interested and rent-seeking groups such as business syndicates.[13] In this landscape, it is not surprising that governments frequently intervene in nonprofits, whether by stimulating their creation and funding or by influencing their operation by assigning representatives to nonprofit boards. While politically connected nonprofits offer opportunities for corruption and patronage, strengthened relationships between governments and nonprofits can create public value. For instance, the Fraunhofer-Gesellschaft (FhG) in Germany, the largest nonprofit organization focused on applied research in Europe, enjoys autonomy from the government in selecting research projects to be funded. However, the nonprofit is subject to some government interference, as the government appoints the FhG's president and some of its board members. The German government provides one-third of the funding, with the remaining two-thirds coming from private funds, competitive grants, and multilateral sources. This collaborative arrangement has facilitated major advances in the automotive industry, as well as in research and development in the fields of micro- and nanoelectronics, and mechatronics, to name a few.[14]

Finally, *cross-sectoral collaborations formed by multiple actors including public, private, nonprofits, and multilateral organizations* are also crucial for specific projects and ongoing activities involving issues requiring resources dispersed across organizations. In these collaborations, each partner is expected to bring different attributes to the table to understand the issues at stake, set priorities, and implement solutions to wicked

[13] See Young (2000).

[14] Please refer to Intarakumnerd and Goto (2018) for more information about research and development institutes in Germany.

problems characterized by multiple stakeholders and complex relationships. Efforts to address HIV/AIDS in Botswana, Africa, are examples of collaborations involving multiple partners. Pharmaceutical companies like Merck, along with local governments and multilateral organizations, engaged in joint actions to provide life-saving medicines, train health professionals to deliver adequate treatment to infected citizens, build diagnosis and treatment infrastructures, and design and manage effective distribution channels to ensure that all items required for treatment are available to targeted populations.[15] As in any complex venture involving different actors, collaborative efforts with multiple organizations from various sectors require a certain degree of coordination. Similar to systems integrators in information technology projects and Engineering, Procurement, and Construction contractors (EPC contractors) in mega infrastructure projects, cross-sector collaborations typically involve intermediaries. These intermediaries play a key role in aligning divergent interests, bridging partners, and mitigating conflicts to facilitate effective collaboration.[16]

Overall, collaborations involving partners from multiple sectors share similarities and differences with private-sector strategic alliances designed to address complex problems. Recognizing both convergent and divergent aspects is crucial for fostering cross-disciplinary dialogues between the strategy and public and nonprofit fields. This understanding can contribute to more effective and mutually beneficial collaborations in addressing major challenges affecting both developed and developing countries. It also holds the potential to reconcile economic and socioenvironmental goals, enabling sustainable approaches to address global challenges.

Strategic Alliances and Cross-Sector Collaborations: Differences and Similarities

For-profit firms also engage in joint actions with other firms to achieve mutual objectives that might be unattainable without collaboration. These actions often take the form of equity and non-equity agreements, falling

[15] Rangan et al. (2006).

[16] Gil and Pinto (2018).

somewhere between vertical integration and arms-length market transactions. Joint ventures, consortia, supply chain networks, special purpose vehicles for specific projects, franchises, and other interorganizational relationships are hybrid forms of organization typically grouped under the construct of strategic alliances.[17]

Strategic alliances are instrumental for many for-profit firms achieving their economic interests. Firms such as Toyota and Honda in the automotive industry are well-known for building partnerships with major suppliers. Increased levels of information sharing and cooperation among firms in the supply chain were pivotal in reducing time to market for new products, lowering prices, and improving quality across various attributes. These collaborative efforts enabled Japanese automakers to gain market share and outperform worldwide giants like Ford, General Motors, Chrysler, and Volkswagen in highly competitive markets.[18]

Other forms of strategic alliances, without the strong control of supply networks by major firms, are indeed possible. In the software industry, the operating system Linux is a product of a network formed by independent organizations in a non-equity alliance. In such arrangements, collaborating parties share resources and capabilities without commitments to equity stakes. In this context, parties are unable to unilaterally define prices, quantities, and quality attributes. Collaborative efforts from several parties provided Linux with attributes such as stability, reliability, and flexibility, enabling it to challenge Microsoft's domination in areas like the operating system market, particularly in segments related to web hosting, cloud computing, and enterprise environments.[19] Unsurprisingly, alliances are central in strategic management thinking, drawing the attention of practitioners such as managers of involved firms, financial analysis, consultants, and strategy scholars.

Yet, more recently, the strategic management field has broadened its focus to diverse types of collaborative efforts beyond those involving firms interested in reaping market-like benefits. Some strategy scholars, concerned with problems affecting firms and markets, have turned their attention to how strategy theories and strategies could be designed and

[17] For a discussion on the aspects involving alliances under a strategic management perspective see the book of Mesquita et al. (2017). An organization economics view on alliances can be found in Ménard (2022).

[18] Dyer et al. (2018).

[19] Gulati et al. (2000) and Jacobides et al. (2018).

implemented to address wicked problems involving pressing social needs. In convergence with previous efforts in the public and nonprofit field, the strategic management field has progressively recognized the importance of cross-sector collaborations (CSC) as hybrid forms of organization that can potentially address major problems affecting businesses and society at large.[20]

While strategic alliances and cross-sector collaborations (CSC) have significant differences, they also share several intersections. Recognizing both the divergent points and the similarities is crucial for conceptual and empirical efforts needed to design and implement effective business and public policies targeted to address wicked problems affecting citizens. Delineating the existing differences is also important to avoid attempts to apply concepts and strategies conceived in the for-profit realm to collaborative arrangements involving actors with different purposes and subject to different incentives and constraints. Indeed, sometimes such attempts, instead of creating value, can lead to value destruction. This may occur either because the resulting outcomes are not mutually beneficial or due to ineffective investments made by partnering organizations, which could have been better utilized in value-creating activities.

Divergent Points Between Alliances and Cross-Sector Collaborations

Strategic alliances and cross-sector collaborations (CSC) diverge in three key features: ***motivation, nature of the partners involved, and*** the way both forms deal with ***uncertainty and specific investments.***

Motivation in strategic alliances is typically business oriented, primarily centered on economic objectives. These objectives often include attempts to gain market share, develop innovative products and services, enter new geographic markets or different industries, create barriers to avoid threats from competitors, and simply survive in competitive environments. For instance, two firms interested in exploring offshore oil and gas might form a strategic alliance to share resources, expertise, and risks in order to reap benefits in this capital-intensive industry.[21] In contrast, cross-sector collaborations are formed by partners with objectives beyond

[20] Quélin et al. (2017).

[21] This example can be found in Harrigan (2003).

economic outcomes and are focused on addressing complex problems that require coordination and collaboration with organizations from different sectors. The products, outputs, and impacts of cross-sector collaborations go beyond financial measures of profits and return on equity. Instead, they can involve indicators related to socioenvironmental goals, benefiting targeted populations and societies in general.

The *nature of partners involved* in strategic alliances, as depicted in the strategy literature, typically consists of for-profit firms. These firms may either operate in the same industry or in different industries, aiming to access or combine resources that allow partners to achieve their economic interests. With clear and unambiguous objectives, firms from related and unrelated areas can design collaborative arrangements with attributes conducive to improved financial performance and corporate goals. For instance, a green energy company focused on wind and solar sources might partner with a telecom company to explore synergies in the free-energy market. In this case, the telecom firm can provide its energy partner access to millions of potential consumers while simultaneously expanding its portfolio of services.[22] In cross-sector collaborations, the presence of organizations from the public, private, and nonprofit sectors can indeed equip the organizational arrangement with resources and capabilities spread across different sectors. This combination can address major problems involving socioenvironmental goals. However, the presence of partners with mixed objectives can pose additional challenges to the effectiveness of collaborative efforts. The diverse goals and motivations of partners from different sectors may require careful negotiation and coordination to align efforts toward shared objectives.

Dealing with uncertainty and specific investments[23]: In most strategic alliances involving private firms, (incomplete) contracts play a leading role in coordinating among partners and preventing opportunism arising from uncertainty and asset specificity. In the latter case, costs of transacting may escalate when dealing with highly specialized assets, such as machines, technologies, control systems, and human capital that cannot be easily

[22] In 2023, Vivo, the Spanish giant in telecom partnered with a renewable energy company to explore the free energy market. See https://www.bnamericas.com/en/news/auren-vivo-sign-contract-to-create-a-jv-with-an-eye-on-the-opening-of-free-energy-market.

[23] I thank Leandro Pongeluppe for the suggestion to include uncertainty and specific investments as a distinctive feature between CSC and strategic alliances.

redeployed to other activities without economic losses. Finding alternative partners, or suppliers in the case of supply chain networks, is not straightforward in these cases, and the shadow of opportunism is present as one party may act opportunistically to reap short-term benefits or pursue other strategic goals outside the scope of the alliance. To protect their investments, parties create clauses and safeguards that can negatively affect alliance performance. These costs can be amplified in settings where the anticipation of environmental changes in supply and demand is costly or unfeasible.[24] Compared to strategic alliances, cross-sector collaborations (CSC) employ some instruments to address opportunism and specific investment issues that may arise in collaborations involving partners from different sectors with potentially conflicting preferences. CSC can endogenously select personnel with altruistic preferences, rely on intrinsic and extrinsic incentives, avoid intrusive monitoring mechanisms, and utilize other non-equity governance mechanisms to address opportunism. Like in some strategic alliances, CSC can reinforce the use of relational ties with partners within existing networks to mitigate reputational risks and gain recognition from relevant stakeholders. These approaches are aimed at boosting mission-driven outcomes and aligning the diverse objectives of partners in the collaboration.[25]

Convergent Points Between Alliances and Cross-Sector Collaborations

Strategic alliances and cross-sector collaborations also present similar features that can facilitate dialogues between strategy and public and nonprofit fields and help practitioners implement effective CSC. Both forms are useful to exploit *resource complementarities*, to *share risks, decision, and property rights*. Their performance is also enhanced by s*electing capable partners* and *designing appropriate governance mechanisms*, especially when attempting to address non-trivial and complex problems, oftentimes characterized by specific investments that are idiosyncratic to the problem to be solved.

[24] See the works of Ménard (2022), Williamson (1991), and Artz and Brush (2000) for a transaction cost perspective in alliances and other hybrid forms.

[25] The works of Alonso and Andrews (2019), Rivera-Santos et al. (2017), and Feilhauer and Hahn (2021) offer a portrait on how the strategy literature has been dealing with contractual issues in cross-sector collaborations.

Resource Complementarities: To achieve the mutual objectives aimed by partners, both strategic alliances and cross-sector collaborations rely on complementary resources and capabilities possessed by dispersed organizations. In a resource dependency perspective, organizations must manage interdependencies with other organizations to succeed. This includes actions to access relevant resources and capabilities that are potentially synergistic and complementary with the resources and capabilities that the organization possesses. Once combined, these resources can be sources of value creation.[26] Similar to alliances in the private sector where partnering organizations share critical resources and capabilities such as distribution channels or technologies, in CSC, organizations can also share resources and capabilities in an instrumental way. Firms engaging in partnerships with nonprofit organizations may seek access to the necessary knowledge about the demands of stakeholder demands as well as expertise to address claims of legitimate stakeholders that may eventually thwart the effectiveness of business policies and instrumental goals. For instance, McDonald's partners with nonprofits like Keep America Beautiful and the World Wildlife Fund (WWF) in its efforts to reduce littering and support circular systems through improved recycling practices.[27]

Indeed, whether in strategic alliances or in cross-sector collaborations, relationships involving complementary resources and capabilities can be an effective way to share risks, particularly when costs for each partner are high and/or when uncertainty is present. This scenario is common in biotech projects, for instance, where a firm possessing skills in researching a new drug may partner with a firm that has expertise in the development process and distribution channels.[28] Similarly, public–private partnerships

[26] The seminal book of Pfeffer and Salancik (2003) is the landmark of the resource dependency theory (RDT). For a review of the application of RDT, especially on mergers and acquisitions, and strategic alliances, see Hillman et al. (2009). For an account of RDT in cross-sector collaborations, see Selsky and Parker (2005).

[27] A description of McDonald's sustainable practices can be seen in https://corporate.mcdonalds.com/corpmcd/our-purpose-and-impact/our-planet/packaging-toys-and-waste.html#:~:text=For%20example%2C%20McDonald's%20USA%20partners,beautify%20communities%20across%20the%20country.

[28] See Vasudeva and Anand (2011).

in infrastructure often involve firms with expertise requiring public supervision and the prior knowledge of civil servants to create public value.[29] In both forms, complementary resources and capabilities can also enable co-investments, not only in assets necessary for the value creation process but in routines to ensure that knowledge between allies is shared. These co-investments can even give rise to self-enforcing and relational governance mechanisms.[30]

Partner selection is a critical and common aspect in both strategic alliances and cross-sector collaborations. The inability to identify capable partners, whether with complementary resources and capabilities or with the necessary willingness to both share their expertise and absorb knowledge from other allies, can impose limits on the effectiveness of collaborative efforts in both forms. Conversely, the capacity to select partners with characteristics conducive to value creation is widely recognized as a factor of success in both alliances and CSC.[31]

Existing research in strategy acknowledges that adequate partner selection involves the ability to recognize in the partner complementary or desirable resources and capabilities. It also emphasizes the importance of finding partners that minimize the potential for losses of status and reputation. Partnering with promising or reputable partners is considered a signal of quality and may endorse future connections, especially in settings characterized by strong interdependencies.[32] Predictably, to avoid failures, organizations involved in cross-sector collaborations tend to prefer partners within current networks. This approach helps avoid failures in the selection process and assures partners that undergo assessments of trustworthiness, being less prone to engage in opportunistic actions. Considering the prevailing resource constraints and the need to achieve internal and external recognition, as well as the reputational risks in cross-sector collaborations, it is common for organizations involved in these

[29] Cabral et al. (2013).

[30] Dyer et al. (2018) and Forrer et al. (2014) develop interesting insights of relational governance arising from complementary resources and capabilities in strategic alliances and cross-sector collaborations, respectively.

[31] Rondinelli and London (2003).

[32] By analyzing the patterns of alliance formation and the choices for high-status partners in the telecom industry Rosenkopf and Padula (2008) provide interesting insights on both the importance and on the drivers of partner selection.

collaborations to rely on recurrent relationships with partners that are already part of existing networks.[33]

Governance also plays a crucial role in the success of collaboration efforts, as recognized in existing literature on both strategic alliances and cross-sector collaborations.[34] Governance in alliances and CSC are also important to mitigate hazards and reduce conflicts that can potentially challenge the attainment of desired mutual gains.[35]

Governance structures in collaborative arrangements encompass formal or informal rules and procedures designed to ensure information and knowledge sharing, allocate decision rights, devise accountability structures, identify common and dissonant goals, and recognize opportunities and threats to attain expected goals. Importantly, they enable a trust-based environment that fosters collaborative efforts in both single-sector and multi-sector collaborations. Examining alliances in the telecommunication industry, Rachelle Sampson found that firms choosing misaligned governance structures experience a performance penalty. For instance, adopting equity structures in settings where non-equity agreements would be more suitable leads to reduced innovative performance for firms involved. This highlights the significance of aligning governance structures with the specific characteristics and objectives of the collaborative effort.[36] Similarly, structures enabling knowledge sharing and knowledge absorption also lead to improved performance in R&D alliances.[37]

The combination of governance structures with other strategic attributes that are present in the partners involved in collaborative efforts is equally relevant for improved performance in cross-sector collaborations. In an analysis of collaborations between local governments, firms, and nonprofit organizations in waste management in the United Kingdom between 2003 and 2014, Rhys Andrews and Jose Manoel Alonso found that governance by targets—those involving payments contingent on the attainment of outcomes—is an effective way to improve

[33] Please refer to Bryson et al. (2006) and Feilhauer and Hahn (2021) to know more about the challenges associated to partner selection in CSC.

[34] Bryson et al. (2015) emphasize the importance of governance in cross-sector collaborations. Similarly, for strategic alliances, Reuer and Devarakonda (2016) and Keller et al. (2021) shed light on the relationship between alliance governance and performance.

[35] See Williamson (1998).

[36] Sampson (2004).

[37] Vasudeva and Anand (2011).

recycling rates. They observed that cross-sector collaborations with target-setting exhibit even higher rates of recycling when diverse partners and accumulated capabilities are involved in establishing such collaborations. This underscores the importance of aligning governance mechanisms with specific goals and contexts in cross-sector collaborations.[38] Certainly, cross-sector collaborations tend to be effective when partners establish governance structures that facilitate the identification of key tasks and focused targets to be attained.[39]

Table 10.1 summarizes the divergent and convergent aspects of strategic alliances and cross-sector.

Table 10.1 Major divergent and convergent points between strategic alliances and cross-sector collaborations

Strategic alliances and cross-sector collaborations	
Divergent points	**Summarized description**
Motivation	Economic outcomes in strategic alliances versus societal needs in CSC
Nature of partners involved	Single sector versus multi-sector partners
Dealing with uncertainty and specific investments	Contractual safeguards versus relational ties[40]
Convergent points	**Summarized description**
Resource complementarities	Pooling synergistic resources and capabilities previously dispersed
Partner selection	Identification of capable and complementary partners as a key attribute for success
Governance	Need of structures and process to assure collaborative efforts and the attainment of common outcomes

[38] Alonso and Andrews (2019).

[39] The collaboration between McDonald's and the Environmental Defense Fund (EDF) to reduce waste, as exemplified by, Rondinelli and London (2003) underscores the importance of well-defined tasks and initiatives within a clear waste-reduction plan, allowing both partners to work toward clear and tangible goals.

[40] While relational contracts are possible in strategic alliances (e.g., keiretsu in Japanese supply chains), social norms based on trust play a more vital role in cross-sector collaborations.

Collaborative Governance in Cross-Sector Collaborations

As suggested by the initial examples in this chapter on childcare and civic festivals, addressing policy issues through cross-sector collaborations often requires an active role for governments as orchestrators of collaborative efforts involving a myriad of public, private, and nonprofit organizations. It is not difficult to imagine how challenging the resolution of wicked problems, characterized by incomplete information, interdependencies, and constant changes in external environments, can be. Considering the complexity of problems with these features and the multiple and conflicting objectives at stake, ensuring that all parties commit to the necessary collaborative efforts in cross-sector collaborations is not straightforward.[41]

In the realm of conflict resolution, political scientists, public administration scholars, public management experts, and urban planning researchers have paid special attention to understanding how collaborative efforts among different actors coalesce in these settings. Existing evidence from the United States documents that some public agencies at the country, state, and local levels have a history of both formal and informal intergovernmental cooperation to implement policy programs in various areas, such as education and transportation, dating back to the nineteenth century.[42]

However, the intensification of cross-sector collaborations after the 1990s has given rise to numerous works focused on understanding the foundations, drivers, components, mechanisms, and structures fostering collaborative efforts to address complex problems. Both practitioners and researchers are particularly concerned with understanding how to stimulate participants to allocate resources in collaborations, how to transition from adversarial and contentious relationships to collaborative negotiations and decision-making, and under which conditions collaborative efforts to address problems that cannot be tackled by a single organization in isolation are likely to succeed. These works can be grouped under the broad umbrella of *collaborative governance*.

[41] Head (2019).

[42] See Elazar (1965).

Attempts to create models and frameworks explaining the governance of arrangements involving organizations from different sectors were largely inspired by cooperative practices observed in the real world. Scholars with various theoretical perspectives undertook efforts in response to this inspiration. Nobel Prize winner Elinor Ostrom and her colleagues of the "Bloomington School of Institutional Analysis" established a comprehensive research agenda to understand how groups in civil society can interact with private and public organizations to address collective action problems. Drawing on examples from common-pool resources like water basins, forests, and marine ecosystems, collaborative efforts occur under polycentricity, wherein governance and decision-making are exercised by multiple centers of authority pertaining to different and overlapping jurisdictions, rather than a centralized and top-down authority.[43] This view has inspired efforts to understand the strategic implications of cross-sector collaborations with collective action dilemmas.[44] The Advocacy Coalition Framework (ACF) is also a well-recognized approach to deal with wicked problems through increased collaboration among actors with similar beliefs to attain common policy objectives.[45]

Public administration and public management scholars have not only contributed to a better understanding of the collaborative process but also provided insights into how to engage participants in collaborative efforts and under what conditions consensus-based decision-making can succeed in cross-sector collaborations. In their models and frameworks,

[43] For further exploration of institutional and polycentric perspectives in collaborative governance, refer to Ostrom (1990), McGinnis (2011), Ostrom and Ostrom (2019), and Araral (2014).

[44] Patala et al. (2022) employ a polycentric approach to analyze circular economy systems in developed countries, focusing on collaborative efforts involving firms, government, and nonprofits. In various arenas of cooperation, the parties involved develop instruments for mutual adjustment, information sharing, and resource sharing. Gatignon and Capron (2023) employ polycentric lenses to explain how private firms can navigate institutional failures, such as limited access to capital and labor markets, in emerging markets. They achieve this by building collective structures with other stakeholders through cross-sector collaborations. These practices enable firms to create trust-based environments, address pressing social dilemmas, and simultaneously reap economic benefits.

[45] Refer to Weible et al. (2011) for an overview of the Advocacy Coalition Framework (ACF). For an attempt to integrate the ACF with collaborative governance theories to foster more collaborative and less adversarial relationships, see Koebele (2019).

several authors have helped identify relevant variables influencing the design, implementation, and assessment of collaborative arrangements. These arrangements often involve governments, through myriad agencies and departments, playing a leading role in enabling solutions that are compatible with democratic and non-adversarial approaches to addressing complex problems, which demand the resources, expertise, and legitimacy of organizations across different sectors. From this perspective, Chris Ansell and Alison Gash define collaborative governance as "*a governing arrangement where one or more public agencies directly engage non-state stakeholders in a collective decision-making process that is formal, consensus-oriented, and deliberative and that aims to make or implement public policy or manage public programs or assets*".[46] Likewise, but with a stronger emphasis on cross-sector collaborations, Kirk Emerson and Tina Nabatchi see collaborative governance as "*the process and structures of public policy decision making and management that engage people across the boundaries of public agencies, levels of government, and/or the public, private, and civic spheres to carry out a public purpose that could not otherwise be accomplished*".[47]

In addition to relying on several factors and constructs familiar to management theories, such as capabilities, strategic leadership, modes of organizing, and trust-building, collaborative governance models developed by public administration and public administration and public management scholars explicitly outline how and why expected changes in the status quo can occur in cross-sector collaborations in a logically structured fashion.[48] These aspects render collaborative governance models actionable and suitable for dialogue with strategic management works on cross-sector collaborations, especially when governments play a pivotal role in these collaborative efforts.

[46] Ansell and Gash (2008, p. 545).

[47] Emerson and Nabatchi (2015, p. 18).

[48] The list of collaborative governance contributions published in the main public administration and public management outlets grew exponentially in the 2000s and 2010s. Major works include Agranoff (2012), Bryson et al. (2006), McGuire (2006), Ansell and Gash (2008), and Emerson and Nabatchi (2015).

The Ansell and Gash Model of Collaborative Governance

With more than 9400 citations in Google Scholar as of December 2023, the collaborative governance model of Ansell and Gash published in the Journal of Public Administration in Theory in 2008[49] is arguably the most recognized model t for understanding why organizations collaborate and why collaborations can succeed or fail.[50] This model, based on an extensive set of real-world cases, consists of three blocks that influence the collaborative process: starting conditions, institutional design, and facilitative leadership. The collaborative process leads to outcomes representing changes.

In the Ansell and Gash model, the collaborative process is influenced by *starting conditions* which consist of power–resource–knowledge asymmetries, incentives and constraints on participation, and the prehistory of cooperation or conflict. The presence of actors with strong power, coupled with a lack of incentives to come to the table and previous records of conflicts and animosity, can negatively influence the effectiveness of the collaborative process.

Equally, the fundamental protocols for collaboration included in *institutional design* affect the collaborative process. Participatory inclusiveness, forum exclusiveness, clear ground rules, and process transparency can motivate stakeholders to participate, serve as elements of trust-building, and ensure that the deadlines of the collaborative process are met.

The third block of the model involves *facilitative leadership*. Similar to the collaborative model developed by John Bryson, Barbara Crosby, and Melissa Stone,[51] who posit that "*for collaborations to thrive, they need ongoing sponsorship from people who have formal authority and championing from people who use mainly informal authority to engage partners in their mutual work*",[52] Ansell and Gash emphasize that the effectiveness of collaborative efforts depends on facilitative leaders who connect antagonistic perspectives and manage interactions among members through arbitration, facilitation, and mediation. Leadership is key in uniting parties and navigating negotiations through challenging situations.

[49] See Ansell and Gash (2008).

[50] Johnston et al. (2011).

[51] See Bryson et al. (2006, 2015).

[52] Bryson et al. (2015, p. 654).

Ansell and Gash conceive the *collaborative process* as a cycle consisting of face-to-face dialogue, trust-building, commitment to process, shared understanding, and intermediate outcomes. In general, communication is central to the collaborative process, allowing stakeholders to perceive opportunities for mutual gain, enable trust, respect, and sense of ownership over the collaborative process. As partners collaborate, they develop a shared understanding on the collaborative process, enabling learning and the attainment of intermediate outcomes, or small wins that can be seen as steps for ultimate *outcomes*.[53]

Collaborative Governance and Performance: The Role of Cross-Sector Capabilities and Public-Public Capabilities for Cross-Sector Collaborations Involving Governments

While numerous qualitative case studies support the feasibility of collaborative governance in addressing wicked problems through cross-sector collaborations, systematic and comparative performance assessments of these experiences are not yet common. In their widely cited book on collaborative governance, Kirk Emerson and Tina Nabatchi acknowledge the challenges of measuring the performance of collaborative arrangements. They note that outcomes are difficult to determine in contexts with multiple goals, and "*the performance of collaborative arrangements* (or collaborative regimes in their definition) *not only occurs over time but also changes over time, making it difficult to observe and evaluate*".[54] Furthermore, observing what happens inside collaborative efforts is not trivial, making it difficult to identify relationships between organizational

[53] Like several works in the literature, Dale Krane and I depart from the Ansell and Gash model to analyze the importance of collaborative governance in civic festivals, as mentioned at the chapter outset. See Cabral and Krane (2018). Kirk Emerson and Tina Nabatchi also develop an interesting framework for collaborative governance in which they identify the drivers of collaboration that influence the choice of the type or organizational arrangement in which the collaboration will take place (collaborative governance regime), the collaboration dynamics, the collaborative actions, outcomes, and the feedback on the system context and collaborative regimes (Emerson & Nabatchi, 2015). Illustrations of the applicability of their model can be seen in the works of Bronen and Chapin III (2013) on the reallocation of indigenous communities affected by climate changes in Alaska and of Gerlak and Heikkila (2011) on an ecosystem restoration program in the Florida Everglades. An additional description of this case can be seen in the Chapter 3 of Emerson's and Nabatchi's above cited book.

[54] Emerson and Nabatchi (2015, p. 183).

elements such as routines, procedures, practices, existing resources, and contextual factors and collaboration outcomes.

Despite the availability of several performance measurement frameworks to support the assessment of collaborative governance outcomes,[55] there is still limited knowledge about what truly makes cross-sector collaborations stemming from collaborative governance arrangements work. To identify performance drivers of cross-sector collaborations, Sergio Lazzarini, Leandro Pongeluppe, Nobuiuki Ito, Felippe Oliveira, and Armen Ovanessoff analyzed 24 public initiatives in Brazil, India, and South Africa across four different areas: education, urban transportation, urban planning, and services to citizens.[56] They developed a rubric to identify evidence of social impact from these initiatives and cases of high and low performance. Using a configurational approach, they identified two distinctive paths conducive to high performance. The first path indicates that high-performing collaborations are associated with strong collaboration within public units (i.e., the initiative is designed and implemented in a system characterized by mutual interdependence with personnel from different public agencies), higher levels of stakeholder orientation in the project, and the presence of strong public capacities. The second path demonstrates that cross-sector collaborations involving for-profit and nonprofit organizations must be combined with strong public capacities to generate high performance.

These results highlight a crucial factor influencing the performance of cross-sector collaborations in settings where governments are central in collaborative efforts: *public capabilities*. This aligns with what we observed in the previous chapter regarding the significance of capabilities for enhanced performance in public–private partnerships. The capabilities inherent in governments are pivotal for the success of cross-sector collaborations involving public organizations.

Private and nonprofit organizations seeking engagement with governments in cross-sector collaborations should assess the presence of two subsets of public capabilities on the government side: the ability to manage cross-sector relationships (*cross-sector capabilities*), similar to the

[55] See Emerson and Nabatchi (2015, Chapter 9) and Noto et al. (2022).

[56] Lazzarini et al. (2020).

contract-management capabilities discussed earlier,[57] and the ability to manage relationships within public bureaucracies, referred to as *public-public capabilities*. Similarly, public authorities and other stakeholders sponsoring or benefiting from cross-sector collaborations must pay special attention to the existence of cross-sector capabilities in governments, as well as the presence of public-public capabilities, before engaging in such collaborations.

Cross-sector capabilities encompass the government's abilities to devise the necessary resources and inputs required for effective collaborations, along with the capacity to articulate, in tandem with partners, the necessary activities and tasks to achieve feasible outcomes that express public value creation. These abilities enable cross-sector collaborations to obtain valuable insights, resources, and efforts from their partners.[58] For this purpose, governments must establish routines to attract and maintain professional and stakeholder-oriented bureaucracies capable of interacting with the cross-sector, understanding their needs and limitations, and translating them into public bureaucracies during both the design and implementation phases of cross-sector collaborations.[59]

In addition to the capacity to attract and retain effective boundary-spanners within public structures, cross-sector capabilities also involve the ability to nurture performance management systems that enable the selection of cross-sector partners, establishment of feasible and realistic goals, monitoring of collaborations, creation of accountability structures, and transparent reporting of progress to watchdog agencies and other relevant stakeholders.[60] Along these lines, having capable personnel to evaluate or

[57] See Brown and Potoski (2003), Cabral (2017), Alonso and Andrews (2019), and Bruce et al. (2019) for more information on contract-management capabilities in public contracting and cross-sector collaborations.

[58] Cabral et al. (2019).

[59] Similar to Lazzarini et al. (2020) and Dentoni et al. (2016) emphasize the importance of stakeholder orientation for effective collaborations.

[60] Lazzarini (2015) sheds light on the importance of capable policymakers that can understand the demands, claims of legitimate stakeholders, and translate them into effective industrial policies involving public, private, and nonprofit organizations that are free of favoritism and patronage. This reasoning can be extended to cross-sector collaborations.

engage with external evaluators to assess the performance of collaborations, preferably using counterfactual assessment methods to ensure that results were caused by the interventions, is also a desirable feature for incentive purposes.[61] Reliable performance assessments can serve as the foundation for reward and sanction structures, encouraging coordinated efforts among cross-sector partners that, when combined, can lead to the creation of public value.[62]

Successful cross-sector collaborations with governments in central roles also require *public-public capabilities*. These capabilities can be defined as the abilities to establish structures and protocols for engaging with other public organizations, whether from the same or distinct levels of government (federal, state/province, or local), enabling the exchange of information, knowledge, and other pertinent resources within public bureaucracies in the pursuit of enhanced collaboration. Public-public capabilities can both balance and shape the interests of myriad stakeholders present in the public sector, including public departments, watchdog agencies, elected officers in legislative bodies, courts, district attorneys, among others, and stakeholders with the capacity to influence or even veto cross-sector collaborations.

Public-public capabilities can help overcome resistance from insulated actors averse to collaboration, include different actors in the collaborative process, foster dialogues in formal or informal forums of collaborations, enable diversity, infuse novel and value-creating perspectives into collaborative arrangements, and increase the costs of boycotts by prominent actors for reasons not related to efficiency, transparency, or public value creation. For that, the presence of empowered and capable actors possessing a public services ethos and willing and able to employ collaborative strategies conducive to aligning objectives and incentives of those involved in intergovernmental collaboration is an important engine to

[61] In joint work with Leandro Nardi and Sergio Lazzarini, I analyze the importance and the main challenges of measuring the performance of cross-sector collaboration, as well as the pros and cons of the different available approaches. Adequate personnel to perform the analysis are deemed as key for effective measurement. See Nardi et al. (2022).

[62] For the importance of counterfactual assessments in cross-sector collaborations involving payments contingent to performance-attainment, such as social impact bonds, pay-for-performance, and outcome-based contracts, refer to Lazzarini et al. (2022).

foster effectiveness in collaborative efforts.[63] Managers with these abilities possess negotiation skills, which tends to be well-evaluated by other members of public bureaucracies and increases the odds of information sharing.[64]

Collaborative Governance and Accountability Issues

Despite the intense use of collaborations in public, private, and nonprofit organizations to excel in a world characterized by volatility, uncertainty, complexity, and ambiguity,[65] it is important to recognize that collaborative arrangements may also give rise to negative consequences. In fact, antitrust agencies worldwide express concern about strategic alliances involving firms. This concern stems from the observation that collusive behavior, aimed at increasing profits at the expense of healthy competition and consumer interests, is not uncommon. Some collaborations have the potential to evolve into cartels, resulting in reduced outputs, increased prices, and diminished quality and innovation, whether through tacit or explicit collusion.[66]

Collusive behavior among collaborating partners is not exclusive to strategic alliances and can also occur in collaborative arrangements within the government realm, leading to severe accountability problems. In collaborative arrangements where partners exchange information and resources, determining who is accountable to whom and identifying the party responsible for high or poor performance is not evident. In some

[63] Andrews and Entwistle (2010) analyze several types of cross-sector collaborations in the UK, highlighting the importance of public-public partnerships for effective collaborations. This result is in line with those found in our study on the carnival in Brazil, as well as those by Lazzarini et al. (2020) in their cross-country analysis and by Quelin et al. (2019) in collaborations in infrastructure projects. The importance of abilities in intergovernmental collaboration is also emphasized in the context of emergency management involving cross-sector partners, see McGuire and Silvia (2010).

[64] See Molenveld et al. (2020) for an assessment of the challenges involved in coordinating the implementation of policy programs with the involvement of several public organizations.

[65] Bennett and Lemoine (2014).

[66] See the Antitrust Guidelines for Collaborations Among Competitors issued by the Federal Trade Commission and the US Department of Justice in: https://www.ftc.gov/sites/default/files/documents/public_events/joint-venture-hearings-antitrust-guidelines-collaboration-among-competitors/ftcdojguidelines-2.pdf.

cases, instead of fostering enhancement, collaboration can lead to the destruction of public value and compromise essential "public values" such as integrity, probity, and rectitude. This is particularly likely in settings where clear and credible rules are lacking, roles and responsibilities are ambiguous, and shared leadership, ensuring the attainment of interests for all relevant stakeholders, proves to be ineffective. In such situations, collusion among members in the collaborative arrangement becomes a significant threat to accountability and the achievement of public value creation.[67]

In simpler terms, collusion within public organizations in collaborative arrangements can be just as undesirable as collusion among private actors. An illustrative example is the collaborative efforts in the Car Wash (Lava Jato) operation in Brazil—a joint effort involving several public bodies, such as the internal control and audit body (CGU), the public prosecutor's office (MPF), the attorney general's office (PGR), the Brazilian Federal Police, the Brazilian revenue service (Receita Federal), and federal courts, working cooperatively.

While the operation unveiled a massive corruption scandal at Petrobras, the Brazilian state-owned company, involving public managers, suppliers, politicians, and others, culminating in the recovery of substantial amounts of embezzled funds and the arrest of several individuals, including the former Brazilian president, Mr. Lula da Silva, the collaborative efforts were highly controversial. In fact, basic protocols of collaborative governance were not adhered to, as demonstrated by a series of leaked messages between Sergio Moro (the judge in charge of the main cases), prosecutors, and judges of the court of appeals. These messages revealed collusion among collaborative partners to fabricate evidence, coercion of plaintiffs to make up stories to incriminate selected individuals, and discussions on strategies to amplify sentences against some investigated individuals. These actions led to biased trials that were eventually ruled as illegal by

[67] Recent research has increasingly focused on the tradeoffs between collaborative governance and accountability. Lægreid and Rykkja (2022) examine the accountability challenges within public organizations and explore problems and solutions in collaborative settings involving public agencies. In a similar vein, Cristofoli et al. (2022) analyze collaborative governance cases in different countries, government levels, and policy domains to identify conditions under which legitimacy and accountability in collaborative arrangements within public agencies occur.

the Brazilian Supreme Court.[68] The consequences of the wrongdoing perpetrated by some collaborating partners were extremely negative, not only from the point of view of the credibility of the justice system but also in terms of the political repercussions that the case sparked.[69]

Conclusion

This chapter explores the importance of cross-sector collaboration in tackling wicked problems that cannot be resolved by individual organizations in isolation. Such issues require information and resource sharing among various actors from public, private, nonprofit, and multilateral organizations.

These collaborations share similarities and dissimilarities with strategic alliances involving private firms. While cross-sector collaborations differ in aspects related to motivation, the nature of partners, and the way both forms deal with uncertainty and specific assets, they converge on the importance of sharing complementary resources, selecting appropriate partners, and governing relationships. In collaborations where governments play a significant role, protocols for collaborative governance among numerous partners are seen as crucial for effective collaborations. Therefore, public bureaucrats with the ability to interact with external partners (cross-sector capabilities) and facilitate collaborative relationships within governments (public-public capabilities) are essential features to address challenging problems through increased collaborations. Yet, as in strategic alliances, enhanced collaborations among public officers may have drawbacks and occur at the expense of accountability, challenging the credibility of collaborative arrangements and their capacity to effectively create public value.

Perhaps, the proverb "*If you want to go fast, go alone; if you want to go far, go together*", takes on new meaning in light of the advances in the

[68] See de Sa e Silva (2022) and https://theintercept.com/2019/06/09/brazil-lula-operation-car-wash-sergio-moro/.

[69] In the words of the law professor of the University of Warwick, George Mészáros: "*(i)n November 2018, the President in waiting, Jair Bolsonaro, offered him the post of Minister of Justice, which he immediately accepted. Given that Bolsonaro benefitted most from Lula's elimination from the election race, many saw Moro's ministerial appointment (upon Bolsonaro's inauguration in January 2019) as a form of payback for services rendered and circumstantial 'proof' of the former judge's lack of impartiality and vaulting political ambitions*" (Mészáros, 2020, p. S68).

literature on cross-sector collaborations in both public administration and strategic management. If so, an alternative proverb could be formulated as follows: "*If you want to go fast, go alone; if you want to go far and effectively change your reality, go together with suitable partners and under appropriate governance.*"

References

Agranoff, R. (2012). *Collaborating to manage: A primer for the public sector*. Georgetown University Press.

Almond, D., Currie, J., & Duque, V. (2018). Childhood circumstances and adult outcomes: Act II. *Journal of Economic Literature, 56*(4), 1360–1446.

Alonso, J. M., & Andrews, R. (2019). Governance by targets and the performance of cross-sector partnerships: Do partner diversity and partnership capabilities matter? *Strategic Management Journal, 40*(4), 556–579.

Andrews, R., & Entwistle, T. (2010). Does cross-sectoral partnership deliver? An empirical exploration of public service effectiveness, efficiency, and equity. *Journal of Public Administration Research and Theory, 20*(3), 679–701.

Ansell, C., & Gash, A. (2008). Collaborative governance in theory and practice. *Journal of Public Administration Research and Theory, 18*(4), 543–571.

Araral, E. (2014). Ostrom, Hardin and the commons: A critical appreciation and a revisionist view. *Environmental Science & Policy, 36*, 11–23. https://doi.org/10.1016/j.envsci.2013.07.011

Artz, K. W., & Brush, T. H. (2000). Asset specificity, uncertainty and relational norms: An examination of coordination costs in collaborative strategic alliances. *Journal of Economic Behavior & Organization, 41*(4), 337–362.

Bennett, N., & Lemoine, J. (2014). What VUCA really means for you. *Harvard Business Review, 92*(1/2).

Bronen, R., & Chapin, F. S., III. (2013). Adaptive governance and institutional strategies for climate-induced community relocations in Alaska. *Proceedings of the National Academy of Sciences, 110*(23), 9320–9325.

Brown, T. L., & Potoski, M. (2003). Contract–management capacity in municipal and county governments. *Public Administration Review, 63*(2), 153–164.

Bruce, J. R., de Figueiredo, J. M., & Silverman, B. S. (2019). Public contracting for private innovation: Government capabilities, decision rights, and performance outcomes. *Strategic Management Journal, 40*(4), 533–555.

Bryson, J. M., Crosby, B. C., & Stone, M. M. (2006). The design and implementation of Cross-Sector collaborations: Propositions from the literature. *Public Administration Review, 66*, 44–55.

Bryson, J. M., Crosby, B. C., & Stone, M. M. (2015). Designing and implementing cross-sector collaborations: Needed and challenging. *Public Administration Review, 75*(5), 647–663.

Cabral, S. (2017). Reconciling conflicting policy objectives in public contracting: The enabling role of capabilities. *Journal of Management Studies, 54*(6), 823–853.

Cabral, S., & Krane, D. (2018). Civic festivals and collaborative governance. *International Review of Administrative Sciences, 84*(1), 185–205.

Cabral, S., Lazzarini, S. G., & De Azevedo, P. F. (2013). Private entrepreneurs in public services: A longitudinal examination of outsourcing and statization of prisons. *Strategic Entrepreneurship Journal, 7*(1), 6–25.

Cabral, S., Mahoney, J. T., McGahan, A. M., & Potoski, M. (2019). Value creation and value appropriation in public and nonprofit organizations. *Strategic Management Journal, 40*(4), 465–475. https://doi.org/10.1002/smj.3008

Cristofoli, D., Douglas, S., Torfing, J., & Trivellato, B. (2022). Having it all: Can collaborative governance be both legitimate and accountable? *Public Management Review, 24*(5), 704–728.

de Sa e Silva, F. (2022). Relational legal consciousness and anticorruption: Lava Jato, social media interactions, and the co-production of law's detraction in Brazil (2017–2019). *Law & Society Review, 56*(3), 344–368.https://doi.org/10.1111/lasr.12620

Delmas, M. A., & Burbano, V. C. (2011). The drivers of greenwashing. *California Management Review, 54*(1), 64–87.

Dentoni, D., Bitzer, V., & Pascucci, S. (2016). Cross-sector partnerships and the co-creation of dynamic capabilities for stakeholder orientation. *Journal of Business Ethics, 135*, 35–53.

Dyer, J. H., Singh, H., & Hesterly, W. S. (2018). The relational view revisited: A dynamic perspective on value creation and value capture. *Strategic Management Journal, 39*(12), 3140–3162.

Economy, C., Carter, E., & Airoldi, M. (2023). Have we 'stretched' social impact bonds too far? An empirical analysis of SIB design in practice. *International Public Management Journal, 26*(3), 413–436.

Elazar, D. J. (1965). The shaping of intergovernmental relations in the twentieth century. *The Annals of the American Academy of Political and Social Science, 359*(1), 10–22.

Emerson, K., & Nabatchi, T. (2015). *Collaborative governance regimes*. Georgetown University Press.

Engle, P. L., Fernald, L. C., Alderman, H., Behrman, J., O'Gara, C., Yousafzai, A., ... & Ertem, I. (2011). Strategies for reducing inequalities and improving developmental outcomes for young children in low-income and middle-income countries. *The Lancet, 378*(9799), 1339–1353.

Feilhauer, S., & Hahn, R. (2021). Firm-nonprofit collaboration: Explaining the rationale behind firms' cross-sector partner choices. *Long Range Planning, 54*(1), 101952.

Forrer, J., Kee, J. J., & Boyer, E. (2014). *Governing cross-sector collaboration.* Wiley.

Gatignon, A., & Capron, L. (2023). The firm as an architect of polycentric governance: Building open institutional infrastructure in emerging markets. *Strategic Management Journal, 44*(1), 48–85.

George, G., McGahan, A. M., & Prabhu, J. (2012). Innovation for inclusive growth: Towards a theoretical framework and a research agenda. *Journal of Management Studies, 49*(4), 661–683.

Gerlak, A. K., & Heikkila, T. (2011). Building a theory of learning in collaboratives: Evidence from the Everglades Restoration Program. *Journal of Public Administration Research and Theory, 21*(4), 619–644.

Gil, N., & Pinto, J. K. (2018). Polycentric organizing and performance: A contingency model and evidence from megaproject planning in the UK. *Research Policy, 47*(4), 717–734.

Gulati, R., Nohria, N., & Zaheer, A. (2000). Strategic networks. *Strategic Management Journal, 21*(3), 203–215.

Harrigan, K. R. (2003). *Joint ventures, alliances, and corporate strategy.* Beard Books.

Head, B. W. (2019). Forty years of wicked problems literature: Forging closer links to policy studies. *Policy and Society, 38*(2), 180–197.

Hillman, A. J., Withers, M. C., & Collins, B. J. (2009). Resource dependence theory: A review. *Journal of Management, 35*(6), 1404–1427.

Intarakumnerd, P., & Goto, A. (2018). Role of public research institutes in national innovation systems in industrialized countries: The cases of Fraunhofer, NIST, CSIRO, AIST, and ITRI. *Research Policy, 47*(7), 1309–1320.

Jacobides, M. G., Cennamo, C., & Gawer, A. (2018). Towards a theory of ecosystems. *Strategic Management Journal, 39*(8), 2255–2276.

Johnston, E. W., Hicks, D., Nan, N., & Auer, J. C. (2011). Managing the inclusion process in collaborative governance. *Journal of Public Administration Research and Theory, 21*(4), 699–721.

Keller, A., Lumineau, F., Mellewigt, T., & Ariño, A. (2021). Alliance governance mechanisms in the face of disruption. *Organization Science, 32*(6), 1542–1570.

Khanna, T., & Palepu, K. (1997). Why focused strategies. *Harvard Business Review, 75*(4), 41–51.

Koebele, E. A. (2019). Integrating collaborative governance theory with the advocacy coalition framework. *Journal of Public Policy, 39*(1), 35–64.

Lægreid, P., & Rykkja, L. H. (2022). Accountability and inter-organizational collaboration within the state. *Public Management Review, 24*(5), 683–703.

Lazzarini, S. G. (2015). Strategizing by the government: Can industrial policy create firm-level competitive advantage? *Strategic Management Journal, 36*(1), 97–112.

Lazzarini, S. G., Cabral, S., Firpo, S., & Teodorovicz, T. (2022). Why are counterfactual assessment methods not widespread in outcome-based contracts? A formal model approach. *Journal of Public Administration Research and Theory, 32*(3), 509–523.

Lazzarini, S. G., Pongeluppe, L. S., Ito, N. C., Oliveira, F. d. M., & Ovanessoff, A. (2020). Public capacity, plural forms of collaboration, and the performance of public initiatives: A configurational approach. *Journal of Public Administration Research and Theory, 30*(4), 579–595.

McGinnis, M. D. (2011). An introduction to IAD and the language of the Ostrom workshop: A simple guide to a complex framework. *Policy Studies Journal, 39*(1), 169–183. https://doi.org/10.1111/j.1541-0072.2010.00401.x

McGuire, M. (2006). Collaborative public management: Assessing what we know and how we know it. *Public Administration Review, 66*(s1), 33–43. https://doi.org/10.1111/j.1540-6210.2006.00664.x

McGuire, M., & Silvia, C. (2010). The effect of problem severity, managerial and organizational capacity, and agency structure on intergovernmental collaboration: Evidence from local emergency management. *Public Administration Review, 70*(2), 279–288.

Ménard, C. (2022). Hybrids: Where are we? *Journal of Institutional Economics, 18*(2), 297–312.

Mesquita, L. F., Ragozzino, R., & Reuer, J. J. (2017). *Collaborative strategy: Critical issues for alliances and networks*. Edward Elgar Publishing.

Mészáros, G. (2020). Caught in an authoritarian trap of its own making? Brazil's 'Lava Jato' Anti-corruption investigation and the politics of prosecutorial overreach. *Journal of Law and Society, 47*(S1), S54–S73. https://doi.org/10.1111/jols.12245

Molenveld, A., Verhoest, K., Voets, J., & Steen, T. (2020). Images of coordination: How implementing organizations perceive coordination arrangements. *Public Administration Review, 80*(1), 9–22.

Nardi, L., Lazzarini, S. G., & Cabral, S. (2022). Impact measurement tools and social value creation: A strategic perspective. In *Handbook on the business of sustainability* (pp. 459–473). Edward Elgar Publishing.

Noto, G., Coletta, L., & Vainieri, M. (2022). Measuring the performance of collaborative governance in food safety management: An Italian case study. *Public Money & Management, 42*(8), 627–636.

Ostrom, E. (1990). *Governing the commons: The evolution of institutions for collective action*. Cambridge University Press.

Ostrom, V., & Ostrom, E. (2019). Public goods and public choices. In *Alternatives for delivering public services* (pp. 7–49). Routledge.

Patala, S., Albareda, L., & Halme, M. (2022). Polycentric governance of privately owned resources in circular economy systems. *Journal of Management Studies, 59*(6), 1563–1596. https://doi.org/10.1111/joms.12810

Pfeffer, J., & Salancik, G. (2003). *The external control of organizations: A resource dependence perspective*. Stanford Business Books.

Quelin, B. V., Cabral, S., Lazzarini, S., & Kivleniece, I. (2019). The private scope in public–private collaborations: An institutional and capability-based perspective. *Organization Science, 30*(4), 831–846.

Quélin, B. V., Kivleniece, I., & Lazzarini, S. (2017). Public-private collaboration, hybridity and social value: Towards new theoretical perspectives. *Journal of Management Studies, 54*(6), 763–792.

Rangan, S., Samii, R., & Van Wassenhove, L. N. (2006). Constructive partnerships: When alliances between private firms and public actors can enable creative strategies. *Academy of Management Review, 31*(3), 738–751.

Reuer, J. J., & Devarakonda, S. V. (2016). Mechanisms of hybrid governance: Administrative committees in non-equity alliances. *Academy of Management Journal, 59*(2), 510–533.

Rivera-Santos, M., Rufin, C., & Wassmer, U. (2017). Alliances between firms and non-profits: A multiple and behavioural agency approach. *Journal of Management Studies, 54*(6), 854–875.

Rocha, R., & Soares, R. R. (2010). Evaluating the impact of community-based health interventions: Evidence from Brazil's Family Health Program. *Health Economics, 19*(S1), 126–158.

Rondinelli, D. A., & London, T. (2003). How corporations and environmental groups cooperate: Assessing cross-sector alliances and collaborations. *Academy of Management Perspectives, 17*(1), 61–76.

Rosenkopf, L., & Padula, G. (2008). Investigating the microstructure of network evolution: Alliance formation in the mobile communications industry. *Organization Science, 19*(5), 669–687.

Sampson, R. C. (2004). The cost of misaligned governance in R&D alliances. *Journal of Law, Economics, and Organization, 20*(2), 484–526.

Selsky, J. W., & Parker, B. (2005). Cross-sector partnerships to address social issues: Challenges to theory and practice. *Journal of Management, 31*(6), 849–873.

Vasudeva, G., & Anand, J. (2011). Unpacking absorptive capacity: A study of knowledge utilization from alliance portfolios. *Academy of Management Journal, 54*(3), 611–623.

Weible, C. M., Sabatier, P. A., Jenkins-Smith, H. C., Nohrstedt, D., Henry, A. D., & DeLeon, P. (2011). A quarter century of the advocacy coalition

framework: An introduction to the special issue. *Policy Studies Journal, 39*(3), 349–360.
Williamson, O. (1991). Comparative economic organization: The analysis of discrete structural alternatives. *Administrative Science Quarterly, 36*, 269–296.
Williamson, O. E. (1998). The institutions of governance. *The American Economic Review, 88*(2), 75–79.
Young, D. R. (2000). Alternative models of government-nonprofit sector relations: Theoretical and international perspectives. *Nonprofit and Voluntary Sector Quarterly, 29*(1), 149–172.

CHAPTER 11

Conclusions

One of the things I like most about academia is the opportunity to engage with practitioners in seminars, lectures, talks, and classes. These occasions allow me to share the scientific knowledge I have accumulated, to make efforts to translate the often complex scientific language into something useful and understandable to non-academics, and to gain insights for my own research.

Not long ago, I was invited to give a talk on evidence-based management to police chiefs responsible for crime investigations. After introducing some concepts related to the relationship between incentives and performance, I presented to almost 40 senior police officers the results of a pay-for-performance program implemented in a different police department. The program aimed to improve crime rates on three performance indicators: violent death, vehicle robbery, and street robbery. To encourage collaboration between officers responsible for patrolling and making arrests, and those conducting crime investigations, a pay-for-performance (PFP) program was implemented.

While the program yielded positive results in preventing live losses, including those stemming from police killings, and decreasing the number of robberies, during my presentation, one senior officer expressed discomfort about the program, despite its evident benefits.[1] He argued that the

[1] More details about this program can be seen in Cabral et al. (2019).

S. Cabral, *Strategy for Public and Nonprofit Organizations*, https://doi.org/10.1007/978-3-031-64969-1_11

primary mission of crime investigation officers was not to prevent deaths or robberies but to conclude investigations, and that officers should be measured and rewarded accordingly. He was not alone in his views, as other police officers also supported his arguments.

In my response, I argued that the investigations conducted by their detectives are crucial for preventing future crimes. By avoiding homicides and saving lives, police forces not only prevent the suffering of families and friends of the victims but also contribute to the potential generation of economic benefits in the future. Individuals whose lives are saved will have the opportunity to continue developing their social and economic activities, thereby contributing to the overall prosperity of society. Additionally, by preventing robberies, police forces alleviate problems for potential victims and discourage illegal supply chains of stolen goods, thus reducing the likelihood of future crimes.

In essence, improving crime rates serves as an engine for creating public value, which is why a pay-for-performance (PFP) program designed to stimulate increased efforts correlated with value-creating outcomes is welcome. Furthermore, policing activities operate in an interdependent fashion and require collaboration and information exchange among different police units. For example, investigation units can provide information about crime hotspots, guiding the allocation of resources for units responsible for patrolling streets. Conversely, officers patrolling streets, who are in direct contact with citizens, can gather valuable information for future investigations. This interconnectedness underscores the importance of collaboration within police departments to effectively address and prevent crime.

While the value of the PFP program is evident, the pushback from some of the police officers attending my talk reflects the strong adherence of many managers in public, private, and nonprofit organizations to an activity- or output-based orientation, rather than an outcome-based one. Indeed, the situation described above is similar to that of blue-collar workers preferring their bonuses to be based on the efficiency of the assembly line rather than contingent on the firm's profits. In both cases, there is a preference for a more tangible and directly measurable metric that aligns closely with individual or departmental tasks and activities. The problem is that these activity and output-based orientations are likely to act as counterforces that hinder organizations from adopting an outcome mindset, which is crucial for creating public value and enhancing the organization's legitimacy in the eyes of prominent stakeholders, particularly in the case of public and nonprofit organizations.

Assuming that the abovementioned police officers prioritize the needs of citizens at least as much as they do their own individual aspirations, if they had the opportunity to carefully read some of the contents of this book, they would likely develop a different opinion about the importance of an outcome-based mindset in benefiting the communities they serve.

My intention with this book was to inform students and practitioners about the significance of strategy lenses in shaping effective public policies and business strategies, which have implications for a wide range of stakeholders. I hope that by reading this book, managers of public, private, and nonprofit organizations, policymakers, and strategists can grasp the distinctions between governments, businesses, and nonprofits and devise appropriate strategies accordingly. I also aim for the concept of public value creation to become central and guide the strategic decision-making of these targeted groups above mentioned. Moreover, I expect that readers will grasp the nuances of value appropriation dilemmas that arise when multiple stakeholders with competing interests are involved. By internalizing this mindset, organizations can develop their own theories of change that have the potential to impact a broader set of stakeholders beyond their immediate targets.

Aligned with such an outcome and impact-oriented purpose, many aspects of this book could prove valuable to readers engaged in strategy within public and nonprofit organizations, or to those who are simply interested in learning more about the topic. For instance, effective policies can exploit the role of intrinsic and explicit incentives to encourage individuals and teams to exert superior efforts, thereby increasing performance standards in dimensions reflecting public value creation. Managers, policymakers, and strategists who are aware of the microfoundations of human behavior, contractual theories, and how individuals exploit existing information asymmetries are better equipped to design and implement policies that are more effective. By understanding that there is nothing more favorable for malicious agents than having uninterested or uninformed principals, strategists can benefit the organizations they serve while also preserving the public interest when designing performance management systems and structures that allocate decision rights within and across organizations.

The process of (public) value creation also relies on the ability to convert planned initiatives into effective policies, which demands successful strategy implementation. Indeed, many policies fail to be implemented because strategists and policymakers often prioritize formulation over execution. Consequently, frustration and value destruction can occur due to the failure to identify critical factors. A deeper understanding of the importance of aligning the organization with its external environment and among its internal variables is crucial for policymakers and managers leading public, nonprofit, and private organizations with significant stakeholder impact to implement strategies effectively. Although intuitive, the dynamic nature of the implementation process and the likelihood of original plans requiring adaptation are surprisingly overlooked. This oversight frequently leads to unsuccessful strategy implementation. Likewise, understanding that implementation efforts are often constrained by inertial forces, stemming from both formal and informal sources of resistance, is also a crucial factor that is often overlooked. Despite abundant examples of failure resulting from resistance rooted in structural and cultural factors, this aspect is frequently ignored. Readers of this book will gain insight into how these inertial forces can be anticipated and how to abort initiatives that are likely to fail, thereby helping organizations avoid wasting valuable resources. I also expect that readers will recognize that inertial forces act as a double-edged sword, impeding the execution of both value-creating and value-destroying strategies. As demonstrated throughout the text, tenured civil servants and bureaucrats can diverge from inept policymakers and hinder the implementation of policies against the public interest, at least temporarily.

In addition to observing relevant strategy contents to address problems related to internal organization, strategists and policymakers must also pay attention to managing relationships with external actors. Recognizing the different types of groups that can affect or be affected by the organization is key to effectively achieving strategic goals and pursuing the public interest, whether for public and nonprofit organizations serving multiple constituencies or for-profit firms aware that failing to address stakeholder needs can thwart their interests. Procedures for mapping relevant stakeholders, identifying their interests in a given public or business policy, and assessing their relative power to support or impede policy implementation become essential for all organizations. Readers of this book can, hopefully, gain an enhanced understanding of the nuances of stakeholders surrounding organizations. They can recognize not only their relative power but also the legitimacy of their claims and the urgency and time-sensitivity of their demands. This understanding allows managers and strategists to prioritize actions and responses to stakeholders who may challenge both organizational survival and the attainment of the public interest.

This book can also be valuable in enhancing understanding of cross-sector boundaries and how organizations collaborate with others from different sectors. In a world where public and nonprofit organizations increasingly resemble private organizations and organizational boundaries are more fluid, many goods and services once provided solely by governments are now delivered with support from private and nonprofit organizations through various contractual modes, including outsourcing, concessions, public–private partnerships, and other collaborative arrangements. With the support of established theories such as transaction cost economics and incomplete contract theories, as well as evidence-based arguments, readers of this book will be equipped to recognize under which conditions governments should delegate or insource activities to preserve the public interest in decisions involving goods and services with varying degrees of consumption rivalry and exclusion likelihood for beneficiaries. Readers will also be able to recognize that effective cross-sector collaborations require collaborative governance among multiple public agencies, making adequate public-public collaboration a prerequisite for effective public–private collaboration. Considering the inherent challenges in terms of finding all the necessary resources within a single organization to address the grand challenges and wicked problems affecting contemporary society, collaborative practices are essential, thus necessitating appropriate governance structures.

Despite these efforts, I acknowledge that there are still some relevant aspects in the relationship between strategy and public and nonprofit organizations that could be further developed. This includes a more extensive discussion about the role of organizational capabilities present in public, private, and nonprofit organizations. Despite my previous work on the capabilities present in both public and private sectors to enable effective public–private collaborations and facilitate public value creation, I was unable to include a more thorough discussion due to space limitations. This would have involved exploring the importance of capable governments in leveraging the value creation potential of private and nonprofit organizations when delivering public services, promoting necessary coordination among stakeholders with distinct preferences, and overseeing external actors to ensure the public interest.

Similarly, I was unable to delve deeper into the institutional strategies performed by private and third-sector organizations to shape their interactions with government bodies and communities. Corporate political actions such as lobbying, campaign donations, and actions to enhance ties with politicians and civil servants in executive, legislative, and judiciary powers are widely used by organizations to influence their outcomes of interest. Considering the existing interdependencies between public and private interests, a closer inspection of these "nonmarket strategies" would benefit readers in understanding what governments must do to take into account the legitimate interests of firms while preserving the public interest. It would also provide an enhanced view for business strategists about how government works and how firms can navigate bureaucratic structures to attain their goals, within the limits of the law.

Despite these gaps, which I may address in future editions, I believe that this book can be valuable in efforts to build bridges across disciplines and assist firms, governments, and nonprofits in improving their performance in key indicators while simultaneously creating public value. This can be expressed in the enhancement of the welfare of those directly and indirectly affected by actions executed by these organizations, either in isolation or through joint collaborative efforts. Overall, although often overlooked, the use of strategic lenses can prove beneficial to governments, nonprofits, and firms, with the potential to generate both positive and negative spillover effects on society.

Reference

Cabral, S., Firpo, S., Costa, M. M. D., Monteiro, J., & Viotti, L. (2019). *Keeping the dream alive: The role of expectancy in pay-for-performance programs*. Paper presented at the Academy of Management Proceedings.

References

Abbington, J. (2009). Music wars: A perspective from the Black Church. *Liturgy, 24*(4), 40–47.

Abdulkadiroğlu, A., Agarwal, N., & Pathak, P. A. (2017). The welfare effects of coordinated assignment: Evidence from the New York City high school match. *American Economic Review, 107*(12), 3635–3689.

Abdulkadiroğlu, A., Pathak, P. A., & Walters, C. R. (2018). Free to choose: Can school choice reduce student achievement? *American Economic Journal: Applied Economics, 10*(1), 175–206.

Abreu, D. (1988). On the theory of infinitely repeated games with discounting. *Econometrica: Journal of the Econometric Society, 56*, 383–396.

Ackermann, F., & Eden, C. (2011). Strategic management of stakeholders: Theory and practice. *Long Range Planning, 44*(3), 179–196.

Adams, S. B. (2005). Stanford and Silicon Valley: Lessons on becoming a high-tech region. *California Management Review, 48*(1), 29–51.

Agranoff, R. (2012). *Collaborating to manage: A primer for the public sector*. Georgetown University Press.

Ahn, T.-S., Choi, Y.-S., Hwang, I., & Hyeon, J. (2018). The effect of information asymmetry and participative target setting on target ratcheting and incentives. *Public Performance & Management Review, 41*(3), 439–468.

Albanese, R., & Van Fleet, D. D. (1985). Rational behavior in groups: The free-riding tendency. *Academy of Management Review, 10*(2), 244–255.

Almond, D., Currie, J., & Duque, V. (2018). Childhood circumstances and adult outcomes: Act II. *Journal of Economic Literature, 56*(4), 1360–1446.

S. Cabral, *Strategy for Public and Nonprofit Organizations*,
https://doi.org/10.1007/978-3-031-64969-1

Alonso, J. M., & Andrews, R. (2019). Governance by targets and the performance of cross-sector partnerships: Do partner diversity and partnership capabilities matter? *Strategic Management Journal, 40*(4), 556–579.

Altamimi, H., Liu, Q., & Jimenez, B. (2022). Not too much, not too little: Centralization, decentralization, and organizational change. *Journal of Public Administration Research and Theory, 33*(1), 170–185. https://doi.org/10.1093/jopart/muac016

Andrews, R., & Boyne, G. (2012). Structural change and public service performance: The impact of the reorganization process in English local government. *Public Administration, 90*(2), 297–312.

Andrews, R., Boyne, G., Law, J., & Walker, R. (2011). *Strategic management and public service performance.* Springer.

Andrews, R., Boyne, G. A., Law, J., & Walker, R. M. (2011b). Strategy implementation and public service performance. *Administration & Society, 43*(6), 643–671.

Andrews, R., Boyne, G. A., Law, J., & Walker, R. M. (2009). Centralization, organizational strategy, and public service performance. *Journal of Public Administration Research and Theory, 19*(1), 57–80.

Andrews, R., Boyne, G. A., Law, J., & Walker, R. M. (2012). *Strategic management and public service performance.* Palgrave Macmillan.

Andrews, R., Boyne, G. A., & Walker, R. M. (2006). Subjective and objective measures of organizational performance: An empirical exploration. In K. J. M. George A. Boyne, Laurence J. O'Toole Jr., Richard M. Walker (Ed.), *Public service performance: Perspectives on measurement and management* (pp. 14–34). Cambridge University Press.

Andrews, R., & Entwistle, T. (2010). Does cross-sectoral partnership deliver? An empirical exploration of public service effectiveness, efficiency, and equity. *Journal of Public Administration Research and Theory, 20*(3), 679–701.

Ansell, C., & Gash, A. (2008). Collaborative governance in theory and practice. *Journal of Public Administration Research and Theory, 18*(4), 543–571.

Ansoff, H. I. (1965). *Corporate strategy: An analytic approach to business policy for growth and expansion.* McGraw-Hill.

Aral, S., Brynjolfsson, E., & Wu, L. (2012). Three-way complementarities: Performance pay, human resource analytics, and information technology. *Management Science, 58*(5), 913–931.

Araral, E. (2014). Ostrom, Hardin and the commons: A critical appreciation and a revisionist view. *Environmental Science & Policy, 36*, 11–23. https://doi.org/10.1016/j.envsci.2013.07.011

Argyres, N. S. (1999). The impact of information technology on coordination: Evidence from the B-2 "Stealth" bomber. *Organization Science, 10*(2), 162–180.

Argyres, N. S., & Zenger, T. R. (2012). Capabilities, transaction costs, and firm boundaries. *Organization Science, 23*(6), 1643–1657.

Artz, K. W., & Brush, T. H. (2000). Asset specificity, uncertainty and relational norms: An examination of coordination costs in collaborative strategic alliances. *Journal of Economic Behavior & Organization, 41*(4), 337–362.

Arvate, P., Cabral, S., Mcgahan, A. M., & Reis, P. R. (2022). Structural advocacy organizations and intersectional outcomes: Effects of women's police stations on female homicides. *Public Administration Review, 82*(3), 503–521. https://doi.org/10.1111/puar.13478

Arvidson, M., & Lyon, F. (2014). Social impact measurement and non-profit organisations: Compliance, resistance, and promotion. *VOLUNTAS: International Journal of Voluntary and Nonprofit Organizations, 25*, 869–886.

Asfaw, S., Davis, B., Dewbre, J., Handa, S., & Winters, P. (2014). Cash transfer programme, productive activities and labour supply: Evidence from a randomised experiment in Kenya. *The Journal of Development Studies, 50*(8), 1172–1196.

Bak, H.-J., & Kim, D. H. (2015). Too much emphasis on research? An empirical examination of the relationship between research and teaching in multitasking environments. *Research in Higher Education, 56*, 843–860.

Baker, G., Stewart, B., Appelbaum, E., & Beer, M. (1993). Rethinking rewards. *Harvard Business Review, 71*(6), 37–49.

Baldi, S., & Vannoni, D. (2017). The impact of centralization on pharmaceutical procurement prices: The role of institutional quality and corruption. *Regional Studies, 51*(3), 426–438.

Barnett, M. L., & King, A. A. (2008). Good fences make good neighbors: A longitudinal analysis of an industry self-regulatory institution. *Academy of Management Journal, 51*(6), 1150–1170.

Barney, J. B. (1991). Firm resources and sustained competitive advantage. *Journal of Management, 17*, 99–120.

Barney, J. B. (1997). *Gaining and sustaining competitive advantage*. Addison-Wesley Publishing Company.

Barney, J. B. (2001). Is the resource-based "view" a useful perspective for strategic management research? Yes. *Academy of Management Review, 26*(1), 41–56.

Barney, J. B. (2005). Should strategic management research engage public policy debates? *Academy of Management Journal, 48*(6), 945–948.

Barney, J. B. (2012). Purchasing, supply chain management and sustained competitive advantage: The relevance of resource-based theory. *Journal of Supply Chain Management, 48*(2), 3–6.

Barney, J. B. (2018). Why resource-based theory's model of profit appropriation must incorporate a stakeholder perspective. *Strategic Management Journal, 39*(13), 3305–3325. https://doi.org/10.1002/smj.2949

Barney, J. B., & Zajac, E. J. (1994). Competitive organizational behavior: Toward an organizationally-based theory of competitive advantage. *Strategic Management Journal, 15*(S1), 5–9.
Baron, D. P. (1995). The nonmarket strategy system. *MIT Sloan Management Review, 37*(1), 73.
Baum, J. A., & McGahan, A. M. (2013). The reorganization of legitimate violence: The contested terrain of the private military and security industry during the post-cold war era. *Research in Organizational Behavior, 33*, 3–37.
Baum, J. R., & Wally, S. (2003). Strategic decision speed and firm performance. *Strategic Management Journal, 24*(11), 1107–1129.
Bencze, M. (2021). Judicial populism and the Weberian judge—The strength of judicial resistance against governmental influence in Hungary. *German Law Journal, 22*(7), 1282–1297.
Bennett, N., & Lemoine, J. (2014). What VUCA really means for you. *Harvard Business Review, 92*(1/2).
Benny, G., Joseph, J., Surendran, S., & Nambiar, D. (2023). On the forms, contributions and impacts of community mobilisation involved with Kerala's COVID-19 response: Perspectives of health staff, Local Self Government institution and community leaders. *PLoS ONE, 18*(6), e0285999.
Berlin, J., Carlström, E., & Karlsson, D. (2023). Backsourcing in the private and public sectors—A systematic review. *Financial Accountability & Management.*
Bertelli, A. M., & Smith, C. R. (2009). Relational contracting and network management. *Journal of Public Administration Research and Theory, 20*(suppl_1), i21–i40.
Best, B., Moffett, S., & McAdam, R. (2019). Stakeholder salience in public sector value co-creation. *Public Management Review, 21*(11), 1707–1732.
Bettinazzi, E. L., & Feldman, E. R. (2021). Stakeholder orientation and divestiture activity. *Academy of Management Journal, 64*(4), 1078–1096.
Bolton, P., & Dewatripont, M. (2004). *Contract theory*. MIT press.
Bonardi, J.-P., Holburn, G. L., & Bergh, R. G. V. (2006). Nonmarket strategy performance: Evidence from US electric utilities. *Academy of Management Journal, 49*(6), 1209–1228.
Bortoluzzi, M., de Souza, C. C., & Furlan, M. (2021). Bibliometric analysis of renewable energy types using key performance indicators and multicriteria decision models. *Renewable and Sustainable Energy Reviews, 143*, 110958.
Bowman, E. H., Singh, H., & Thomas, H. (2002). The domain of strategic management: History and evolution. In A. Pettigrew, H. Thomas, & R. Whittington (Eds.), *Handbook of strategy and management* (pp. 31–51). Sage.
Bozeman, B. (2007). *Public values and public interest: Counterbalancing economic individualism*. Georgetown University Press.
Brandenburger, A. M., & Stuart, H. W., Jr. (1996). Value-based business strategy. *Journal of Economics & Management Strategy, 5*(1), 5–24.

Bresnahan, T. F., Brynjolfsson, E., & Hitt, L. M. (2002). Information technology, workplace organization, and the demand for skilled labor: Firm-level evidence. *The Quarterly Journal of Economics, 117*(1), 339–376.

Brickley, J. A., Smith, C. W., & Zimmerman, J. L. (2001). *Managerial economics and organizational architecture* (2nd ed.). McGraw-Hill.

Bridoux, F., & Stoelhorst, J. (2022). Stakeholder theory, strategy, and organization: Past, present, and future. *Strategic Organization, 20*(4), 797–809.

Bromiley, P., & Rau, D. (2014). Towards a practice-based view of strategy. *Strategic Management Journal, 35*(8), 1249–1256.

Bronen, R., & Chapin, F. S., III. (2013). Adaptive governance and institutional strategies for climate-induced community relocations in Alaska. *Proceedings of the National Academy of Sciences, 110*(23), 9320–9325.

Brown, J. D., Earle, J. S., & Telegdy, A. (2006). The productivity effects of privatization: Longitudinal estimates from Hungary, Romania, Russia, and Ukraine. *Journal of Political Economy, 114*(1), 61–99.

Brown, T. L. (2010). The evolution of public sector strategy. *Public Administration Review, 70*(s1), s212–s214.

Brown, T. L., & Potoski, M. (2003). Contract–management capacity in municipal and county governments. *Public Administration Review, 63*(2), 153–164.

Bruce, J. R., de Figueiredo, J. M., & Silverman, B. S. (2019). Public contracting for private innovation: Government capabilities, decision rights, and performance outcomes. *Strategic Management Journal, 40*(4), 533–555.

Bryson, J. M. (1988). A strategic planning process for public and non-profit organizations. *Long Range Planning, 21*(1), 73–81.

Bryson, J. M. (2004). What to do when stakeholders matter: Stakeholder identification and analysis techniques. *Public Management Review, 6*(1), 21–53.

Bryson, J. M. (2018). *Strategic planning for public and nonprofit organizations: A guide to strengthening and sustaining organizational achievement*. Wiley.

Bryson, J. M., Ackermann, F., & Eden, C. (2007). Putting the resource-based view of strategy and distinctive competencies to work in public organizations. *Public Administration Review, 67*(4), 702–717.

Bryson, J. M., Crosby, B. C., & Bloomberg, L. (2015). Discerning and assessing public value. In J. M. Bryson, B. C. Crosby, & L. Bloomberg (Eds.), *Public value and public administration* (pp. 1–21). Georgetown University Press.

Bryson, J. M., Crosby, B. C., & Stone, M. M. (2006). The design and implementation of Cross-Sector collaborations: Propositions from the literature. *Public Administration Review, 66*, 44–55.

Bull, C. (1987). The existence of self-enforcing implicit contracts. *The Quarterly Journal of Economics, 102*(1), 147–159.

Burton, R., Håkonsson, D. D., Larsen, E. R., & Obel, B. (2020). New trends in organization design. *Journal of Organization Design, 9*, 1–2.

Cabral, S. (2006). "*Além das grades*": *uma análise comparada das modalidades de gestão do sistema prisional* (Doctoral Dissertation [Phd in Management]), Federal University of Bahia, Salvador, Bahia, Brazil.

Cabral, S. (2007). Sobre a participação privada na gestão e operação de prisões no Brasil: uma análise à luz da nova economia institucional. *Organizações & Sociedade, 14*, 29–47.

Cabral, S. (2017). Reconciling conflicting policy objectives in public contracting: The enabling role of capabilities. *Journal of Management Studies, 54*(6). https://doi.org/10.1111/joms.12269

Cabral, S. (2023). Public–private partnerships. In *The Brazilian way of doing public administration: Brazil with an's'* (pp. 97–106). Emerald Publishing Limited.

Cabral, S., Firpo, S., Costa, M. M. D., Monteiro, J., & Viotti, L. (2019). *Keeping the dream alive: The role of expectancy in pay-for-performance programs.* Paper presented at the Academy of Management Proceedings.

Cabral, S., Mahoney, J. T., McGahan, A. M., & Potoski, M. (2019b). Value creation and value appropriation in public and nonprofit organizations. *Strategic Management Journal, 40*(4), 465–475.

Cabral, S., Ito, N., & Pongeluppe, L. (2021). *The disastrous effects of leaders in denial: evidence from the COVID-19 crisis in Brazil.* Available at SSRN 3836147.

Cabral, S., & Krane, D. (2018). Civic festivals and collaborative governance. *International Review of Administrative Sciences, 84*(1), 185–205.

Cabral, S., & Lazzarini, S. G. (2015). The 'guarding the guardians' problem: An analysis of the organizational performance of an Internal Affairs Division. *Journal of Public Administration Research and Theory, 25*(3), 797–829.

Cabral, S., Lazzarini, S. G., & Azevedo, P. F. (2010). Private operation with public supervision: Evidence of hybrid modes of governance in prisons. *Public Choice, 145*(1–2), 281–293.

Cabral, S., Lazzarini, S. G., & De Azevedo, P. F. (2013). Private entrepreneurs in public services: A longitudinal examination of outsourcing and statization of prisons. *Strategic Entrepreneurship Journal, 7*(1), 6–25.

Cabral, S., Quelin, B., & Maia, W. (2014). Outsourcing failure and reintegration: The influence of contractual and external factors. *Long Range Planning, 47*(6), 365–378.

Cabral, S., & Santos, M.-F. (2018). Accountability mechanisms in public services: Activating new dynamics in a prison system. *International Public Management Journal, 21*(5), 795–821.

Cabral, S., & Saussier, S. (2013). Organizing prisons through public-private partnerships: A cross-country investigation. *BAR-Brazilian Administration Review, 10*, 100–120.

Calabrese, T. (2013). Running on empty: The operating reserves of US nonprofit organizations. *Nonprofit Management and Leadership, 23*(3), 281–302.

Callaghan, R. C., Vander Heiden, J., Sanches, M., Asbridge, M., Hathaway, A., & Kish, S. J. (2021). Impacts of Canada's cannabis legalization on police-reported crime among youth: Early evidence. *Addiction, 116*(12), 3454–3462.

Capano, G., & Lippi, A. (2021). Decentralization, policy capacities, and varieties of first health response to the COVID-19 outbreak: Evidence from three regions in Italy. *Journal of European Public Policy, 28*(8), 1197–1218.

Capano, G., & Toth, F. (2023). Thinking outside the box, improvisation, and fast learning: Designing policy robustness to deal with what cannot be foreseen. *Public Administration, 101*(1), 90–105.

Cardoso, R. L., Azevedo, R. R. d., Pigatto, J. A. M., Fajardo, B. d. A. G., & Cunha, A. S. M. d. (2023). Lessons from Brazil's unsuccessful fiscal decentralization policy to fight COVID-19. *Public Administration and Development, 43*(2), 106–119.

Carrillo, J. D., & Gromb, D. (2007). Cultural inertia and uniformity in organizations. *The Journal of Law, Economics, & Organization, 23*(3), 743–771.

Cecchini, S. (2023). The hidden impact of conditional cash transfer programs on state capacity. In K. J. Baehler (Ed.), *The Oxford handbook of governance and public management for social policy* (pp. 983–999). Oxford University Press.

Chandler, A. D., Jr. (1962). *Strategy and structure: Chapters in the history of the American industrial enterprise* (1ed ed.). MIT Press.

Chaudhury, N., & Parajuli, D. (2010). Conditional cash transfers and female schooling: The impact of the female school stipend programme on public school enrolments in Punjab, Pakistan. *Applied Economics, 42*(28), 3565–3583.

Chioda, L., De Mello, J. M., & Soares, R. R. (2016). Spillovers from conditional cash transfer programs: Bolsa Família and crime in urban Brazil. *Economics of Education Review, 54*, 306–320.

Chowdhury, R., Doukas, J. A., & Park, J. C. (2021). Stakeholder orientation and the value of cash holdings: Evidence from a natural experiment. *Journal of Corporate Finance, 69*, 102029.

Coase, R. (1937). The nature of the firm. *Economica, 4*, 386–405.

Coase, R. (1974). The lighthouse in economics. *The Journal of Law and Economics, 17*(2), 357–376.

Cohen, K. J., & Cyert, R. M. (1973). Strategy: Formulation, implementation, and monitoring. *The Journal of Business, 46*(3), 349–367.

Copeland, M. T. (1958). *An mark an era: The history of Harvard Business School*. Little Brown and Company.

Cristofoli, D., Douglas, S., Torfing, J., & Trivellato, B. (2022). Having it all: Can collaborative governance be both legitimate and accountable? *Public Management Review, 24*(5), 704–728.

Crittenden, V. L., & Crittenden, W. F. (2008). Building a capable organization: The eight levers of strategy implementation. *Business Horizons, 51*(4), 301–309.

Dachs, B., Kinkel, S., & Jäger, A. (2019). Bringing it all back home? Backshoring of manufacturing activities and the adoption of Industry 4.0 technologies. *Journal of World Business, 54*(6), 101017.

De Brauw, A., Gilligan, D. O., Hoddinott, J., & Roy, S. (2015). The impact of Bolsa Família on schooling. *World Development, 70*, 303–316.

De Brauw, A., & Hoddinott, J. (2011). Must conditional cash transfer programs be conditioned to be effective? The impact of conditioning transfers on school enrollment in Mexico. *Journal of Development Economics, 96*(2), 359–370.

De Janvry, A., He, G., Sadoulet, E., Wang, S., & Zhang, Q. (2023). Subjective performance evaluation, influence activities, and bureaucratic work behavior: Evidence from China. *American Economic Review, 113*(3), 766–799.

de Sa e Silva, F. (2022). Relational legal consciousness and anticorruption: Lava Jato, social media interactions, and the co-production of law's detraction in Brazil (2017–2019). *Law & Society Review, 56*(3), 344–368.https://doi.org/10.1111/lasr.12620

Delmas, M. A., & Burbano, V. C. (2011). The drivers of greenwashing. *California Management Review, 54*(1), 64–87.

Dentoni, D., Bitzer, V., & Pascucci, S. (2016). Cross-sector partnerships and the co-creation of dynamic capabilities for stakeholder orientation. *Journal of Business Ethics, 135*, 35–53.

Dixit, A. (2002). Incentives and organizations in the public sector: An interpretative review. *The Journal of Human Resources, 37*(4), 696–727.

Donaldson, L. (2001). *The contingency theory of organizations*. Sage.

Donaldson, T., & Preston, L. E. (1995). The stakeholder theory of the corporation: Concepts, evidence, and implications. *Academy of Management Review, 20*(1), 65–91.

Dorobantu, S., Henisz, W. J., & Nartey, L. (2017a). Not all sparks light a fire: Stakeholder and shareholder reactions to critical events in contested markets. *Administrative Science Quarterly, 62*(3), 561–597.

Dorobantu, S., Kaul, A., & Zelner, B. (2017b). Nonmarket strategy research through the lens of new institutional economics: An integrative review and future directions. *Strategic Management Journal, 38*(1), 114–140.

Dorobantu, S., & Odziemkowska, K. (2017). Valuing stakeholder governance: Property rights, community mobilization, and firm value. *Strategic Management Journal, 38*(13), 2682–2703. https://doi.org/10.1002/smj.2675

Durand, R. (2023). From the boardroom: Making purpose research relevant for practice. *Strategy Science, 8*(2), 149–158. https://doi.org/10.1287/stsc.2023.0182

Durand, R., Grant, R. M., & Madsen, T. L. (2017). The expanding domain of strategic management research and the quest for integration. *Strategic Management Journal, 38*(1), 4–16.

Durand, R., & Huysentruyt, M. (2022). Communication frames and beneficiary engagement in corporate social initiatives: Evidence from a randomized controlled trial in France. *Strategic Management Journal, 43*(9), 1823–1853.

Dyer, J. H. (1997). Effective interfirm collaboration: How firms minimize transaction costs and maximize transaction value. *Strategic Management Journal, 18*(7), 535–556.

Dyer, J. H., Singh, H., & Hesterly, W. S. (2018). The relational view revisited: A dynamic perspective on value creation and value capture. *Strategic Management Journal, 39*(12), 3140–3162.

Early, G. L. (2004). *One nation under a groove: Motown and American culture.* University of Michigan Press.

Economy, C., Carter, E., & Airoldi, M. (2023). Have we 'stretched'social impact bonds too far? An empirical analysis of SIB design in practice. *International Public Management Journal, 26*(3), 413–436.

Elazar, D. J. (1965). The shaping of intergovernmental relations in the twentieth century. *The Annals of the American Academy of Political and Social Science, 359*(1), 10–22.

Emerson, K., & Nabatchi, T. (2015). *Collaborative governance regimes.* Georgetown University Press.

Engle, P. L., Fernald, L. C., Alderman, H., Behrman, J., O'Gara, C., Yousafzai, A., ... Ertem, I. (2011). Strategies for reducing inequalities and improving developmental outcomes for young children in low-income and middle-income countries. *The Lancet, 378*(9799), 1339–1353.

Fama, E. F., & Jensen, M. C. (1983). Separation of ownership and control. *The Journal of Law and Economics, 26*(2), 301–325.

Fan, C. S., Lin, C., & Treisman, D. (2009). Political decentralization and corruption: Evidence from around the world. *Journal of Public Economics, 93*(1–2), 14–34.

Farley, R., Danziger, S., & Holzer, H. J. (2000). *Detroit divided.* Russell Sage Foundation.

Faulk, L., Pandey, S., Pandey, S. K., & Scott Kennedy, K. (2020). Donors' responses to profit incentives in the social sector: The entrepreneurial orientation reward and the profit penalty. *Journal of Policy Analysis and Management, 39*(1), 218–242. https://doi.org/10.1002/pam.22179

Fei, T., & Rainey, H. G. (2003). Total quality management in Malaysian government agencies: Conditions for successful implementation of organizational change. *International Public Management Journal, 6*(2), 145–172.

Feilhauer, S., & Hahn, R. (2021). Firm-nonprofit collaboration: Explaining the rationale behind firms' cross-sector partner choices. *Long Range Planning, 54*(1), 101952.

Felin, T., & Zenger, T. R. (2017). The theory-based view: Economic actors as theorists. *Strategy Science, 2*(4), 258–271.

Ferlie, E., & Ongaro, E. (2015). *Strategic management in public services organizations: Concepts, schools and contemporary issues*. Routledge.

Ferlie, E., & Ongaro, E. (2022). *Strategic management in public services organizations: Concepts, schools and contemporary issues*. Routledge.

Festinger, L. (1954). A theory of social comparison processes. *Human Relations, 7*(2), 117–140.

Fitzsimmons, A. B., Qin, Y. S., & Heffron, E. R. (2022). Purpose vs mission vs vision: Persuasive appeals and components in corporate statements. *Journal of Communication Management, 26*(2), 207–219.

Flammer, C. (2015). Does corporate social responsibility lead to superior financial performance? A regression discontinuity approach. *Management Science, 61*(11), 2549–2568.

Flammer, C., & Kacperczyk, A. (2016). The impact of stakeholder orientation on innovation: Evidence from a natural experiment. *Management Science, 62*(7), 1982–2001.

Forrer, J., Kee, J. J., & Boyer, E. (2014). *Governing cross-sector collaboration*. Wiley.

Frank, D. H., & Obloj, T. (2014). Firm-specific human capital, organizational incentives, and agency costs: Evidence from retail banking. *Strategic Management Journal, 35*(9), 1279–1301.

Freeman, R. E. (1984). *Strategic management: A stakeholder approach*. Pitman.

Freeman, R. E. (1994). The politics of stakeholder theory: Some future directions. *Business Ethics Quarterly, 4*(4), 409–421. https://doi.org/10.2307/3857340

Freeman, R. E. (2017). Five challenges to stakeholder theory: A report on research in progress. In *Stakeholder management* (pp. 1–20). Emerald Publishing Limited.

Freeman, R. E., & Phillips, R. A. (2002). Stakeholder theory: A libertarian defense. *Business Ethics Quarterly, 12*(3), 331–349.

Freixas, X., Guesnerie, R., & Tirole, J. (1985). Planning under incomplete information and the ratchet effect. *The Review of Economic Studies, 52*(2), 173–191.

Friesl, M., Stensaker, I., & Colman, H. L. (2021). Strategy implementation: Taking stock and moving forward. *Long Range Planning, 54*(4), 102064.

Galiani, S., Gertler, P., & Schargrodsky, E. (2005). Water for life: The impact of the privatization of water services on child mortality. *Journal of Political Economy, 113*(1), 83–120.

Gatignon, A., & Capron, L. (2023). The firm as an architect of polycentric governance: Building open institutional infrastructure in emerging markets. *Strategic Management Journal, 44*(1), 48–85.

Gatignon, A., Clement, J., Pongeluppe, L. S., & Wassenhove, L. V. (2023). *Resource-poor but network-rich: A configurational approach to stakeholder engagement for scaling social inovvation*. Working paper.

George, B. (2021). Successful strategic plan implementation in public organizations: Connecting people, process, and plan (3Ps). *Public Administration Review, 81*(4), 793–798.

George, B., Walker, R. M., & Monster, J. (2019). Does strategic planning improve organizational performance? A Meta-Analysis. *Public Administration Review, 79*(6), 810–819.

George, G., Fewer, T. J., Lazzarini, S., McGahan, A. M., & Puranam, P. (2024). Partnering for grand challenges: A review of organizational design considerations in public–private collaborations. *Journal of Management, 50*(1), 10–40.

George, G., Haas, M. R., McGahan, A. M., Schillebeeckx, S. J., & Tracey, P. (2023). Purpose in the for-profit firm: A review and framework for management research. *Journal of Management, 49*(6), 1841–1869.

George, G., McGahan, A. M., & Prabhu, J. (2012). Innovation for inclusive growth: Towards a theoretical framework and a research agenda. *Journal of Management Studies, 49*(4), 661–683.

Gerlak, A. K., & Heikkila, T. (2011). Building a theory of learning in collaboratives: Evidence from the everglades restoration program. *Journal of Public Administration Research and Theory, 21*(4), 619–644.

Gil, N., & Pinto, J. K. (2018). Polycentric organizing and performance: A contingency model and evidence from megaproject planning in the UK. *Research Policy, 47*(4), 717–734.

Gil, N. A. (2023). Cracking the megaproject puzzle: A stakeholder perspective? *International Journal of Project Management, 41*(3), 102455.

Gomes, R. C., Liddle, J., & Gomes, L. O. M. (2010). A five-sided model of stakeholder influence: A cross-national analysis of decision making in local government. *Public Management Review, 12*(5), 701–724.

Govindarajan, V. (1988). A contingency approach to strategy implementation at the business-unit level: Integrating administrative mechanisms with strategy. *Academy of Management Journal, 31*(4), 828–853.

Granovetter, M. (1982). The strength of weak ties: A network theory revisited. In P. V. Marsden & N. Lin (Eds.), *Social structure and network analysis* (pp. 105–130). Sage.

Grossman, S. J., & Hart, O. D. (1986). The costs and benefits of ownership: A theory of vertical and lateral integration. *Journal of Political Economy, 94*(4), 691–719.

Gulati, R., Nohria, N., & Zaheer, A. (2000). Strategic networks. *Strategic Management Journal, 21*(3), 203–215.

Tavares, G. M., Marcolino, A. C., & Cabral, S. (2024). Câmeras nos Uniformes Reduzem Mortes Decorrentes de Intervenção Policial? Avaliando Potenciais Mecanismos Explicativos. *Administração Pública e Gestão Social*. https://doi.org/10.21118/apgs.v16i1.15774

Guth, W. D., & MacMillan, I. C. (1986). Strategy implementation versus middle management self-interest. *Strategic Management Journal, 7*(4), 313–327.

Hackman, J. R., & Wageman, R. (1995). Total quality management: Empirical, conceptual, and practical issues. *Administrative Science Quarterly*, 309–342.

Hadani, M., & Schuler, D. A. (2013). In search of El Dorado: The elusive financial returns on corporate political investments. *Strategic Management Journal, 34*(2), 165–181.

Hameduddin, T., Fernandez, S., & Demircioglu, M. A. (2020). Conditions for open innovation in public organizations: Evidence from Challenge. gov. *Asia Pacific Journal of Public Administration, 42*(2), 111–131.

Hannan, M. T., & Freeman, J. (1977). The population ecology of organizations. *American Journal of Sociology, 83*(929–984).

Hannan, M. T., & Freeman, J. (1984). Structural inertia and organizational change. *American Sociological Review, 49*(2), 149–164. https://doi.org/10.2307/2095567

Hardin, G. (1968). The tragedy of the common. *Science, 162*, 1243–1248.

Harrigan, K. R. (2003). *Joint ventures, alliances, and corporate strategy*. Beard Books.

Hart, O. (2003). Incomplete contracts and public ownership: Remarks, and an application to public-private partnerships. *The Economic Journal, 113*(486), C69–C76.

Hart, O., Shleifer, A., & Vishny, R. W. (1997). The proper scope of government: Theory and an application to prisons. *The Quarterly Journal of Economics, 112*(4), 1127–1161.

Hartog, J., Ferrer-i-Carbonell, A., & Jonker, N. (2002). Linking measured risk aversion to individual characteristics. *Kyklos, 55*(1), 3–26.

Head, B. W. (2019). Forty years of wicked problems literature: Forging closer links to policy studies. *Policy and Society, 38*(2), 180–197.

Healy, P. M., & Palepu, K. G. (2003). The fall of Enron. *Journal of Economic Perspectives, 17*(2), 3–26.

Heinrich, C. J. (2007). False or fitting recognition? The use of high performance bonuses in motivating organizational achievements. *Journal of Policy Analysis and Management, 26*(2), 281–304. https://doi.org/10.1002/pam.20244

Heinrich, C. J., & Marschke, G. (2010). Incentives and their dynamics in public sector performance management systems. *Journal of Policy Analysis and Management, 29*(1), 183–208.

Helfat, C. E. (2000). *Guest editor's introduction to the special issue: The evolution of firm capabilities* (Vol. 21, pp. 955–959). Wiley Online Library.

Heller, P., Harilal, K., & Chaudhuri, S. (2007). Building local democracy: Evaluating the impact of decentralization in Kerala, India. *World Development, 35*(4), 626–648.

Higgins, J. M. (2005). The eight 'S's of successful strategy execution. *Journal of Change Management, 5*(1), 3–13.

Hill, C. W., & Jones, G. R. (2011). *Essentials of strategic management*. Cengage Learning.

Hillman, A. J., Withers, M. C., & Collins, B. J. (2009). Resource dependence theory: A review. *Journal of Management, 35*(6), 1404–1427.

Hofstede, G. (1997). *Culture and organizations: Softwares of the mind*. McGraw Hill.

Holmström, B. (2017). Pay for performance and beyond. *American Economic Review, 107*(7), 1753–1777.

Hölmstrom, B. (1979). Moral hazard and observability. *The Bell Journal of Economics, 10*, 74–91.

Holmstrom, B., & Milgrom, P. (1991). Multitask principal–agent analyses: Incentive contracts, asset ownership, and job design. *The Journal of Law, Economics, and Organization, 7*(special_issue), 24–52.

Homonoff, T., Spreen, T. L., & Clair, T. S. (2020). Balance sheet insolvency and contribution revenue in public charities. *Journal of Public Economics, 186*, 104177.

Hood, C. (1991). A public management for all seasons? *Public Administration, 69*(1), 3–19.

Hood, C. (1995). The "new public management" in the 1980s: Variations on a theme. *Accounting, Organizations and Society, 20*(2–3), 93–109. https://doi.org/10.1016/0361-3682(93)E0001-W

Hoskisson, R. E., Wan, W. P., Yiu, D., & Hitt, M. A. (1999). Theory and research in strategic management: Swings of a pendulum. *Journal of Management, 25*(3), 417–456.

Hrebiniak, L. G. (2006). Obstacles to effective strategy implementation. *Organizational Dynamics, 35*(1), 12–31. https://doi.org/10.1016/j.orgdyn.2005.12.001

Hurwicz, L. (2008). But who will guard the guardians? *American Economic Review, 98*(3), 577–585.

Inoue, C. (2020). Election cycles and organizations: How politics shapes the performance of state-owned enterprises over time. *Administrative Science Quarterly, 65*(3), 677–709.

Intarakumnerd, P., & Goto, A. (2018). Role of public research institutes in national innovation systems in industrialized countries: The cases of Fraunhofer, NIST, CSIRO, AIST, and ITRI. *Research Policy, 47*(7), 1309–1320.

Jacob, B. A., & Levitt, S. D. (2003). Rotten apples: An investigation of the prevalence and predictors of teacher cheating. *The Quarterly Journal of Economics, 118*(3), 843–877.

Jacobides, M. G., Cennamo, C., & Gawer, A. (2018). Towards a theory of ecosystems. *Strategic Management Journal, 39*(8), 2255–2276.

Jensen, M. C., & Meckling, W. H. (1976). Theory of the firm: Managerial behavior, agency costs and ownership structure. *Journal of Financial Economics, 3*, 305–360.

Johnson, L. K. (2014). Intelligence shocks, media coverage, and congressional accountability, 1947–2012. *Journal of Intelligence History, 13*(1), 1–21.

Johnston, E. W., Hicks, D., Nan, N., & Auer, J. C. (2011). Managing the inclusion process in collaborative governance. *Journal of Public Administration Research and Theory, 21*(4), 699–721.

Jones, B. D., & Baumgartner, F. R. (2005). *The politics of attention: How government prioritizes problems*. University of Chicago Press.

Jones, M. B. (2007). The multiple sources of mission drift. *Nonprofit and Voluntary Sector Quarterly, 36*(2), 299–307.

Jones, T. M., & Wicks, A. C. (1999). Convergent stakeholder theory. *The Academy of Management Review, 24*(2), 206–221. https://doi.org/10.2307/259075

Kale, P., Dyer, J. H., & Singh, H. (2002). Alliance capability, stock market response, and long-term alliance success: The role of the alliance function. *Strategic Management Journal, 23*, 747–767.

Kandel, E., & Lazear, E. P. (1992). Peer pressure and partnerships. *Journal of Political Economy, 100*(4), 801–817.

Kaplan, R. S. (2001). Strategic performance measurement and management in nonprofit organizations. *Nonprofit Management and Leadership, 11*(3), 353–370.

Kapucu, N. (2006). Public-nonprofit partnerships for collective action in dynamic contexts of emergencies. *Public Administration, 84*(1), 205–220.

Katic, I. V., & Hillman, A. (2023). Corporate political activity, reimagined: Revisiting the political marketplace. *Journal of Management, 49*(6), 1911–1938.

Keller, A., Lumineau, F., Mellewigt, T., & Ariño, A. (2021). Alliance governance mechanisms in the face of disruption. *Organization Science, 32*(6), 1542–1570.

Khaneman, D., & Tversky, A. (1982). *Judgment under uncertainty: Heuristics and biases*. Cambridge University Press.

Khanna, T., & Palepu, K. (1997). Why focused strategies. *Harvard Business Review, 75*(4), 41–51.

Kim, S., & Schifeling, T. (2022). Good corp, bad corp, and the rise of B Corps: How market incumbents' diverse responses reinvigorate challengers. *Administrative Science Quarterly, 67*(3), 674–720.

Koebele, E. A. (2019). Integrating collaborative governance theory with the Advocacy Coalition Framework. *Journal of Public Policy, 39*(1), 35–64.

Kreps, D. M. (1990). Corporate culture and economic theory. In J. Alt & K. Shepsle (Eds.), *Perspectives on positive political economy* (pp. 90–143). Cambridge University Press.

Kucinskas, J., & Zylan, Y. (2023). Walking the moral tightrope: Federal civil servants' loyalties, caution, and resistance under the Trump administration. *American Journal of Sociology, 128*(6), 1761–1808.

Lægreid, P., & Rykkja, L. H. (2022). Accountability and inter-organizational collaboration within the state. *Public Management Review, 24*(5), 683–703.

Lawrence, P. R., & Lorsch, J. W. (1967). *Organization and environment: Managing differentiation and integration.* Richard D. Irwin.

Lazzarini, S. G. (2015). Strategizing by the government: Can industrial policy create firm-level competitive advantage? *Strategic Management Journal, 36*(1), 97–112.

Lazzarini, S. G. (2020a). The nature of the social firm: Alternative organizational forms for social value creation and appropriation. *Academy of Management Review, 45*(3), 620–645.

Lazzarini, S. G. (2020b). Social impact bonds in São Paulo's state public school system: New modality of public-private partnership in Brazil: Commentary. *Education Policy Analysis Archives, 28*, 112. https://doi.org/10.14507/epaa.28.5148

Lazzarini, S. G. (2022a). *The right privatization: Why private firms in public initiatives need capable governments.* Cambridge University Press.

Lazzarini, S. G. (2022b). *The strategic imperative: Do we need moral considerations in strategic theories of stakeholder engagement?* Available at SSRN.

Lazzarini, S. G., Boehe, D., Pongeluppe, L. S., & Cook, M. L. (2020). *From instrumental to normative relational strategies: A study of open buyer-supplier relations.* Paper presented at the Academy of Management Proceedings.

Lazzarini, S. G., Cabral, S., Firpo, S., & Teodorovicz, T. (2022). Why are counterfactual assessment methods not widespread in outcome-based contracts? A formal model approach. *Journal of Public Administration Research and Theory, 32*(3), 509–523.

Lazzarini, S. G., Cabral, S., Pongeluppe, L. S., Ferreira, L. C. d. M., & Rotondaro, A. (2021). The best of both worlds? Impact investors and their role in the financial versus social performance debate. In *A research agenda for social finance.* Edward Elgar Publishing.

Lazzarini, S. G., Pongeluppe, L. S., Ito, N. C., Oliveira, F. d. M., & Ovanessoff, A. (2020). Public capacity, plural forms of collaboration, and the performance of public initiatives: A configurational approach. *Journal of Public Administration Research and Theory, 30*(4), 579–595.

Lazzarini, S. G., & Zenger, T. (2023). Strategy as (a causal) theory of change. *Academy of Management Proceedings, 2023*(1), 11924. https://doi.org/10.5465/AMPROC.2023.11924abstract

Legg, A. (2010). A taxonomy of musical gesture in African American gospel music. *Popular Music, 29*(1), 103–129.

Leiblein, M. J., Reuer, J. J., & Zenger, T. (2018). What makes a decision strategic? *Strategy Science, 3*(4), 558–573.

Lipscomb, M., & Mobarak, A. M. (2016). Decentralization and pollution spillovers: Evidence from the re-drawing of county borders in Brazil. *The Review of Economic Studies, 84*(1), 464–502.

Litwack, J. M. (1993). Coordination, incentives, and the ratchet effect. *The RAND Journal of Economics, 24*, 271–285.

Lopez-Arana, S., Avendano, M., Van Lenthe, F. J., & Burdorf, A. (2016). The impact of a conditional cash transfer programme on determinants of child health: Evidence from Colombia. *Public Health Nutrition, 19*(14), 2629–2642.

Lumineau, F., & Henderson, J. E. (2012). The influence of relational experience and contractual governance on the negotiation strategy in buyer–supplier disputes. *Journal of Operations Management, 30*(5), 382–395.

Lynch, S. E., & Mors, M. L. (2019). Strategy implementation and organizational change: How formal reorganization affects professional networks. *Long Range Planning, 52*(2), 255–270. https://doi.org/10.1016/j.lrp.2018.02.003

Lyon, T. P., Delmas, M. A., Maxwell, J. W., Bansal, P., Chiroleu-Assouline, M., Crifo, P., ... & Lenox, M. (2018). CSR needs CPR: Corporate sustainability and politics. *California Management Review, 60*(4), 5–24.

Mahoney, J. T., McGahan, A. M., & Pitelis, C. N. (2009). Perspective—The interdependence of private and public interests. *Organization Science, 20*(6), 1034–1052.

Mankins, M. C., & Steele, R. (2005). Turning great strategy into great performance. *Harvard Business Review*, p. 2607.

Manolitzas, P., & Yannacopoulos, D. (2013). Citizen satisfaction: A multicriteria satisfaction analysis. *International Journal of Public Administration, 36*(9), 614–621.

Massoud, M. A., Fayad, R., El-Fadel, M., & Kamleh, R. (2010). Drivers, barriers and incentives to implementing environmental management systems in the food industry: A case of Lebanon. *Journal of Cleaner Production, 18*(3), 200–209.

Mazzucato, M. (2013). *The entrepreneurial state: Debunking public vs private sector myths*. Anthem Press.

Mazzucato, M. (2018). Mission-oriented innovation policies: Challenges and opportunities. *Industrial and Corporate Change, 27*(5), 803–815. https://doi.org/10.1093/icc/dty034

McCarthy, M. (2013). The young musicians of Motown: A success story of urban music education. *Music Educators Journal, 99*(3), 35–42.

McGahan, A., & Pongeluppe, L. S. (2023). There is no planet B: Aligning stakeholder interests to preserve the Amazon rainforest. *Management Science, 69*(12), 7860–7881. https://doi.org/10.1287/mnsc.2023.4884

McGahan, A. M. (2020). Where does an organization's responsibility end? Identifying the boundaries on stakeholder claims. *Academy of Management Discoveries, 6*(1), 8–11.

McGahan, A. M. (2021). Integrating insights from the resource-based view of the firm into the new stakeholder theory. *Journal of Management, 47*(7), 1734–1756.

McGahan, A. M. (2023). The new stakeholder theory on organizational purpose. *Strategy Science, 8*, 245–255.

McGahan, A. M., Zelner, B. A., & Barney, J. B. (2013). *Entrepreneurship in the public interest: Introduction to the Special Issue* Vol. 7, pp. 1–5. Wiley Online Library.

McGinnis, M. D. (2011). An introduction to IAD and the language of the ostrom workshop: A simple guide to a complex framework. *Policy Studies Journal, 39*(1), 169–183. https://doi.org/10.1111/j.1541-0072.2010.00401.x

McGuire, M. (2006). Collaborative public management: Assessing what we know and how we know it. *Public Administration Review, 66*(s1), 33–43. https://doi.org/10.1111/j.1540-6210.2006.00664.x

McGuire, M., & Silvia, C. (2010). The effect of problem severity, managerial and organizational capacity, and agency structure on intergovernmental collaboration: Evidence from local emergency management. *Public Administration Review, 70*(2), 279–288.

McKevitt, D. (2015). Debate: Value for money—In search of a definition. *Public Money & Management, 35*(2), 99–100.

McLaughlin, J. A., & Jordan, G. B. (2015). Using logic models. In K. E. Newcomer, H. P. Hatry, & J. S. Wholey (Eds.), *Handbook of practical program evaluation* (4th ed., pp. 62–87). Wiley.

Megginson, W. L., & Netter, J. M. (2001). From state to market: A survey of empirical studies on privatization. *Journal of Economic Literature, 39*(2), 321–389.

Meier, K. J., O'Toole, L. J., Boyne, G. A., Walker, R. M., & Andrews, R. (2010). Alignment and results: Testing the interaction effects of strategy, structure, and environment from miles and snow. *Administration & Society, 42*(2), 160–192.

Mello, U. (2022). Centralized admissions, affirmative action, and access of low-income students to higher education. *American Economic Journal: Economic Policy, 14*(3), 166–197.

Ménard, C. (2022). Hybrids: Where are we? *Journal of Institutional Economics, 18*(2), 297–312.

Mesquita, L. F., Ragozzino, R., & Reuer, J. J. (2017). *Collaborative strategy: Critical issues for alliances and networks*. Edward Elgar Publishing.

Mészáros, G. (2020). Caught in an authoritarian trap of its own making? Brazil's 'Lava Jato' anti-corruption investigation and the politics of prosecutorial overreach. *Journal of Law and Society, 47*(S1), S54–S73.https://doi.org/10.1111/jols.12245

Metricis, I. (2022). *Guide to the assessment of socio-environmental impact for use in impact-oriented projects and investments: general guide focused on and verification of additionality.*

Miles, R. E., Snow, C. C., Meyer, A. D., & Coleman, H. J., Jr. (1978). Organizational strategy, structure, and process. *Academy of Management Review, 3*(3), 546–562.

Milgrom, P., & Roberts, J. (1990). The economics of modern manufacturing: Technology, strategy, and organization. *The American Economic Review, 80*, 511–528.

Milgrom, P. R., & Roberts, J. (1992). *Economics, organization and management*. Prentice-Hall.

Miller, G. J. (1992). *Managerial dilemmas: The political economy of hierarchy*: Cambridge University Press.

Mintzberg, H., Ahlstrand, B., & Lampel, J. B. (2020). *Strategy safari*. Pearson.

Mirel, J. (1999). *The rise and fall of an urban school system: Detroit, 1907–81*. University of Michigan Press.

Mitchell, D. (2022). Bought in? The contingent effect of stakeholder support upon strategic implementation success in American municipalities. *Public Management Review, 24*(5), 773–798.

Mitchell, R. K., Agle, B. R., & Wood, D. J. (1997). Toward a theory of stakeholder identification and salience: Defining the principle of who and what really counts. *Academy of Management Review, 22*(4), 853–886.

Molenveld, A., Verhoest, K., Voets, J., & Steen, T. (2020). Images of coordination: How implementing organizations perceive coordination arrangements. *Public Administration Review, 80*(1), 9–22.

Moloney, K., & Moloney, S. (2020). Australian quarantine policy: From centralization to coordination with mid-Pandemic COVID-19 shifts. *Public Administration Review, 80*(4), 671–682.

Moore, M. H. (1995). *Creating public value: Strategic management in government*. Harvard University Press.

Moore, M. H. (2000). Managing for value: Organizational strategy in for-profit, nonprofit, and governmental organizations. *Nonprofit and Voluntary Sector Quarterly, 29*(1_suppl), 183–204.

Mossman, K., Onil Bhattacharyya, M., McGahan, A., & Mitchell, W. (2017). Expanding the reach of primary Care in Developing Countries. *Harvard Business Review*.

Murphy, M., & Arenas, D. (2010). Through indigenous lenses: Cross-sector collaborations with fringe stakeholders. *Journal of Business Ethics, 94*, 103–121.

Nag, R., Hambrick, D. C., & Chen, M. J. (2007). What is strategic management, really? Inductive derivation of a consensus definition of the field. *Strategic Management Journal, 28*(9), 935–955.

Naranjo-Gil, D., & Hartmann, F. (2007). How CEOs use management information systems for strategy implementation in hospitals. *Health Policy, 81*(1), 29–41.

Nardi, L., Lazzarini, S. G., & Cabral, S. (2022a). Impact measurement tools and social value creation: A strategic perspective. In *Handbook on the business of sustainability* (pp. 459–473). Edward Elgar Publishing.

Nardi, L., Zenger, T., Lazzarini, S. G., & Cabral, S. (2022b). Doing well by doing good, uniquely: Materiality and the market value of unique CSR strategies. *Strategy Science, 7*(1), 10–26.

Neilson, G. L., Martin, K. L., & Powers, E. (2008). The secrets to successful strategy execution. *Harvard Business Review, 86*(6).

Ni, X., Song, W., & Yao, J. (2020). Stakeholder orientation and corporate payout policy: Insights from state legal shocks. *Journal of Banking & Finance, 121*, 105970.

Nickerson, J. A., & Zenger, T. R. (2002). Being efficiently fickle: A dynamic theory of organizational choice. *Organization Science, 13*(5), 547–567.

Nickerson, J. A., & Zenger, T. R. (2008). Envy, comparison costs, and the economic theory of the firm. *Strategic Management Journal, 29*(13), 1429–1449.

Nie, M. (2004). State wildlife policy and management: The scope and bias of political conflict. *Public Administration Review, 64*(2), 221–233.

Noble, C. H. (1999). The eclectic roots of strategy implementation research. *Journal of Business Research, 45*(2), 119–134.

North, D. (1990). *Institutions, institutional change and economic performance*. Cambridge University Press.

Noto, G., Coletta, L., & Vainieri, M. (2022). Measuring the performance of collaborative governance in food safety management: An Italian case study. *Public Money & Management, 42*(8), 627–636.

Nutt, P. C. (1986). Tactics of implementation. *Academy of Management Journal, 29*(2), 230–261.

Nyberg, A. J., Maltarich, M. A., Abdulsalam, D. D., Essman, S. M., & Cragun, O. (2018). Collective pay for performance: A cross-disciplinary review and meta-analysis. *Journal of Management, 44*(6), 2433–2472.

O'Reilly, C. A., Caldwell, D. F., Chatman, J. A., Lapiz, M., & Self, W. (2010). How leadership matters: The effects of leaders' alignment on strategy implementation. *The Leadership Quarterly, 21*(1), 104–113.

Ocasio, W., Kraatz, M., & Chandler, D. (2023). Making sense of corporate purpose. *Strategy Science, 8*, 123–138.

Odziemkowska, K. (2022). Frenemies: Overcoming audiences' ideological opposition to firm–activist collaborations. *Administrative Science Quarterly, 67*(2), 469–514.

Ohrling, M., Solberg Carlsson, K., & Brommels, M. (2022). No man is an island: Management of the emergency response to the SARS-CoV-2 (COVID-19) outbreak in a large public decentralised service delivery organisation. *BMC Health Services Research, 22*(1), 371. https://doi.org/10.1186/s12913-022-07716-w

Oliveira, C. A., Carneiro, J., & Esteves, F. (2019). Conceptualizing and measuring the "strategy execution" construct. *Journal of Business Research, 105*, 333–344.

Olson, M. (1965). *The logic of collective action*. Harvard University Press.

Olson, Z., Clark, R. G., & Reynolds, S. A. (2019). Can a conditional cash transfer reduce teen fertility? The case of Brazil's Bolsa Familia. *Journal of Health Economics, 63*, 128–144.

Osborne, D., & Gaebler, T. (1992). *Reinventing government: How the entrepreneurial spirit is transforming the public sector*. Addison-Welsey.

Ostrom, E. (1990). *Governing the commons: The evolution of institutions for collective action*. Cambridge University Press.

Ostrom, V., & Ostrom, E. (2019). Public goods and public choices. In *Alternatives for delivering public services* (pp. 7–49). Routledge.

Paik, Y., Kang, S., & Seamans, R. (2019). Entrepreneurship, innovation, and political competition: How the public sector helps the sharing economy create value. *Strategic Management Journal, 40*(4), 503–532. https://doi.org/10.1002/smj.2937

Park, S., & Berry, F. (2014). Successful diffusion of a failed policy: The case of pay-for-performance in the US federal government. *Public Management Review, 16*(6), 763–781.

Patala, S., Albareda, L., & Halme, M. (2022). Polycentric governance of privately owned resources in circular economy systems. *Journal of Management Studies, 59*(6), 1563–1596. https://doi.org/10.1111/joms.12810

Peteraf, M. A. (1993). The cornerstones of competitive advantage: A resource-based view. *Strategic Management Journal, 14*(3), 179–191.

Pfeffer, J., & Salancik, G. (2003). *The external control of organizations: A resource dependence perspective*. Stanford Business Books.

Piening, E. P. (2011). Insights into the process dynamics of innovation implementation: The case of public hospitals in Germany. *Public Management Review, 13*(1), 127–157.

Pigou, A. C. (1920). *The Economics of welfare*. Macmillan.

Pollitt, C. (2007). Decentralization: A central concept in contemporary public management. In E. Ferlie, L. E. Lynn, & C. Pollitt (Eds.), *The Oxford handbook of public management* (pp. 371–397). Oxford University Press.

Pongeluppe, L. S. (2022). The favela effect: Spatial inequalities and firm strategies in disadvantaged urban communities. *Strategic Management Journal, 43*(13), 2777–2808. https://doi.org/10.1002/smj.3414

Poppo, L., & Zenger, T. R. (2002). Do formal contracts and relational governance function as substitutes or complements? *Strategic Management Journal, 23*(8), 707–726.

Porter, D. O., & Olsen, E. A. (1976). Some critical issues in government centralization and decentralization. *Public Administration Review, 36*, 72–84.

Porter, M. E. (1980). *Competitive strategy*. The Free Press.

Porter, M. E. (1990). The competitive advantage of nations. *Harvard business review*(March-April), 73–93.

Porter, M. E. (1996). What is strategy? *Harvard Business Review, November–December*, 61–78.

Power, M. (2003). Evaluating the audit explosion. *Law & Policy, 25*(3), 185–202. https://doi.org/10.1111/j.1467-9930.2003.00147.x

Power, M. (2021). Modelling the micro-foundations of the audit society: Organizations and the logic of the audit trail. *Academy of Management Review, 46*(1), 6–32.

Prendergast, C., & Topel, R. H. (1996). Favoritism in organizations. *Journal of Political Economy, 104*(5), 958–978.

Quelin, B. V., Cabral, S., Lazzarini, S., & Kivleniece, I. (2019). The private scope in public–private collaborations: An institutional and capability-based perspective. *Organization Science, 30*(4), 831–846.

Quélin, B. V., Kivleniece, I., & Lazzarini, S. (2017). Public-private collaboration, hybridity and social value: Towards new theoretical perspectives. *Journal of Management Studies, 54*(6), 763–792. https://doi.org/10.1111/joms.12274

Rajala, T., Laihonen, H., & Vakkuri, J. (2018). Shifting from output to outcome measurement in public administration-arguments revisited. In E. A.-P. E. Borgonovi & C. Bianchi (Ed.), *Outcome-based performance management in the public sector* (pp. 3–23). Springer.

Rangan, S., Samii, R., & Van Wassenhove, L. N. (2006). Constructive partnerships: When alliances between private firms and public actors can enable creative strategies. *Academy of Management Review, 31*(3), 738–751.

Rasella, D., Aquino, R., Santos, C. A., Paes-Sousa, R., & Barreto, M. L. (2013). Effect of a conditional cash transfer programme on childhood mortality: A nationwide analysis of Brazilian municipalities. *The Lancet, 382*(9886), 57–64.

Reis, P. R. C., Cabral, S., & Arvate, P. (2023). Fostering agility through public procurement reforms: The role of experienced procurement officers. *International Journal of Public Administration*, 1–12. https://doi.org/10.1080/01900692.2023.2205048

Reuer, J. J., & Devarakonda, S. V. (2016). Mechanisms of hybrid governance: Administrative committees in non-equity alliances. *Academy of Management Journal, 59*(2), 510–533.

Rezaie, R., Frew, S. E., Sammut, S. M., Maliakkal, M. R., Daar, A. S., & Singer, P. A. (2008). Brazilian health biotech—Fostering crosstalk between public and private sectors. *Nature Biotechnology, 26*(6), 627–644.

Ring, P. S., & Perry, J. L. (1985). Strategic management in public and private organizations: Implications of distinctive contexts and constraints. *Academy of Management Review, 10*(2), 276–286.

Rivera-Santos, M., Rufin, C., & Wassmer, U. (2017). Alliances between firms and non-profits: A multiple and behavioural agency approach. *Journal of Management Studies, 54*(6), 854–875.

Roberts, J. (2010). Designing incentives in organizations. *Journal of Institutional Economics, 6*(1), 125–132.

Rocha, R., & Soares, R. R. (2010). Evaluating the impact of community-based health interventions: Evidence from Brazil's Family Health Program. *Health Economics, 19*(S1), 126–158.

Rogers, P., & Blenko, M. (2006). Who has the D. *Harvard Business Review, 84*(1), 52–61.

Rondinelli, D. A., & London, T. (2003). How corporations and environmental groups cooperate: Assessing cross-sector alliances and collaborations. *Academy of Management Perspectives, 17*(1), 61–76.

Rosenkopf, L., & Padula, G. (2008). Investigating the microstructure of network evolution: Alliance formation in the mobile communications industry. *Organization Science, 19*(5), 669–687.

Sampson, R. C. (2004). The cost of misaligned governance in R&D alliances. *Journal of Law, Economics, and Organization, 20*(2), 484–526.

Savas, E. S. (2000). *Privatization and public-private partnerships*. Seven Bridges Press.

Schoen, C., Buttorff, C., Andersen, M., & Davis, K. (2015). Policy options to expand Medicare's low-income provisions to improve access and affordability. *Health Affairs, 34*(12), 2086–2094.

Schwerdt, G., Messer, D., Woessmann, L., & Wolter, S. C. (2012). The impact of an adult education voucher program: Evidence from a randomized field experiment. *Journal of Public Economics, 96*(7–8), 569–583.

Selsky, J. W., & Parker, B. (2005). Cross-sector partnerships to address social issues: Challenges to theory and practice. *Journal of Management, 31*(6), 849–873.

Shei, A., Costa, F., Reis, M. G., & Ko, A. I. (2014). The impact of Brazil's Bolsa Família conditional cash transfer program on children's health care utilization and health outcomes. *BMC International Health and Human Rights, 14*, 1–9.

Shenhar, A. J. (2001). One size does not fit all projects: Exploring classical contingency domains. *Management Science, 47*(3), 394–414.

Shin, J., & Choi, Y. K. (2019). Organizational innovativeness and its determinants in South Korean nonprofit human service organizations. *Nonprofit Management and Leadership, 30*(1), 51–68.

Shirley, M. M. (1999). Bureaucrats in business: The roles of privatization versus corporatization in state-owned enterprise reform. *World Development, 27*(1), 115–136.

Siggelkow, N. (2001). Change in the presence of fit: The rise, the fall, and the renaissance of Liz Claiborne. *The Academy of Management Journal, 44*(4), 838–857. https://doi.org/10.2307/3069418

Sigman, H. (2005). Transboundary spillovers and decentralization of environmental policies. *Journal of Environmental Economics and Management, 50*(1), 82–101.

Simon, H. A. (1965). Administrative decision-making. *Public Administration Review, 25*(1), 31–37.

Simon, H. A. (1973). Organization man—Rational or self-actualizing. *Public Administration Review, 33*(4), 346–353.

Simon, H. A. (1991). Bounded rationality and organizational learning. *Organization Science, 2*(1), 125–134.

Skinner, R. M. (2017). Water policy in a time of climate change: Coping with complexity. *Public Administration Review, 77*(1), 13–16.

Smith, A. (1999 [1776]). *The wealth of nations*. Penguin.

Soule, S. A., & Dyke, N. V. (1999). Black church arson in the United States, 1989–1996. *Ethnic and Racial Studies, 22*(4), 724–742.

Spulber, N. (1997). *Redefining the state: Privatization and welfare reform in industrial and transitional economics*. Cambridge University Press.

Stühlinger, S., & Hersberger-Langloh, S. E. (2021). Multitasking NPOs: An analysis of the relationship between funding intentions and nonprofit capacities. *VOLUNTAS: International Journal of Voluntary and Nonprofit Organizations, 32*(5), 1042–1053.

Suchman, M. C. (1995). Managing legitimacy: Strategic and institutional approaches. *Academy of Management Review, 20*(3), 571–610.

Suykens, B., Meyfroodt, K., Desmidt, S., & Verschuere, B. (2022). Does performance-based accountability impact how non-profit directors perceive organizational performance? Insights from rational planning. *Public Management Review, 24*(9), 1355–1382.

Tawse, A., & Tabesh, P. (2021). Strategy implementation: A review and an introductory framework. *European Management Journal, 39*(1), 22–33. https://doi.org/10.1016/j.emj.2020.09.005

Teece, D. J., Pisano, G., & Shuen, A. (1997). Dynamic capabilities and strategic management. *Strategic Management Journal, 18*(7), 509–533.

Teodorovicz, T., Lazzarini, S., Cabral, S., & McGahan, A. M. (2023a). Investing in general human capital as a relational strategy: Evidence on flexible arrangements with contract workers. *Strategic Management Journal, 45*, 902–938.

Teodorovicz, T., Lazzarini, S., Cabral, S., & Nardi, L. (2023b). Can public organizations perform like private firms? The role of heterogeneous resources and practices. *Organization Science, 34*(4), 1527–1553.

Thaler, R. H., & Ganser, L. (2015). *Misbehaving: The making of behavioral economics*. Nash Format.

Touchton, M., Knaul, F. M., Arreola-Ornelas, H., Porteny, T., Sánchez, M., Méndez, O., … Rosado, J. A. (2021). A partisan pandemic: State government public health policies to combat COVID-19 in Brazil. *BMJ Global Health, 6*(6), e005223. https://doi.org/10.1136/bmjgh-2021-005223

Uzzi, B. (1996). The sources and consequences of embeddedness for the economic performance of organizations: The network effect. *American Sociological Review, 61*, 674–698.

Vakili, K., & McGahan, A. M. (2016). Health care's grand challenge: Stimulating basic science on diseases that primarily afflict the poor. *Academy of Management Journal, 59*(6), 1917–1939.

Van Slyke, D. M. (2007). Agents or Stewards: Using theory to understand the government-nonprofit social service contracting relationship. *Journal of Public Administration Research and Theory, 17*(2), 157–187. https://doi.org/10.1093/jopart/mul012

Vasudeva, G., & Anand, J. (2011). Unpacking absorptive capacity: A study of knowledge utilization from alliance portfolios. *Academy of Management Journal, 54*(3), 611–623.

Wageman, R. (1995). Interdependence and group effectiveness. *Administrative Science Quarterly, 40*, 145–180.

Weible, C. M., Sabatier, P. A., Jenkins-Smith, H. C., Nohrstedt, D., Henry, A. D., & DeLeon, P. (2011). A quarter century of the advocacy coalition framework: An introduction to the special issue. *Policy Studies Journal, 39*(3), 349–360.

Weimer, D., & Vining, A. (2017). *Policy analysis: Concepts and practice*. Routledge.

Weiser, A.-K., Jarzabkowski, P., & Laamanen, T. (2020). Completing the adaptive turn: An integrative view of strategy implementation. *Academy of Management Annals, 14*(2), 969–1031.

Wicks, A. C., & Harrison, J. S. (2017). Toward a more productive dialogue between stakeholder theory and strategic management. In *Stakeholder management* (Vol. 1, pp. 249–273). Emerald Publishing Limited.

Williamson, O. (1985). *The economic institutions of capitalism*. Free Press.

Williamson, O. (1991). Comparative economic organization: The analysis of discrete structural alternatives. *Administrative Science Quarterly, 36*, 269–296.

Williamson, O. E. (1998). The institutions of governance. *The American Economic Review, 88*(2), 75–79.

Williamson, O. E. (1999). Public and private bureaucracies: A transaction cost economics perspective. *Journal of Law, Economics and Organization, 15*(1), 306–342.

Winter, S. G. (2003). Understanding dynamic capabilities. *Strategic Management Journal, 24*(10), 991–995.

Wong, E. M., Ormiston, M. E., & Tetlock, P. E. (2011). The effects of top management team integrative complexity and decentralized decision making on corporate social performance. *Academy of Management Journal, 54*(6), 1207–1228.

Wood, D. J., Mitchell, R. K., Agle, B. R., & Bryan, L. M. (2021). Stakeholder identification and salience after 20 years: Progress, problems, and prospects. *Business & Society, 60*(1), 196–245.

Young, D. R. (2000). Alternative models of government-nonprofit sector relations: Theoretical and international perspectives. *Nonprofit and Voluntary Sector Quarterly, 29*(1), 149–172.

Young, S., & Macinati, M. S. (2012). Health outsourcing/backsourcing: Case studies in the Australian and Italian health sector. *Public Management Review, 14*(6), 771–794.

Zarychta, A., Grillos, T., & Andersson, K. P. (2020). Public sector governance reform and the motivation of street-level bureaucrats in developing countries. *Public Administration Review, 80*(1), 75–91.

Zenger, T. (2016). *Beyond competitive advantage: How to solve the puzzle of sustaining growth while creating value*. Harvard Business Review Press.

Zenger, T. R. (1994). Explaining organizational diseconomies of scale in R&D: Agency problems and the allocation of engineering talent, ideas, and effort by firm size. *Management Science, 40*(6), 708–729.

Zenger, T. R. (2002). Crafting internal hybrids: Complementarities, common change initiatives, and the team-based organization. *International Journal of the Economics of Business, 9*(1), 79–95.

Zucco, C., Jr. (2013). When payouts pay off: Conditional cash transfers and voting behavior in Brazil 2002–10. *American Journal of Political Science, 57*(4), 810–822.

Index

A
Abdulkadiroğlu, Atila, 131
Ackerman, Colin, 208
Advocacy Coalition Framework (ACF), 269
Africa, 193
Agarwal, Nikhil, 131
Agency costs, 76
Agle, Bradley, 203
Airport, 175
Air traffic control, 147
Alban, Marcus, x
Alesia, Mark, 171
Alonso, Jose Manoel, 266
Amazon Forest, 8
Analytic Hierarchy Process, 122
Andersson, Krister, 140
Andrews, Rhys, viii, 266
Ansell, Chris, 270
Ansoff, Igor, 28
Arms-length contracts, 236
Arvate, Paulo, 182
Asset specificity, 226, 262
Astra Zeneca, 8
ATT, 171
Auctions, 168
Audit explosion, 77
Australia, 132, 201
Australian government, 161

B
Backsource, 162
Bahia State Symphonic Orchestra (OSBA), 112
Baker, George, 73
Balanced scorecards, 165
Balancing centralization and decentralization, 145
Baldi, Simona, 143
Barney, Jay, 168
Baron, David, 15
Battered Women Fighting Back (BWFB), 170
Baum, Joel, 228
B Corps, 59
Belgian municipalities, 167
Belgium, 172
The Benevolent Society, 252

S. Cabral, *Strategy for Public and Nonprofit Organizations*,
https://doi.org/10.1007/978-3-031-64969-1

Best, Bernadette, 202
Better-than-average effect, 120
Bettinazzi, Emanuele, 196
Beyoncé, 253
Biles, Simone, 171
Bill & Melinda Gates Foundation, 257
BioNTech, 8
Biotech projects, 264
Black Baptist, 6
Black culture, 253
Blanc, Honoré, 149
Bloomberg, Laura, 64
Bloomington School of Institutional Analysis, 269
Body-Worn Cameras (BWCs), 114
Bolsonaro, Jair, 132
Bono Vox, 253
Boston, 170
Boston Consulting Group, 30
Botswana, 193, 259
Bounded rationality, 95
Boyne, George, viii
Bozeman, Barry, 56
Brandenburger, Adam, 54
Brazil, 171
Brazilian favelas, 205
Brazilian Supreme Court, 278
Brickley, James, 116
Bryson, John, viii, 41
Business-nonprofit, 256
Business syndicates, 258

C

Cable TV, 243
Canada, 134
Canadian Cannabis Act, 134
Capable partners, 263
Capable suppliers, 241
Capron, Laurence, 257
Cardoso, Ricardo, 142
Carneiro, Jorge, 163
Carnival, ix
Carnival of Salvador, 253
Carville, James, 73
Car Wash (Lava Jato) operation, 277
Challenge.gov, 166
Chandler, Alfred, 28
Charitable funds, 118
Cheating, 118
Checks and balances, 155
Chen, Ming-Jer, 33
Chicago public schools, 118
Chief Executive Officers (CEOs), 143
Chile, 64
China, 122
Chrysler, 260
Cliff, Jimmy, 253
Climate change, 183
Coase, Ronald, 30, 226
Coercion of plaintiffs, 277
Collaborative arrangements, 236
Collaborative governance, 268
Collective action, 203
Collective goods, 227
Collusion, 277
Common goods, 231
Commonwealth Bank of Australia, 252
Community benefits agreements (CBA), 205
Complementarities, 177
Conditional cash-transfer, 52
Configurational approach, 273
Conner, Bart, 171
Consortia, 260
Context-setters, 209
Contingency approach, 173
Contracting lead-times, 168
Contract-management capabilities, 242
Contractual incompleteness, 95, 225
Control rights, 225

Corfo, 8
Corporate purpose, 60
Corporate social responsibility (CSR), 16
Corporativism, 36
Cost-benefit analysis, 56
Cost savings, 246
Counterfactual assessment, 38
COVID-19, x
Crime hotspots, 286
Criterion for selecting effective measures, 126
Crittenden, Victoria, 170
Crittenden, William, 170
Crosby, Barbara, 64
Cross-sector collaborations, x, 25, 253
Cultural inertia, 181

D
Danone, 59
da Silva, Lula, 277
de Azevedo, Paulo Furquim, x
Decentralization
  benefits of, 136
  problems of, 141
Decision-making process, 156
Decision rights, 134
Defense, 236
de Janeiro, Rio, 171
de Janvry, Alain, 122
Deming, W. Edwards, 108
Demircioglu, Mehmet Akif, 166
Democratic Republic of the Congo, 193
de Oliveira, Carla Albuquerque, 163
Diamond Model, 29
Disenfranchised stakeholders, 206
Distortions in subjective measures, 121
Donaldson, Lex, 174
Donaldson, Thomas, 203
Dorobantu, Sinziana, xi, 195
Drivers of successful implementation, 165
Dual chain of command, 156
Durand, R., 18

E
E-commerce firms, 205
Economies of scale, 143
Eden, Fran, 208
Electricity, 243
Embraer, 233
Emerson, Kirk, 270
Emilia-Romagna, 132
Enfranchisement of stakeholders, 207
Enron, 117
Environmental changes, 175
Environmental, social, and governance (ESG), 16
EPC contractors, 259
Esteves, Felipe, 164
Eswatini, 193
Evans, Tim, 171
Excludability, 229
External fit, 173
Externalities, 15, 227

F
Fama, Eugene, 148
Familia, Bolsa, 52
Family Welcome Center (FWC), 131
Fan, C. Simon, 142
Fei, Teddy, 170
Feldman, Emilie, 196
Ferlie, Ewan, viii, 26
Fernandez, Sergio, 166
Fishing, 191
Five Forces Framework, 29
Flammer, Caroline, 196
Ford, 260
Foreign affairs, 240

Fourth sector, 59
Fraunhofer-Gesellschaft (FhG), 258
Freeman, Edward, 195
Freeman, John, 180
Free-market, 239
Free-riding, 36, 92
Frontline workers, 133
Full government provision, 233

G
Gaming, 36, 117
Gash, Alison, 270
Gatignon, Aline, 193
Gekko, Gordon, 200
General human capital, 18
General Motors, 260
George, Bert, 167
Germany, 162
Gil, Gilberto, 253
Goal ambiguity, 37
Goal setting, 169
Gold-mining, 195
Gordy, Berry, 4
Governance mechanisms, 263
Government-nonprofit, 256
Government Performance and Results Act (GPRA), 25
Government responsiveness, 168
Grand challenges, 16
Grayling, Chris, 219
Greenpeace, 9
Greenwashing, 257
Grillos, Tara, 140
Grossman, Sanford, 225
Group-based incentives, 88
Guarding the guardians problem, 149

H
Hambrick, Donald, 33
Hameduddin, Taha, 166
Hannan, Michael, 180
Hardin, Garrett, 231
Hartmann, Frank, 165
Hart, Oliver, 225
Harvard Business School, 27
Healthcare, 57
Henisz, Witold, 195
Herod, 77
Hersberger-Lang, Sophie E., 114
Hill, Charles, 163
HIV/AIDS, 193
Homicides, 286
Honda, 260
Hospitals, 143
House of Representatives, 12
Hrebiniak, Lawrence, 164
Human behavior, 109
Human capital, 177
Hunting, 191
Hybrid arrangements, 232
Hybrid multidivisional form, 154

I
Implementation of performance management systems, 109
Implementation problems, 162
Incentive distortions, 113
Incentive intensity, 120
Incentives, 12, 13
Indianapolis Star, 171
Indigenous communities, 205
Influence costs, 122
Information sharing, 276
Information technology projects, 259
Inoue, Carlos, 206
Insper Metricis, 126
Institutional strategies, 290
Intelligence, 12
Inter-American Development Bank (IDB), 124
Intergovernmental cooperation, 268
Internal Affairs Divisions, 119

Internal fit, 177
Internal revenue, 111
International Finance Corporation (IFC), 124
Intersectional approaches, 206
Ito, Nobuiuki, 273

J
Jackson, Michael, 253
Jacob, Brian, 118
Jarzabkowski, Paula, 163
Jensen, Michael, 148
John Bryson, 43
Johnson, Shawn, 171
Joint ventures, 260
Jones, Gareth, 163
Jones, Quincy, 253
Jones, Thomas, 198
Jordan, Michael, 51

K
Keep America Beautiful, 264
Keiretsu, 100
Kellogg, 171
Kenya, 193
Key performance indicators (KPIs), 126
Krane, Dale, 254
Kwiatkowski, Marisa, 171

L
Laamanen, Tomi, 163
Law, Jeniffer, viii
Lazzarini, Sergio, x, 119, 169
Leadership styles, 169
Lebanon, 165
Legitimacy, 63
Lesotho, 193
Levitt, Steven, 118
Li Li Leung, 172
Lin, Chen, 142
Linux, 260
Local supply chains, 253
Long-term outcomes, 118
Low-powered incentives, 35

M
Machiavelli, Nicolau, 26
Macinati, Manuela, 161
Make-or-buy, 241
Malawi, 193
Malicious agents, 13
Managerial practices and resources, 169
Managing stakeholders, 202, 207
Marchesini, Marcelo, xi
Marcolino, Antonio Cesar, 114
Market failures, 227
Matrix forms, 154
Matthew, the tax collector, 77
McAdam, Rodney, 202
McDonald, 264
McGahan, Anita, x, 16
Médicins Sans Frontières, 9
Mega infrastructure projects, 259
Melo, Ursula, 132
Merck, 259
Meyer, Kennett, 41
Milgrom, Paul, 177
Mill, John Stuart, 228
Mining, 205
Mission, 37
Mission drift, 61
Mitchell, Ronald, 203
Modes of provision of public services, 234
Moffett, Sandra, 202
Monteiro, Guilherme Fowler, xi
Moore, Mark, vii
Moral and normative ethics, 197
Moro, Sergio, 277

Motivations for privatization, 238
Motown, ix
Motown Records, 3
Mozambique, 193
Multicriteria decision analysis (MCDA), 122
Multidivisional forms (M-form), 151
Multitask, 36, 113
Murray-Darling Basin River system, 201

N
Nabatchi, Tina, 270
Nag, Rajiv, 33
Naranjo-Gil, David, 165
Nardi, Leandro, 169
Nartey, Lite, 195
National Basketball Association (NBA), 51
National Probation Service (NPS), 220
Natura, 8
Natural monopolies, 227
Nebraska, 138
New Public Management (NPM), 35, 135
New South Wales, 201
New stakeholder theory (NST), 203
New York University, 131
New Zealand, 132
Nie, Martin, 192
Nike, 51
Noble, Charles, 163
Nonmarket strategies (NMS), 15, 290
North, Douglass, 30
North Star Alliance, 193
Nutritional education, 58
Nutt, Paul, 163
NYC Public Schools, 131

O
Objective measures, 110
Odziemkowska, Kate, 205
Oliveira, Felippe, 273
Olympic Games, 171
Ongaro, Edoardo, viii, 26
Operational capacity, 66
Opportunism, 233
Orbán, Viktor, 183
Organizational cohesion, 154
Organizational design, 13
Organizational inertia, 182
Organizational mission, 60
Organizational purpose, 198
Organizational scope, 223
Organizational structures, 12, 148
Organizational values, 37
Ostrom, Elinor, 8
Ostrom, Vincent, 228
O'Toole, Peter, 41
Outcome-based contract, 81
Out-of-home care, 251
Output measures, 111
Outsourcing, 161
Ovanessoff, Armen, 273

P
Paraná, 221
Parker, Barbara, 256
Pathak, Parahg, 131
Pay-for-performance programs, 36
Peer pressure, 93
Performance assessment, 110
Performance-contingent payments, 36
Performance management, 13
Perry, James, 35
Petrobras, 277
Pfizer, 8
Philanthropic, 108
Philips, Robert, 204
Piening, Eric, 162

Pigou, Arthur, 227
Plato, 81
Polar modes, 232
Police chief, 152
Police forces, 111
Police officers, 73
Policing activities, 286
Policy Cycle, 37
Policy design, 38
Policy evaluation, 38
Political turfs, 254
Pongeluppe, Leandro, 34
Porter, Michael, 29
Power-Grid Model, 208
Preston, Lee, 203
Primary infancy, 251
Principal-Agent, 74
Prison services, 57
Private goods, 229
Privatization, 222
Probation services, 219
Probity, 207
Procter & Gamble, 171
Procurement officers, 182
Property rights, 224
Public capabilities, 273
Public goods, 231
Public-private collaborations, 256
Public–private partnerships, 43
Public–private performance gap, 169
Public procurement, 43
Public-public capabilities, 274, 275
Public schools, 6
Public security, 112
Public supervision, 87
Public value, 12, 56
Public value creation, 57
Public value governance triangle (PGVT), 65
Python, 137

Q
Quasi-experimental methods, 126
Queensland, 201
Quélin, Bertrand, xi

R
Rainey, Hal, 170
Ratchet Effect, 115
Recidivism, 219
Regression discontinuity design, 205
Regulation, 87
Reintegration, 220
Reis, Paulo, 182
Relational contracts, 88
Relational governance, 265
Rent-seeking, 87
Reputation, 101
Research Triangle, 7
Residual costs, 77
Resilient Families, 251
Resource-based view, 64
Resource complementarities, 263
Ridesharing services, 175
Ring, Peter, 35
Risk-averse, 41
Rivalry in consumption, 229
Roberts, John, 115, 119
Roman Empire, 77
Route 128, 7

S
Sabotage, 120
Sampson, Rachelle, 266
Samuelson, Paul, 228
Savas, Emanuel, 228
Selecting the mode of delivery, 244
Selsky, John, 256
Senate, 12
September 11, 138
Sexual abuse, 171
Sex workers, 193

Shleifer, Andrei, 225
Short-term orientation, 118
Silicon Valley, 7
Simon, Paul, 253
Singapore, 64
Six-Sigma, 169
Skinner, Rob, 201
Small and medium enterprises (SMEs), 168
Smith, Adam, 149, 227
Social comparison, 120
Social Impact Bonds (SIB), 252
Social media, 112
Social norms, 101
South Africa, 193
Soviet Union, 116
Special purpose vehicles, 260
Sports facilities, 246
Stakeholder analysis, 207
Stakeholder identification, 210
Stakeholder management, 17, 194, 199
  instrumental approach to, 197
Stakeholder-oriented, 34
Stakeholder salience, 210
Stakeholder theories, 195
State-owned enterprises, 117
Strategic alliances, 259
Strategic intentions, 162
Strategic leadership, 170
Strategic management, ix
Strategic planning, 11
The Strategic Triangle, 62
Strategizing, 10
Strategy, 33
Strategy and public and nonprofit management, ix
Strategy execution, 38
Strategy formulation, 38
Strategy implementation, 38
Street robbery, 285
Structural inertia, 180
Stuart Jr, Harborne, 54
Stühlinger, Sara, 114
Subjective measures, 111
Subway, 237
Suchman, Mark, 63
Supply chain networks, 260
Sustainable Development Goals (SDGs), 8
Sweden, 138

T
Taiwan, 132
Tanzania, 193
Tavares, Gustavo, 114
Taxi drivers, 176
Telecom Italia, 233
Tensions between flexibility and accountability standards, 182
Teodorovicz, Thomaz, 18, 169
Theory-based view, 10
Theory of change, 123
Toll goods, 230
Top-management teams, 143
Total quality management (TQM), 169, 178
Toyota, 260
Trade-Related Aspects of Intellectual Property Rights (TRIPS), 17
Tragedy of the commons, 231
Transaction Cost Economics (TCE), 30
Transaction costs, 95
Tresman, Daniel, 142
Trio elétrico, 253
Tri-sectoral collaborations, 256
Truck drivers, 193
Trump, Donald, 183
Tzu, Sun, 26

U
Uganda, 193

Uncertainty, 41
Unitary form (U form), 150
United Nations, 8
United States, 171
University of Pennsylvania, 164
US Gymnastics, 170

V
Vaccines, 236
Vakili, Keyvan, 16
Value appropriation, 76, 287
Value creation, 52
Value for money, 56, 237
Vannoni, Davide, 143
Vehicle robbery, 285
Veloso, Caetano, 253
Veneto, 132
Victoria, 201
Vining, Aidan R., 229
Violent death, 285
Vishny, Robert, 225
Vision, 37
Volkswagen, 260
Von Clausewitz, Carl, 26
Vouchers, 239

W
Wales, 219
Walker, Richard, viii, 41
Waste management, 266
Weak incentives, 119
Weimer, David, 229
Weiser, Ann-Kristin, 163
Westpac Banking Corporation, 252
Wicked problems, 255
Wicks, Andrew, 198
Wildlife management, 192
Williamson, Oliver, 30, 226
Win-win-win situation, 252
Women police stations, 206
Wood, Donna, 203
The World Bank, 123
World War II, 27
World Wildlife Fund (WWF), 264
Wrongdoing, 278

Y
Young, Dennis, 258
Young, Suzanne, 161

Z
Zambia, 193
Zarychta, Alan, 140
Zenger, Todd, 33, 120
Zimbabwe, 193

SPRINGER NATURE

GPSR Compliance

The European Union's (EU) General Product Safety Regulation (GPSR) is a set of rules that requires consumer products to be safe and our obligations to ensure this.

If you have any concerns about our products, you can contact us on ProductSafety@springernature.com

In case Publisher is established outside the EU, the EU authorized representative is:

Springer Nature Customer Service Center GmbH
Europaplatz 3
69115 Heidelberg, Germany

The manufacturer's authorised representative in the EU is Springer Nature Customer Service Centre GmbH, Europaplatz 3, 69115 Heidelberg, Germany. If you have any concerns regarding our products, please contact ProductSafety@springernature.com

Printed and bound by CPI Group (UK) Ltd, Croydon, CR0 4YY
01/10/2026
02225903-0014